Centennial

NINETEEN HUNDRED & EIGHTY-SEVEN

1987

EXCLUSIVE TO THE EX:

ANCISCO ALWAYS
ES A PARTY
ST GAVE IT ONE ON
'RACK EVERY DAY'

III

grandfather and so missed the chance to sit
ut newspapers. My Dad tells me I sat on
2, but no memory remains of that potential
eath in 1951, we summer vacationed at San
Simeon and the place formed my enduring
impression of the style and ideas of its
creator.

Many years later, watching "Citizen
Kane" for the first time in college, I was
struck by the difference between the
fictional gloom of Xanadu as compared to
the real color and sweep of San Simeon.

The force that placed the castle on
that hillside was ultimately the millions
of people who read those papers. Nowa-
days, we are accustomed to think of the
dia as powerful but that position rests

LAWYERS & OTHER CRIMINALS

BY HARRY JUPITER

(Harry Jupiter, an Examiner staffer, heard much of the lore and glory of the San Francisco bar at one of the great ones — the Kearny Street establishment run by Cookie Picetti.)

BACK IN the days before every home had a television set, the most gripping dramas in town ran daily in the courtrooms at the Hall of Justice and City Hall.

There was no admission charge, but the audience often had to show up early to be assured of a seat.

Generations of young attorneys packed the courtrooms when a spectacular trial was in session.

There were superstars of the bar, lawyers whose every appearance caused a buzz in the hallways and brought reporters and hangers-on rushing to courtrooms.

Attorneys waiting for their own cases to be heard joined the rapt audiences.

Some of the great names have been forgotten by all but veteran lawyers, but there were indeed

---

BY WILLIAM KENNEDY

WORKING FOR HEARST

'SON,' HE SAID, 'YOU'RE IN THE WRONG BUSINESS, THE WRONG TOWN AND THE WRONG NEWSPAPER'

AVERILL PARK, N.Y., 1987 — Charlie Davis was an old and amiably cynical newspaperman

who had the falsest set of false teeth I ever saw, who had genius when he played high-low seven-card stud, who owned a bad stomach (every night he drank a cup of soup, every night he threw it up), a backwardly sloping bald pate with straight white threads hanging off it like icicles, a belly like a bowling pin, a talent for making up a front page so that you wanted to read every story, a reverence for authority that came from a lifetime of working

THE HEARSTS: FATHER AND SON

THE
HEARSTS
FATHER AND SON

WILLIAM RANDOLPH HEARST, JR.
with
JACK CASSERLY

ROBERTS RINEHART PUBLISHERS

Copyright © 1991 by William Randolph Hearst, Jr., and Jack Casserly
Published by Roberts Rinehart Publishers
Post Office Box 666 Niwot, Colorado 80544

Published in the United Kingdom and Europe
by Roberts Rinehart Publishers
3 Bayview Terrace, Schull, West Cork
Republic of Ireland

Published in Canada by Key Porter Books
70 The Esplanade
Toronto, Ontario M5E 1R2

International Standard Book Number 1-879373-04-1,
1-879373-10-6 (limited edition)
Library of Congress Catalog Card Number 91-61285
Printed in the United States of America

All photographs courtesy of the Hearst
Corporation and Mr. & Mrs. W. R. Hearst, Jr.,
unless otherwise noted

The first 250 copies of this book have
been set aside as limited editions, slip-cased
and containing a bookplate bearing Mr. Hearst's signature.

For Austine

CONTENTS

Photos follow pages 48, 112, 208, and 304

PREFACE

THE THOUGHT of writing this book has been on my mind for about ten years. I've fought it all that time. The reason is my father would have done a much better job if he had chosen to write of his life and our family. He was a finer reporter and editor than I have ever been. Also, since Pop never answered his enemies or critics, I knew that I would have to reveal and explain some of his private life. I've always been reluctant to do that.

I finally undertook this book at the urging of my wife, Austine, because my father deserves a more accurate and definitive public account of his turbulent career. I'm his last close link, apart from my brother Randy. If one of us didn't write about him and our family, an intimate look at not only my father but our extraordinary grandparents would be lost.

At the age of eighty-three, I needed someone to bang the drum and keep me marching. Jack Casserly, a veteran reporter, author, and my editorial assistant, did that and more.

This work is an accounting of my stewardship in the news game while following in the footsteps of my father. Pop plays a major role in the book because he stamped such a large imprint on our family and, indeed, on the media of the twentieth century.

My father was one of the most powerful and controversial Americans of our times. At the pinnacle of his career, he may have been the most influential.

A score of books, thousands of magazine and newspaper articles, store-houses of photos, a major movie, and millions of other words in The Congressional Record, speeches, and private papers have attempted to capture the character of my father and the life of our family. Among these are numerous inaccurate accounts, false judgments, and unfounded riddles which have been created about Pop and the rest of us over the years. It's time to set the record on a straighter course. I hope to do that fairly, with decency and, above all, truthfully.

I take a firsthand look at my father's life and that of five generations of Hearsts over the past 125 years or so. Most of the material written and spoken about my father has been by people who never met him. They presumed not only to understand him but to expound on his innermost thoughts and emotions. Two authors did know him: Mrs. Fremont Older and Adela Rogers St. Johns; each was informative and accurate within the scope of her knowledge.

My father has been described as the personification of evil genius. That is a tragic oversimplification. He was a score of men in one, an extraordinarily complex character who reflected the contentious times in which he lived. Pop was a man of countless hues, an incredibly adventurous individual with a boundless spirit and outlook. He also was very patriotic.

The old man was a flamboyant editor and publisher. He lived for headlines and national press battles. Yet Pop prized privacy even more. That was one of the most difficult things to comprehend about him. Even as he sought tranquility in his retreat at San Simeon, Pop was continually buffeted by public storms which he created in editorials, his political and socioeconomic views, and his personal life. He attracted national and international attention with these strong convictions while running some ninety different businesses.

I lived in my father's shadow all my life. For much of four decades we lived and laughed alongside one another. I was not only his son but his student.

This book is being published almost to the day that Pop died forty years ago on August 14, 1951. The coincidence convinces me beyond any logic that I have done the right thing in writing it. This marks the first time in these four decades that any of our father's sons publicly discusses Pop or our family in any real depth. That includes our relationship with my father's mistress, Marion Davies.

It's not easy coming out of the old man's shadow and writing of the lives of my mother, my four brothers, and myself. But, after such a long wait, the time seems right. And time is running out on me.

I've been a newspaperman for more than sixty years, the only one of my father's five sons who has been a lifetime reporter and editor. My father's life and mine stretch from the Civil War to the present. I will describe much of it—from my boyhood in New York and California to our family relationship with Pop and my life as a newspaperman. That career led me around the globe, beginning in World War II, to meet most world leaders and witness many important events.

The bond between Pop and me has endured, but let no one think that I haven't charted my own course. I disagreed strongly at times with the old man. Let this book, however imperfect, speak for both of us in our own ways. And may it give some guidance and meaning to those young reporters who will, above all, inherit and rejoice in the free press which we and others have left them as a legacy. And may it offer some insight to all my fellow Americans into this and the twenty-first century.

William Randolph Hearst, Jr.
New York 1991

ACKNOWLEDGMENTS

MANY PEOPLE who contributed to this book are no longer with us—my mother and father; my brothers George, John, and David; my grandparents, George and Phoebe Apperson Hearst; Frank Conniff, my best friend; Julia Morgan, our architect at San Simeon; and many others—friends, fellow newsfolk across the country, and people I met along the way. My love and gratitude to all.

No one, however, deserves more credit for this undertaking than my wife, Austine. For ten years, she persisted, insisting that I owed this firsthand recollection to my family—past, present, and future. I finally relented and with the help of our sons, William Randolph Hearst III and Austin, reconstructed my life and that of our family.

No one worked harder on this book than Joy Ruth Casserly, our able and experienced researcher, who found thousands of long-forgotten family letters, office correspondence and memos, legal documents, photos, and other information at Hearst headquarters in New York, at the ranch in San Simeon, the Joseph A. Moore Collection at the Library of Congress in Washington, the Bancroft Library at the University of California in Berkeley, and the Julia Morgan Collection in the Robert Kennedy Library at California Polytechnic State University in San Luis Obispo. Much of the material is newly discovered. A hearty thanks to those library staffs and my New York colleagues as well.

To jog my memory of people, places, and long-ago events, we used the New York Public Library's Newspaper Annex, where past editions of the *New York Journal-American* are on microfilm. We also delved into material at the *Journal-American* morgue in the Humanities Research Center at the University of Texas in Austin. Ken Craven, the director, was especially helpful.

I also browsed through books, old magazines, and other material related to our family. They reminded me of how forgetful one can become.

Many others helped us: Catherine Hearst, Randolph A. Hearst, Hope Hearst, Paul McNamara, Joseph Kingsbury-Smith, Mrs. Frank Conniff and her son, Michael; Harvey Lipton, Dick Deems, Helen Gurley Brown, John Mack Carter, Eleanor Lambert, Gus Engelman, Frank Carpozi, Jr., Doris Kaplan, Jack O'Brien, Frank Borsky, Mildred Schindler, Rosemarie Ziegler, Mike Pearl, Martin Steadman, Joseph Hagan, Pete Kriendler, Joan Hanauer McKenna, Marvin Sleeper, Professor John Hazzard, John "Bunky" Hearst, Larry Newman, Edward Hymoff, Max McCrohon, Bob and Yuri Horiguchi, Norma Barzman, Allen Berg, Bill Umstead, Joseph Singer, Jim O'Donnell, Taylor Coffman, Bob Brandes, Barbara and Bill Atkins, Nancy Lovaglio, and Oscar Collier.

We may have missed some people who helped us, and we regret any omissions. However, they are as much a part of this book as anyone listed here.

As a lifetime newspaperman, I accept full responsibility for this story. Thanks again to one and all who pushed and pulled me along the way. That includes my colleague Jack.

I
ROOTS

San Simeon is a little siesta town on the Pacific Ocean midway between the rolling riptides of Los Angeles and San Francisco. No place in the world brings back so many memories to me. San Simeon has been the crossroads of our family history for more than a century. Many of my own early struggles began on its now famous hilltop where my father built a "castle" and so many dreams.

The Santa Lucia Mountains are often covered by an early morning fog, but the sun usually burns it off by about ten o'clock. The baked-brown hills climb out of the mist as the sun rises and reaches above the ocean. They seem to stretch forever against the sky. Local folk still walk the beaches to watch the Pacific tide rise and fall as it has for centuries.

Unlike most of the crowded California coastline, only a few hundred people live here. Many of them work in the tourist hotels and restaurants scattered along the few miles of village shore. Other hundreds work at what the state of California calls the Hearst Castle. My father and our family simply called it "the ranch." A dozen homes, which my father had built long ago for permanent workers, are still lived in by those who are employed at the ranch. Sadly, the old pier, used for unloading ships that carried materials to build the castle, was torn down in 1947. The Hearst Corporation donated that land, and more nearby, for a public campground.

I've returned here virtually every year since I was ten—except during World War II—and I'm now eighty-three years old. It has been a pilgrimage in search of myself—my youth, my mother and father, my grandmother, and the horizons of a young man early in this century. Now, in the twilight of my life, I often sit on the front porch of our cottage here and reflect on that long journey. How lucky I've been to do much of my growing up in this part of the country, and later to have been a reporter during the most interesting century in history.

I saw America's earliest cars and planes. I first drove a car in 1920, when I was only twelve years old. Before twenty, I was a licensed pilot. My generation spanned the development of electricity and the telephone; radio and television; penicillin and the antipolio vaccine. We fought and witnessed four American wars, the birth of atomic and nuclear energy, the conquest of outer space with Americans walking on the moon, organ transplants, and the leap into supercomputers. Not the least of these incredible events was the rise and fall of communism, and the victory of freedom and democracy. I regret that my father did not live to see all of it. He would have had a grand time covering these great stories.

Despite the vast changes that have redrawn the face of California, the sweeping panorama that attracted the first Hearst, my grandfather, has changed little. George Hearst began buying land along this central coast about 125 years ago to raise cattle and horses. Grandpa amassed about 50,000 acres before he was finished. His wife, Phoebe, purchased another 50,000 acres. And my father added yet another 150,000. Nevertheless, that total has since greatly decreased through the sale, donation, and trading of acreage.

My father introduced my mother, Millicent, to the ranch in 1904, a year after they were married. Years later, in 1918, he brought out the entire family—my mother and us five sons. Pop casually mentioned to us that he might one day build a family bungalow on Camp Hill. (He called it that because his parents—and later we—camped on the highest hill in tents.) The area seemed an endless wilderness amid lonesome mountains and valleys. The meadows and forests were virtually untouched. Native deer watered at small streams, while peregrine falcons and hawks swooped overhead. Distant gulls soared over the white-tipped ocean rocks. Birds and animals roamed everywhere. Sagebrush and wild flowers covered the countryside.

Our family began crossing the country to California by train for the summer months while I was still a small child. We actually came to see my grandmother, Phoebe Apperson Hearst, who lived in San Francisco. She eventually moved to Pleasanton, which is about 225 miles northeast of here. My father had owned a hacienda in Pleasanton, which Grandma appropriated from him when he later moved to New York. Pop really didn't mind. He was always more interested in San Simeon. My father was mesmerized by the wildly beautiful hills and canyons along the coast-line. He was rarely able to visit grandmother without returning to San Simeon.

I remember one of our early trips here. We had taken the train from New York to Los Angeles, then switched to another train for San Luis Obispo. As we rode by car to San Simeon, Pop talked to Mom about building a family summer home, but I didn't pay much attention. It seemed like such a distant dream.

None of us realized at the time, not even my father, that he was undertaking an adventure that would last three decades. Nor did we have the faintest idea that the project would cost perhaps $30 million to $40 million. The total, of course, ranged over many years. But the continuous expense was still so breathtaking that, like the great architecture and art that accompanied it, the staggering sums were difficult for anyone to comprehend in those days. That was Pop—a man whose unexpected leaps into the unknown were buttressed by an unquenchable optimism. Unfortunately, none of us was blessed with such an adventurous spirit, although I tried to adopt one.

I went to school mostly in New York, but also attended a little, one-room grade school in San Simeon for a while. That was because my skinny frame always seemed to attract whatever illness was making the rounds back East. The climate was warmer here.

I had many boyhood friends at San Simeon—Tarpy Lanini and the Robinson boys, Jack and Harry; the Villa brothers, Charley and Doc; Pete Sebastian and Virginia Summers. It's strange what one remembers—for example, that Tarpy was a good fisherman but couldn't pronounce the word "handkerchief." He said "hankicef." The Robinsons lived at San Simeon Point, where their father had a plant that processed seaweed for fertilizer. The Sebastians owned the local general store, built in 1852. The place is still open for business in the old village, although it has been designated a state historical monument. And I had a crush on Virginia Summers.

We had our share of scrapes. One summer my brother Jack, Pete Sebastian, and I got in a lot of hot water—or was it cold? We filled the horses' water trough with rocks. Some of the workers caught us. Mr. Lee, the ranch manager, made us take out all the rocks, carry them away, wipe out the trough, and fill it with buckets of clean water. We sure learned something about the back-breaking work of a farm hand. I never forgot it.

I still remember the sternest lecture that our father gave my brothers and me at San Simeon. We were talking with Señor Francisco Estrada, whose family had sold part of their Santa Rosa ranch to my grandfather. Señor Estrada lived on the land down near the stable. He was really a dignified old cowboy, always smiling, a truly fine horseman who also performed wonderful rope tricks. Señor Estrada came from an old Mexican family and was highly respected by Pop. We had been calling him by his nickname "Pancho." Our father was furious. He insisted that we call the old gentleman either Don Pancho or Don Estrada—not merely by his nickname. "Don" is the Spanish equivalent of "sir" and a mark of respect. From that day forward, I addressed Señor Estrada in one word: DonPancho!

The ranch originally comprised two Mexican land grants. The other half belonged to the Pico family and was named Piedra Blanca (White Rock), after the rocks in the waters just off the beach whose color came from the droppings of sea gulls over the centuries.

Many people have now discovered the Hearst Castle. The Casa Grande and three guest houses, which once were the private quarters of our family and friends, today welcome tourists from all over the world. They come by car and busload to view what Pop called La Cuesta Encantada (The Enchanted Hill). Young and old want to see the extraordinary setting— the hilltop looking across mountains and down to the ocean—and the thousands of beautiful art treasures filling hundreds of rooms in the four buildings.

The works of art at San Simeon have long represented perhaps the greatest private collection in the history of the United States. It was one man's dream—to put Old World artistic accomplishments in a purely American setting. As Hedda Hopper, the Hollywood columnist, once wrote: "It was like a visit to a Never-Never Land. Never have we seen its like, and never will we again." George Bernard Shaw joked that it was what God would have built if He had had the money.

After Pop died in 1951 our family and the executors of the estate were in a quandary about the future of the huge, costly complex. No member of the family or the corporation was in a position to maintain it. My father had told me several times that he expected this. He hoped that the University of California would accept the house and gardens as a gift. However, the university declined. After much discussion, the main buildings and grounds were offered to the state of California. The 137-foot-high Hispano-Moresque Casa Grande and its great bell towers, the three guest houses, and the sprawling majestic gardens, terraces, and pools had become a white elephant. However, our family and the Hearst Corporation wanted to retain the huge acreage around the buildings as a cattle ranch.

The state accepted the 123-acre complex and placed it under the direction of the California Park System. The park system opened the grounds and buildings to the public in 1958. The site officially became the Hearst San Simeon State Historical Monument. The castle has now become one of the largest tourist attractions in the United States, with some 1.1 million visitors a year. The state has translated informational brochures on it into seven foreign languages: Spanish, German, French, Italian, Japanese, Korean, and Hebrew. The enterprise provides California with more than $1 million in annual revenues. The white elephant is now a golden goose.

The present complex is surrounded by a 80,000-acre working cattle ranch owned by the Hearst Corporation. Four generations of us have tended what was once fifty, and now fifteen, miles of magnificent California coastline as part of our family heritage. (In 1940, a big chunk of the ranch's sweeping acreage was sold—as an act of patriotism, not profit—to the federal government and became the U.S. Army's Hunter-Liggett Reservation.)

Every summer my wife, Austine, and I live here in a cottage near Pico Creek, about a mile from the ocean. We are inexorably drawn back by the history of the place, our love of the land, and memories echoing from past years. I have thought long and hard, looking out at the vast stretch of land, that such holdings are always transitory. Grandfather and Pop are long gone. The land—not man—ultimately prevails. We, like the

American Indian and Spanish conquistadors, are its keepers for only a brief time.

When I reflect on the past—our family history—I think of my grandmother. I remember Phoebe Apperson Hearst as I do no other person in my life except my father. She taught me the fundamentals of real life. For all her gracious unpretentiousness, she was a very shrewd, practical individual. And she seemed to be everywhere at once. From the time I was able to compose a simple letter, I wrote to her. We had a very close bond, and all my correspondence to her reflected that. This was a typical letter, written at the age of nine, dated the day after Christmas, 1917:

Dear Grandma:

I just received your nice long letter. I was sorry to hear that you were not well, and that you could not come out for Chirstmas.

Thank you very much for that nice little [bird] cage that you sent me, and the book. I think the cage is very pretty with the two little doors. Papa gave me a beautiful bag with all the fittings of silver. Mama also gave me a little desk set with little sailors on top. We had a big tree and everybody was there. Everything would have been twice as nice if you had been there.

I am awfully pleased that you did not kill the turkey. I am sure that we will have lots of fun with it. If it is as tame as you say, I know that Jonny [a worker at the hacienda] would not kill it. I am sure that "Bessie" is lonesome but I will soon be there to ride her.

I suppose you got my telegram [which] I sent last night. I have not had a cold since I have been here. John says he will write you this evening. Give my love to Miss Reid [a governess], and lots of love to you and hoping you will soon get well.

Love from all,
William

I never met my grandfather, who died in 1891, seventeen years before I was born in 1908. But I knew him from Grandma, who seemed to know everything, including the most minute details of our family history. She explained to me the origin of our family name. Genealogists traced it back to the lowlands of Scotland in the Middle Ages. The original Anglo-Saxon was spelled "Hyrst." A hyrst was a thicket. The family later went to Ireland, from where they emigrated to America about 1680. John

Hurst, who changed the spelling of the family name, settled and farmed in Virginia. Some of his sons later moved to Abbeyville County, South Carolina. In 1808, William G. Hearst (early in the eighteenth century, the family changed the spelling again) rode up to Franklin County, Missouri, where he farmed, operated a store, and later married. William was the father of my grandfather, George, who was born in 1820.

It was not my father but my grandparents, George and Phoebe, who began the Hearst dynasty—if that is what it is. Pop probably would never have envisioned either his media empire or San Simeon were it not for those two Missourians who scaled the first mountaintops. They became mine owners, large land owners, and ultimately multimillionaires. Their lives were truly remarkable.

Grandpa Hearst began with no more than a pick and shovel on his shoulder. He had little formal schooling. Young George began work on his father's Missouri farm. One of his jobs was to drive hogs, which his father sold, to a lead-mining settlement about fifteen miles away. George was fascinated by mining, and hung around the settlement asking endless questions. He continued to spend much of his spare time at this and other diggings in the area. He also borrowed and pored over books that explained the mining of minerals. He thus added technical knowledge to his uncanny instinct about mining. Phoebe told me that local Indians described him as "the boy to whom the earth talked."

At the age of thirty, on May 12, 1850, George left the meager life of his family farm and headed for the gold fields of California. Some relatives and friends had departed ahead of him. Since he was alone, George's mother and sister rode with him for the first two days on the road west. Grandpa later said: "I would not have thought of going on. Nothing would have induced me to leave them the way I did, if it had not been for pride. I felt it [that he would strike it rich] in my bones."

It wasn't easy for George to leave home. His father had died in 1846, leaving a widow, daughter, two sons, and several thousand dollars of debt. George became responsible for all of them. He paid off most of the debt while still working the farm, and later sent his family money from California.

He had bouts with cholera and fever on the 2,000-mile trip. Phoebe said he was so ill in Wyoming that he prayed to die. But George was rugged. He picked himself up and trudged on. His first California stops were Placerville, Jackass Gulch, and Eldorado. Other colorful digs followed: Red Dog, Delirium Tremens, and Hell-Out-for-Noon City.

George eventually became a great miner. He discovered, bought into, traded, and rediscovered some of the richest mines in American history. These included the Homestake, where he and his partners built the town of Lead, South Dakota. The town and mine are still alive. It became the most lucrative gold mine in America, pouring out a profit of between $4 million and $6 million a year. His biggest strike was the Anaconda in Montana, where George discovered the largest and richest vein of copper in the world. Also the Comstock Lode in Nevada, a vein of silver and gold up to eighty feet wide and two miles long, plus the Ontario in Utah.

George was a strong man, slightly over six feet tall and bearded. He cussed at times and drank his share of rotgut whiskey. He was not noted for bordello-hopping or for cheating any of his fellows. By all accounts, he was an upright person whose word was his bond. Perhaps that wasn't difficult, because he was not a big talker. Grandma said a lot of folks saw him as a soft touch.

In 1860, a decade after George had left home, he received a letter from his family saying his mother was ill. Grandpa was now a rich man, and felt it was time to wipe out the last dollars of debt and put his family in order. So he returned home, comforted his mother by paying off the final bills, and remained until she died. He told no one outside the family of his wealth.

During this time George met pretty little Phoebe. She was eighteen and he was forty. Actually, the two distant cousins had first met when Phoebe was nine years old. The families had been neighbors and friends. She had been named after George's mother, Phoebe Elizabeth. Young Phoebe's parents, the William Appersons, were successful farmers who discouraged the courtship because of the age difference. They also were concerned that George would bring their daughter into the rough camp life of California miners.

Phoebe deliberated long and hard. She told me that she also was lured by the prospect of a faraway land with a golden rainbow. Grandma saw George as a handsome dreamer who would find gold. So they eloped. The two were married in Steadman, Missouri, on June 15, 1862. She was nineteen and he was forty-one. They remained in Missouri for four months to settle the estate of George's mother. By the time they left for California—a honeymoon trip by train to New York, a boat to Panama, across the isthmus, and another ship to San Francisco—Phoebe was pregnant. On April 29, 1863—in the midst of the Civil War—Phoebe gave birth to her only child, William Randolph Hearst, in her San Francisco bedroom.

The couple's life, like most mining experiences in those days, was boom and bust. George was often away in the California hills or Nevada desert, searching for new strikes of gold or silver. After his first bust, Phoebe was forced to adjust from owning a big home to renting a modest dwelling. She told me it never bothered her. Like George, she always saw other nuggets beyond a new rainbow. Both were lifelong dreamers and optimists. Sure enough, more strikes came and the family was back on top of San Francisco's hills in a large new mansion. Grandma told me she never doubted that George would make it. He became not only one of the richest men in the country but, later, a U.S. senator and newspaper owner. George died in 1891, leaving his entire estate to Phoebe.

After her husband died, Grandma controlled one of this country's largest mining and land fortunes. But her real interest was young Willie. That was clear from the chats she had with me about my father. Phoebe laughed one time and told me this story:

Willie had an Irish governess by the name of Eliza Pike. The young Irish woman was a Catholic and uncomfortable with the fact that Phoebe had not yet had her child baptized.

One day, while Grandma was out of San Francisco looking for a California home for her parents, Eliza swooped up Willie and raced to a Catholic church, where she had a priest baptize the boy.

Later, Eliza confessed her deed to Phoebe, who mildly protested that she was an Episcopalian. The governess replied, "It doesn't matter so long as the baby is a Christian."

Grandma burst into laughter. Eliza apparently thought there were Christians and christians.

Phoebe told me that Willie was quite intelligent, but his forte was an irrepressible imagination. He loved mischief. She sighed and said Willie wasn't easy to discipline. He was courteous one minute and exploding firecrackers the next. He liked acting and singing, but once sprayed his dancing teacher with the water hose.

Phoebe also had quite an imagination for a woman of her day. When Willie was ten, the two of them sailed for Europe. A private tutor came along. For the next year and a half the pair discovered European art in the finest museums and galleries of Germany, Italy, France, and England. Grandma laughed when she told me of the trip, "The teachers at home never would have believed it. They thought Willie was a barbarian!" Grandma knew this was the most impressionable and character-building time in my father's upbringing. He would continue to be a prankster through college, but she had motivated him in another direction for the rest of his life—toward being an admirer and collector of great painting, sculpture, and other art.

That was precisely what Phoebe did in Europe: admire. And buy, buy, buy. Actually, George was having hard financial times at home, but she continued buying, forever the optimist. To ease Grandpa's concerns, she wrote him daily letters saying their one-time "holy terror" was becoming a gentleman. And, she hoped, a scholar.

After returning home, Pop discovered theater—from sturdy old American plays to *Hamlet*. He was wild about minstrels and song-and-dance acts. He memorized songs and learned to imitate some of the dance steps. Willie stepped lively in his formal education too, moving from school to school and tutor to tutor. He exhausted his teachers, friends, and acquaintances with pranks and pratfalls.

Grandma took Willie to Europe again, with a tutor, when he was sixteen. She returned to her old museum and gallery haunts across the continent. However, Phoebe galloped so swiftly that she finally collapsed and was put in bed. When Grandma realized she would be out of action for some time, she shipped Willie home to St. Paul's School near Concord, New Hampshire. The discipline, including three Episcopal church services daily, did little to improve Willie's behavior. He wrote his mother, still resting in Germany, that he would mellow if only she would spring him from this prison.

Phoebe finally returned home. She faced Willie and told him that, if he continued at St. Paul's and behaved himself, she would send him to Harvard. To inspire her son, Grandma even took Willie there for a visit. Nonetheless, desperate to flee St. Paul's and the New Hampshire deep-freeze, Willie again resorted to a long series of pranks, and the school finally bounced him out the door. Willie raced to the train and (as he later

told his mother) sang all the way back to San Francisco. He finished high
school under tutors at home.

Willie enrolled at Harvard with some misgivings. He apparently never
intended to do much studying. (Unfortunately, his professors soon recognized this.) Instead, he became business manager of the *Lampoon*, the
university humor magazine, and of Hasty Pudding, the theater-production
group. Pop put the *Lampoon* on its financial feet with various advertising
gimmicks. He was a sometime actor in Hasty Pudding productions, and
a full-time leader of rowdy beer blasts that kept the actors in the pudding.
Pop raised a lot of hell.

In 1885, during his junior year, Pop got tired of acting like a student.
He decided to bow out with an ingenious, suspenseful final act—sending
chamber pots to his profs with their individual names embellished on the
bottom of each. Harvard rang down the curtain.

Grandma said Pop never once expressed a regret or misgiving about
Harvard. He never looked back. He had other aims and didn't like wasting time. These goals were in a state of flux—from buying a newspaper
to taking another trip to Europe. But the thrust of his character remained:
Never be idle.

In the spring of 1886 the governor of California appointed Grandpa
to fill the unexpired term of U.S. Senator John T. Miller, who had died
in office. Phoebe and George went to Washington, and purchased a large
home there. George implored his son to return to the family roost and
run one or more of its businesses—which included the 1,000-square-mile,
million-acre Babicora Ranch that he had bought in Mexico.

But Pop was now far more committed than his parents realized to
becoming a newspaper owner and editor. He became a reporter on Joseph
Pulitzer's *New York World*. Pop was attracted by Pulitzer's odd combination of idealism and circulation-raising stunts. Many New Yorkers
considered the *World* sensational—and it was, featuring juicy scandal and
murder—but the paper also exposed corruption and other local injustices.

My father was already versed in many aspects of journalism because of
his prolonged visits to the *Boston Globe* while at Harvard. The *World*
widened his technical knowledge and honed his editorial skills. He was
ready to assume direction of his own newspaper. And where else but at
his father's own dull, money-eating *San Francisco Examiner*. Grandpa had

purchased the paper in 1880 after staking it to several loans. He was active politically, and thought the *Examiner* would help his fellow Democrats.

In 1887 George realized a lifetime ambition—he was appointed to a full six-year term in the Senate. At that point he finally relented and turned the *Examiner* over to his twenty-three-year-old son. Grandma said George did it because of a remarkably persuasive letter that Willie wrote to his father:

> I have just finished and dispatched a letter to the editor of the *Examiner* in which I commented on the illustrations, if you may call them such, which have lately disfigured the paper.
>
> I really believe that the *Examiner* has furnished what is thus far the crowning absurdity in illustrated journalism, in illustrating an article on the chicken show by means of the identical Democratic roosters used during the late campaign.
>
> In my letter to the editor, however, I did not refer to this for fear of offending him, but I did tell him that in my opinion the cuts that have recently appeared in the paper bore an unquestionable resemblance to the Cuticura Soap advertisements; and I am really inclined to believe that our editor has illustrated many of his articles from his stock of cuts representing gentlemen before and after using that efficacious remedy.
>
> In case my remarks should have no effect and he should continue in his career of desolation, let me beg of you to remonstrate with him and thus prevent him from giving the finishing stroke to our miserable little sheet.

Nevertheless, Pop insisted he was fond of the paper—as a mother loved a deformed offspring. He didn't want to see the *Examiner* die and was convinced he could run it successfully. He explained:

> It would be well to make the paper as far as possible original. To imitate only some such leading journal as the *New York World* which depends for its success upon enterprise, energy and a startling originality, not upon the wisdom of its political opinions or the lofty style of its editorials. To accomplish that, we must have active, intelligent and energetic young men.

Pop said the *Examiner* would have to be publicized from Oregon to Mexico to raise its prestige and increase its advertising, even if that meant lowering rates. He stressed the importance of illustrations, concluding:

"All these changes [must] be made not by degrees but at once so that the improvement will be very marked and noticeable."

The *Examiner* claimed a circulation of more than 23,000 when Pop assumed control. Even that skimpy total was artificially boosted by freebies. The young publisher aimed to change that when, on March 4, the same day his father was sworn in, he stayed up most of the night to publish his first edition. Pop eventually made the *Examiner* the Word of the West. This was his code: promote public service, support the underdog, and raise circulation. In all three areas, he raised hell.

Pop had moved into a house across the bay at Sausalito with Tessie Powers. She had been his mistress at Harvard, and apparently in Washington and New York. He had met her through a friend while she was a waitress in Cambridge. By all accounts, Tessie was pretty and fun, and adored Willie. Pop never hid his living with Tessie and, later, actress Marion Davies—except from Grandma. He didn't wish to be known as a hypocrite. Yet, he was essentially a private man—to his mother, and then to his wife and children, his business associates, and most who knew him.

One of my father's greatest faults was that he always went out and did what he damn well pleased. Grandma and Grandpa had long ago learned that hard, cold fact. George once said of his son, "When he wants cake, he wants cake, and he wants it now. I have noticed that, after a while, he gets the cake."

Some people described the *Examiner* as a three-ring circus. Wrong. It was a one-ring circus with Pop as the ringmaster. The headlines were the largest and loudest on the West Coast. He would splash a big local fire across the entire front page and much of the second. Pop would cover a California disaster with a trainload of reporters who would wring every cry and tear from the tragedy. He would send another team to expose a Chinese opium den. The young editor was a walking firecracker who hired brass bands, boats, and trains in various journalistic exploits. He not only loved the hurly-burly but created much of it.

Grandma said Willie's finest quality was loyalty to his people. He was courteous and charming but formal, calling everyone "Mister" or "Miss." But that formality never lessened his commitment to his employees. Pop hired several women reporters, which was unheard of in those days. Some became "sob sisters"—or, more accurately, the mothers of many a weepy story. The first was the *Examiner*'s Winifred Sweet, who later became

Winifred Black Bonfils. She wrote under the byline of Annie Laurie. Winifred wrote heartrending yarns of little orphans, fallen angels, runaway children, and lovable lost dogs.

Grandma liked Winifred's human interest scoops. Her favorite was the time Winifred faked fainting on a downtown San Francisco street and was taken to the City Receiving Hospital. She wrote a sensational exposé of what happened to her and other patients. They were carted to the emergency room in filthy wagons, ill treated by drunken male attendants, and harassed by other staff members. The exposé shocked the city. It brought about regular ambulance service and cleaned out some of the rotten hospital staff.

Many were later to follow Winifred on the *New York Journal-American* and other Hearst newspapers, but none was better. Some said she could make a stone weep. And, of course, circulation jumped. Winifred was with us for some fifty years.

Critics said that, as editor of the *Examiner,* Pop became a peddler of journalistic shock and sensationalism. That is, to a large extent, true. As a matter of fact, old-time *Examiner* editor Arthur McEwen is often quoted for his sprightly summary of the paper's style. McEwen wanted readers to say "Gee whiz!" on seeing the front page. They were to holler "Holy Moses!" on glancing at the second page. And by Page Three, they should leap from their seats and shout "God a'mighty!" Somebody once said, "San Franciscans went to a party every time they picked up the *Examiner.*"

Pop was not only the first West Coast editor to splash big, bold headlines but he ran racy stories on the front page as well. However, the *Examiner*'s boldest story of the day was often of great significance—from exposing political graft to detailed reporting on health. He hired the best reporters and writers for the paper at the highest salaries. These included Mark Twain, Jack London, and Ambrose Bierce, to name a few. And some of the country's best artists—from Thomas Nast to Frederick Remington, Charles Russell, and Walt Disney.

Pop's biggest battles were against the California utilities and the Southern Pacific Railroad. The toughest fight, which raged for years, involved the railroad. Pop attacked the "unscrupulous power" of Southern Pacific, which was in undisputed control of California state government. Democrats and Republicans alike had caved in to railroad magnate C. P. Huntington. Political corruption was so rampant that one article in the

Examiner said: "You couldn't pass the Lord's Prayer in this legislature without money."

Virtually every newspaper in the state was, to one degree or another, controlled by the railroad. When Pop challenged the Southern Pacific, he was also declaring war on state government and other newspapers. Old-timers admired his guts. Some historians tended to be somewhat cynical about his motivations. But no one challenged his courage. Pop was ultimately responsible for forcing the railroad to repay the federal government about $120 million in interest on loans. The young editor also forced gas and water companies to lower their prices because they were robbing the public.

He championed the building of the Panama Canal, a stronger U.S. Navy, union labor, and usually supported whoever happened to be the underdog at the moment. He was a very outspoken Progressive at first, perhaps as much as Wisconsin's Senator Robert La Follette. Pop later became a Democrat with pronounced socialist views. Ultimately, he joined the Republican party and became a leading anti-Communist. Grandma was proud that Willie dedicated the *Examiner* to many public service projects. She even prompted some of them.

Phoebe and George knew that Pop worked harder than anyone at the paper. Perhaps that's why the two pleased parents allowed their Willie to put the bite on them for more than $300,000 during the first year that he owned and edited it. He bought new presses, raised salaries, and organized attention-grabbing stunts to improve the *Examiner*'s circulation and prestige. As for reports that Willie danced a jig in the city room when one of his reporters broke an outstanding story, Grandma and Grandpa ignored them.

I found it interesting that Grandma saved the front page of Willie's first edition of the *Examiner* in 1887. These are the stories that covered it:

- The opening of a new German parliament in Berlin.
- The golden jubilee of England's Queen Victoria.
- A report on the Roman Catholic Church's views concerning organized labor.
- An exposé of negligence at San Francisco institutions for foundling babies.

That coverage could hardly be termed sensational. It was mostly Pop's brashness that made him enemies. He challenged not only many notions of journalistic practice but also turn-of-the-century business and political ethics. Leaders in all these fields were furious with him. Pop's individualism and independence were to make him enemies all his life.

In fewer than five years, Pop transformed the *Examiner* from a listless little sheet into a lively, news-and-feature-packed, increasingly influential, and financially successful newspaper. The enterprise attracted national attention because, among other reasons, it was the most attractive newspaper west of the Mississippi. By the time of my grandfather's death in 1891, the *Examiner*'s circulation and advertising had more than tripled. The paper was now equal to or better than any competitor.

Pop was ready for New York.

My father left San Francisco in 1895. He never forgot the *Examiner*, though. When the newspaper suffered some $2 million in damages in the 1906 earthquake, Pop wrote: "Everything has been destroyed except that indomitable American pluck, the unconquerable American spirit which will not be subdued. In a month, there will be the beginning of a new and splendid city; in a year it will have assumed shape; and in three to five years it will be built and busy, greater than ever." Pop's first act was to express loyalty to *Examiner* employees. His second was to find new presses. He discovered them in Salt Lake City, and paid twice their worth. The unassembled parts were loaded on two railroad cars and attached to a San Francisco-bound express train; Chicago mechanics were rushed by train to San Francisco to assemble them. Pop had done it all between lunch and dinner in New York. Within days of the quake, the *Examiner* was publishing again. Grandma cheered.

Phoebe was as busy as her Willie. Since the death of George, she had funded innumerable charities. Despite her unassuming ways, Grandma had become a powerful force in education and other fields. She was a devoted patron of the arts, and gave generously to historical institutions and other worthy causes. She also was the behind-the-scenes, multimillion-dollar force that propelled her son into building the largest media empire in the country.

As Pop launched his New York career in 1895, Phoebe moved from San Francisco to his one-time hacienda at Pleasanton, a farming area in the hills of Alameda County. She called it the Hacienda del Pozo de Verona—the House of the Well of Verona. The beautiful fountain adorning the well was designed and sculpted in Italy before the United States was born. Grandma wanted to live more quietly than the bustle and noise of San Francisco would allow. Also, she was getting older and more concerned about her health. The trip to Pleasanton, round about in those days, was about forty miles. Grandma continued to maintain her apartment above the *Examiner,* and lived there when business and other needs demanded. But the hacienda became home.

From the time I was a child, I spent several months each year with Grandma at her hacienda. I had a lot of colds and bronchitis in New York, so Mom and Pop thought it best that I live with her in the milder California climate. She was to become my second mother. I really grew up on both the East and West coasts. About the age of five, I began spending the entire summer with Grandma. That is the earliest and clearest remembrance of my childhood. I have no recollections of the house where I was born on January 27, 1908, at Twenty-eighth Street and Lexington Avenue in Manhattan.

Grandma had such an enormous influence over me because she rarely, if ever, preached. That is, with words. I was so impressed by the way she stood, and spoke—and rode in her huge Pierce Arrow limousine—that I was completely fascinated. It was a huge, polished, very grand contraption, and assumed an even more distinguished aura with a uniformed chauffeur sitting in the front seat. She invited us for a ride only when she wanted company going to San Francisco. Years earlier, when I had first met her, she used a stylish carriage pulled by highstepping trotters.

I used to say that whatever derring-do I had as a youngster I inherited from Grandma. None of us was ever sure what she was going to do next. I remember her telling me of the big summer of 1912 at her hacienda at Pleasanton. Grandma decided to build the first permanent camp for the Young Women's Christian Association. I thought that was a wonderful gift until she told me *where* she planned to build—a camp for nearly 300 girls on the grounds of the hacienda!

First, Grandma sketched out for a contractor precisely what she wanted done—including the piping and draining of water as well as the electrical supply. Then she mapped the exact area for a large platform, to be covered with a massive tent, that would serve as a dining area for 350 people. Some seventy-three tents, each with sleeping cots and dressing tables for four girls, were set in the shade under nearby oak trees. Other needs, including the china and entire equipment for the "chow hall," were chosen and purchased by Phoebe. Grandma was determined to win the support of all her neighbors for the project. So she ordered all the food for the camp from nearby farmers—fresh fruit, vegetables, eggs, fresh milk, butter, poultry, beef, lamb, and pork.

Phoebe made the place jump, but preferred to stay in the background. She told me her enjoyment came in surprising people.

A few years after I began spending my summers with Grandma, I noticed that, when I was safely tucked away for the night, she would go to her sitting room and work. In later years, I saw that her lights would sometimes be on until two or three o'clock in the morning. In high school, I finally figured out what she was doing.

When Grandfather passed on, he had left her one of the country's largest companies and she was now running it—extensive silver and gold mines, the ranches at San Simeon and in Mexico, the *Examiner* and the growing newspaper chain of her son, as well as other investments. She was her own accountant and knew the financial status of each enterprise. She scheduled meetings at the hacienda with foremen and others running these businesses. Grandma hired and fired, promoted and demoted, and watched every move my father made. She was his top banker. I began to realize, to my utter astonishment, that Grandma was one of the richest women in America.

Phoebe was all the more remarkable because of her plain, homespun background. She was born on December 3, 1842, on a farm near the town of St. James in Franklin County, Missouri. Her parents were neither rich nor poor. They had migrated there from Virginia and South Carolina. Phoebe became a schoolteacher and, before she married George Hearst, her most daring accomplishment was a study and sightseeing trip to St. Louis.

Based on that rural background, she adhered to three unbendable rules: Be on time, have good manners, and respect older people. This was demonstrated virtually every day at afternoon tea. My brothers and I were expected to be in her sitting room at four o'clock on the dot. Her tea and our milk and cookies would be served at precisely that hour, not a minute later. Each of us was to greet Grandmother, showing her proper respect. Then, we would proceed to our individual chairs and take up our napkins. We would not grab, no matter how hungry we might be, but wait until the cookie plate was passed. Our napkins were to be folded properly across our knees, and we were to be relatively quiet until everyone was served.

Grandma opened the conversation by asking us what we had done during the day. Each of us, in turn, would respond.

She frequently had guests for tea, which meant don't be a second late! These were often prominent people—the governor, the president of a university, a distinguished poet, and perhaps several bright university students who had caught her eye. The tea talk was often way over my head. She would discuss European art, archeology, poetry, opera, whatever was appropriate for the guests. We were expected to show our interest by asking questions if we wished, but we were not to interrupt the speaker. We were to remain until Grandma rose, the signal that tea was over. We were to fold our napkins appropriately, shake hands graciously with each guest, and depart with a minimum of running and shouting.

Grandma knew precisely what her place was and what ours were—and ran her roost with a velvet voice and a withering look of disapproval. I believe she was the only person on earth who ever scared my father. She never raised her voice, although she sometimes lectured him in a soft but authoritative tone.

If Phoebe was a teacher, she was also a student—of almost everything. She loved birds and liked to chitchat about the activities of the Audubon Society. She hired special tutors to teach us about nature and the environment. As a result, I've been a lifetime bird watcher and nature lover. Her favorite subject was anthropology. She spoke often and knowingly of man's origins, traditions, and cultures. Phoebe was reared an Episcopalian and believed children should have religious education. She talked about right and wrong, but in terms of hard work, self-improvement, and a strong family life. In essence, life had a purpose.

These chats were warm and outgoing, never in the form of a lecture. Her soft sweetness and easy charm, as she discussed such profundities as good and evil, constantly impressed me. The thing that distinguished Phoebe from most people I met was that she had an extraordinary presence. Everything she said and did seemed important, and you remembered it.

Grandma had an unusual habit that confounded me the entire eleven years I knew her. She started to buy Christmas presents in January, when her current tree was still up. She would see something that seemed particularly appropriate for a certain person and buy it. She reserved some closets for only Christmas gifts and would fill every one of them by June or July. I was never tempted to sneak a look in any of them because I thought I might get killed in an avalanche if I opened any of the closet doors. Every year, Phoebe shopped until the very day before Christmas. Once, a certain San Francisco department store was about to close before the holiday, but she had not completed her shopping. They kept the entire store open for her alone until she finished.

Although the feminist movement as we understand it today did not exist in her time, Phoebe was extremely active in aiding young women's causes—from help for the YWCA to constructing women's buildings at the University of California at Berkeley. She gave many individual scholarships to young women in various fields: medicine, engineering, architecture, music, and others. Phoebe also joined and marched with O.H.P. Belmont to win American women the right to vote.

One of these student protégées, Julia Morgan, was among the first women engineering graduates at UC Berkeley, and later became the first woman to graduate from the École des Beaux-Arts in Paris, long recognized as the world's top architectural school. Miss Morgan worked for Phoebe, designing additions to her hacienda. Julia was later to become the architect of Pop's enormous construction project at San Simeon. This native San Franciscan worked with my father for about thirty years.

Phoebe not only sponsored an international architectural competition to enhance the development of UC Berkeley but funded a women's gymnasium, a mining school as a memorial to her husband, and other projects on that campus.

Grandma never forgot her days as a Missouri school teacher. She founded and sponsored free kindergartens before they were part of the national education system. She built and maintained a kindergarten and library at her husband's mines in Lead, South Dakota, and Anaconda, Montana. She and her friend, Alice Birney, founded and helped support the first Parent Teachers Association.

She became involved with various San Francisco hospitals, and soon sought to offer women the opportunity to study and practice medicine at them. She visited these hospitals regularly, often paying nurses' salaries, offering extra payments to doctors for special work, and covering other hospital expenses, including payment for medicines and baby clothes. Grandma gave $10,000 to San Francisco's Hahnemann Hospital when it opened, and became one of the largest benefactors of Children's Hospital. She also contributed to the San Francisco Infants' Shelter and Old People's Home, as well as to orphan asylums. And she was always mailing checks to poor folks back in Missouri.

Phoebe improved her already good French and visited all the great art galleries and museums of Europe to become a connoisseur; she achieved the same mastery of opera and symphonic music. At the same time, she was sending young men and women to college, even abroad. The students included violinists, pianists, painters, sculptors, architects, and writers. She had become a patron of young ambition, especially among women.

Phoebe sponsored archeological digs at the San Antonio Mission near her hacienda. Later, in 1948, the Hearst foundation provided $500,000 to help restore the California missions.

When her husband became a U.S. senator, and the family moved to Washington, D.C., she immediately established free kindergartens for the poor. Phoebe also helped build both the National Protestant Episcopal Cathedral and the National Cathedral School for Girls. She gave $175,000 for the construction of the school alone. When it was discovered that construction would eventually cost much more, Grandma assumed the total cost. She completed the final payment on the entire Mount St. Albans tract of land. Phoebe cared little or nothing about what religion an individual might belong to or, to be even more precise, whether they practiced any faith at all.

Grandma decided to help restore George Washington's home at Mount Vernon. After it began crumbling into ruins, the old place had been purchased by a group of women known as the Mount Vernon Ladies Association of the Union. The association was one of the first national women's groups in the country. After Phoebe was settled in Washington, she not only helped to restore the house and 200-acre estate but assisted in organizing the group to raise more funds. She also hunted for the Washington family's old furniture and other pieces that had been sold or removed. She found many and returned them to their proper places in American history. Phoebe also spent $250,000 to restore the estate's old sea wall, to prevent it from being washed away. The ladies' association praised her work and elected her a regent. However, Phoebe's contributions remained generally unrecognized. A bishop finally learned of her activities and wrote her a letter of thanks. She treasured the letter and kept it among her papers.

My father bought Abraham Lincoln's 62-acre farmstead and offered it to the state of Illinois, but Phoebe provided the funds. It's not generally known but, through Phoebe's friends, he also gave 400 acres and $100,000 to Oglethorpe University in Georgia.

As if all that were not enough, Phoebe underwrote archeology digs in Egypt, Italy, Russia, Peru, Greece, Mexico, and even Florida. She sponsored a five-year dig in Egypt and, in 1905, she went there to see for herself and spent months at the excavation. She also co-founded the Travelers Aid Society.

Although she liked fine clothes and other amenities, Phoebe spent the overwhelming part of her fortune on others. She was very practical, studying situations and people closely before she offered financial aid or reward.

Perhaps it seems I'm boasting about Grandma's generosity. She herself went to great pains to conceal it, but that was often impossible. Many projects became public. Still, she was able to keep private scores of scholarships and similar assistance. It's estimated that she gave away somewhere between $21 million and $25 million during her lifetime. That was when a dollar was real money, and there were no tax benefits in giving to charity. Many of Phoebe's charitable works, and those of my father too, have never been made public.

If Phoebe had one big disappointment in life it was not having more children. She casually mentioned that to me several times. She loved my father deeply, and proudly told me he was named after his paternal and maternal grandfathers. He became the light of her life. She wanted other children who would be named after other relatives, but they never came.

Grandma caught influenza during an epidemic in the early spring of 1919. My brother Jack and I were living with her in the hacienda at the time. For the next several weeks she kept getting weaker. Jack was then stricken with appendicitis and hospitalized. I was the only grandson with her.

When Grandma's health suddenly deteriorated sharply, Mom and Pop took the train west to join us. Phoebe lingered on but never regained her strength. She was very calm, though, and I kept telling her that she would pull through. Shortly after my parents arrived, Phoebe died. It was Easter Sunday, April 3, 1919. This was the first time that I had looked death in the face. I wept for days. The whole world had fallen and crashed into smithereens for this eleven-year-old boy. I could not envisage life without her. That was the end of my boyhood innocence. I never looked at life quite the same way again.

II

THE LITTLE SULTANS

Pop married Millicent Veronica Willson in 1903. He loved the theater and beautiful women. Millicent fit the billing—she was very pretty and a dancer in New York musicals with her sister, Anita. The Willson family were entertainers and lived near Gramercy Park in Manhattan. On the day Pop and Mom were wed, he was one day shy of forty and she was twenty-one.

Grandma was not too happy about the match, however. With her down-home, Missouri farm upbringing, Grandma didn't view big-city entertainers as reliable enough for a stable marriage. It was only after Mom began to present Grandma with five grandchildren—George, myself, John, and the twins, Randolph and David—that Phoebe reversed field. By the time mother had the twins, Phoebe and Mom were engaged in a charming correspondence. It was one of the few times in Grandma's life that she was wrong. Mom and Pop sent Phoebe this note shortly after my birth:

> He [my brother George] looked the baby over very carefully, patted it when it cried, and named it at once his "Brother Weeyum." Weeyum is a fine, big baby. He has blue eyes and rather blond hair, a fine voice, a good appetite, and a disposition to sleep his senses away.
>
> Milly and Will

About a year after I was born, we moved from Twenty-eighth Street and Lexington Avenue in Manhattan to Eighty-sixth Street and Riverside Drive on the west side of town. Our new place, which we rented, covered the top three floors of the Clarendon Apartments. It overlooked the Hudson River. That was Pop's response to Mother's request for more room. It was like a royal palace. The lowest of the three floors was a dining room and big-domed living room. Pop often used one end of the large living room as an office. The two top floors were made into a banquet hall for parties and a ballroom for dancing. The ballroom had a balcony at each end. There were two apartments on each floor. Mom and Pop, who entertained a lot, lived on the middle floor. Our parents had a retinue of maids, butlers, and cooks.

Our home was to become even larger. The owner wouldn't allow Pop to expand our apartment, so my father bought the entire building for about $1 million. He had much of it redecorated. When all the work was finished, some people said we owned the largest private apartment in New York and likely the world. It was a little like living in Madison Square Garden.

Pop proceeded to buy a lot of real estate in Manhattan, especially around Columbus Circle in midtown. These purchases continued for many years. In today's market, they would be worth billions of dollars.

Our parents weren't home very much. When they did entertain, they didn't want five noisy boys roughhousing underfoot. They also were concerned about all the valuable paintings, statuary, and armor in the place. So we boys lived downstairs with our cousins—August and Mamie Mayer and their two boys, Charlie and Billy, and daughter, Millicent. Mr. Mayer was a detective on the New York City police force.

However, my brother Jack and I were often invited upstairs, where we met the cream of New York society. Jack and I were almost like twins. We did nearly everything together because of our close age. Our eldest brother, George, was four years older than I. The family's real twins were much younger. Jack and I liked the vaudeville song-and-dance teams that often entertained guests after dinner. Edgar Bergen, the ventriloquist, and his dummy, Charlie McCarthy, were wonderful. But Jack and I preferred comedians like Bert Lahr and Ed Wynn. I loved Wynn and for weeks tried to imitate him.

We had governesses, nannies, and private tutors—even bodyguards when my father feared we might be kidnapped. That was the custom of rich, prominent men at the time. They chose the best guardians and schools they could find and then turned their children over to them.

We saw Mom virtually every day during our grade-school years in New York. She could not have been more devoted to us. I loved my mother dearly and still do. But most of her time was given to my father, to charities, and necessary social events. Mom's most distinctive characteristic was her terrific sense of humor. She passed some of that on to me.

My father, like many other parents, would step in when we had study or deportment problems, but, for the most part, we came under the direction of others. We were really a type of American aristocracy, styled along the lines of the British upper class. In those days, many wealthy American parents allocated time to their children only when there was good reason and available time.

None of us knew the meaning of financial need. We asked, and things simply appeared. We attended the best private schools, wore the best clothes, and had our own chauffeur to drive us around town. We often invited pals and tooled around Manhattan like little sultans.

At the age of six I was marched off to what we called the Dutch School. That was because the Dutch Reform Church was its founder and located next door. Presidents Theodore Roosevelt and Franklin D. Roosevelt had gone to church there. Its proper name was the Collegiate School. It's still educating there on West Seventy-seventh Street. Collegiate was known for its high teaching standards and strict discipline. It also had military training under a former French army officer. He taught us French as well.

All of us wore the same cap. It was shaped like a Union Army hat— dark blue and flat on top. I learned the cap would hold water and you could drink out of it. I was caught, of course, as was the case in most of the antics I pulled. I, and others, concluded I was not cut out to be a general.

Pop assigned Chris MacGregor, a mild-mannered young fellow from his newspaper, to watch over us. Chris drove us to school and picked us up every day. He often took us to the Riverside Drive and Van Cortlandt parks, where he watched over us as we played on the swings and merry-go-round. Sometimes we would play stickball with neighborhood pals in the streets near our home. We used mop handles and broomsticks to hit a soft rubber ball. The cops would often chase us off the streets, and we would take it on the lam like any other red-blooded roughnecks.

The old man himself nailed us in one escapade. My brothers and I somehow got our hands on a stage spotlight. We hooked it up inside our apartment and began shining it on horses, cars, and people below. Some people got rather sore. Finally we made out the figure of a man walking toward us in the darkness. We gave him the full treatment. It was Pop! Wow, did we stand to attention on that one!

I later played first base on local sandlot teams. My idol was Bill Terry, the first baseman of the New York Giants. When the Giants moved to San Francisco, I was devastated. But the blow was cushioned, because San Francisco was part of our family history.

Even though I had decided not to become a general, I had not informed Pop. So when I was ten, he sent me to a military school, St. John Manlius, near Syracuse, New York. It was war from the start. The place struck me as an igloo just this side of the polar ice caps. I was a frail, skin-and-bones kid. I was convinced that one begins freezing at thirty-five degrees Fahrenheit. Pop called an armistice after one semester and yanked me out of the cooler. That's when I started going out to Grandma's hacienda in California, where the climate was milder and tutors came to the house.

I was always somewhat in awe of Grandma, her hacienda, and its beautiful gardens. The gentle slopes and green fields made the landscape seem like an old-world fairyland. The flowers were spectacular—pergolas filled with purple and white Japanese wisteria, with roses and tropical jasmine climbing above and shading the cloisters of a nun's walk. There was a beautiful grove of oaks, tall trees from one to three centuries old, standing like sentinels on the hill above the hacienda. Grandma gave receptions (under large tents when there was a threat of rain) for as many as 300 guests in the gorgeous outdoor gardens.

I still see the hacienda today in an old photograph taken there with two of my brothers. I cherish it more than any other remembrance of my childhood. It shows me saddled on a pony near the hacienda. My brother George is sitting on a larger pony in a leather saddle. Jack is in a tub-shaped wicker basket, with his legs sticking out through the sides. He could not have been more than three. That photo always makes me smile.

The hacienda was a long residence that rambled more than 500 feet from one end to the other. It overlooked the Livermore Valley. The roof level rose and fell as Grandma built new sections and added second stories to provide quarters for us and guests. A ballroom stood near one end, with bedrooms above it. Beyond the ballroom, up a flight of stairs, were a half-dozen bedrooms where we slept. Next to the ballroom, a long hall led into a billiard room. And adjacent to that was a long living room with an adjoining dark-blue sitting room. Grandma spent much of her day in the sitting room and usually went there after dinner. She received guests there and in the library.

My brothers and I had our own dining room across from the living room. Grandma usually ate with us. However, when she had guests, Phoebe entertained them more formally in the large dining room. Our dining room led out into a pantry area and into the kitchen, which must have been fifty feet long. Downstairs, below ground level, was a cool room where Grandma slept in the summer. She used a bedroom at the other end of the house, in the wing over the music room, during winter.

The hacienda had a great banquet hall, perhaps sixty feet by thirty feet, for formal occasions. It was a magnificent Spanish-style room with grilled doors of carved bronze that Grandma found in an ancient Spanish castle. She bought the door on one of her trips to Europe and had it transported to California. Phoebe bought many art objects in Europe and had them shipped to the hacienda. Her collection was formidable in its own right, since the purchases spanned about forty years.

Grandma had great parties, often fifty people for an entire weekend and 300 for a wedding, christening, or outdoor dinner. She used the music room and ballroom indoors, and the spacious garden for outdoor gatherings. Phoebe entertained foreign dignitaries as well as senators and other Washington leaders, California politicians, educators, poets, physicians, archeologists, musicians, writers, and, especially, young people. She loved the vitality and spontaneity of the young.

Although small, Phoebe was very regal in long, high-collared, lace-trimmed dresses. She dressed that way every day, all day. Her favorite color was lavender and she wore it often. I wondered about her dress because, most of the time, just us family were out there in the hills—nowhere, really—and she comported herself like a queen.

Beyond the music-room end of the house, Grandma built a fifty-foot playroom for our use on rainy days. An indoor swimming pool sparkled in blue-white just off it. A tennis court stood outside. A rear warehouse stopped stray balls and pinged them back to us. A grape arbor meandered along the tennis court, and also ran past the front of the hacienda.

In one of the storehouses at the rear of the residence, Grandma kept dozens of trunks of beautiful costumes. When young people came for an education conference or some other get-together that she would sponsor,

Grandma would open the trunks at the end of the meeting and host a costume party. The young crowd—dressing as queens, knights, and court jesters—loved it.

In back of the warehouse we had a sandpile with swings, rings, kiddy cars, and other playthings. In those early days, Jack and I had a German governess who tried to keep us out of trouble. When we outgrew our sandpile, Grandma built a two-story boys' house for us. It was a barracks-type building where we could holler and battle out of her hearing. The place had a balcony with three bedrooms on either side and a couple of bedrooms at each end. It had pool and billiard tables, reading rooms, and places for visitors. I used to read Jules Verne there, and thought he was a pretty far-out guy with his science-fiction yarns on going to the moon and submarine trips to the depths of far-away oceans. Of course, we had no radios, TV, or videos, so Verne was very exciting stuff.

I mention these details about Grandma's place to indicate that the five of us lived in the lap of luxury on both the East and West coasts. Surprisingly perhaps, we didn't see ourselves as rich or exceptional kids. We simply had not been exposed to how most families lived. We discovered the real world much later in life, and it came as a big shock to some of my brothers.

The Fourth of July at Grandma's was always special. Pop, who was a firecracker nut, would set off so many explosions and soaring rockets that Grandma would hide. We had an Airedale by the name of Punch. That dog had an uncanny ability to know the Fourth was about to explode. On the afternoon before the fireworks, he would run for the hills and not return until the following morning. I'm not sure what tipped him off, but it may have been a few sparklers that we tested in the afternoon.

We had a great time at the hacienda, riding the ponies and, later, the horses, swimming, playing pool, and eventually learning about cars. That was my youthful downfall. I fell head over heels in love with everything on four wheels.

I had a car, as I have mentioned, at the age of twelve. It was a Saxon. The large acreage of Grandma's place allowed me to drive it on the grounds. Of course Pop bought it, but I called it mine. Few people today have ever heard of a Saxon. It was a compact, open vehicle about the size of today's smallest car. I bounced all over Grandma's spread in it, staying off the outside roads, although I was always tempted to drive to San Francisco Bay, which was only about 20 miles away.

I returned to Collegiate from 1920 through 1922 because Grandma had died. After that, to improve my health, I returned to California. I learned that Pop had sold the hacienda a year after Phoebe's death. I had never been angry with my father, but I was furious with him after being told of the sale. I was upset because we had spent such wonderful times there, and Grandma had dedicated part of the hacienda as the boys' house. That made the place sacred. I wept bitterly.

I finished high school in Berkeley, where my brother George and I lived with cousins. I transferred to Hitchcock Military Academy at San Rafael, but did not graduate. Then I went to a cramming school so that I could take the entrance exam at the University of California at Berkeley. I entered Berkeley at seventeen and spent the next two and a half years studying liberal arts there. I was an average student and a member of Phi Delta Theta fraternity, but more interested in the real world than the lecture halls, fraternity house, or books.

My leaving the university didn't mean a whit to Pop. He was never impressed with a college education. The old man was actually pleased when I told him that I wanted to go to work for him on the *New York American*. It would get me off my duff and bring in some income.

During these years of growing up, I remained a car nut and deep in the old man's pocket. He bought me a sporty Packard with bucket seats and later a twelve-cylinder convertible Packard coupe. The last car the old man purchased for me was an open Studebaker touring car. I tried to talk him into a foreign sports car—the girls loved those—but he nixed that, saying America built the world's best cars. Meantime, I was souping up engines and modifying each vehicle to make it run faster and look sportier.

In those days, having your own car was like owning a large yacht today. To have one at my age was a gift of the gods. When I was born, in 1908, the General Motors Company was just being formed and Henry Ford announced the Model T. Before that, cars were too expensive to create a mass market. The road system was very bad. The U.S. automotive industry built only 65,000 "machines" that year. By 1914 the entire industry was producing only a half-million cars. Two years later, the country was astounded when the Ford Motor Company alone built 500,000 vehicles. Henry Ford was seen as an industrial and social revolutionary with his assembly-line production, an unheard-of five-dollar-a-day wage for workers, and a low-priced car.

Yet there were few gas stations on the roads. Lubricating your car was a long, dirty job. We had mostly open vehicles until 1915 or so, when closed cars began to outnumber them. That was a great advance for most families, whose Sunday picnic was often rained out before it started.

The first radios, clamped to the steering wheel, didn't appear until 1929. In 1930, Cadillac introduced the first V-6 engine. We didn't have automatic transmissions until 1937. It wasn't until 1948 that the first tubeless tire was sold.

In those years I could name every vehicle on the road. My life revolved around them until, in my late teens, I told Pop that I was hopelessly in love. He always chuckled at my youthful romances, but I told him that this time it was serious—airplanes. That made him sit up.

Pop was crazy about flying. Although not a pilot himself, he loved to go up and see the country. He was building a mile-long airstrip to fly himself and guests to and from San Simeon. He bought a tri-motored Stinson, a Douglas DC-3, and finally a converted B-23 that Douglas had built as a bomber. So the old man could hardly refuse to pay for my flying lessons.

I took lessons from Eddie Bellande, who had been a World War I navy pilot, and Pat Patterson, who later moved to Hong Kong, where I always tried to visit him on my trips to the Far East. The two risked their necks teaching me the basics of flying at Rogers Air Field, then on the outskirts of Los Angeles. The field has since disappeared in a cluster of homes and shopping centers along Crenshaw Boulevard.

I learned to fly in a Travelair biplane with two open-air cockpits. Eddie or Pat would sit in the front and use hand signals to me to keep my nose or wing up or down. The Travelair was smaller than the famous old fighting "Jenny" of World War I, but had the same engine. It boasted all of 90 horsepower. I soloed in 1927 when I was nineteen. There is no other feeling in the world like a solo flight—except perhaps when you become a father for the first time!

Flying was a lot easier in those days. You didn't have to work a radio and get tangled up in a lot of instruments. When you landed one of those little biplanes, you just sighted right along the top of the fuselage. That's unlike today, when you sit way up in the nose of the plane with what seems like miles of ship behind you.

I don't fly anymore, and drive a car only occasionally in daytime. My sight has given me problems since two cataract operations about twenty years ago. And my hearing has slipped over an even longer period. The noise from years of flying in open cockpits, together with more than a decade of underwater swimming in California, severely damaged my hearing. Even though I'm an old duffer, I miss both of them.

So I was going to work for the old man. I would be not only his son but also an employee. This would be an entirely new relationship. It meant accountability in a professional world. His world.

The old man was already a living legend. A giant in journalism. But who *was* he? Who was William Randolph Hearst, the newspaper owner, publisher, editor, and international art collector—this man of the world?

III
POP: THE MAN
AND THE MYTH

He was a Caesar. He had an inferiority complex.
He was a Charlemagne. He was shy and unassuming.
He was a Napoleon. He was indecisive.

He was a megalomaniac. He was a reserved, restrained, private man.

He was ruthless, reckless, a rogue. He was a keen competitor but a man of principle (his word was his bond), demonstrably kind, a gentleman of impeccable manner and speech.

He was one of the most hated men in America. He was a man of vision and greatness.

He was a muckraking sensationalist, a terror in print. He was one of the greatest technical innovators and public crusaders in the history of American journalism.

He was an enigma, two different men, a human contradiction. He was many things, but one for certain: a genius.

Those clashing characterizations have portrayed my father for a century—from when he became owner and publisher of the *San Francisco Examiner* in 1887 to his death in 1951 and even after his passing. He was all of those things. And none. Pop was simply a man of his times. He could be ahead of those times, as in his profession, and he could be deliberately behind, as in his courtly manners and love of art. But my father was essentially of the years and milieu in which he lived and worked.

When he left San Francisco to purchase the *New York Journal* in 1895, Pop was thirty-two years old. He deliberately chose to challenge the most powerful newspaper interests in the nation by entering its largest and most competitive market. It was, by any measure, a daring decision. He was risking professional and financial disaster.

The nation was economically troubled at the time, although New York appeared to be prosperous. Tens of thousands of workers across the land were unemployed and their number was increasing. Public protests and other discontent swept like a prairie fire across the country. Farmers torched wheat they were unable to sell; strikers, seeking higher pay for workers, rose in number; there was a call for silver currency; and a continuous tide of immigrants poured into the nation.

The New York metropolitan area was a Goliath compared to San Francisco—more than ten times the population of the Bay Area. Elevated trains, cable cars, hordes of delivery wagons, and bread lines filled the streets with a rushing, clamorous vitality. Gentlemen sported derbies and grand mustaches, and the ladies wore cartwheel hats and long skirts while riding in their horseless carriages. The city also swarmed with foreign poor who spoke little or no English and were struggling to survive. Tens of thousands of illiterate and ignorant aliens spoke three dozen different languages. These were the backroom seamstresses, sweatshop tailors, carpenters and painters, cobblers and fruit-stand vendors—Irish, Italian, Jewish, German, Chinese, and scores of others. A fair-paying permanent job was a gift of the gods.

Pop said that New York was the most American city—a great melting pot of people from across the world, all seeking freedom of opportunity, speech, and religion. These were his customers. He was going to help make them Americans—teach them how to read and write, and understand the city and nation in which they were strangers. He had to publish a newspaper that they could read and comprehend. My father saw this as a great adventure—and, if he himself were to survive, it could be profitable as well.

The three dominant newspapers in the city at the time were the *Sun, Herald,* and *World.* The *Times* and the *Tribune* lagged far back of the Big Three in circulation and earnings. Dragging in the rear were the *Recorder, Press, Advertiser,* and *Morning Journal.*

Pop purchased the *Morning Journal,* the only newspaper for sale at the time, for $180,000. The *Journal* was called the "chambermaid's paper," because it covered mostly gossip about the rich and famous. It had been owned for about a year by John R. McLean, a seasoned Ohio publisher, who bought it for $1 million. The paper had a German edition. McLean had, however, let the *Journal* slide, and it was ready to slip soundlessly into the nearby East River if the paper's news coverage, advertising, and earnings fell any further.

The *Journal* was located on two floors of a dingy structure on Printing House Square in lower Manhattan. This was Park Row—more like Newspaper Row, since most papers were situated there—across from City Hall. The two-story plant had old presses, musty offices, fading leadership, and lost direction. It sold about 30,000 copies a day.

The *World,* where up-to-date presses poured out a half-million copies daily, was located in the large, modern Pulitzer Building one block north. The building was named after its legendary owner, Joseph Pulitzer. Pop was soon editing the *Journal* from rented offices in a top floor of Pulitzer's own modern headquarters. In a pique of competitive fever, Pulitzer later evicted Pop from his property. My father then rented offices at the Tribune Building. He was ultimately to build his own newspaper plant on South Street, overlooking the East River.

Pulitzer's *World,* a crusading and often sensational paper featuring explosive exposés of all types, had been Pop's model. He had learned at Pulitzer's feet as a reporter there. Pulitzer also appealed to my father because he was enthusiastic about the news, prompted by an extraordinary curiosity about everyday life.

Now Pop prepared to challenge the newspaper king with his own, new brand of newspapering. He would reach out to even more of the masses—the underdogs, the ignorant, the lost—and bring them not only into the fold of his newspaper but into society itself. The old man was passionate about that society. He was an idealist who believed deeply that American democracy was the best form of government on earth. Other newspapers catered to the educated and rich, but Pop did not believe those times would sustain such journals or that they would have much effect on the life of the city.

Pop and Pulitzer exploded the fiercest newspaper war in American history, fought over the pennies of Irish and Jewish working girls and German and Italian common laborers. They were the masses who dreamed of speaking English, finding a better job, fighting those who bilked and then ignored them, seeking a voice in their economic, social, and political futures. Pop became the foremost publisher in the nation to champion so many causes of the underclass. From promoting fairness in the courts to halting police harassment and seeking hospital care for the needy, he supported the entire range of social initiatives affecting the poor.

In the fierce battle, Grandma gave Pop $7.5 million, an astonishing sum in those days, and my father spent every dime of it in the first three years of his struggle against Pulitzer. All her advisers cautioned Phoebe against such an expensive and—they thought—unwinnable battle. But she was galvanized by the fact that she had reared a very hard-working son. Diligence was a frontier virtue. She prized it.

Pop fired the first shot in the war by cutting the price of the *Journal* to one penny. The *World* sold for two cents. Within the inner workings of the *Journal,* he adopted this business slogan: "There is no substitute for circulation." Pop brought his top editors and writers from San Francisco to New York. He hired the best available local talent, doubling and tripling their salaries. He stressed—and this has long been the battleground on which his legend and legacy have been fought—stories of basic human appeal.

Pop's human approach to news was based on a more precise premise than the vague concept of "human interest." He often said that each reader had five basic interests—himself, others, the world around him, where he came from, and where he was going. If a publication satisfied those needs and desires, he believed it would succeed. He never separated those aspects of success. He saw no nobility in going broke. Less than two months after he took the helm of the *Journal,* its circulation soared from 30,000 copies to about 100,000.

Pop did not seek to invent fantasies, as some papers of those days did in writing about the human condition. He suggested no miraculous cures or supposed sightings of people from other planets. He always maintained that truth was stranger than fiction. Rather, the new owner aimed to depict the people of New York and their daily lives in all their realities. He sought human interest on a scale that had never been envisaged by his competitors and, when they saw the *Journal*'s meteoric rise in circulation, they attacked him as a sensationalist. The no-holds-barred battle with Pulitzer featured news of financial and political chicanery, horror stories about sweatshops, tear-jerkers written by sob sisters, sex stories of runaway girls and other fallen angels, and crime scoops from murder to robbery shootouts.

On the national scene, Pop attacked bigness—from corporate monopolies to bankers—in favor of the little guy. He went all out to help start the Spanish-American War in 1898. In reaction, so did Pulitzer. My father's angry headlines and stories on the sinking of the U.S. battleship *Maine* in Havana Harbor virtually ignited the conflict. He accused Spain of blowing up the *Maine,* although we now know that it's more likely the ship went down because of a fire in its bunker. The U.S. Navy has never fixed definitive blame for the sinking. The important thing to Pop was, however, that more than 250 American seamen perished in a U.S. naval vessel that had been sunk.

Pop believed in the rebel cause of ousting Spain from Cuba. The old man saw it as patriotic American policy. He went further—we should drive them eventually from the entire hemisphere. He wanted to rid the Americas of European colonialism. His news competitors attacked almost every move he made. My father sailed to Cuba himself to cover the battles, and came under fire several times according to eye witnesses. The claim that he touched off the war merely to boost the *Journal*'s circulation didn't go far enough. Pop wanted a free Cuba then as much as I wish for a liberated Cuba today. So he attacked Spanish rule there as well as its potential threat to this country. He wanted to export American democracy.

Unlike some of his competitors, Pop always looked for heroes and heroines. He did that in Cuba and elsewhere. That is what his sob sisters and other feature writers were all about. His entire philosophy was summarized in the fair dictum: Portray the human condition as it is and offer a special accolade to the brave. He would rather put the triumph of an ordinary man or woman on the front page than a famous robber or a crooked big-name politician. Newspapering was always an adventure to him, not merely a job. He saw Cuba as one of his greatest exploits. Perhaps, who knows, he was looking for the hero in himself?

Pop believed the war did produce a hero—one of his *Journal* reporters, James Creelman. Creelman begged army officers to allow him to join their charge on a fort. On launching the attack, they motioned the reporter to follow. In the fight Creelman captured the first Spanish flag of the war. He said the *Journal* deserved it because the paper had played such an important role in the conflict. Creelman waved the flag at furious Spanish soldiers, who fired, wounding him in the left arm. The newsman was carried down the hill with other wounded, and someone draped the flag over his body. Creelman passed out and awoke to see my father kneeling over him. The reporter later recounted that my father wore a Panama hat with a bright ribbon around it, and his face was "radiant with enthusiasm." Pop said, "I'm sorry you're hurt, but wasn't it a splendid fight? We beat every paper in the world."

The war also produced one of the great footnotes in journalistic history. Before hostilities began, Pop had sent the famous artist Frederick Remington to Havana to portray the action. Remington got bored sitting around hotel beaches and cabled this message to my father: "Everything is quiet. There is no trouble here. There will be no war. I wish to return. Remington."

Pop's biographers, most of whom never consulted him, quoted him as replying: "Please remain. You furnish the pictures and I'll furnish the war. W. R. Hearst." It's a wonderful story, of course, and has gotten many a wry chuckle. The only trouble is, it's not true. Pop told me he never sent any such cable. And there has never been any proof that he did. But with headline salvos against Spain, he did in fact help to furnish the war. In any case, Remington stayed, and his later sketches of the conflict filled full pages in the *Journal*.

My observations about those days of sensational journalism are not intended to reflect on Pulitzer or any other competitor; my father always respected Pulitzer and the others. Rather, they are to indicate the times in which the circulation war was fought, a time of no radios, no TV, no movies—and no holds barred. Pop was out to win, and he saw the news formula for victory as not only informing but entertaining readers, since they wanted both.

The growth of America's newspapers must be seen in perspective to understand those times. Up to about 1830, the major newspapers in New York and the rest of the country had appealed to commercial and political interests, the elite of the nation. Most were little more than commercial bulletin boards, stories handed them by businessmen. As metropolitan populations climbed, newspapers turned more attention to immigrants and the middle class. Politics, education, health, crime, courts, and eventually sports began to be featured. Local reporters were hired at ten to twenty dollars a week—relatively modest salaries—to write these stories.

That is how the Penny Press began. It broke down geographical, class, and cultural barriers. It stressed increased advertising as the major source of revenue. This helped take papers out of the hands of political parties, robber barons, and others. Such papers expressed only one viewpoint and/ or controlled the reporting of political fraud and other crimes against the public. Historians mark this time as a switch between "views" papers and "news" papers. The Penny Press grew as English-speaking urban populations increased. Technology offered faster printing, mechanized typesetting, and more reasonably priced newsprint. The business and editorial functions became separate, although each influenced the other.

While some editors featured the sensational, others spent much time mocking the rich and famous and picking editorial fights with other newspapers. Each was searching for a news formula that would make it New York's newspaper leader. This was a complete departure from the old days of printers putting out staid, stale news. Newspapers assumed more wide-open editorial directions to appeal to more of the masses. The rise of the middle class and its new importance in advertising increased pressures for greater readership.

Gifted editors and writers were attracted to the field, particularly in New York. These included James Gordon Bennett of the *Herald*; Benjamin Day and, later, Charles A. Dana of the *Sun*; Horace Greeley of the *Tribune*; Adolph Ochs, who bought the *Times* in 1896; and, later, the Sulzberger family, when an Ochs daughter, Iphigene, married Arthur Hays Sulzberger. These newsmen had different approaches to the business. Yet one didn't exclude the other. People often read two or three different papers. The fundamental difference among the dailies was their separate appeal to distinct audiences—from the well-read to the foreign-born and poorly educated.

Bennett and Greeley reflected the split personality of papers divided by various stages of in-depth, serious news coverage and popular success. Bennett covered murder and other crimes personally and wrote about them in gruesome detail. Yet he also stressed significant national and international coverage. Greeley also covered crime and sex extensively, yet strove for intellectual excellence with significant coverage. He accepted patent medicine and other questionable advertising. In those days newspaper advertising often functioned on the basis of "let the buyer beware."

These were times that led the way to Pulitzer and Pop. But "sensationalist" news coverage had been an integral part of American journalism before the two men came on the scene. The early history of a free and independent press in Europe and elsewhere had been full of the sensational, and was later transported here. The rivalry between Pop and Pulitzer became even more intense. Their competition was reflected in greater technical innovation, much more editorial enterprise, higher costs, more advertising, and circulation battles that might have seemed more like a circus were they not so financially critical.

Pulitzer had become a publishing giant in New York after a successful career in St. Louis. Born in Hungary, he understood the needs and hopes of immigrants and other poor. At the start of the Civil War, he bought the *World*, which was tottering, for $346,000. The *World* plodded along for years. It wasn't until some twenty years later that Pulitzer decided to seize circulation leadership of the city's papers.

Pulitzer hired top reporters and editors. These included Arthur Brisbane, Herbert Bayard Swope, Heywood Broun, and Walter Lippmann. The *World*'s front-page exposés of various kinds of skulduggery became famous. So did Pulitzer's attacks on the "intellectual elite" and his crusades against bigotry. The around-the-world trip of reporter Nellie Bly (Elizabeth Cochrane) brought the *World* sensational national attention. Pulitzer's headlines became bigger and bolder proclamations of blood and death.

Someone said that NEWS—North, East, West, and South—had become like the four winds. The reader never knew which way the news wind was going to blow—true, false, probable, or maybe. Editors and newspapers often overreacted to attract attention.

When Pop began challenging Pulitzer in the late 1890s, the old man set a course that he followed at all the papers he purchased across the country. My father not only hired the best talent available but doubled and tripled their salaries. This included Arthur Brisbane and Morrill Goddard from the *World*. Also Mark Twain, Stephen Crane, Richard Harding Davis, James Creelman, Dorothy Dix, Susan B. Anthony, and many others.

He used the latest technology, including his own innovations and changes, perhaps more than any other publisher in America. Among Pop's many innovations were:

- New techniques to synchronize type, text, and illustrations.
- Improvements in printing presses and printing-plate making. His

straight-line production techniques were adopted throughout the industry.

- The first halftone photographs printed on newsprint.
- He was the first to print a complete section of comics in colors. My father had the best cartoonists and comics—from the "Katzenjammer Kids" to "Puck."
- He mass-produced newspapers on such a scale that people compared him to Henry Ford's assembly-line car manufacturing.
- He produced layouts with big, bold headlines and up-front positioning of flamboyant stories. His innovations were so imaginative and audacious that publications of every type around the world imitated them.
- He purchased for his publications virtually every mechanical device that could assist them as soon as each came on the market.
- He organized the nation's largest chain of newspapers (thirty-two at one time), and formed international news (International News Service), photo (International News Photos), and feature (King Features Syndicate) services to support each of them. These services also sold material to other U.S. and foreign newspapers and magazines.
- He created a stable of top national and international magazines in a host of fields—from motoring to fashion and from popular mechanics to sophisticated living. He recruited the top talent here and abroad.

Pop eventually owned and operated the largest publishing business in the world. He had nearly 40,000 employees at one time, after adding staffs at new radio and television stations.

Out of the Pulitzer-Hearst battle came the infamous term "Yellow Journalism." This was a reference to a character named the "Yellow Kid" in the comic strip "Hogan's Alley." The kid was a sympathetic young fellow dressed in a flour sack. Pop hired the original cartoonist from the *World* and featured him and "Hogan's Alley" in the *Journal*. Pulitzer countered by hiring another illustrator to draw a comic strip on the "Yellow Kid." The phrase originated at the *Tribune* and *Press*, both of which were losing considerable circulation to the *Journal* and *World*. It was born of professional antagonism and perhaps jealousy.

The central criticism of Yellow Journalism was that it believed in nothing (not the poor and not the voiceless) but selling papers. Yet Yellow Journalism, as it developed, served two very useful purposes. It led to beneficial muckraking reporting. Also, reporters were given public credit for their work. Previously, only editors and publishers had received public notice. Richard Harding Davis became a celebrity with his national and international datelines. He spoke of a "new school of yellow kid correspondents." His words were an accolade.

Many of the new breed sought not only to *cover* great stories; they also wanted to help make them. They would go looking for the Dr. Livingstons in other jungles, blow open scandals in police departments and prisons, and find skeletons in the closets of political leaders—all with great personal daring. These were the nation's first intrepid globe-trotting correspondents and muckraking, investigative reporters. A good number were fiercely committed to probing serious public issues and, indeed, offering solutions to them. To suggest that Yellow Journalism merely lowered public taste to attain increased circulation is an oversimplification.

Even a casual reading of my father's *Journal* and *American* in the early part of this century will show that both papers were clearly concerned with improving American society. Prominent leaders in various fields regularly contributed to them. These included Émile Zola and Stephen Crane on literature; Ignace Paderewski and Walter Damrosch on music; George Bernard Shaw, Charles Edward Russell, and Edward Markham on sociopolitical trends, as well as Susan B. Anthony and Helen Keller on women. Brisbane himself offered readers wide selections from philosophers Hegel, Kant, Darwin, and Spencer.

In bringing readers these leaders through the printed word, Pop was teaching the less educated about American life as well as how to read. The old man brought school into the living rooms of Chinese, Russian Jews, Italians, and Germans. Lydia Commander, a social commentator at the time, wrote that Yellow Journalism might not always be nice and proper, but neither were the readers who followed and needed it. I don't entirely agree with that comment, however. Many of the lower-middle-class working people in New York and San Francisco at the turn of the century and into the 1900s were religious, basically decent people.

A good many authors have since written that the muckraking journalism of my father and others did more for American education than all the universities and other institutions of higher learning at the time. The old man emphasized social and economic justice. But he did it without advocating violence or radicalism that could well have exploded among the nation's urban masses. The Hearst newspapers stressed the welfare of its readers—from better labor and union practices to coverage of illnesses and health clinics, as well as eating habits, the need for proper clothes, and spending leisure time well.

As Yellow Journalism grew, newspapers began to stand on their own feet. Independent editors and publishers launched crusades and more penetrating investigations. They were the puppets of no pressure group. Papers would rise or fall on the opinion of the reading public. One result was that the U.S. news business rose more rapidly than in any other nation of the world. It became one of the country's industrial pacemakers. Pop and Pulitzer led the way into this new era.

It was in the midst of their circulation fight that Arthur Brisbane quit Pulitzer and joined Pop. He was a hard-hitting editorial writer and columnist who was to fire his broadsides from our organization for the next forty years. Pop and Brisbane needed all of their six-foot two-inch frames to withstand the returning shells. Brisbane was to become the most-read columnist in America. The two men formed an unbreakable alliance that lived up to the motto of the many commentators since: "To comfort the afflicted and afflict the comfortable."

In the years that I knew Brisbane, before his death at dawn's light on Christmas Day of 1936, I found that his entire success was based on simple but passionate writing. Anyone could understand Brisbane's short, simple sentences and thoughts. And no one misunderstood the anger, defiance, contempt, and compassion that he poured out on hundreds of subjects. Brisbane's fundamental formula made him one of the highest-paid columnists in U.S. history.

Brisbane defended Yellow Journalism in these words: "Whatever is new, especially if it succeeds, disturbs old-fashioned people, above all if it compels them to pay their employees more, from top to bottom. That's what Yellow Journalism does when it's successful." I have never liked the expression "Yellow Journalism." The word "yellow" smacks of cowardice. There is an implication that Pulitzer and Pop, instead of being men of strong conviction, may have had a yellow streak down their backs. The truth is that both men were quite courageous.

Brisbane loved to heat up the Hearst-Pulitzer war. He used the "Yellow Kid" comic to deliberately provoke the *World* about it. Arthur sometimes sent old Joe into orbit. It was all great for circulation. The war with

Pulitzer blazed ahead in big headlines featuring political fights, all types of exposés, and chilling crime coverage.

The basic criticism of Pop and Pulitzer was that they were putting out newspapers that were really entertainment sheets. But, as the history of New York journalism has clearly shown, Pop's *Journal* (and, later, *Journal-American*) covered local news as well as if not better than the city's most serious and, at times, tiresome papers. Indeed, the *Journal* and *World* regularly scooped them.

Just two years after my father became publisher of the *Journal*, then with both morning and evening editions, his paper soared to a circulation of more than 700,000 copies, while Pulitzer's morning and evening *World* passed 800,000. Each of the four remaining newspapers sold 100,000 copies or less.

The battle with competitors exploded on a national level. Pop opposed President William McKinley's reelection in 1900. The Republican candidate had accepted large campaign funds from the Southern Pacific and other railroads who opposed the then Nicaragua (later the Panama) Canal. If any such canal were dug, they would lose millions of dollars in freight revenues.

Pop was virtually under siege by William Jennings Bryan and other Democratic leaders to support Bryan as the party's presidential candidate. They also wanted him to start a new newspaper in the Midwest, since no major paper in the area supported the Democrats. Pop didn't want to start a Midwest paper. He told Bryan and others that, although Chicago was the largest and most influential city in the area, it was a very tough newspaper town, with the bloodiest circulation wars in the country. Good publishers had failed there. He wanted no part of it. His reluctance also was based on the conclusion that Bryan would, in any case, be defeated by William McKinley, which he was. Nevertheless, under rising pressure from Bryan and other Democrats, Pop relented and started the afternoon *Chicago American*. Its morning companion, the *Examiner*, was launched two years later. As my father predicted, the street battles in Chicago over circulation were the roughest he ever fought.

Some have long suggested that my father went into Chicago and other cities to build a news organization that would propel him into the White House. Actually, he began the Chicago operation to support the Democratic party.

Brisbane had told Pop that he had the stuff to be president. Perhaps that caused him to think about such a run, but he never indicated that to my mother or later to any of his sons. There is nothing in all our family records—or any conversation that I am aware of—to support the claim that the old man secretly planned a chain of papers so that he would ultimately sit in the Oval Office. His dedication to newspapering is at odds with that premise. If one doubts that reasoning, my father's open affair with Marion Davies closed the door to the presidency at a time when critics claimed he was still waiting for presidential lightning to strike. Pop was not so foolish as to believe the affair would allow him to somehow slip in the back door of the White House.

In 1901, after his election, the *New York Journal* continued to attack McKinley and, unfortunately, the editorial used these words: "If bad institutions and bad men can be got rid of only by killing, then the killing must be done." In the same issue, Ambrose Bierce also quoted in his column a refrain he had written a year earlier about Kentucky governor William Goebel:

> The bullet that pierced Goebel's breast
> Can not be found in all the West;
> Good reason, it is speeding here
> To stretch McKinley on his bier.

Bierce and others at the *Journal* insisted Pop never knew of the editorial or column before they were published. Bierce said my father never discussed the matter with him. He learned of the editorial—but not the column—only after the presses had begun to run. The old man ordered the presses halted and the reference to "killing" eliminated. However, some of these early papers did hit the streets and, when rival newspapers and other critics saw both the editorial and column, they launched all-out attacks on my father. Pop quickly contacted McKinley. He told the president that he would drop from his newspapers any future article that McKinley might view as personally offensive. The president sent him a letter of thanks.

In September of 1901, during a reception stop in Canton, Ohio, a young man shot McKinley, and the president later died. My father's rivals believed they now had enough rope to hang the old man. Many rushed reporters to interview the assassin, Leon Czolgosz. It's a matter of record that they tried to get him to say he shot the president because the Hearst papers caused him to hate McKinley. But the killer replied: "I never saw a Hearst paper. I am sick. Why did I do this? I wish I hadn't. I was crazy."

The uproar rocked the nation. Competing papers continued to assail my father. Some people still believed he was the cause of McKinley's death. Pop was burned and hanged in effigy. He received many death threats. Hearst newspapers were burned, banned from some establishments, and hurled from newsstands. Also leading the charges against him were the political bosses of Tammany Hall. He was branded not only an assassin but an anarchist.

Although some of these assaults were incredibly intemperate, Pop took the heat and never replied to a single critic. He later explained to me that criticism goes with the territory of journalism. He said it was an essential part of the business. We did it every day in our editorial columns. He told me he loved a good fight. These attacks never upset him. Pop said the best thing was to give attackers no credence—and continue fighting for what you believe in. I personally believe that my father suffered from some of these attacks, although he never gave the slightest hint of it. He was sensitive and compassionate, and it would simply be contrary to such a nature to fail to be affected by such vilification.

After McKinley's death, Pop changed the name of the *Morning Journal* to the *American*, with the afternoon *Journal* retaining its masthead. It may have seemed an insignificant change to many, but not to the old man. He was reaffirming his creed and record as a patriotic American.

Despite the McKinley experience, Pop became even more deeply involved in politics. He was furious that Tammany Hall and other parts of the Democratic machine were fleecing the New York public of millions of dollars, and newspapers seemed powerless to stop or even curtail them. That stung my father. Up to that point in his life, most newspapers had been victorious in their public fights. The character of both my father and Tammany guaranteed that their battle would be a dog fight. To many politicians, there was only one way to settle a score: personally. Those were the rules. The old man did not make them.

New York politicians were either so entrenched through payoffs that they ignored the papers, or they threatened newsmen, even with bodily harm. Politics was the dirtiest business in the city. Pop knew that, but its full impact took some time to sink in. He told me one time that, the more he tried to wash away the political dirt, the deeper he seemed to slip into it.

My father decided to run for Congress in 1902, seven months before marrying Mom. (She had nothing to say about it then, but she sure did later on.) Tammany leaders supported the old man. He didn't reject their backing. The liaison was only a matter of convenience, a temporary party truce, and both knew it. The two understood they would eventually go to war. The old man was elected to a two-year term. And "Uncle Joe" Cannon, a longtime Democratic kingpin, and others continued to believe they ruled by divine right—the dollar.

My mother pleaded with Pop not to get any deeper into politics. She later told me how she begged him to forget any such thoughts. Mom warned Pop that he wouldn't be able to run politics as he had his newspapers—by doing what he felt right and best. She described the compromises he would have to make for political backing, support he would first choke on before being able to swallow it. Mom insisted he didn't have the flexible make-up and elastic principles that were the essence of politicians. This was a New York girl who truly understood the turf. And she was right.

My father was never comfortable in politics. He disliked giving speeches, although he eventually became good at it. He detested compromises, as Mom had warned, yet found himself in the midst of many. The old man had always avoided personal publicity. To be elected, he had to court it. That was one of the most difficult aspects of his life. He didn't like intrusions into his private life; nor did he seek to infringe on the lives of others, unless there was an overriding need. He felt interrupting people with handshakes and phony backslapping was degrading.

Pop was eventually elected to a second term in Congress in 1904, but was miserable in the job. He liked Washington, but found much of the work boring and he missed many votes. The old man kept both feet in the news business by buying the *Boston American* and *Los Angeles Examiner* after founding the *Chicago American*. Nevertheless, the political bug had bitten him. Later that year Pop allowed the California delegation to nominate him as a presidential candidate at the Democratic national convention in St. Louis. Pop was forty-one years old. The Republicans had earlier nominated Theodore Roosevelt in Chicago.

Clarence Darrow, the great trial lawyer, led the Illinois delegation in seconding Pop's nomination. My father received 263 convention votes, far

short of nomination, but he rectified his "greatest political mistake"—
proposing that all senators henceforth be elected by direct vote of the
people, not by state legislatures, as he had once supported. Judge Alton
B. Parker became the Democratic nominee. Roosevelt won in a landslide.

Pop ran for mayor of New York in 1905. He didn't want to run, but
critics of city hall corruption and corporate dominance insisted he was the
only man who could throw the rascals out. The old man would not have
wished such a campaign on anyone. As he put it in print at the time:

> I appeal to them all [members of the Independence League] to unite
> against the traitors in office, and the franchise thieves back of them.
> You know what kind of government this city has. Whose fault is it?
> It isn't the fault of the corporations. It isn't the fault of [Charles F.]
> Murphy or [Benjamin B.] Odell [Tammany bosses] or their puppets.
> You are like a sleeping giant pillaged by pygmies.

He denounced Tammany night after night. His life was repeatedly
threatened. My mother later told me she feared for both their lives. She
said my father had no doubts. He would survive. But just to be certain,
armed bodyguards protected him. Pop said many times during the campaign, "I don't want the office of mayor. I certainly don't want the salary.
What I want is your good opinion. Vote for the entire ticket!"

The Bowery and East Side, longtime Tammany strongholds, rallied to
him. Both turned out large, thunderous campaign crowds. That was a
signal to Tammany that they were in serious political trouble. Fore-
warned, they set out to scuttle my father. And did. Eyewitnesses told of
ballot boxes being thrown off the Brooklyn Bridge. Hundreds of witnesses
reported other fraud. The most ominous sign of all came late on election
evening. Tammany would not permit any more ballots to be counted and
reported. In a period of about an hour the dirty work was done. The dead
voted; repeaters followed them; ballots were dumped; Hearst poll
watchers were offered bribes and those who refused were run off election
premises; votes for Hearst were declared invalid; Tammany thugs roamed
from precinct to precinct far into the night. Mayor McClellan was
reelected.

Protest rallies erupted, but they were of no consequence. My father
called off these rallies because of shootings. The wounded were taken to
hospitals. He didn't wish to see any further bloodshed. Out of the uproar,
twenty-four small fry were convicted, most charged only with creating a

Phoebe Apperson Hearst as a young woman.

George Hearst.

Phoebe Hearst.

William Randolph Hearst, Sr., aged eight.

Senator George Hearst.

William Randolph Hearst, Sr., as a young publisher in New York.

Millicent as a young woman.

Mother and son on the front porch of Phoebe's hacienda near Pleasanton, California.

The original home built by George and Phoebe Hearst at San Simeon.

Congressman Hearst and his wife Millicent at the House of Representatives in 1902.

Mr. and Mrs. William Randolph Hearst, Sr., 1910.

Grandma—Phoebe Apperson Hearst—marches for the women's right to vote in San Francisco.

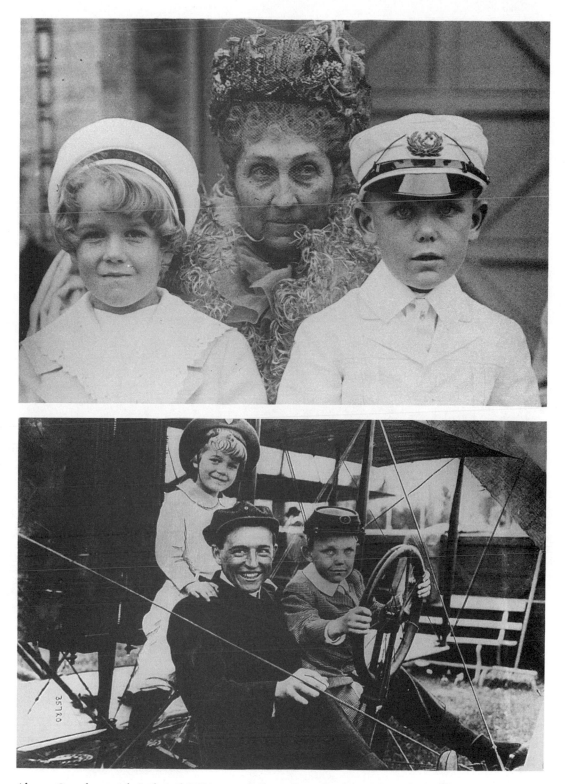

Above: Grandma with Jack and Bill in new sailor suits at her hacienda. *Below:* Bill's interest in aviation began early. This 1915 photo shows the author seated to the right of Art Smith, a famous aviator of the day, while Jack stands behind.

Bill fishing with George (left) and pal on the McCloud River at Wyntoon.

William Randolph Hearst, Jr., aboard ship for a trip to Europe in 1919.

Sons Bill and Jack flank William Randolph Hearst, Sr., on the return voyage from Europe.

Randy and David wave farewell on yet another trip to the hacienda at Pleasanton.

The Hearst family in 1923. Left to right are John, WRH, David, Millicent, Randy, George, and Bill.

public disturbance. A few, however, were sent up to Sing Sing prison for beating some voters bloody. Tammany had stolen the election, and everybody in New York knew it.

In 1906 Pop ran for governor of New York. He was backed by Democrats (but not Tammany) and Independents. He ran on this platform: New York City and New York State must no longer be ruled by political bosses and large corporations. His election slogan called for popular rights over special privileges. The Republicans made an issue of "Hearst wearing collars made in Paris." Charles Evans Hughes, who was later to become famous as a U.S. Supreme Court justice, defeated the old man by nearly 60,000 votes of about 1.5 million cast. Pop conceded defeat in these words: "I congratulate the bosses on their foresight in defeating me, for my first act as governor would have been to lift the dishonest officials by the hair of their unworthy heads. I am enlisted in this fight against the control of government by the trusts and corrupt corporations, and I will fight it out to the end."

I caused a brief interlude in Pop's political wars. Mom brought me into the world on January 27, 1908—a sure vote for the old man, but he would have to wait a few years. I was puny and sickly from the start. It was only a year before I got pneumonia. Mom and Pop didn't think their young offspring was going to make it. I did, but was plagued with one illness or another much of my life—from ear problems to ulcers to failing eyesight. Good health has been a struggle for me. With that background, I am sure that Pop never put any political hopes in me. Nor did I.

In 1909 Pop once again ran for mayor on an impossible platform: He said he didn't wish to be elected. As the Independence League candidate, he told the voters of New York: "I do not ask you to elect me, but this is one of the most disgraceful Tammany tickets ever nominated in the city. I do ask you to vote for the ticket of able men I have the honor to head, and against the Tammany rogues and rascals whom I have the honor to oppose."

The Tammany crowd was not about to allow anyone near its juicy pie; the city budget had sweetened to about $800 million. They divided slices of that among themselves and their supporters. Tammany also was being paid off big by the utilities; water rates were four times those of other municipalities, while power and gas were ten times higher. The pie had become a mountain of goodies. Judge William Gaynor, a Tammany toad, was elected mayor. Mom later said that my father never dwelt on the defeat except to pledge his continued opposition to Tammany. The old-time pols continued stealing, and laughed all the way home.

Pop began losing confidence in both parties. He looked more than ever toward a third party, growing out of the Independence League that he had formed. It could eventually become a winner, but, if not, might well force important concessions from both parties. The old man had become a leader of the Progressive Movement. Like Bob La Follette and others, he sought political reform and the revitalization of economic competition in the country.

Pop was powerful not because he was active in politics but because he exerted wide influence on the nation's thinking through his growing chain of newspapers and magazines. Multimillions got their politics from him and his colleagues because radio, motion pictures, and television had not yet arrived on the scene. Upset because of my father's broad national appeal, the *New York Times* and other newspapers maintained that he represented an ignorant public opinion. The issue, if there was one, centered on whether Pop adequately informed his readers. Once again, Yellow Journalism became a point of public contention.

Some critics were describing my father as a firebrand socialist. Industrial and other financial leaders called him a "radical." Yet no radical or socialist organization in the country supported him. The old man was actually his own brand of capitalist. As he defined it, "The prosperity of the businessman depends on the prosperity of the people." He was convinced that American capitalism might be destroyed unless it was drastically changed. By that he meant sweeping out some assumed prerogatives of the wealthy—primarily monopolies and trusts that reneged on democratic competition.

Many of the nation's wealthy took refuge in individual initiative. The old man saw through that camouflage, and maintained that the rights of individuals must be balanced by the needs and rights of society. To counterbalance big business, my father supported big labor, and consistently backed the demands of unions. Pop always said that trusts would drive unions into politics.

In those years the old man also praised big government. He advocated government ownership of public utilities, railroads, telegraph, and similar powerhouses. He would have exerted executive authority to bring about welfare reforms. In championing the rights of the have-nots, my father was ostracized by his own social class. Many such leaders would not work or socialize with him. A good number hated him.

Pop became a conservative in later years. He explained the change this way: "It's more important to be correct than consistent."

Pop's political fights became legendary—with Teddy Roosevelt, Al Smith, Woodrow Wilson, and Franklin D. Roosevelt. The reasons were as varied as the men themselves. They ranged from political corruption to war issues and whether FDR should have run for a third term. In all cases, the debates exploded into national controversy. But if my father ever had any long-term political ambitions, he began pulling back as America approached World War I.

Teddy Roosevelt succeeded McKinley and played to the national mood, indirectly attacking Pop over McKinley's death. He opposed my father when Pop ran for mayor in 1905 and governor in 1906. Later, Pop assailed Teddy for holding a stick over the heads of many of the nation's trusts on one hand while taking their campaign contributions with the other.

My father fought Woodrow Wilson's nomination as the Democratic presidential candidate in 1912. Pop had a foreboding about Wilson, whom he viewed as an ivory-tower, unrealistic professor. He believed Wilson's lack of shrewdness might well lead the country into some kind of national catastrophe.

Wilson prepared for war. Pop's battle against our entry may have postponed it six months. He fought not only Wilson but also England with a series of exposés on British censorship. The government killed legitimate stories concerning its policies and conduct of the war. My father attacked France and other Allied powers as well as influential Americans who were trying to get us into the war. It was an extraordinary spectacle—one American publisher taking on European governments and various U.S. leaders. In response to inquiries from Congress, he concluded a telegram to one lawmaker with the declaration: "AMERICA FIRST AND FOREVER. HEARST." Some of the feeling against my father's stand became, as observers later admitted, "almost hysterical."

After the war, he criticized the Treaty of Versailles and the League of Nations. He believed they entangled the United States in foreign interests and alliances, and that we should retain our independence of thought and action. The *New York Tribune* questioned my father's loyalty to America. In one editorial it said the Hearst newspapers printed seventy-four attacks on America's allies and seventeen articles in defense or praise of Germany. Years later, the author of the editorial indicated that he was ashamed of the fierceness of his assault. Although he disagreed with my father's views, he said he had never doubted Pop's patriotism.

In 1922 Al Smith refused to run for governor on the same ticket with my father as the Democratic U.S. Senate candidate. Pop had not been endorsed, and it was not certain that he would run if the Democrats decided to nominate him. Smith set out to destroy whatever chance there might be of his candidacy at that year's state party convention in Syracuse.

Smith had come up through the patronage system of Tammany Hall. Born beneath the Brooklyn Bridge in lower Manhattan, he had eventually become governor in 1918. Smith attacked my father in what was then billed as one of the greatest vendettas in the history of New York politics. The fierceness with which the two fought one another over various issues hung like a pall over the two men for years. It wounded the political lives of both. Smith later ran for the presidency in 1928 against Herbert Hoover and lost. His political war against my father haunted that campaign. In 1932 Pop swung convention delegates against Smith, guaranteeing the nomination of Franklin D. Roosevelt.

FDR and Pop were close friends in the beginning. The president said he would launch many of my father's proposed economic and other reforms. For the most part, he never did. Roosevelt planned, among other changes, to place controls on the media under the National Recovery Act. Pop thought that was a dangerous idea and told the president so. Pop and Roosevelt patched up their differences at various times, and their relationship would blossom anew. Nevertheless, their rapport became increasingly uneasy. My father was becoming more and more conservative. He fought the increased and costly effect of federal red tape on business. The longer Roosevelt was president, the more my father believed he was leading the country down the road toward socialism. Pop believed that Roosevelt would bring the country into World War II as soon as he could.

Various motives have been ascribed to my father's opposition to both world wars. Most of them are wrong. Pop saw World War I as a useless fight among intermarried royal houses for greater personal spoils; he based that on a very clear understanding of the history of European conflicts. Regarding World War II, he believed that we should think of American interests and our sons first, not bleed the nation's youth and U.S. Treasury for others who would certainly think twice about bailing us out.

Pop said he would go to war only if the American people wanted it. My father maintained that he represented the views of most Americans. "It is their fight," he said of the Europeans to the family, "not ours. We ran to escape their follies." No national figure of equal prominence took such a public position. Pop's convictions flowed from his deep feeling about the country and an almost reverent respect for the Constitution.

He was assailed as an American Firster, a pro-Nazi, and an English hater. The first charge was true; he helped found the America First movement to protect U.S. international interests. But the latter two claims are demonstrably false from the testimony of many other sources. As for being pro-Nazi, nothing could have been further from the truth. In 1934 Pop took a crowd of family and friends to Europe, including my brother George and his wife, as well as my then wife, Lorelle, and me. We sailed on the *Rex* to Spain. After a brief tour there, Pop chartered a plane to fly us to England for a visit to St. Donat's Castle, which he had purchased nearly a decade earlier. None of us had ever seen it. The castle was an eight-century-old structure situated on some 1,300 acres on the Bristol Channel near Cardiff. All of us were awestruck by the place. Then we left for Germany, where Pop was to have an interview with Hitler.

My father had earlier expressed an interest in meeting Hitler for two reasons—he thought such an interview might be a big scoop for our papers, and it would be a favor to his good friend, Louis B. Mayer. Before we left the States for Europe, the Hollywood movie mogul had seen the old man privately and asked him to intercede with Hitler for Germany's Jews, who were already suffering under the Führer. Pop liked Mayer and told him he would do anything he could. Mayer repeated his request while we were traveling in Europe. My father again promised he would do his best.

The German government was anxious to have Pop meet Hitler. German leaders hoped my father would continue warning against our entry into the war. Hitler also wanted to speak personally with an American who could tell him more about the way that U.S. public opinion was formed and its effect on our national policy. Ernst "Putzie" Hanfstaengl, whose father knew Pop well, had become a hanger-on in the Hitler entourage. My father had purchased many art objects through the elder Hanfstaengl and had met the son. Putzie angled hard for the meeting once Pop arrived in Bad Nauheim to take the baths.

Pop saw Hitler in Berlin and, without telling anyone, kept his promise to Mayer. He told the German leader that he and his policies would find more acceptance in the United States if persecution of the Jews and other minorities would halt. Hitler disclaimed any special targets, but pointed out that the New Socialism would serve Germany better if the opposition behaved themselves. Pop saw the warning in such a reply, confirming a judgment he had already made: Hitler was an unpredictable demagogue.

I wanted to attend the meeting, but Pop nixed it. He knew there would be a burst of outrage among many Americans after the interview, and he wished to keep me clear of it. Critics branded Pop a "fascist" for seeing Hitler. Characteristically, he said nothing.

On return to the United States, he told Mayer, other Jews, and his news colleagues that naziism was spreading in Germany while fascism was becoming stronger in Italy and elsewhere. The question was whether the two would unite. If they united, world war seemed inevitable. He was deeply concerned about Hitler's attitude toward the Jews. Pop eventually saw the inevitability of our entering World War II, as we had the first world war. The threat to the United States had become too great. But he clearly preferred America to remain at peace as long as it could.

In 1936 he turned to Kansas governor Alfred M. Landon to oust FDR from the Oval Office. It was obviously a big mistake. Landon lost in a landslide, carrying only two states, Maine and Vermont. I remember the Kansan's defeat only too vividly. My brother Jack and I went to Jack White's Late Night Club in Manhattan for dinner the day after the election. When we walked in Jackie Gleason was playing master of ceremonies and chortled to one and all, "Well, folks, here come Maine and Vermont!"

My father opposed FDR's third term. He didn't believe any man should have more than two terms in the White House. Pop told me that, if given the chance, FDR would run for a third, fourth, fifth, and sixth term. Pop joined the Republicans in an attempt to thwart Roosevelt.

Before Brisbane died, he and I discussed my father's switch from the Democrats to the GOP. The columnist said to me, "If you're not a bit radical when you're young, there's something the matter with you. And if you're radical when you're old, there's also something the matter with you."

Brisbane was a very urbane, shrewd, sophisticated man who knew Pop as well as anyone. He believed that my father was a "man of destiny." He also was convinced that Pop saw himself in that light, that he was born to bring great influence on our national life. I would put less personal emphasis on that concept than Brisbane did, although my father did see himself as an opinion maker. Pop's emphasis was not on himself but on the United States as a nation of Manifest Destiny. His thinking reflected that belief. He was utterly convinced that the American people and system of government were created to become the leaders of the world, nothing less.

Despite the fact that Pop saw Roosevelt as less noble than his high calling—as indeed a danger to the nation—he and FDR basically liked one another. My father praised FDR as a great American at the time of his death. The president regularly sent his regards to Pop through reporters and others.

From the mid-1930s onward, my father became increasingly disturbed about the growing Communist influence in the country. He was very concerned about Communist underground activities here. The Communists were infiltrating some labor unions as well as branches of the federal government. Before World War II even began, Pop saw Stalin as a tyrant and dictator at home and an international conspirator abroad. My father viewed the potential spread of communism as the most dangerous political virus he had ever seen. He called a spade a spade—communism meant death to democracy and God. Pop said so in blunt terms, touching off a storm of national debate that was to last more than three decades.

My father was hated by Soviet leaders and by members of the Communist party in the United States. The old man felt that Roosevelt—but not other Americans and not Churchill—had been taken in by Stalin. When Senator Joseph McCarthy warned of the dangers of communism at home, Pop believed it was time that Americans be awakened. Communists and their fellow travelers then boycotted the Hearst newspapers. The struggle to alert Americans became a vitriolic, vicious fight. Liberals across the country—many college professors, others in the media, a number of Hollywood and other leftists—assailed the old man because he supported McCarthy's investigations.

In the midst of all this Pop received a phone call from Jim Richardson, an exceptionally fine city editor on the *Los Angeles Examiner*. Richardson explained that the managing editor wanted to fire one of his reporters, Norma Barzman, because of her and her husband's political views. Norma wore a Roosevelt button in the office, and was a member of a Soviet-American friendship society. She and her husband, Ben, also were allegedly active among groups said to be fellow travelers of the Reds.

Pop remembered Barzman. For one thing, she was once the only female reporter on the *Examiner*. The old man liked women reporters. He also recalled a little-boy-and-dog story she had written. Barzman had befriended them when they were homeless. Pop told Richardson, "I don't care what she or her husband are. The question is: Is she a good reporter? If she is, she stays." Richardson hung up and, as Norma later related it, "He turned to me in his taciturn way and said: 'The Chief says you stay.'"

Barzman's husband, a Hollywood screenwriter, was later blacklisted. It involved his refusal to testify before a congressional committee investigating communism in Hollywood. My father heard about it but said nothing. He came to the *Examiner* around Christmas to wish the staff a happy holiday and was introduced to Barzman. The two had never met before, but Pop said: "Yes, I know. Don't look so glum. It's OK. Just keep on doing a good job of reporting. Everything will be fine." Norma and Ben later went on a self-imposed exile to France for thirty years. When they returned to Los Angeles, she went back to work for us, writing a column on the elderly for the *Examiner*. Ben has recently passed away. Today, some forty-five years after that office Christmas party, Norma still vividly recalls Pop's consoling words.

There are many such stories about my father's loyalty to his people. He had placed Norma's fidelity to her job—not his convictions about communism—at the crux of his decision. He saw her commitment to honest reporting as loyalty to him. A reporter could disagree with my father about many things, but he or she had to maintain basic reportorial integrity.

Pop continued his battle against communism until he died in 1951. Perhaps no American fought communism harder than my father. I believe that is one of the reasons why some of his critics have been so harsh for so long. Many liberals in this country have never forgiven the old man for his anticommunism. He smoked out their support and made fellow travelers accountable for their backing of Red causes. History is now setting the record straight. My father's judgments have finally been vindicated. Communism has failed and is now in decline all over the world. I often feel that somehow the old man knows about it.

Through the years, Pop continued to buy newspapers, magazines, and other media outlets across the country and abroad. By the mid-1930s we owned papers in such cities as New York, Albany, Boston, Pittsburgh, Baltimore, Washington, D.C., Detroit, Chicago, Milwaukee, Los Angeles, San Francisco, Seattle, and San Antonio. The magazines included *Good Housekeeping, Harper's Bazaar, Connoisseur, Redbook, Town & Country, House Beautiful, Popular Mechanics, Sports Afield, Cosmopolitan, Motor Magazine, Motorboating & Sailing,* as well as International News Service and International News Photos, King Features Syndicate, radio and television stations, Hearst Metrotone News, book and movie companies. He also had large mine, real estate, and timber holdings. And he continued to spend considerable sums in adding to the buildings at San Simeon and their vast art and other collections.

Despite his wealth, my father had little interest in money as such. It was only a blank space to be filled in on a check to accomplish a specific aim. It was the goal that mattered, not the money or even, at times, the astronomical cost. Obviously, he ran his companies so they would be profitable and survive. But he rarely if ever discussed with anyone what he owned or the extent of his personal wealth. Pop had only one aim: build, build, build. If he was greedy, it was for power, not money.

Pop and Pulitzer eventually declared a truce in their circulation war. The *Journal* surpassed the *World* in readership. Pulitzer, his health failing, died aboard his yacht in 1911. The *World* continued until 1931, when it was purchased by the Scripps-Howard chain. Pop was sad to see Pulitzer leave the news scene, because he enjoyed their battles. He wrote these words as part of Pulitzer's obituary: "A towering figure in national and international journalism has passed away; a mighty democratic force in the life of the nation and in the activity of the world has ceased; a great power uniformly exerted in behalf of popular rights and human progress is ended. Joseph Pulitzer is dead."

In 1936 the Depression was strangling not only the American economy but the Hearst empire as well. The Hearst Corporation was then subdivided into three dozen different companies. My father had twenty-nine newspapers in eighteen cities in 1936, as well as ten American magazines and three in Britain. But Pop continued spending. His top executives received higher salaries than most in the industry, and he refused to ask that reporters and others on his papers take wage cuts. In fact, Pop was not listening much to anyone until John W. Hanes, former assistant secretary of the treasury under President Roosevelt, finally convinced him after much argument to undertake drastic savings measures.

Hanes was known as a man who brought order out of chaos—and the corporation was more than $125 million in debt. The company had been making about $15 million a year and Pop was spending every dime of it. Pop gave Hanes the nod. But Hanes had his work cut out for him because my father was one of the country's biggest spenders. He owned not only San Simeon but probably the finest collections of old silver, antique furniture, architectural parts, stained glass, Greek pottery, Mexican saddles, and American Indian artifacts anywhere. (His collection of woven Navajo blankets was shown at major exhibitions in Washington.) My father was the largest private art collector in the world. He also had borrowed regularly through the years. During her lifetime, Grandma also wrote out checks of $10,000 a month to Mom and Pop for living expenses.

In 1937, with massive Depression debt and more bills piling up for the company, the Securities and Exchange Commission denied us an application to issue $35 million in debentures. A consortium of seventeen banks moved in and imposed a trusteeship. The news sent a shock of surprise through the organization, because my father was viewed as one of the richest men in the world. It was almost as if John D. Rockefeller had asked someone for a dime.

Clarence J. Shearn, a former company employee, was appointed trustee. He quickly began to dismantle the empire and, within two years, had either sold or axed six daily newspapers, including the *New York American,* which was merged with the *Journal.* Eight other papers later followed. He killed Universal News Service and closed down film production. Executive salaries were slashed in half. Everyone in the family took one cut or another.

Hanes and, later, John Neylan, an attorney, stepped in to defend the company from what they considered a plan to wreck my father. Neylan related that Shearn tried to get Harry Chandler, owner of the *Los Angeles Times* and no friend of Pop's, to foreclose on a $600,000 mortgage that Chandler had obtained, without my father's knowledge, on the San Simeon estate. Chandler extended the loan.

One aspect of all this remains clearest in my mind. I was working in New York as the publisher of the *Journal-American* at the time. Part of Pop's fabulous collection of art, purchased in Europe and elsewhere over decades—but stored in warehouses in the Bronx and its vicinity—was put up for sale at Gimbel's department store. More than 10,000 of these art objects covered about 100,000 square feet in the store. Mobs of bargain-hunting shoppers swarmed through three floors of the store. It was bedlam as they rubbernecked and then grabbed this or that to take home and be able to say: "Old man Hearst owned this. I bought it for ten bucks." I was sick about it, so ill that I went to bed. I avoided passing Gimbel's. It seemed like all of us had sold out.

Some of the collection had already been sold at earlier offerings in London, New York, and other U.S. cities. It appeared that everything was now going—from more than 10,000 crates of stones from a Spanish monastery to canvases by Rembrandt, Van Dyck, and Rubens. The Clarendon, our home on Riverside Drive, was sold. St. Donat's Castle in England was taken over by the British government as a military training center. Even the tiniest objects were up for grabs. Prices ranged from thirty-five cents for some to thousands of dollars for others. The sale was like a Broadway hit show and lasted from 1941 through 1945.

Perhaps the most heartrending sale of all was that of the stones from the Spanish monastery. The cost of shipping alone from Europe had been estimated at about $400,000. The stones were sold for $19,000 and moved to Miami, Florida, where they were reconstructed as a monastery. I've heard it is now a tourist attraction, but haven't seen it. Still, there are limits to everything. When Pop's famed collection of Georgian silver was put up for auction at Christie's in London, he had an agent buy some of it back for him.

During this time, Eleanor "Cissy" Patterson, a longtime friend of Pop's, lent him $1 million at 5 percent. Marion Davies lent him another million, which he later paid back in full. That help from associates and good friends saved the old man.

In the wild financial atmosphere of the times, I speculated that my father might hole up in San Simeon and never return to the business. But Pop was one tough old bird, and he hung in there with these words, "I'm a newspaperman. That's all I am, and all I ever want to be. The only thing I really seek now is to be a better newspaperman."

Neylan said Shearn attempted to sell the company's profitable magazines at giveaway prices. He constantly thwarted Shearn and, finally, in 1945, the company turned the corner and the financial crisis was over. The empire had been sliced by about 40 percent, but the old man still owned sixteen big-city dailies with a combined circulation of more than 5 million. Eight magazines survived—including *Cosmopolitan, Good Housekeeping,* and *Harper's Bazaar*—and they were generating about $50 million in annual revenues. Other parts of the empire managed to hang on as well.

Many explanations have been offered as to how the company pulled out of the crisis. In my judgment, there were two heroes: Hanes and my father. Neylan and Serge Semenenko, a Russian immigrant who became a top Boston banker, also deserve great credit for their unstinting efforts. It was Semenenko's Bank of Boston that put up the money in those critical days of saving the corporation.

Semenenko later told me of going out to San Simeon to see my father. He told Pop that he would have to cut his living expenses by 70 percent. He mentioned that the upkeep on San Simeon was costing thousands a day. My father seemed staggered. Many newspapers were in trouble and so on. Semenenko recalled that my father went to a window overlooking the blue Neptune swimming pool and looked out on the gardens beyond the colonnades. Pop turned and Semenenko immediately saw on my father's face that he had finally accepted losing his battle to keep spending. Pop said, "I have been remiss. I will follow your advice as to what I must do." Semenenko said tears came into his eyes. Not Pop's; his.

For the old man to accept the drastic surgery on all he had built over the years, including his art treasures, was perhaps the lowest moment of my father's life. Semenenko told me, "Only one man saved Mr. Hearst: Mr. Hearst." If Pop was upset by all the turmoil, he never showed it. It was only money, he said, not life or death. I presume he sold more than $100 million in various properties to survive. But, typically, he said nothing. He never made one excuse. To me, that was a profound part of his character and, to this day, I have tried to live with similar guts.

The critical financial factor in our resurgence was a leap in new advertising. That resulted from economic expansion during World War II. With millions of Americans, including many women, holding defense jobs, the nation's spending accelerated, and we were saved.

As the United States entered World War II, Pop took on more and more work as he directed his papers and the rest of the company from California. Perhaps in answer to those who said he was finished, Pop began writing his own column in 1940. With Brisbane gone, there was no one who expressed his views as cogently.

My father lived with Marion Davies for two years at Wyntoon, located on the Oregon-California border, during the war. After the conflict, he returned to San Simeon and made his headquarters there until 1947. He then moved to Marion's house in Beverly Hills, for two reasons. Following a stroke, he became concerned about his health, and his heart specialist lived there. Also, Marion wanted to get away from the isolation of San Simeon and be closer to her Hollywood friends.

One of the reasons that Pop was able to run his empire from California was Joe Willicombe, his faithful secretary of more than twenty-two years. Willicombe would send messages on the Hearst wire, telegrams and written memos to executives, with these three opening words, which became bywords in the organization: "The Chief says." Willicombe had been a reporter and had learned stenographic dictation to cover stories. Pop learned of that and made him his secretary. A very efficient individual, Joe was on call throughout the day and night. No one was closer to Pop on a day-to-day basis than Willicombe. My father and Willicombe grew old together and formed their own special bond. Perhaps it is the ultimate tribute to Joe to say he knew my father's mind so well that he answered many inquiries himself.

Another model of efficiency was Adela Rogers St. Johns, who was one of our reporters for about thirty years. I recall speaking with her for the last time. She reminisced about the assassination of Mahatma Gandhi. Within hours of Gandhi's death in 1948, Pop phoned and asked Adela to write a series of articles on his life. My father said that Gandhi had been the most important man of the times and we should explain his concept of democracy. Adela agreed. Pop wanted the first article in five hours! He told her, "I want to beat everybody else. I want it in tomorrow's papers." Adela wrote the first installment of 2,500 words and beat the deadline by eleven minutes.

Adela phoned Pop from her California home when the motorcycle driver had roared away with her last article on Gandhi. She told me there was silence on the other end of the line. Finally, Pop said, "I have always been glad I persuaded that editor not to fire you when you were so young." That was all Adela could remember of the conversation. She said to me: "I loved your father. We were both loyal people. I knew that my newspaper life had ended with the Gandhi series. Time and deadlines had run out on me. But I would live my old days working with him over and over again."

Journalism historians have made much of how Pop managed his newspapers from California—his comparison of the news and photo coverage of each, catching errors in layout and photo format, and spotting good writing and reporting. Pop was asked late in his sixty-five-year journalistic adventure what was the greatest improvement in journalism during his career. He unhesitatingly told *Editor & Publisher,* the bible of the business, that it was illustration. He referred primarily to improvements in pictorial reproduction. My father loved good photography and was convinced more than anyone else in his time that good journalism also meant exceptional pictures.

In my four decades of writing a Sunday column, I have received countless letters about my father. Allow me to share parts of two of them from 1989. I chose a couple from the many that arrive each year about the time of the death of my father on August 14, when I always write about him. One was dated August 16 and came from Virginia Wright of Sequim, Washington:

> In the late 1930s, as we clawed our way out of the Depression, I was a fortunate kid. I had a job with the *Los Angeles Examiner.* However, misfortune struck when unexpected emergency surgery confined me to a hospital and home for eight weeks.
>
> Group health insurance was non-existent and money was scarce. But it was not a problem in my case. Each and every week, a paycheck was in my mailbox. The generosity must have had the stamp of approval of Mr. Hearst.
>
> It gave me a warm sense of security belonging to a family which cared. It has been remembered through the years.

Indeed, she remembered for more than a half century.

On August 17, 1989, Mary Alice Yelverton of Boerne, Texas, wrote in part: "I learned quite a bit through the years about your father. He was one of the heroes of the San Francisco earthquake disaster when the Hearst newspapers sent numerous (I think it was thirty) train loads of blankets, clothes and medicine to the victims. It was fantastically generous.''

Another remembrance of Pop is framed on my office wall. It is a faded clipping of long ago from a column in one of our newspapers. The unsigned columnist wrote:

> Newsboy Novelette: It happened some time ago. We just encountered it. A newspaper publisher was revising some editorials in his apartment one hot, humid night. He decided to take a stroll around the block for some fresh air. He went out coatless, no hat, his shirt opened at the collar, wearing old trousers and his slippers . . . He walked for half a mile and paused to buy the midnight editions of the morning papers. "Oh," he told the newsboy (a kid of about 13), "I left my money at home." So saying, he put the papers back on the stand. "That's all right," said the kid, "you have an honest face." "But," said the man, "you can't always judge by a face, you know." "Well," said the lad, "yours looks all right to me, Mister." This touched the Old Boy so deeply that when he got home he phoned one of his top brass and instructed him to get the boy's name and address. "But don't tell him why!" Shortly after, that newsboy was sent to a military prep academy and then to college. He is now an officer in the army. He never knew the name of his benefactor—William Randolph Hearst.

Pop never knew about the article until it was published. He was not especially pleased because it sounded as if he might be blowing his own horn. I believe he was somewhat embarrassed, as he never referred to the article again.

The thing I remember most about my father was his boundless mentality. He never saw his life or dreams fenced in by any frontiers. He had an immeasurable, almost infinite belief in himself and America.

My father was a very calm, logical person, the epitome of the old-fashioned gentleman. He often made his points with humor. In more than forty years I never saw him lose his temper, although he often had reason to be upset. He didn't believe in personal confrontations and took pains to avoid them. The old man, clearly referring to outside critics, kept this quotation from George Washington among his most important private papers: "To persevere in one's duty and be silent is the best answer to calumny."

In public Pop was outspoken, colorful, fearless, and driven by inexhaustible energy. In private he was a caring and trusted confidant of this sometimes erring son. I loved him. At times, however, that love was like trying to hold onto a hurricane. I was swept along in a career of 150-mile-an-hour winds. I desperately reached for safe ports much of the time. My two biggest lifelines were my father and grandmother—and yet Pop was creating much of the storm!

All of us in the family felt he should have given us more of his time. My brothers and I felt we needed the reassurance of his presence and more personal guidance while we were growing up. But he chose to express much of his caring—although by no means all—in years of letters, telegrams, phone calls, presents, and other ways. Excerpts from a letter to me and my brothers illustrate one example:

> Success is a frame of mind—a mental posture—an immutable conviction—an unalterable determination.
>
> Circumstances have nothing to do with success. When you have made up your mind, success is certain. But, if you only half make up your mind, you will never get anywhere.
>
> You have to know you can succeed, and be determined to succeed. You must keep your mind on the objective, not on the obstacles.

His silences toward us were often difficult to understand and bear. The only reasonable explanation that I have been able to come to over the years was his far-flung company and other responsibilities. Of course, that's not a complete rationale because he had time to undertake projects other than work. He loved many things. His horizons were too great.

In not spending more time with his wife and children, my father made the biggest mistake of his life. It left an emptiness in all of us. However, in my mind it created an iron-willed determination that I would be a better father to my own children.

Yet he was not a womanizer, not a boozer, never knew laziness, and had great financial integrity. He liked the best in everything—from gifted editors and writers to fine artists, outstanding architecture, great men and women, and good gardeners. It is often said that the individual who loves gardening must be a good person. Add animals to that. My father loved them more than anyone I ever met.

The old man was never merciless, yet often merciful. He never asked for forgiveness but gave it abundantly.

He was in his own way like Pearl Buck, who loved the land and peasants of China. My father loved the land and the lower ranks of Americans. Unlike FDR, who was a glad-hander, he was a true populist. He also appreciated hard work and was attracted to go-getters who wanted to accomplish something with their lives. He was, in the end, his own man.

These reflections are the first time in more than a century that I—the only one of us to do so—have lifted a word or voice about our inner family circle. My father chose to remain private throughout his life.

It may be too idealistic a view, that he was overcome by his own limitless destiny. However, that would explain his enormous drive and direction, despite the many crosscurrents in his life.

Some will always see my father as an exile on his own St. Helena. However, history may yet look up to see him standing tall on his enchanted hill above San Simeon.

IV
THE MAGNIFICENT
OBSESSION

T he experts told Pop that it couldn't be done. No one could build
an adequate foundation for a large home up there on the crest
of that steep hill overlooking the Pacific and the little village of
San Simeon. There was no proper building material available—no
lumber, no nearby steel or iron. Even if such materials were carried by
boat to the pier, a rising, curving road would have to be constructed out
of the wilderness. And it was more than a five-mile pull up the 1,600-
foot grade to the mountaintop. Frosty winter weather could make such
a twisting route treacherous to climb, especially with heavy, unstable
loads.

Where would the skilled workmen come from? Where would they be
housed? How would they be fed? And where would sufficient drinking
water be found? There also was no place for workers to go and nothing
for them to do during their spare time in this far-off no-man's-land
between the ocean and the Santa Lucia Mountains. They would take to
drinking, fighting—and then quitting. It was a crazy idea. The experts
told the old man to forget it.

History agreed with them. From its earliest times, San Simeon had
always been a backwater. Almost all the early Spanish explorers sailed
past the small inlet. Only Juan Rodriguez Cabrillo, a Portuguese in service
to the king of Spain, may have set foot on the soil in 1542. No one is

certain who first came to the area. The bay of San Simeon is said to have been named by a devout, early Spanish settler. It was in honor of an old man in the New Testament who was one of the first to hail Jesus as the Messiah.

In later years Spain's Sebastian Vizcaino, England's Sir Francis Drake, and other explorers sailed past San Simeon many times as they searched for safe ports and places to colonize. For more than two centuries the Spanish forgot about San Simeon and their California claims. In 1771 Father Junipero Serra came and built a Franciscan mission at San Antonio de Padua, over the hills from San Simeon in a river valley. He had constructed two earlier missions, at San Diego and Monterey. In 1797 the Franciscans built San Miguel Arcangel, their sixteenth mission, which also was not distant from San Simeon.

It was not until 1840 that Don José Jesús de Pico received a Mexican grant covering part of the San Miguel mission lands, vast acreage he called Rancho Piedra Blanca. In the next two years, two large sections of acreage were granted to Julian and José Ramon Estrada. Julian named it Rancho Santa Rosa. These were the largest spreads later bought by my grandfather, George Hearst.

In 1822 Mexico broke away from Spain. California became a province of the new republic, and a Mexican governor arrived in Monterey. At the time, the missions controlled 8 million acres of prime land, and more than 150,000 head of horses, cattle, and sheep. Thousands of Indians worked for the missions. Rising numbers of new American settlers in California were anxious to buy some of this land. In 1846 a group of Americans took a Mexican general captive and declared a "Yankee Republic." Captain John Sutter and his local army garrison proclaimed themselves leaders of the "Bear Flag Republic." The discovery of gold at Sutter's Creek sparked the gold rush of 1849. The Stars and Stripes soon replaced the banner of the "Bear Flag Republic." Americans everywhere proclaimed that California now belonged to the United States.

Mexico went to war. The Americans, under General Winfield Scott, won the conflict in sixteen months. As a result of the Treaty of Guadalupe Hidalgo and the Gadsden Purchase, which followed, the United States added California, Nevada, Utah, almost all of Arizona, much of Texas, southwest Wyoming, the westernmost part of Colorado, and western New Mexico to its spreading domain. California became a state in 1850.

The United States moved relentlessly toward the Pacific as American leaders heralded the nation's doctrine of Manifest Destiny. Later, the Homestead Act of 1862 opened up the High Plains. Small armies of sodbusters poured across the desert. The Land Grant Act of 1882 transferred millions more acres of public lands into private hands. The West— from the Mississippi River to Texas and California—exploded with railroad barons, mining millionaires, cattle kings, land-hungry ranchers, and farmers.

To understand my father, one must comprehend the lure and the promise of Manifest Destiny, which didn't look to the crowded, urban East but rather to a limitless land of new pioneers and new opportunities in the West. His boyhood was shaped around the idea of an unbounded land with immeasurable potential. That was his outlook as a man. My father once said to me of San Simeon and the West, "I love it. I just love it. My father brought me to San Simeon as a boy. I had to come up the slope hanging on to the tail of a pony. We lived in a cabin on this spot and could see forever. That's the West—forever."

Many easterners never clearly understood what made Pop and his fellow westerners tick. Their America was yet to be discovered—a land and people of incalculable hope amid endless horizons. My grandfather had been part of the stampede west. In 1865 he began not only buying land but putting up warehouses on the shore of San Simeon for provisions and feed for the cattle and racehorses he planned to breed. He would later train racehorses there. The little local harbor had already become a busy port for whale hunters. George later built a wharf and pier so local farmers and ranchers could ship their produce. The 100,000 acres purchased by George and Grandmother Phoebe came to be known simply as the Hearst Ranch.

George left his entire estate to his widow, and nothing to his son. I'm not certain what Pop thought of that at the time. He may have chafed at the decision, although his letters to Phoebe don't bear that out. Indeed, he indicated it was a smart move. Pop could blow a lot of dough. He would splurge a thousand bucks taking his reporters on a yacht party. Or another grand searching for an errant editor who had disappeared on a long toot. A thousand dollars in those days could buy half a house. If you put a fine painting in front of him, there was no telling how wide he might open his checkbook.

In any case, when Phoebe died she passed on vast lands to my father—not only the San Simeon property but a million-acre ranch in Mexico, a thousand square miles of Mexican land in Vera Cruz and the Yucatan, and thousands of acres of timber forest on the McCloud River near Mount Shasta in northern California. She also owned a fortune in gold mines and other assets. Their worth at the time was estimated at about $20 million, but that is a gross understatement. Most of the mines and other properties were still appreciating and yet to pay off.

My father had the money, therefore, to build almost anything on the mountaintop. Pop first told us he would build a family cabin and later a bungalow—a ranch house in western terms. Within months, however, he was planning to construct something larger, and larger. Eventually, a complex of buildings was planned. This is what came to be known as the Hearst Castle.

Pop was convinced that all the nay-sayers were wrong. Something grand, even grandiose, could and would be built. But why, oh, why, so many people have asked over the past half century, did your father construct such an extraordinary estate—and at San Simeon of all places—and furnish it with such a rich treasure-house of the world's art? In Pop's own words to me: "I just wanted to. Period. I loved the place."

My father said he wanted to bring together many things—the Spanish-Moorish architecture, the great rooms full of fine paintings, sculpture, silver works, tapestries, woodwork, vases, and all the rest of old Europe—to set them all in the one place he loved most. To him, assembling an art collection was not much different from collecting stamps—except that it was a lot more expensive! As time went on the work became a passion and, at times, all consuming. He simply could not stop building and furnishing the place.

To do so he moved mountains—sometimes literally. He also transported across the Atlantic Ocean European castles, a Spanish monastery stone by stone, and tons of art that were to fill not only the estate at San Simeon but large warehouses in New York. He did it all with something not even a fortune could buy: his imagination. Pop had a romantic vision of troubadours and trumpets, artists and ageless heroes, damsels and minstrels, and countless court jesters. He loved the laughter and theater of it all. In many ways, Pop was a medieval man.

He was fifty-six years old when construction began in 1919 and, with easy wit, he said he no longer wished to live in tents. It was toward the close of that year that Pop abandoned his bungalow plan and decided on a much bolder one. He would construct a group of buildings with a towered main structure that would resemble a Spanish hill town. He wanted the central residence built first, so we could move into it by the following summer. He soon changed his mind, as he was often to do over the next three decades. Three smaller houses, eventually for other members of the family, relatives, and guests, would encircle our home and be constructed first. We would move into the one ready for our visit the following summer. Each house was to have at least one spectacular view— either of the Santa Lucia Mountains, the ocean, or a fuller sun. Actual construction began several months later, during the winter of 1920.

Shortages of all kinds plagued the project, from building materials to skilled workers, but my father saw them as mere inconveniences. We lived in tents the following summer while Pop and his architect, Julia Morgan, struggled with endless problems.

My mother was as excited as Pop about the project, only for a personal reason. She had long had, as a New York City girl, her fill of sleeping on cots and balancing family meals on rickety outdoor tables at San Simeon. Mom wanted a firm bed and a strong table. But she was a good sport about all of it—even the long horse rides. Pop loved these rides and picnics and, nearly every day, Mom would struggle onto a horse and hope her heart and seat would hold out.

I remember one camping trip in which we rode about a dozen miles up a mountain called Pat Garrity's. Mom always rode astride, in full-cut breeches and boots, since sidesaddles were seldom available in the West. We camped out. About 4:30 A.M. we kids woke up and began making a racket. That woke up Mom and Pop, much to their consternation, and everybody was soon dressed and anxious for breakfast.

We rode down the mountain, never easy in those steep hills, and finally arrived at a natural pool in the Arroyo de la Cruz. Poor Mom was sweating, but all us kids dashed in first, leaving her to sit and wait until it was safe to swim. We got back on the horses with Mom aching all over and hours yet to ride. Being the trouper she was, Mom never said a word until we arrived back on top of our hill. Then, getting down from her horse, she looked in Pop's direction and sighed, "He told me it was going to be a short ride!" All of us burst into laughter.

If my father was crazy to undertake the project, so was Julia Morgan, a tiny but strong-willed woman who was bold enough to agree with his vision and accept the job as architect. Julia was one of the first women to graduate in civil engineering from the University of California at Berkeley. In 1902, after two attempts by the French to keep her out of the school, Julia became the first woman to graduate from the École des Beaux-Arts in Paris. It had long been recognized as the world's top architectural institution.

Julia was about five feet two inches tall and weighed no more than a hundred pounds. She wore horn-rimmed glasses and usually dressed in tailormade suits with handmade Parisian blouses. Always prim and proper, she topped her understated yet distinctive garb with a trim, dark hat affectionally called the Queen Mary style. Underneath that impeccable attire and highly professional air was a steel-trap mind and a will of iron.

I used to listen to her and the old man go at it in her small office at the top of the hill. She and Pop had some real squawks, let me tell you, but both were so formal and low-keyed that an outsider would hardly have noticed. Indeed, through all the years she always called him "Mister Hearst" and he referred to her as "Miss Morgan." At the end of most discussions she deferred to him as the client. But not without forcing my father to consider all the questions in her mind, the cost, and the new architectural problems created.

Julia wrote Pop hundreds of long letters and notes about every aspect of the work. She managed to cajole, plead, demand, and warn Pop in the most courteous, professional language. But, if one read carefully between the lines, she caught the old man up short many a time and indicated she would not retreat on her view unless he had a darn good answer. Some of this correspondence is still preserved. Several times their views were so far apart that Julia quit, but Pop simply would not hear of it. They would come to some kind of compromise, and she would soon be drawing a new sketch. Julia was as totally committed to the project as my father.

Pop loved to go round and round with her because he was, at heart, an amateur architect. I have always said that if the old man had never become a newspaperman, he would have been a good architect. Julia and Pop referred to one another as "fellow architects" and both got great laughs out of that.

Julia's incredible devotion to the work at San Simeon was demonstrated in her schedule. For many years, on most weekends she left her San Francisco office at the close of business on Friday and took the night train to San Luis Obispo. A waiting car would transport her fifty miles over rough roads to the construction site. She would get to bed after midnight and rise at dawn to oversee the entire project. Julia would return to San Francisco on Sunday night the same way, arriving just in time to start work in her office on Monday morning.

Julia herself hired, oversaw, and paid the many artisans and laborers who worked at San Simeon—sometimes as many as 150. She dealt with stone casters, ornamental plasterers, woodcarvers, tile designers, tapestry workers, and others. In effect, she worked as the architect and contractor. Pop authorized her to pay premium wages despite the Depression. I often saw her tiny figure bent over some part of the work, then nimbly climbing over barricades and other obstacles to inspect another job. She was like a rabbit, hopping hither and yon; but as she straightened up in her suit, a regal lady arose.

The two had an extraordinary adventure together: thousands of crucial decisions, then changes; costs and more costs; selecting the most appropriate art for each of the hundreds of rooms; finding California and other American artists to duplicate the wood and paintings of European masters, so ceilings and other areas would match; planning the extremely complex landscaping; and seeing that thousands of other details fit in the enormous jigsaw puzzle.

Their work extended to Wyntoon, the large place that Grandma built beneath Mount Shasta, near the California-Oregon border. The main house and other structures burned to the ground in the winter of 1929–30. Julia was chosen to resurrect Wyntoon. Pop would let only Julia take complete charge. She built a delightful Bavarian village—four gingerbread houses painted with murals—along the rushing McCloud River. The estate today covers about 67,000 acres. It is owned by the Hearst Corporation. For several years during World War II, my father and Marion Davies moved from San Simeon and lived at Wyntoon (Marion called it "Spitoon"). He had been warned that Japanese submarines might try to shell the castle. It was of course a false alarm, but there was a lot of wartime hysteria about the Japanese.

My wife and I still go to Wyntoon for short visits. It is cooler than San Simeon during the summer. The gingerbread houses create a dreamy, idyllic atmosphere. I always take an afternoon to commune spiritually with the old man. I tell him it will not be too long before we are together again. We will do a lot of cracker-barrel reflecting about world events and share some laughs.

In these later years of my life, I have thought about Julia—the reserved spinster who preferred anonymity; the consummate professional who refused to submit her name for architectural prizes and other recognition, although she designed and built some 700 structures in her career. Her only glory was to be a "working architect," a monument to self-effacement and personal grace. It has often been said and written that Julia even burned her blueprints, drawings, and files before she died in 1957. That's inaccurate. The misunderstanding came from Julia's repeated observation that her work should "speak for itself."

Morgan's secretary, Mrs. H. C. Forney, retained many of Julia's papers. Forney's daughter has given many Morgan drawings to UC Berkeley. Julia herself kept a good number of her office records—later passed to her nephew, Morgan North—and these were given to California Polytechnic State University at San Luis Obispo. The university has a Julia Morgan Collection. The letters between Julia and my father demonstrate the close and congenial collaboration between the two. They also show a little-mentioned aspect of their work—how difficult it was to exchange ideas and plans by letter and telegram at a distance of 3,000 miles, and keep work on schedule.

Julia died peacefully in San Francisco, and the newspapers briefly noted that a local architect had passed away. She had said little of herself and spent her last years quietly seeing only a few close friends. Yet the sparse mention was appropriate from her viewpoint. Her highest accolade was the respect she earned from other architects.

Little by little, from the start of the century, Pop had been buying European art during visits to the continent, and through dealers and auctions in Europe and New York. Since he and Julia had decided that the architecture of the estate would be Spanish Renaissance, Pop bought even more Spanish art. He has often been criticized because the general decor didn't flow smoothly. That was because he saw fit to combine their styles with the predominantly Spanish.

Some drew caricatures of the old man waltzing around Europe throwing money at castles, sculptures, and paintings. The truth is, he purchased much of the art through dealers in New York, such as Duveen, which stored antiques there. At that time, New York buyers toured Europe and bought ancestral collections of the war-ravaged continent—at most reasonable prices. Of course it is true that my father bought a lot of other art on personal trips to Europe, and perhaps paid too much at times. But he always used to say, "The price is often what the object is worth to you."

From 1920 until the Depression years of the 1930s, Pop shipped boats and rail cars full of art to Miss Morgan at San Simeon. His purchases became such a flood that some had to be held in New York warehouses. On arrival at San Simeon, these items were placed in warehouses that Julia had constructed near the docks. She had to reinforce the wharf and build a railroad siding so the material could be moved there. By 1930 the San Simeon warehouses were full, but much material remained in New York until a decision was made on what to do with it. Loads, literally, of art objects were never shipped west. Much of this was sold at Gimbel's during the company's financial crisis. Julia described the first shipments in 1921—the art itself as well as what my father was attempting:

So far we have received from him, to incorporate in the new buildings, some twelve or thirteen carloads of antiques, brought from the ends of the earth and from prehistoric down to late Empire in period, the majority, however, being of Spanish origin.

They comprise vast quantities of tables, beds, armoires, secretaries, all kinds of cabinets, polychrome church statuary, columns, door frames, carved doors in all stages of repair and disrepair, over-altars, reliquaries, lanterns, iron-grille doors, window grilles, votive candlesticks, all kinds of chairs in quantity, and six or seven well heads.

I don't see myself where we are ever going to use half suitably, but I find the idea is to try things out and if they are not satisfactory, discard them for the next thing that promises better. There is interest and charm coming gradually into play.

Pop's purchases became more in keeping with the actual site as the buildings took shape. Julia's natural reserve was disappearing in the exhilaration of it all. She called on art dealers to locate "finer and more important" pieces. But Julia never forgot how it all began. In her correspondence and conversations with Pop, she constantly referred to the project as "the ranch."

Pop became even more enthralled. He began to refer to the rising complex as a museum. In using that lofty language, he was also implying something broader than the interests of our family. To him, the concept of a museum was an artistic achievement to be shared with others. That is precisely what the great galleries of Europe had taught him. He was saying that we would use the place for a while, temporarily, but one day it would belong to the American people. And he believed in giving them a good show in a breathtaking American setting—an enchanted castle and gardens created in the European grand manner. That is borne out in his conversations with me and with Julia and her architectural colleagues.

In the summer of 1921 the family moved into the Casa del Mar (House of the Sea) for the first time. It was the first of the half moon of guest houses around the Casa Grande (Big House) to be finished. The Casa del Monte (House of the Mountain) and Casa del Sol (House of the Sun) were completed by 1924. Neither my father nor Julia, by the way, referred to them as "guest houses." They were adjoining structures or buildings.

The Casa Grande, begun in 1922, was ready for partial use by 1926, though some later sections were not completed until the 1930s. One of the most remarkable feats of engineering by my father and Julia Morgan is the water supply of San Simeon. A giant-sized pipe, two feet in diameter, runs from a distant mountain, across hills, to a reservoir—all by the force of gravity—to the twin towers of the Casa Grande. Each tower actually hides a giant water tank that had to be built strong enough to withstand such pressure.

Each of the thirty-six carillon bells in the two castle towers has an electric motor. A clapper, similar to a small hammer, is attached to every motor. It strikes the bell from about two inches away and, since each bell is a different size, every one has an individual tone. The bells have inscriptions on them. Part of one reads:

Tuned be its Metal Mouth Alone to Things Eternal and Sublime.
And as the Swift Wing'd Hours Speed on, May it Record the Flight of Time.

Christmas eve of 1925 has often been called the castle's grand opening. That isn't accurate, since Pop continued to stay at the Casa del Mar during his sporadic visits. Nevertheless, on that Christmas vigil, he held a housewarming dinner for our family (our mother and all five sons attended) and friends in the large Assembly Room.

It was a very festive occasion. The guests, surprised and even stunned by the array of great art, were swept up in the beauty of the room. A baroque portal stood at the entrance to the Casa Grande and led across a Pompeian mosaic to a large main vestibule. In a single sweep guests immediately saw a French fireplace sixteen feet high, Flemish tapestries, Italian-carved Renaissance choir stalls and ceilings, timeless wall reliefs, bronze European sculptures and, atop very large, antique walnut refectory tables, high silver candlesticks and a great, crystal jewel casket.

My father had concealed a private elevator, which descended from his personal suite and opened into this room, where he would suddenly appear among the guests. For two decades he enjoyed surprising his visitors this way. It was his little joke to start the evening.

As a young fellow I was dazzled by the beautiful actresses and big-name movie stars from Hollywood who visited. Many other friends and some of Pop's top editors also came. Many told me that, despite its ornateness, they found the room warm and relaxing. I've found that original impression repeated by countless visitors through the years.

Other comforts were added to the Assembly Room later: permanent card tables with decks for any kind of game, jigsaw puzzles, tables for checkers, chess, and dominoes. (Pop loved to play dominoes.) It had large, deep, comfortable chintz-covered chairs and sofas.

That was the last Christmas we had dinner together as a family. My mother had a big Christmas party for local youngsters before we returned to New York. Then Marion Davies moved in openly.

The Casa Grande was never completed. Pop continued to get new ideas from photos in various architectural publications to improve the buildings and site. He changed the outdoor pool, gardens, and other parts of the landscape several times. The endless project became a magnificent obsession with him. San Simeon was like his own flesh and blood. It was, in some ways, his heartbeat.

During the late 1920s Pop visited San Simeon more and more often. He stayed in the Casa del Mar, the most ornate of the three guest houses. In 1928 my father moved into the newly completed Gothic Suite of the Casa Grande. By 1930 Pop lived more at San Simeon than anywhere else.

He spent more than 200 days there that year. It was soon to become his permanent home and working headquarters.

The family always referred to Casa del Mar as "A" House. That was its name in the planning stage. It is larger and more richly decorated than the other houses and, in some aspects, even more so than the Casa Grande. One enters through a magnificent set of carved doors. It has walls covered in antique red velvet and has stunning, gold-leaf trim on all the windows, window and door frames, and ceilings. Every piece of furniture is a priceless antique except for the overstuffed chintz-covered sofas and armchairs.

The house, located on the side of a hill, is on three levels. The lowest level contains a loggia with magnificent ancient Roman mosaics. A table, inlaid with various types of precious marble, carries the Medici family crest. Among the many works of art throughout is a bronze plaque of Napoleon, made when he was a young French officer during the Italian campaign. Pop always retained a particular fondness for "A" House, and returned to live there during his last years at San Simeon.

Casa del Monte was "B" House. It is the smallest of the three, a splendid Renaissance villa. The house faces the summit of the Santa Lucia Mountains, the Junipero Serra Peak. The mood of the rooms is Spanish and Italian Renaissance.

The Cardinal Richelieu bed in "B" House, set in a mountain-view bedroom, became, over the years, perhaps the most famous individual object at San Simeon. It is an elaborately carved Italian baroque piece that has caught the eye of many a guest—and, later, tourist. Some well-known guests like David Niven and Cary Grant boasted in their memoirs and interviews that they had slept in the cardinal's bed. Not true. In a whimsical moment, Camille Rossi, the construction chief during most of the 1920s, created the fable just for the fun of it. The bed apparently belonged to a prelate of the church, but not Richelieu. The fable caught everyone's imagination and was transformed into fact.

The Casa del Sol was called "C" House. It sits between the two smaller buildings and looks west toward the old lighthouse. There is a mixed flavor to the place—Persian rugs and carpets and Oriental vases vie with Italian pieces for predominance. As in the other houses, many works are 500 to 1,000 years old.

Many people today refer to the Casa Grande and the entire complex as the "castle" because of its European character. Some have compared the Casa Grande to a European cathedral. Its twin towers are copied from a cathedral in Spain. Even I can sometimes get lost in its labyrinthine corridors and more than 100 rooms. That includes, with an added new wing, about forty bedroom suites.

The Assembly Room dominates the first floor. The nearby dining room, which Pop called the Refectory as the monks had, has four antique Italian walnut matching tables, placed end to end, with a fifth, from England, last. These normally seated forty guests. However, the tables have been known to accommodate as many as fifty. Some of its Dante chairs are antiques, while others are copies made in Europe and New York. I like the multicolored Palio banners from Siena that hang from the ceiling. The Refectory features art from various ages. Saints and madonnas create a spiritual mood. The huge, impressive ceiling, carved with saints in full relief, comes from Siena. Along the walls are fifteenth-century choir stalls. Part of the renowned silver collection makes the room truly unique, with great candlesticks, serving dishes, and wine cisterns dating from the eighteenth century.

After dinner Pop usually invited guests to a small movie theater to view pre-release or new films. He always sat in the front row with his dachshunds at his feet and a phone to the projectionist at his side. The theater was decorated with a considerable amount of gold leaf, and the walls were covered with specially woven red damask made by Franco Scalamandre, founder of the celebrated textile firm. Scalamandre told me that the damask order from my father gave him sufficient funds to set up his looms in New Jersey and start his own business in this country. The firm has since furnished materials for many U.S. historic shrines.

A carillon keyboard is still used to play the Casa Grande's thirty-six bells. The twin bell towers were modified in 1926–27 to allow installation of a Belgian carillon. Each tower has eighteen bells, which were installed a few years later. In the nearby billiard room hangs a great tapestry, "Hunt of the Stag." Tapestries similar to this series grace the walls of the Cloisters, a part of New York's Metropolitan Museum of Art.

The Doge's Suite, largest in the castle, is set on the mezzanine level. It is patterned after suites in the Doge's Palace at Venice. The room has a splendid Venetian Gothic loggia. The Morning Room and the Cloisters adjoin the Doge's Suite. All are filled with various treasures, from carved mantelpieces to marble arches and palace doors.

My favorite areas in the Casa Grande are the two great libraries on the second and third floors, and my father's Gothic Suite on the third. Pop's library is one of the largest yet most serene rooms in the place. The library walls are covered with Renaissance-style bookshelves, which still contain many original works and fine volumes. (When my father passed away, the trustees and I agreed that a major part of the valuable book collection should go to the Bancroft Library at UC Berkeley. Bancroft was prepared to care for and make these works available to scholars.) Above the bookshelves are ancient Greek vases of pottery. All are more than 2,000 years old. My father's Greek vase collection was perhaps the most complete private collection in the world. When Pop died, some of the vases were purchased by New York's Metropolitan Museum to complete its own collection.

Pop's Gothic Suite is the most spiritual—perhaps even religious—area in the entire complex. It presents a side of my father that few ever came to know. I have always felt that this suite represented the idealistic inner man. He was very spiritual, privately, as I have come to realize in later years. This was manifest in his lifetime pursuit of artistic excellence. These rooms were Pop's retreat, his monastic cell, his one private place in the world. He lived with pictures of his mother and father in this room. He also kept a small madonna, given him by his lifetime friend Eleanor "Cissy" Patterson, a veteran newswoman. I believe these choices mirrored much of the man.

The bedroom, library, and sitting rooms contain many of Pop's favorite works of art. Austine and I and the children often stayed there. Almost everything is of museum quality: ceilings, paintings, statues, mantelpieces, doors, candlesticks, and pieces of bronze, brass, and ivory. The size of Pop's bedroom is modest compared to other parts of the suite and the rooms below. He made the rooms comfortable with large chintz-covered chairs and sofas. Marion Davies' suite was separated from his by a sitting room.

I never visited the private area of my father and Marion. The thought never occurred to me. I walked up there only after the two left for Beverly Hills in 1947. Even then I was uncomfortable. My relationship with Marion was never close. Of course we were polite, spoke casually whenever we met, but I kept my distance. I loved my mother and, to me, Marion was an interloper. This had been our hill, our land, our family home from the time of our grandparents. However, Pop enjoyed Marion's company and the two got along well. My relationship with Marion underwent strong swings in later years, and was to end in disaster.

Each year, swallows come and build mud nests under the eaves of the castle. After the eggs hatch and the birds fly away, the abandoned nests have dirtied the fancy wooden eaves, so workmen wash away the mess with hoses from fire trucks. The castle grounds, with their thousands of beautiful flowers, seem to become a bee colony at times. Hives are discovered in the most unusual spots. And, when pushed to vacate, some of the brave bees do not leave quietly.

A new wing—a three-level section on the north side of the Casa Grande, with a wine cellar and bowling alley—completes the complex, except for the outside temple, statuary, and landscaping. The new wing also has an impressive array of European and other art.

The outside terraces and esplanade are filled with wellheads, fountains, sculptures, Italian columns, and many freestanding pedestals from all parts of the world, all carved from marble and stone. These are surrounded by palms, oaks, magnolias, azaleas, roses, and hundreds of other flowering bushes and trees.

Pop cherished trees. He happened to be visiting nearby Paso Robles one day and noticed more than a score of thirty-foot Italian cypresses. He was appalled on learning they were about to be destroyed. He purchased them immediately, but had to wait a year to move them to San Simeon. Meantime, he ordered that a box be built around each tree to ensure its safety. All were later transported thirty miles across the mountains to the estate. The massive undertaking took two years before all stood in a terraced row. Only heaven knows the cost.

Pop would not allow any tree to be cut down. I remember one time when workmen were about to saw down a 100-year-old oak to make way for some project. The old man somehow heard about it, and both of us rushed down to the site. He asked the men to move the oak but not cut it down. They said that could not be done. My father ordered the work held up until he devised a plan to move the tree. The oak was dug up and jacked slowly along a trench until it was inside a three-sided concrete flower pot. Great care was taken so as not to damage the tree roots. The fourth side was attached once the oak was securely contained. Then the giant pot was lifted by crane to another spot. The fourth side of the pot was again removed and the tree inched outside into a hole. The undertaking cost Pop about $40,000. The bill never fazed him because he had saved the old oak. The estate had, by the way, nearly two dozen gardeners during most of his years there.

Winston Churchill loved the landscape at San Simeon. When he visited us in 1929, he spent considerable time studying it from different views. We didn't know it, but he planned to paint several scenes. Churchill was actually writing for the Hearst newspapers at the time and happened to be visiting Hollywood, so Pop invited him up from the movie colony.

During the Churchill visit, Pop and one of his financial advisers were conferring inside the Casa Grande. A maid rushed past them, apparently saying that the British guest was "fainting" and wanted some "turpentine." Pop was perplexed and hurried out on a terrace where Churchill was painting—not fainting. He had asked for turpentine to thin his oils. The old man got the drift immediately and started laughing. Churchill could not figure out why; he just puffed on a cigar and went back to work on his landscape.

The massive outdoor Neptune Pool is graced by an early Roman temple, and the indoor Roman Pool glistens with thousands of glass tiles from Venice. The fabulous Neptune setting, with its colonnaded pavilions at each end, is perhaps the most memorable outdoor backdrop at San Simeon. Neptune holds 345,000 gallons of fresh spring water, while the Roman Pool holds 205,000. The movie *Spartacus* was filmed with Neptune and its temple as a backdrop.

Pop also loved animals, so he created a 2,000-acre outdoor zoo on the place, beginning in late 1924. He then purchased some forty Montana buffalo. These were followed by everything from elephants and llamas to zebras and emus. We had the largest privately owned, free-roaming animal kingdom in the world. No one was allowed to drive fast up the hill lest they hit an animal. If anyone did, the old man would hardly speak to him.

Also off the main grounds of the estate, he constructed a mile-long pergola with grape vines and espaliered fruit trees covering the entire length—just in case someone wanted to ride or take a walk without being bothered by a hot sun. It is a good place from which to study the castle above. The pergola is high and wide enough for two horsemen to ride abreast.

The estimated cost of all that went into the estate at the time ranges from $30 million to $40 million. I am unsure as to the total. If it were possible to replicate it today, the price of the estate would climb into the billions of dollars. The expense is now unimportant. It seems clear, though, that no man—no matter how much money he might have—will ever attempt such a herculean adventure in America again. Few would be as artistically prepared as my father to undertake the task, and perhaps fewer still would have the will to remain at the job for so long.

La Cuesta Encantada, the entire complex on top of the hill, was honored in 1976 when the U.S. Department of the Interior designated it a National Historic Landmark. It was thus enrolled in the National Register of Historic Places.

The nooks and crannies of the place recall almost forgotten boyhood adventures. I remember wandering through each house and every floor as each building was being constructed. In later years, when the estate was finished, I enjoyed making the same rounds, greeting guests and telling them of our early tent years there. I got to know most of Pop's business associates and many of the Hollywood stars who came for weekend parties.

I lived in both "A" House and the Casa Grande for many years. My brothers and I had the complete run of the buildings and grounds. We swam, played a lot of tennis, and rode. I never thought much about the lavishness of the surroundings. That may sound peculiar, but it's the truth. Nor did I think of the place as a museum, as some guests did. I accepted the "castle" as I had our massive apartment in Manhattan or Grandma's hacienda. It was simply there.

There usually seemed to be something going on. Pop was constantly involved in new construction in and around the houses as well as placing new trees and flowers in the gardens. New animals arrived for the outdoor zoo and more cattle for the ranch. The number of workers rose as did the number of visitors.

We had our own ice cream maker in the kitchen. I was always afraid of spilling ice cream on one of the Persian rugs. Believe me, the old man would have lectured us if I or any of my brothers ever tossed a baseball or football inside; we never did because the weather was usually good. However, we played pool, cards, and sneaked down to the basement cellar to study the wines. We never uncorked any. That was definitely out of bounds. I accidentally let it slip one time that we had seen the wine cellar, and noticed the place was kept locked after that.

As the years passed, however, the castle took on a mystique, a presence, that became for me the spirit of my father.

Perhaps the most moving moment of all the years that I spent there came in August of 1957. As editor-in-chief of the Hearst newspapers, I wrote a Sunday column on San Simeon. Excerpts from the one I wrote on the sixth anniversary of Pop's death indicate how deeply I felt about my father and our home there:

> I am writing this column, sitting at my father's desk in his study on the third floor of this big castle at San Simeon. Out of the window, I can look over the brown hills rolling miles down to the Pacific, 1,600 feet below. At the horizon, the water blends into the lighter blue of the sky.
>
> My heart is heavy and aching, and the beautiful panorama gets blurry once in a while, as I know this is the last time that we shall ever come here as our home. Later this year, the castle and all of its treasures and lovely gardens will be given to the state of California, and from next summer on it will be open to the public to come, see and admire. If you are ever out this way, by all means make a point of stopping by.
>
> On the wall of my father's bedroom next door is the following quotation from Sir Edward Bulwer Lytton's "The Lady of Lyons," which could have been written about this place:

> A palace lifting to eternal summer
> Its marble walls, from out a glossy bower
> Of coolest foliage musical with birds.
> And when the night came—the perfumed light
> Stole through the mists of alabaster lamps,
> And every air was heavy with the sighs
> Of orange groves and music from sweet lutes,
> And murmurs of low fountains that gush forth
> In the midst of roses.

The column recalls four decades of visits—from the first half-dozen long, brown canvas tents and a much larger tent—sixty by twenty feet—that served as a combination dining room and living room. It remembers the antiquities coming up the hill—Roman, Egyptian, Greek, French, Spanish, and others—the tapestries, rare silks, and books, and the huge crates of European furniture. The column recalls the many years it took for the complex to assume its present form. There was no hurry, as Pop studied the plans and blueprints with care. On several occasions, partially completed structures—the great, white marble pool comes most readily to mind—were completely torn down and reconstructed more to his liking. The column continued:

When Pop was in residence here, it was the headquarters for his many and varied business activities. News tickers from the International News Service, the Associated Press, our own Hearst wire, a 24-hour-a-day switchboard, and short-wave radio communication were part of the equipment.

Company executives and celebrities from every field of endeavor, from national politics to movies, were forever coming and going. Pop had a tremendous capacity for work, combined with a knack for being able to turn from work to play, whether it was horseback riding or hunting, swimming or playing tennis with us.

Parts of the building are still in an uncompleted state and, frankly, had he lived another 10 years, I don't think he would ever have put the final touches to it, as he enjoyed creating, designing, building and decorating so very much.

It was not that he was superstitious about finishing it—he was a perfectionist. He could always see ways in which, artistically or decoratively, improvements could be wrought.

For to me, the place will always be Pop's master work, representing him as much or more than any of his newspapers or magazines or better known accomplishments.

I feel Pop's presence very strongly here—every block of stone, every piece of wood, every flower, every tree is here because he put it here. . . . I will miss living here as I miss him.

Pop had known that the state would probably become its eventual owners. In fact, he wanted to give the place to the University of California. He told me that he would be delighted to have that happen. He didn't believe the company would wish to keep up the expense of the complex, particularly because it would no longer be a working part of the firm, and thus would be an added tax expense. Neither of us related these thoughts to anyone because it was not time to suggest he might be leaving. He was very serene about it. I remember rising from the conversation and being a little weak at the knees. He was smiling, however, and I knew that he had long reconciled himself and was pleased that so many people would one day enjoy the place. As events unfolded, the university decided not to accept the offer, but some farsighted people in state government saw the castle's tourist possibilities, and the park system took over.

Looking down the hill today, one can see tourist buses descending to the state offices below. The castle complex, which the park system still manages, actually covers only about 123 acres. Another thirty acres are an animal park. The state area is completely surrounded by the large Hearst ranch. The Hearst Corporation has since purchased about 70,000 acres of farm and cattle-raising land over the Santa Lucia Mountains, about twenty-five miles beyond the city of Paso Robles.

Earlier, as World War II approached and the U.S. Army sought large training sites, the federal government had purchased about 150,000 acres of the Hearst acreage. It became the Hunter-Liggett Reservation. The old man reserved the right to repurchase the property when the government no longer needed it. However, the Army has upgraded the land to Fort Hunter-Liggett and still retains it.

About the same time as the government purchase, Pop donated about 5,000 acres in the Big Sur area of Monterey County to the Boy Scouts for a camp.

I have often sat up on the hill to catch the warm rays of the late afternoon sun. In summer, the hilltop is as much as thirty degrees warmer than the seashore below. I have been concerned about the beautiful flowers because there has been a local drought in recent years. Water is gravity-fed from springs some five miles away. The reservoir holds about 1.5 million gallons, but, when it gets low, water must be carried up the hill in trucks.

The little cottage Austine and I live in is down the road. The place is quite modest—two bedrooms with baths, a living-dining room with a fireplace, and a kitchen. It's on a stream that flows down and joins the ocean not far distant. We call it the Pico Cottage because it is on Pico Creek. The cottage was once a stagecoach stop. The stage ran from San Luis Obispo to Cambria and finally San Simeon. It was a minor stop, just to change horses. The sweaty chargers would be fed and rested in a nearby hay field.

When we or the company have guests, we send them a few miles up the road to a large Victorian house that my grandfather built for himself and Phoebe in the 1870s. It is a well-maintained, comfortable old place that says we have been around these parts for a long time.

I like to picnic with Austine up in these hills. It's not only because of the panoramic view of the area but also the sweep of birds above and the running animals below. I've been a birdwatcher since I was a boy, when Phoebe hired a teacher on the environment for us. Until recently, Austine and I often rode horses up to a nearby height called Arbor Hill. It's my favorite spot to picnic because one can see the beautiful rolling countryside for many miles in every direction. Now, because of breaking my hip, Austine drives me up the hill in a car.

I spend time up here because there is still so much to see and remember. The old harbor juts out to sea but is no longer used for commerce. People play on the beach, but few swim because the water is too cold. When I was a kid, it was never too cold. Black Angus and Hereford cattle loll in the distance. Those 4,000 to 5,000 head are the major source of revenue for the ranch.

Arabian horses munch on the grass near our cottage. I remember when Pop had three stables. One was behind the Casa Grande, where about forty horses were kept for guests. Quarter horses were stabled down near the airstrip at the bottom of the long road up here. Champion Arabians and palominos grazed here, near Pico Creek. They were hidden, like our cottage, in a valley whose steep slopes are covered with ancient live oaks and rare Monterey pines. Austine still raises Arabians here. The horses are great company for us as we've been riding since we were children.

I still remember Pop's old poultry ranch and dairy. He raised turkeys, chickens, ducks, guinea and cornish hens, quail, and other game birds for the family and guests. The dairy had prize Jersey cows that supplied milk, butter, and cheese to the castle and the families that lived in the village of San Simeon. A large vegetable garden was situated on the horse ranch.

I notice that many of the pine trees have disappeared. There used to be about 1,000 acres of Monterey pines nearby, but unfortunately these grand specimens are fast falling due to old age and disease. Whenever I look at these dying trees, I think of the passing of Pop's vast outdoor animal park. He was forced to sell off most of his animals to zoos and other collectors around the country because the company needed cash and fewer debts. It really made him heartsick.

I remember the time after Pop's death when a lot of the zebras, which had roamed free, were to be sold to an animal dealer. They were penned in preparation for being trucked away. We had been having great rainstorms at the time, and many of the foals were up to their bellies in mud. Austine and I slipped down to the pens and freed the lot of about twenty. We knew that Pop would have approved.

There are a lot of pelicans and gulls in the sky these days. At one time, however, we thought both were in danger here. DDT and other poisons used in agriculture drained down from farms to the sea, where the pelicans and gulls laid their fragile eggs. These poisons are being used less here now, and the birds are making a comeback.

San Simeon has many unique plants. A good number of them exist nowhere else in the world. We must not let them die, and I'm going to fight for them as long as I live.

It's never easy for me to go down the hill. It's like turning your back on a friend. I sometimes close my eyes until we turn left on the highway and head toward Pico Creek. When I open my eyes, the ocean suddenly sweeps in front of me with the mountains at my left elbow. I usually get sentimental and think about the incredible legacy that my father and grandparents left for me, my wife, and my children. And for the people of America. It is a slice of paradise, and how fortunate we have been to be able to leave some footprints here on the hills and sand.

V
BAPTISM IN INK

I once told a friend that if my brothers and I ever got out of bed before ten o'clock in the morning, someone should hold a parade. None of us ever came close to our father in disciplined working habits. Nor did any of us have the talent or drive of the old man. Pop carried an excitement about news and public issues in his bones. I inherited some of that and developed a great interest in reporting. However, neither I nor any of my brothers mastered the technical aspects of the newspaper business even remotely as well as he did. In retrospect, I don't believe any of us could have filled the shoes of our father. His name will be spoken as long as reporters and editors recall individual journalistic leadership and innovation.

The old man gave us riches, but he wanted something back from his investment. He was a taskmaster. He made it clear from our high school years that each of us would have to pull his own weight in life, especially if we went to work for him. He was pleased whenever we expressed an interest in the newspaper business, but that was not a sign that he was going to hold our hands. Our father had no favorites among us. If one of us worked hard at school or at our jobs, Pop would eventually compliment him. He offered no praise lightly to any son. If one of us didn't work hard, he would make a mental note of it, and, in one way or another, let him know about it later. When Pop indicated I was his journalistic heir, he became much more demanding of me. He never seemed to let up.

My father believed that "money invariably kills ambition." He wrote many editorials about that conviction. Yet we were obviously wealthy. He countered that by insisting that we begin at the bottom and work our way up in the business. That meant salary, too. We later figured prominently in the organization primarily because the old man wanted the company to perpetuate his name. Pop practiced the conviction of his mother and father that people should have a purpose in life. That mission was to contribute to society. If anyone felt that life had dealt him a free ride, my father turned his back on that individual.

I never knew what it was to be poor, nor did my father. At the same time, the old man had private contempt for anyone who would not work diligently for his pay. Pop repeatedly warned us that he would not treat us like a rich man's sons. Each of us was told he would have to prove himself to my father's satisfaction. He concluded in an even sharper warning: "That is the only way you will be promoted or inherit my properties." For that reason, the tenure of some of my brothers at the top of the company was relatively brief and rocky.

I felt much the same way he did—and still do. We should get our cake only after we have earned our daily bread.

None of us completed college. That did not seem to bother Pop, since he was not graduated from Harvard. George spent a year at UC Berkeley; John dropped out of Oglethorpe; Randy left Harvard; and David didn't go to college at all. I left UC Berkeley after two and a half years.

Pop wrote two letters that reflected his ambivalence about education. The first was written to our mother while my twin brothers, Randolph and David, were away at Lawrenceville (prep) School in New Jersey:

> They do not take kindly to education. This is probably a defect, but Brisbane says, "It takes a good mind to resist education." Anyway, a certain kind of good mind does resist education.

He wrote the second to the twins themselves when they were teenagers at Lawrenceville:

> You have had a good time at Palm Beach [on vacation]. I expect something more of you than to be playboys. This is not a good period in the world's history for playboys. Things are too serious. Situations

are too dangerous, and I want you two boys, who are now getting to be men, to begin to take a man's view of life. You will have to work and work hard. You might as well be learning how to work now. You have got to get an education that will make you able to take care of yourselves. No one knows whether you will inherit anything or not; but if you are not able to make money, you will not be able to keep money. If you are not trained for the contest that is ahead of you, you are likely to bring up the rear of the procession.

Actually, those letters were messages to all five sons.

Our five lives took different directions. George eventually became publisher of the *San Francisco Examiner* and held other top posts in the organization. I later became publisher of the *New York Journal-American.* John held many different jobs in the company, including a management position at *Cosmopolitan* magazine in New York. Randy and David ultimately became publishers in San Francisco and Los Angeles. Randy is now chairman of the Hearst Corporation board of directors. However, only Randy and I retained an abiding interest in the working of the company—he on the business side and I in news. I was the only son to spend most of his working life as a daily newsman.

As publishers and managers, all of us shared power with senior executives. I divided the publishing responsibilities with Edmond Coblentz at the *Journal-American.* In reality, my father had the last word at all the papers as long as he lived. He kept in contact with his chief executives across the country on an almost daily basis.

Some of my brothers were surprised and, at times, shocked at what they perceived as a hard-nosed attitude on our father's part when it came to their work. Pop tested the ability of each of us to perform, independent of our being his sons. Coming of age was a very disturbing time for each of us. We had been sheltered from many of life's cruelties, despite various warnings by Pop that making a living was no easy business. Most of us felt we needed more time and greater warning from him before facing the problems of a career. The working world came as a cold and perhaps even cruel blast of new air. My brothers felt that Pop treated us harshly.

The relationship between our father and us is most clearly reflected in some of the telegrams and letters that we exchanged over the years. They concern various problems of each son. On June 8, 1926, my oldest brother, George, telegraphed Pop from New York in care of the *Los Angeles Examiner*:

> WOULD LIKE VERY MUCH TO JOIN WESTCHESTER [New York] BILTMORE CLUB. THE DUES AND INITIATION FEES COME TO TWENTY-TWO HUNDRED DOLLARS. WILL YOU PLEASE PUT ME IN? GEORGE.

The following telegram was to George, at the *San Francisco Examiner,* on March 16, 1927:

> YOU MUST POSITIVELY BE MORE ECONOMICAL. I HAVE PAID OUT TEN THOUSAND DOLLARS FOR YOUR EXPENSES IN NEW YORK. I HAVE GIVEN YOU ONE HUNDRED DOL-LARS PER WEEK INCREASED SALARY ON EXAMINER AND I HAVE JUST ORDERED YOU PAID TWENTY-FIVE HUNDRED DOLLARS. I CANNOT DO ANY MORE. YOU MUST LIVE WITHIN YOUR SALARY, WHICH IS LIBERAL CONSIDERING YOUR YOUTH AND INEXPERIENCE. BE SENSIBLE AND MAKE BUSINESSMAN OF YOURSELF. POP.

This is a letter from Pop to George on September 16, 1927:

> I hate to bother you but I feel it is my duty as your father to write this letter.
>
> You are getting dangerously stout. Health is important, and if you do not take pains to keep from getting dangerously fat, you are going to pop out some time soon with fatty degeneration of the heart or kidneys or something of that kind. Getting fat is in 99 cases out of 100 a matter of eating too much. You eat heavily and you eat often; then you drink a good deal; and you like beer and fattening drinks of that kind; and that is the reason you are getting stout. People who eat a lot WANT to eat a lot. It is just like any other habit—it is hard to break yourself of it, but it can be done. Furthermore, you do not take any kind of regular exercise.
>
> You have everything to live for. Put yourself in condition to live.
> Affectionately, Pop.

Another letter from Pop to George on September 23, 1927:

I am sending $5,000 to the Army and Navy Club, but you really ought not to involve me or yourself in such absurd expenditure. It is childish.

The club is of no use to you and you have not any $5,000 to give to it and what you did was merely to commit me to a $5,000 payment that I don't want to make and that I get no benefit from, and that you get no benefit from, and that I only make because I do not want to see you disgraced.

Do try to have a little judgment about money and don't go off at half cock about things on your own account, and when it comes to matters in which I am involved, please try to consult me. Sincerely, Pop.

Telegram from George to Pop on March 7, 1928:

MOM HAS OFFERED ME ONE HUNDRED DOLLARS FOR EVERY POUND I LOSE. WHAT IS YOUR OFFER AS I HAVE A FEW BILLS TO PAY? SURELY YOU WON'T LET MOM OUTDO YOU? JUST RETURNED AND AM BACK ON THE JOB HEAD OVER HEELS IN WORK. HOPE TO SEE YOU SOON. GEORGE.

Telegram from Pop to George on the same day in response to the above:

IF YOU WON'T LOSE WEIGHT FOR YOUR OWN HEALTH AND GOOD LOOKS, YOU WON'T LOSE IT FOR A FEW DOLLARS. MOREOVER I THINK MOM IS WASTING HER MONEY BECAUSE IF YOU LOSE A FEW POUNDS YOU WILL TAKE IT RIGHT BACK ON AGAIN AND ONLY SOLUTION IS FOR YOU TO KEEP YOUR WEIGHT DOWN BY MODERATE EATING AND VIGOROUS EXERCISE. I WILL GIVE YOU A CHANCE TO MAKE A LITTLE MORE MONEY. YOU MAY HAVE FIVE PERCENT OF NET PROFITS OF SAN FRANCISCO EXAMINER UNDER PRESENT CONDITIONS. THIS SHOULD GIVE YOU SEVENTY-FIVE THOUSAND DOLLARS A YEAR OR MORE. YOU WOULD BE VERY WISE TO CULTIVATE POLICY OF INTELLIGENT ECONOMY. WISE PEOPLE WHO SAVE MONEY HAVE JUST AS MUCH SATISFACTION OUT OF SAVINGS AS JACKASSES HAVE OUT OF SPENDING IT. W. R. HEARST.

Joe Willicombe, my father's secretary, sent the following telegram to George on February 5, 1929:

YOUR FATHER DIRECTED ME TO SEND YOU THE EN-
CLOSED ARTICLE BY HERBERT KAUFMAN, ENTITLED
"FOOLS, MONEY AND MONARCHIES."

This is a brief excerpt from a letter that Pop wrote George on September 24, 1929:

Whether you form the habit of thrift or not, I want you to realize that
you are getting an enormous amount of money [salary of between
$75,000 and $80,000 per year] for a young fellow—more than anyone
that I know of at your age and that I am not going to give you any
more except as you earn it. Affectionately, Pop.

From Pop to George at the *Los Angeles Examiner* on February 4, 1940:

The color work this morning was simply atrocious.

Letter from Pop to George on October 25, 1940, after George moved
to radio station KYA in San Francisco and asked to have equal authority
with the manager:

Somebody has to be in charge of the station. You have not demonstrated the ability to run a station. Mr. Meyer has.
   Please be careful, son, not to make yourself unwelcome in San Francisco, because they will not take you back in Los Angeles and you
would have nowhere to go. And please realize, son, that you have to
make a record of some creditable kind, at least of a willingness to work
and cooperate, before you will be advanced to any kind of a responsible
position. Affectionately, Pop.

Pop sent the following telegram to Mom from San Simeon on January
20, 1927, regarding John:

JOHN HAS NOT BEEN TO A TO ZED SCHOOL SINCE OPEN-
ING. IT IS USELESS TO KEEP HIM THERE. I AM SENDING HIM
EAST. ENTER HIM AT SOME BOARDING SCHOOL. I DO NOT
CARE WHERE, THE STRICTER THE BETTER. W. R.

John telegraphed our father in California on September 13, 1927:

WELL HERE I AM ALABAMY BOUND MUCH TO MY DISGUST
BUT AS YOU SAY QUOTE MUCH MUST BE SACRIFICED IN
THE QUEST OF KNOWLEDGE UNQUOTE DONT FORGET IT

WONT BE LONG BEFORE I AM A YEAR OLDER AND AS A BIRTHDAY GIFT TO MYSELF I BECAME ENGAGED TO DOROTHY. LOVE FROM YOUR WELL MEANING BUT BLUNDERING SON JOHN.

Pop responded to John with this telegram a day later:

I AM HAPPY TO HAVE YOU GO AROUND WITH A NICE GIRL LIKE THAT INSTEAD OF THOSE BUM FELLOWS THAT YOU HAVE BEEN GOING WITH. LET ME KNOW HOW YOU GET ON AT OGLETHORPE AND IF YOU CANNOT MAKE IT THERE WE WILL SEE WHAT WE CAN DO SOMEWHERE ELSE. W. R. HEARST.

Pop to John in Atlanta on September 17, 1927:

WILL SEE WHAT I CAN FIND IN WAY OF RING FOR DOROTHY. IT IS TOO SOON TO TALK ABOUT AN AUTOMOBILE. YOU DONT KNOW WHETHER YOU ARE GOING TO GET INTO OGLETHORPE. POP.

John to Pop on September 19, 1927:

I AM ENTERED IN THE UNIVERSITY OF OGLETHORPE, MY CREDITS BEING OKAY. SCHOOL STARTS THE TWENTY-EIGHTH. AM GOING TO NEWYORK OVER MY BIRTHDAY. CAN I BUY THE MACHINE THERE? YOUR STUDIOUS SON JOHN.

Pop replied to John by telegram a day later:

NOW JOHN LISTEN TO YOUR FATHER. PLEASE BE A LITTLE SENSIBLE. YOU AND YOUR AUTOMOBILE ARE LIKE A CHILD WITH A WHOOP. YOU OUGHT TO BEGIN TO BE GROWN UP SINCE YOU ARE ENGAGED. I WILL GET YOU AN AUTO WHEN I AM CONVINCED YOU ARE SETTLED DOWN AND ARE TAKING YOUR RESPONSIBILITIES SERIOUSLY. DONT GO TO NEW YORK. STICK AROUND AND GET READY FOR COLLEGE. POP.

Pop to John on September 24, 1927:

I HAVE BOUGHT A LOVELY RING FOR DOROTHY. POP.

Pop to John on October 8, 1927:

WILL LET YOU GET MARRIED IN SUMMER OF NINETEEN TWENTYEIGHT IF YOU DO YOUR WORK PROPERLY AT COLLEGE.

Pop wrote to John on November 26, 1928, after John returned to New York, married Dorothy, and began to work for him:

The whole trouble is you want too large and expensive an apartment for a young couple starting out in life. Your income is large but it is not large enough for the standard you have set for yourself. Better plan more simply and reasonably, son. You can get an adequate hotel apartment for six or eight thousand dollars and I guess you better do that. Pop.

Pop wrote to John on September 29, 1932, after John failed to show up for his job on our Atlanta newspaper:

I am not going to urge you, because what you might do at my urging would not be of any use. You must do something now at your own initiative. Otherwise, you will be like George—just a flop. Affectionately, Pop.

For the next two years, Pop and John exchanged correspondence about John not showing up for work. On January 19, 1939, Pop wrote again to John:

Are you carrying out my instructions faithfully to report at the [Los Angeles] *Examiner* office every morning at nine o'clock, lay out your program for the day, and attend to that program assiduously, and get some results?

To the best of my knowledge and belief you are not doing this, and if you do not do it there is only one of two courses open to me—either you have to pack your bags and baggage and go back East, where nobody wants you or will have anything to do with you, or else put you on a percentage basis.

I do not like to be drastic with you, but there does not seem to be any other alternative. Affectionately, Pop.

Pop wrote to John on November 6, 1941:

I am sorry, but I am NOT going to allow you any expenses. You are on your own—sink or swim in New York. If you don't like the job, don't take it. You are not an infant any longer, swinging on a pap bottle. I am sorry I did not see you. In fact I seem never to see you except when you want something. And you even try to arrange for that over the phone. Good luck, Pop.

Memo from Pop to New York Hearst executive J. D. Gortatowsky on June 13, 1942:

Pay John if and when he works. W. R. Hearst.

On June 23, 1942, Pop wrote to John:

Nobody is going to get paid except for service rendered. In other words, "No tickee, no shirtee" is the unvarying motto of the institution.

I secured for you a good position—an enviable position—in the management of the *American Weekly* [magazine]. Since then you have been either ill or absent more than half the time. If you do not like the job, son, you should resign and get a job in some other service.

If you do like the job, you must work at it consistently and earn your salary. Otherwise you will not be paid. Otherwise you will not be retained. But if you are going to stay in our organization, you must work and earn your compensation. Affectionately, Pop.

Pop wrote a fatherly letter to David on May 3, 1932:

You ought to write more, whether you like to write or not. You ought to write letters constantly to me and your mother and your friends. You ought take every opportunity to write essays and other writing tests at your school. You ought to try to get on your school paper and, furthermore, you ought to read—not a lot of trash but some good books.

I do not know how good you are at arithmetic, you certainly have never been taught either to read or to write. It is important that you should do both. Now go to it, son, and let's get somewhere. Affectionately, Pop.

David to Pop from Palm Beach, Florida, on June 17, 1932:

HAVE SELECTED STUDEBAKER AT NINETEEN HUNDRED AND SEVEN DOLLARS. PLEASE WIRE CHECK AT ONCE AS WE WISH TO LEAVE PALMBEACH TOMORROW MORNING. PRICE INCLUDES INSURANCE. LOVE DAVID.

Pop to David at his school in Princeton, New Jersey, on June 15, 1935:

IF YOU ARE UNABLE TO ENTER COLLEGE YOU MAY WANT TO GET SELF-SUPPORTING JOB SOMEWHERE. BETTER COME WEST AS SOON AS YOU CAN AND DISCUSS YOUR PLANS. FATHER.

My father telegraphed Mom about David on September 26, 1935:

Can he not take special courses elsewhere than Columbia? I detest that communistic college.

There was not much correspondence between Pop and my brother Randy. However, a telegram from Pop to Randy, and thoughtful gifts, indicate the old man's interest in Randy's intellectual life and career. On February 17, 1935, Pop telegraphed Randy in New York:

I THINK YOU BETTER GO ON JOURNAL AS REPORTER AND LEARN TO WRITE. ALSO, SON, READ GOOD BOOKS, ESPE- CIALLY DICKENS AND THACKERAY FOR STYLE, AND MORE MODERN BOOKS LIKE "MICROBE HUNTERS," "STORY OF PHILOSOPHY," "MEN OF ART," ETCETERA, FOR INFORMA- TION. PLEASE TRY HARD TO BE GOOD NEWSPAPERMAN. POP.

Joe Willicombe sent Randy the following note on April 17, 1935:

Chief is sending you by express, in care of the [San Francisco] *Examiner,* two books that he would like you to read and discuss with him when you next see him. The books are CHARLES THE FIRST by Hilaire Belloc and MARIE ANTOINETTE by Stefan Zweig.

Pop put a personal twist on my leaving college and going to work. I was on vacation in Palm Springs in 1928 with some college buddies. I mentioned that I had a small yacht. Several of them cooked up the idea that I should phone Pop and tell him that I wasn't breathing too well and the doctor prescribed a boat trip. We would take a semester off from school and see the world. After a few beers the idea began to look like it might sail.

I phoned Pop at San Simeon and told him that a doctor said I should take a boat trip for my health. He asked, "What ails you?"

We had not rehearsed a precise answer to that question, so I quickly stuck my head out of the public phone booth and hollered, "Quick! What the hell is wrong with me?"

"Sinus!" somebody shouted.

I closed the booth door to the outside chatter and said as nonchalantly as I could, "It's sinus, Pop."

He replied, "Well, you've got a crazy doc because people usually go to the desert, not the sea, for sinus."

I gulped and there was a long silence. Finally, the old man said calmly, "Bill, I think you're telling me that you would just as soon quit college and go to work."

I knew he was right and swallowed hard. Pop quietly asked, "Am I correct?"

"Yes," I replied.

"Let me know what you decide," the old man said soberly.

The world voyage had run aground. I phoned him later to say that I wanted to work for the *New York American* and learn the business from the ground up. Thankfully, I have never gotten sinus in my life.

Pop was as frank and tough with me as with my brothers. For example, I got married when I was twenty years old to Alma Walker, whom I met while a student at UC Berkeley. She was a fine girl from a good family in Piedmont, California.

My father never tried to dissuade me from the marriage, although I was still far from mature. But he did caution me to be as certain as I could so as not to regret the decision later. After the wedding we moved to New York and I began working as a reporter on the *American*.

I never felt at home in those early months. Alma had met an artist, Alex Calder, who said he would brighten our apartment by painting it. He sure did. Alex completed a three-dimensional mural that ran through several rooms. Wires stuck out of our walls; so did plastic bananas and other fruit as well as wild beasts of the jungle. I would sit down to a meal and see these horror shapes in purple, blazing yellow, or black and blue. It was like living in a haunted house. I paid his asking price: a case of beer. I eventually removed the wires and bananas, and painted over the jungle with a nice old-fashioned white. Of course, Calder later became a famous artist.

The marriage proved to be puppy love and broke up after four years. Pop was right. I simply hadn't listened to him and examined my reasons as carefully as I should have.

My job took over my life. I thought only of making it—driving my father nuts with letters, phone calls, and sometimes visits. I often sharply disagreed with the old man. I fired off this letter after he sent me a copy of an editorial about money killing ambition:

> Not necessarily. Necessity makes a person work a lot harder, that is true. But if it is a worthy ambition, it takes more than money to kill it.
>
> I'll tell you what my ambition is. It is to be able to help you in your business, to be capable to do my part, and then some. You may think I am saying this to please you, but it really is the truth.
>
> I'll bet a lot of people in New York wouldn't do a thing for us if we went broke. All of us appreciate what you have done for us, and I am sure we are not made of the stuff of a fellow who will not work if he does not have to.

One letter Pop wrote had special significance because it affected all five sons. He sent it to Tom White, general manager of our newspapers, on November 10, 1935. In it Pop named the company executives whom he wanted on a board of directors for the newspapers, adding:

> Regarding the boys, I would like to make their admission to the Board of Directors conditional on a record of hard work and actual achievement. I think this will have a beneficial effect.
>
> I think that Bill can be speedily admitted on this basis, but I do not think that John can, and I do not propose to appoint him until he has proved he has something of value to contribute.
>
> The twins will be along in a year or so, and I want the same conditions to apply to them. In fact, in all probability, David will remain in the newspaper business and not go to college. And Randolph will probably finish his first year in college and then go into the newspaper business.
>
> I do not want either David or Randolph to acquire the habit of idleness, which is apparently all that college has to teach my children.

Despite reservations, Pop decided to give George a big chance. He made him publisher of the *San Francisco Examiner* when our eldest brother was only twenty-five. My father wanted the Hearst name to remain prominent in San Francisco. Other executives actually made most decisions, but Pop wanted to see how George would handle himself under business pressure.

George stayed a few years, had a good time, and got married. He divorced, married again, and eventually had five wives. Pop moved him about in the organization, but George never settled down to hard daily work. He died in his late sixties.

My closest brother, Jack, didn't work consistently, either. His health was never good, and he also died young. The twins, David and Randy, were harder workers. David put in a lot of effort as publisher of our old Los Angeles paper; he lived to be about seventy. As publisher of the San Francisco paper, Randy improved the *Examiner*. He had five daughters by his wife, Catherine. The kidnapping of their daughter Patty took a lot out of Randy, and he eventually moved to New York. Of the five sons, only Randy and I survive today.

Pop wrote to me more than to his other sons. He kept the pressure on. On July 7, 1938, the old man wrote me at the *Journal-American* from San Simeon:

I don't say our printing is better on the Coast. Our 30-lb. paper is exceedingly light and difficult to print on. But our engraving is clearer and more brilliant, and the result is better pictures in spite of handicaps. Concentrate on your engraving and you will beat us. Pop.

Pop wrote to me on July 9, 1938:

Please note the details of this picture. This can only be gotten by good etching. Sometimes I am told that the light is better on the Coast. Well, the light isn't better at night. Pop.

He wrote to me on December 15, 1938:

Referring to the motto on the bottom of the *Journal-American* letter paper—"TELL US AND WE'LL TELL A MILLION."

I do not like this motto at all. There is something cheap and slangy about it. We had a much better motto: "A quality newspaper with over a million circulation." This has much more dignity and impressiveness. Please restore the former motto—and live up to it. Affectionately, Pop.

On March 23, 1940, Pop had Willicombe write to me regarding the *Journal-American*:

The paper is dirty typographically and needs cleaning up generally.

Pop wrote to me on April 13, 1942:

Referring to the memorandum dated April 2nd telling of gain in undis-play classified for the first quarter of 1942: This is exceedingly bully. You know I am a classified bug and that nothing pleases me more than the fine gains in that department. Sincerely, W. R. Hearst.

Pop later urged his editors to hire more young people. He was also addressing his sons:

To be convincing as a newsman, you must be convinced yourself.

To be interesting, you yourself must be interested. To be exciting about the news, you must first be excited about it.

Get rid of the blasé crowd. Get young people to whom it is not all a dreary routine. Give them a chance. Let them be young. Let them make mistakes. Maybe the public will like mistakes. Maybe we are making the mistake of not being vital enough.

I am getting old—running down—going to sleep like a top before it keels over. We must not let the papers run down. They must not go to sleep.

Yet, at various times, each one of us felt alone—some more than others. But my commitment to Pop and the business never caused any real dis-tance between my father and me. If I felt alone—and I did—it was momentary.

One time I did feel keenly on my own was when, at the age of seventeen and in college, I got a union card and worked during the summer as a "fly boy," pulling newspapers from presses at the *New York Daily Mirror*. I stripped down to my bare chest and sweated through a summer of backbreaking labor. The guys working with me were wonderful. I made good friends, and we shared some laughs and cold beer after work. This became a pattern in my life. My best friends were fellow newspaper people.

Thus began my training in the mechanics of printing. Pop insisted that all of us learn about the total process of getting out a newspaper or magazine.

In 1928, at the age of twenty, I became a full-fledged New Yorker and began to cover city hall as a young reporter on the *American*. Charlie Bayer, already a star reporter on the paper, was covering that beat. He took me under his wing and became my teacher. Charlie knew everything—not only where all the bodies were buried but even those whose funeral was coming in a month or two! He had an uncanny street savvy that could not be learned in any school. Charlie sized people up, then either swallowed them or spit them out. He was a straight, no-nonsense guy who seemed to be at home almost anywhere.

We did not write our stories back then. Most papers were putting out six or more editions a day with tight deadlines. Charlie and I phoned stories in to a battery of rewrite men in the *American* city room. They took the bare facts and turned them into deathless prose. All of us were constantly fighting the clock. Sometimes it was possible to get only a few paragraphs of a story in the paper for one edition. The competition with a dozen other papers on stories, even from edition to edition, was fierce.

As a young reporter I received no bylines. So it was not fame but the thrill of the business that kept me on my toes. Charlie and I would almost die if another paper had a good story that we missed. Perhaps it would have been just as well if we had dropped dead some days, because there were times when the city editor was ready to kill us with his bare hands, when somebody had beaten us on a story.

James J. Walker, a Tammany Hall dandy, was mayor from 1926 to 1932. Jimmy was a fun-loving guy who would rather bounce a showgirl on his knee than balance the city budget. He loved the theater and spent much of his time on Broadway. The dapper little Irishman was also a frustrated songwriter whose eyes would grow misty when he hummed "Danny Boy" or "When Irish Eyes Are Smiling." Both were written by a beginning songwriter named Ernest R. Ball. Jimmy would probably have given up the mayor's job if he could have written those melodies.

Jimmy hit so many nightspots that society and gossip columnists wrote as much about him as the city hall reporters did. I was jealous that Jimmy's night life was getting more news play than his more important work, which I covered. Jimmy was often late and sometimes did not even show up for work. He once arrived at an official city function, stepped out of his car, and fell flat on his face—dead drunk. The pause was only momentary. His driver and pals lifted Jimmy back into the car and took him home. Or to another place of revelry. Walker usually had a witty remark to cover his tracks.

Jimmy personified the Roaring Twenties in New York. The stock market rocketed upward. The big bats of Babe Ruth and Lou Gehrig powered the New York Yankees into becoming known as the Bronx

Bombers and Murderers Row. Flappers and Flaming Youth lit up Broadway like a five-alarm fire. Walker led the merry-go-round—loads of illegal booze, a lively penchant for hellbent fun, and lots of financial dreams.

Jimmy took up with Betty Compton, a former show girl, after separating from his wife, a devout Catholic. They led a merry nightly parade through restaurants, the theater, entertainment joints, and Madison Square Garden. Jimmy flaunted the romance, and some critics roundly condemned him for it. He fired back saying there were a lot of hypocrites around town and he had the special blessing of not being one of them. Jimmy and Betty eventually married, but were divorced after about ten years.

Fiorello La Guardia, who hoped to unseat Walker as mayor, heard of many of Jimmy's wilder escapades. He told his political lieutenants, "Don't let anybody know about that. It'll get Walker another hundred thousand votes!"

Jimmy hated to make political speeches. He ran for reelection in 1929 only after he got his Tammany cronies to agree that he did not have to deliver any talks. Nevertheless, in the waning days of the campaign they forced him to make a dozen speeches. On the last day Walker had to deliver no less than five. He began imbibing after the first that morning and wound up pretty well oiled by the time of the last talk that evening. He could barely walk to the podium, but delivered one of the most memorable speeches in the history of New York politics:

> Ladies and Gentlemen, I was driving up to this last big and most important rally of my campaign. A man on one side was telling me about all the things I was doing for the Negro while I was in the state assembly. A fellow on the other side was telling me of all the things I did for the Negro while I was mayor of New York.
>
> Well, I'll tell you the truth. In all my political life, I never did anything for the Negro. I never did anything for the Catholics, either. Or the Jews or the Italians or the Germans. Because, ladies and gentlemen, I don't know the difference. Good night!

Jimmy was forced to resign in 1932 amid corruption charges. Walker's flights into fancy were unforgettable—and sometimes unfathomable. Even for New York, a mayor with a doll on his arm, a drink in his hand, and a joke on his lips was a bit much.

I remember my reporting days at city hall as a rat race. I ran, ran, ran all day. I was ready to shoot Alexander Graham Bell a few times, because our phone always seemed to be ringing. I heard it in my sleep.

After I left city hall La Guardia became mayor. He made big government news almost every day, championing one cause or another. He was a feisty, colorful little guy who took no back seat or back talk from anyone. Yet the "Little Flower" managed to pull off reading the funny papers to kids on the radio every Sunday morning while pulling no punches on the issues. He was a rare bird: a New York Republican.

I felt great on being transferred to the police beat. But there, unfortunately, the phone rang even more. Stories were tougher to cover because they happened in all parts of the city and sometimes many people were involved. I worked with Johnny Shine of the *American,* but I was much more on my own, covering the cops, than I had been at city hall. You had to track down a lot of different people: crime victims, arresting officers, sometimes the accused, their lawyers, and witnesses. The jigsaw puzzle was hard to put together. If I ran on the city hall beat, I leaped from story to story covering police.

In my early years as a reporter, one story stands out like a loaded gun— the police shootout with "Two-Gun" Crowley in 1931. Crowley was one of a long list of local hit men and tough guys like "Dutch" Schultz, "Waxey" Gordon, and Jack "Legs" Diamond. These guys killed like they were swatting flies in Hell's Kitchen. Crowley not only had a reputation for rubbing out some of the citizenry but he was also supposed to be half nuts.

I heard the cops had trapped him in a ground-floor apartment on upper Broadway, so I raced up there in my car. An army of police had completely surrounded the place, pouring gunfire and tear gas into the apartment. I stood out of range because, every so often, Crowley would open up with several blasts through one of the windows. When things momentarily became quiet, Crowley's voice would blast from inside the place: "You'll never take me alive, coppers, never!" Both sides fired intermittently, and the stand-off continued.

Several hours later, Detective Johnny Broderick suddenly appeared on the scene. I knew Johnny because, when we were kids, my father had hired him to accompany us on our train trips to the West Coast. Pop feared we might be kidnapped. If Crowley and the other gangsters were tough, Broderick was fearless. He took tough guys, dumped them in garbage cans, put the lid on, and had them delivered that way to a police station. Johnny had won numerous medals for valor and took no guff from anybody. "Two-Gun" now faced a cop who put the fear of God in armed crooks with only his fists.

The shooting had stopped, but I was still biting my nails. Johnny talked with the captains in charge. He thought he could take Crowley alive. He asked that his fellow officers not fire while he approached Crowley. The captains passed the word.

Johnny began walking toward the apartment. At first Crowley did not see him. He kept sniping away. Then he spotted Johnny, but the big detective continued walking unhurriedly toward the apartment. Crowley knew Johnny and quit firing. Johnny knocked on the door. Crowley yelled something back. Johnny introduced himself like it was some social meeting under the clock at the Biltmore in Grand Central Station. Crowley acknowledged.

"Listen, pal," Johnny shouted, "you ain't got a chance. Come out here now, and I'll see that nothing happens to you. Otherwise . . ." His voice trailed off.

Crowley finally opened the apartment door. He meekly handed Johnny his gun. The two walked slowly into the middle of the street. Several officers rushed up, handcuffed Crowley, and led him to a paddy wagon. He eventually died in the electric chair.

I ran madly to find a phone and call the *American*. I was so excited I could hardly speak. The patient rewrite man told me to calm down and start slowly. After several deep breaths, I composed myself and dictated the facts. It was a front-page banner splash. I received no byline, but for twenty-four hours I was on top of the world.

It seemed that half the town slid down their flagpoles when the stock market crashed in 1929. Tens of thousands of New Yorkers were out of work and many had lost their life savings, including their homes. But Pop did not, and he would not slash salaries during the first three or four years of the Depression. He felt deeply about paying people fairly. Finally, with the red ink looking like a bucket of blood, the accountants forced him to cut salaries and curb many business expenses.

I worked inside for a couple of years—on rewrite, the copy desk, and learning about the workings of story assignments and the city desk. I followed the managing editor and others around, observing how various editors and departments interrelated.

While bouncing off these ropes, the "crime of the century" was committed in nearby New Jersey. The Lindbergh baby was kidnapped from the new family home just north of Hopewell on March 1, 1932. Colonel Charles Lindbergh and his wife, Anne, were grief-stricken. The whole country was not only deeply shocked but angry. Lindy was a national hero after his solo flight to Paris. It was, to put it mildly, a helluva story.

Betty Gow, nursemaid to the child, first discovered that Charles, Jr., was missing. The twenty-seven-year-old Scottish woman had placed the baby in his nursery crib immediately after supper because he had just gotten over a cold. Mrs. Lindbergh played with her son briefly before turning out the nursery light.

Miss Gow returned to the room about ten o'clock to check on the baby. He was not there. She rushed to Anne and then the colonel to see if either had removed him from the crib for any reason. Lindbergh ran upstairs to the nursery and, finding the baby gone, raced to his bedroom and grabbed his Springfield rifle. He rushed outside, looking for kidnappers, but saw no one in the darkness. Lindbergh then phoned police and, by midnight, the news had been flashed around the world.

The New York manager of INP, the Hearst international photo service, assigned his entire staff to the story. He chartered two ambulances and filled them with photographers and a makeshift darkroom. The photos were developed as the ambulances, with sirens screaming, raced back to New York each day for weeks.

The *American* assigned a dozen reporters to cover it. I volunteered because I had met Lindbergh twice. He might talk with me if I could get to see him. The first time I met him was when my father asked Lindy, after his famous flight, to write for our papers. Lindy had to turn down the offer because he already had a writing commitment. We met again on a train to the West Coast. Lindy introduced himself to me. I had already recognized him, of course, but explained that I did not want to intrude on his privacy. Lindbergh liked that, and we had a nice chat. So I felt there was a real chance he would see me. I devised a plan.

I drove to Hopewell and took two of our fellows with me. Windsor McKay was a draftsman, not a cartoonist or caricaturist, who illustrated the *American* editorial page. We wanted him to draw precise layouts of the Lindbergh home and property. Eddie Malsby was, to the best of my recollection, a photographer. I told neither of them what I intended to do.

We arrived at the Lindbergh estate, but the family wouldn't answer the doorbell. A handful of reporters stood around waiting to question anyone entering or leaving. Soon, scores of newsmen were arriving, and hundreds more were on the way from all parts of the country. It was to become, as I had anticipated, a teeming, screaming mob of men, microphones, cameras, and movie-house newsreel crews.

By afternoon a small army of news people swarmed over the Lindbergh property. They took copious notes and pictures of the house, the baby's nursery window, the grounds, and surrounding properties. They were actually obliterating footprints and other clues to the kidnapping. The crush and hollering was now so intense that the normally calm countryside was approaching a state of bedlam. The state police finally established a headquarters in and around the Lindbergh garage.

I drove to a deserted lane and began putting my plan into action. I took off my overcoat and suit coat and put on a Western Union jacket and hat. Then I motored up, as nice as you please, to the Lindbergh front door. A maid answered, and I said I had a personal telegram for the family; the colonel or Mrs. Lindbergh would have to sign for it. I was told to come inside and wait. No one returned. Police were combing every inch of the house. Finally one of the officers ordered me out to the garage, where their office was set up, to wait there. I sat down in a vacant chair.

The police trusted no one and began to eye me suspiciously. They also were getting tired of looking at me. There were only a few seats in the place, and I was certainly not one of their priorities. Finally, one of the commanders came over and snapped, "Beat it, kid." I remember looking at him in amazement—because he called me "kid" (I was twenty-four years old), and I was startled by his abrupt command. Anyway, I did not answer or move. So he shot at me again, "Listen, kid, I told you to beat it."

What a come-down! Here I was, a full-fledged reporter. An old hand who had covered the mayor and city council of New York. A seasoned police reporter who had nailed the "Two-gun" Crowley shootout above the masthead on the front page of the *New York American*. A veteran of the toughest news battlefield in the country. And on my biggest story this cop was calling me a "kid" and telling me to "beat it."

Yet, dressed like a Western Union messenger, I sure as hell was not about to tell him that I was William Randolph Hearst, Jr. He might have run me in for impersonation. So I quietly buried my pride, picked up my rear end, and trudged mournfully to my car. It was quite a put-down, but I was not defeated. I would call Lindbergh until I got him on the phone.

After many tries—and using my name—I finally spoke with Lindy. I was trying to help and told him: "This is a very big national story. In fact, it's now international. We have reporters here from the biggest papers—not only New York, Newark, Philadelphia, and Washington but Los Angeles and San Francisco. And reporters are coming in from Europe and elsewhere. Won't you please hold a press conference? Tell us every so often what you can. Otherwise, we're going to camp like an army outside your house and follow you wherever you go. If you plan to leave the state, also let us know; we've got guys watching your house around the clock and if you suddenly make a run for it, they will set off an alarm. Then we'll all come bundling out of bed and chase you like a horde of bloodhounds. We could, without knowing it, upset your apple cart . . ."

Lindbergh replied, "No. And from now on, you won't get the news not only from here." (The state police soon moved the press headquarters from the Lindbergh garage to the state capital.)

I felt very sorry for Lindy and understood his reluctance to deal with us. The life of his child hung in the balance. Nevertheless, I said, "I think you're making a mistake. The reporters are going to follow you, and the fuss could cause you some problems."

As a matter of fact, that is just what happened. Lindy later went to investigate a report about the baby being buried in a nearby area. Newsmen piled into cars and followed him down the road as if it were the caravan of some big politician running for public office, not a private mission of mercy. No scene could have been more out of character for Lindbergh, a reserved individual. When Lindy got there he discovered the report was a false alarm.

The incident created a lot of frustration all around. It was an impossible relationship; we had our job to do, but he wanted to handle things his own way. That conflict with reporters—despite the fact that the media had had much to do with making him a hero—characterized Lindy's relations with news people for the rest of his life. I was very disappointed about this, because Lindbergh was a real gentleman. And his wife was very much a lady. Their tragedy was profound and I could not help but sympathize with them. However, Lindy was a strong-willed individual—that was the strength that had made him great—who did not bend easily if he believed he was right. Obviously, in this case, he thought he was. I had failed as a peacemaker and was heartsick about it.

Meantime, the bedlam went from bad to worse. There were no big developments in the case, but reporters were required to write about the kidnapping every day. INS, the AP, and UP were each pouring out about 10,000 words daily. The public could not get enough of the story. Reporters blew up minor and sometimes even meaningless happenings into big stories. There were endless speculations, rumors, and theories about the how, why, and who of the abduction. This created constant tension among newsmen, the Lindberghs, and police.

The first and second ransom notes arrived through the mail. The Lindberghs publicly announced that they would meet the demands, and they appealed to the kidnapper not to harm their son. Lindbergh himself secretly delivered $70,000 in cash to the spot demanded in the final note.

The story reached a national and international crescendo in May when the body of the Lindbergh baby was found in a nearby woods. The infant had been murdered. The senseless, cold-blooded violence of the crime, especially after a ransom had been paid, shocked the world.

The Lindberghs soon moved to Englewood, New Jersey, and never returned to Hopewell. In August of 1933, with much public cheer, Anne gave birth to another son, John Morrow Lindbergh. However, still bitter about the kidnapping, and seeking privacy, the family began to live reclusively.

From the time when the child's body was discovered in 1932 until the arrest of Bruno Richard Hauptmann in September of 1934, and his execution in 1936, the case was rarely out of the newspapers. Many of the stories concerned the ransom money. The serial numbers of those bills had been recorded and listed with banks and businesses across the nation. Finally, Hauptmann, a German-born carpenter living in the Bronx, was arrested after he passed one of the ransom bills at a New York City gas station.

Lindbergh identified Hauptmann's voice—a foreign accent—from their brief conversation during the ransom delivery. (The kidnapper had hidden his face.) A wood expert pinpointed and helped trace some lumber the kidnapper had bought at a Bronx hardware store. Hauptmann's purchase linked him to the kidnap ladder.

Once again, international attention focused on the case. Hundreds of newsmen poured into Flemington, New Jersey, where the trial began on

January 2, 1935, in the small Hunterdon County courthouse. Only a limited number of reporters were able to enter the courthouse each day. Those outside were later briefed. Every word of testimony was reported, and then some. The trial became a global spectacle. More than a million words were transmitted around the world each of the trial's thirty-two days. Nearly seventy telegraph operators were busy around the clock.

I returned to work at the *American*, and the paper's big guns were assigned to cover the trial: Arthur Brisbane, Walter Winchell, Damon Runyon, and Adela Rogers St. Johns. Jimmy Kilgallen, who later became one of my pals during the war in Europe, covered for our INS.

Some six weeks later, on February 13, Hauptmann, still pleading his innocence, was convicted of murder in the first degree by an exhausted jury. There was no recommendation of leniency. The Associated Press flashed that Hauptmann was given a life sentence. INS clients across the country began phoning our New York headquarters and screaming bloody murder at Barry Faris, who was the INS editor-in-chief. Where was the INS flash on the verdict? Faris was steaming because Kilgallen had filed nothing, but he refused to panic. He had faith in Kilgallen and would not allow our wire to send out a word without hearing from Jimmy.

As things turned out, the AP reporter had misunderstood a prearranged signal from a source close to the jury and flashed the wrong verdict. Then the AP sent word around the world that Hauptmann had been convicted but that the jury had recommended clemency. Jimmy had had his own prearranged signal-maker and was the first to flash correctly: "Hauptmann gets death." When I learned of Kilgallen's triumph, I smiled, just as I knew Jimmy himself had done when he heard of his big scoop.

Jimmy, a master of understatement, told me later, "Some of the guys in the office gave me a bit of a squeeze play, asking for a verdict, but I had my own source and trusted him."

I said, "Jimmy, you call it a 'squeeze play,' but the whole world was watching and listening."

"I know," he said with his perennial half-smile, "but I like to keep things simple. If you keep them simple, you'll be all right." I never forgot Jimmy's half-smile. He even wore it in his casket when he died at ninety-four.

Hauptmann was electrocuted at the New Jersey state penitentiary on April 3, 1936.

I continued to learn the ropes at the *American,* and got a few pay raises, but not much. For the life of me, I cannot remember exactly how much I made as a reporter—it was a half-century ago—but I was not paid any more than the other newsmen. If I had to guess, it was at most about thirty bucks a week, with a few small raises as I moved from one training job to another. These ranged from general assignments to make-up editor in the *American* composing room, to assistant city editor, and on to various slots in the advertising and, finally, the business departments.

Our newspapers operated on the star system in those days. We featured great writers and reporters. Damon Runyon, a writer on the *American* for twenty-seven years, was New York's star columnist-reporter. Somebody called him Broadway's Boswell because he wrote so much and so well about the Big Street and the characters who peopled it.

Broadway was not so much a street as a state of mind—a crazy assortment of people who lived and died in a time of wonderful nonsense. They were rich and poor, rogues and geniuses, bookies and beautiful babes, down-and-outers and do-gooders, stars and bit players, gangsters and good parish priests with the gift of forgiveness. Many of these characters died every dawn, but rose every evening to cavort under the bright lights.

Damon had come from papers in Pueblo and Denver, Colorado. New York was the mecca of newspapermen and writers, and Runyon struck gold on Broadway instead of in a ghost town on some dry Colorado creek. He captured the ways and characters of the bright lights like no one then or since. Damon wrote a lot of fiction, short stories that commanded not only the highest praise but top dollar. Many of these delightful yarns were made into movies—stories like "Guys and Dolls," "Butch Minds the Baby," and "Little Miss Marker." Damon's characters—from Apple Annie to the Lemon Drop Kid and Jack O'Hearts—are legendary. We will never see their likes again because Runyon's Broadway has long since disappeared.

I knew Damon fairly well because both of us worked on the *American* and saw much of each other around New York. Damon never said much. When he did, he often had a sharp tongue. I never would have equated Runyon the person with Runyon the writer.

Runyon was a compulsive gambler, betting mostly on the nags. He knew a lot of jockeys. I figured he had a lot of hot tips. But not true. Damon regularly lost, sometimes big. I never heard him cry about a large bet, though. Instead, he would go out and buy himself a couple of ex-

Marion Davies as a young star.

Marion posing at San Simeon with Helen, William Randolph Hearst's favorite dachshund, for a Cosmopolitan-Warner Brothers publicity still.

William Randolph Hearst, Sr., and Helen at Wyntoon.

Millicent Hearst with Mrs. Franklin D. Roosevelt in 1934.

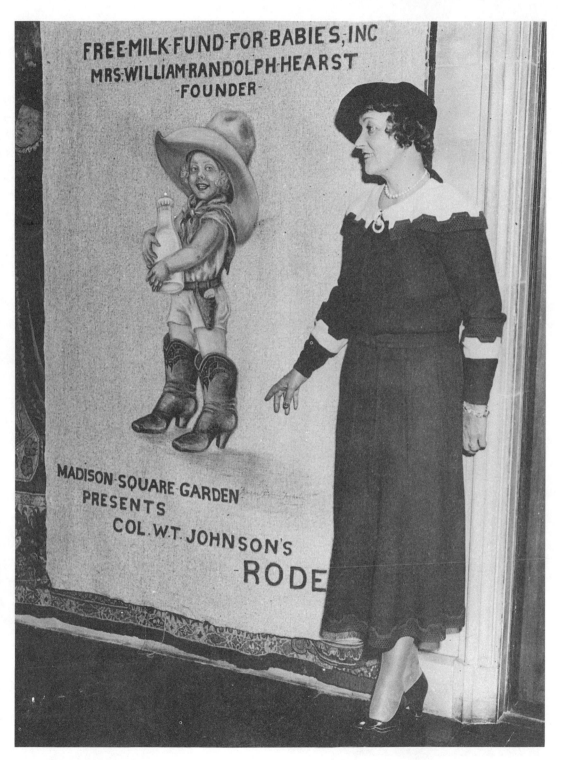

Millicent working on her favorite New York charity in 1933.

Newspapermen at work. William Randolph Hearst, Sr., seems to be casting a watchful eye on Bill Jr., getting his "baptism in ink" on the presses of the New York *Journal* in 1924. The younger Hearst is seated at the center of the photograph at right.

William Randolph Hearst, Jr., with Arthur Brisbane, the legendary Hearst columnist whose commentary was "front-paged" by the senior Hearst for nearly forty years. This photo was taken in 1928 when Bill was just starting out as a reporter at the age of twenty.

Airplanes proved to be an early fascination for Bill Hearst, and he quickly made use of their speed for beating competitors to the news. The photo above shows the Hearst Company's Sikorsky Amphibian delivering *Journal-American* photos from the Coney Island fire of July 1933 to Manhattan. In a lighter moment, the photo below depicts novice airman Hearst with instructor Eddie Bellande at Old Clover field in Los Angeles in 1927.

Bill lands his own light plane near South Street Seaport in Manhattan, just blocks from
the offices of the *Journal-American*.

William Randolph Hearst, Sr., and two friends—Winston Churchill and film studio executive Louis B. Mayer—pause on the street during a visit to New York in the 1930s. Hearst would later oppose Churchill's efforts to get the U.S. involved in World War II, but, ironically, confronted Hitler about his treatment of the Jews as early as 1934—mostly at Mayer's urging.

"La Cuesta Encantada"—more commonly known as Hearst Castle or San Simeon—looks nearly complete in this photo of the 1930s.

Hearst's birthdays at San Simeon always called for costumes. Pictured here with their father are (from left to right) Randy, George, and Bill.

David, John, Bill, George and Randy pose with gaucho WRH at another San Simeon fctc.

A party at San Simeon of course brought out the stars. Pictured here with hostess Marion Davies are Gloria Swanson, Joan Bennett, and Jean Harlow.

Gary Cooper poses with Marion and the diminutive Mary Pickford at San Simeon.

Bill, John, and George following a game of tennis with their father.

Above: Although it's often been claimed that Millicent Hearst never visited San Simeon, this photograph from the 1930s—the last taken of the family together—proves otherwise. From left to right are Randy, David, George, Millicent, WRH, Bill, and John. *Below:* San Simeon was not the only gathering place for the stars as this 1940 photo from Wyntoon indicates. Pictured here are Cary Grant, Marion Davies (who derisively referred to the Northern California Hearst estate as "Spitoon"), sculptress Hanna Gaertner (her fountain above), WRH, and two friends of Marion's.

Although San Simeon was always "home" for William Randolph Hearst, Sr., he spent much of his time during World War II at Wyntoon (above). His other estates included St. Donat's Castle in Wales, shown in the photo below, and a "cottage" at Santa Monica, shown on the opposite page before and after demolition.

Three Hearst sons (Bill, David, and Randy) join their father on a voyage to Europe in 1936.

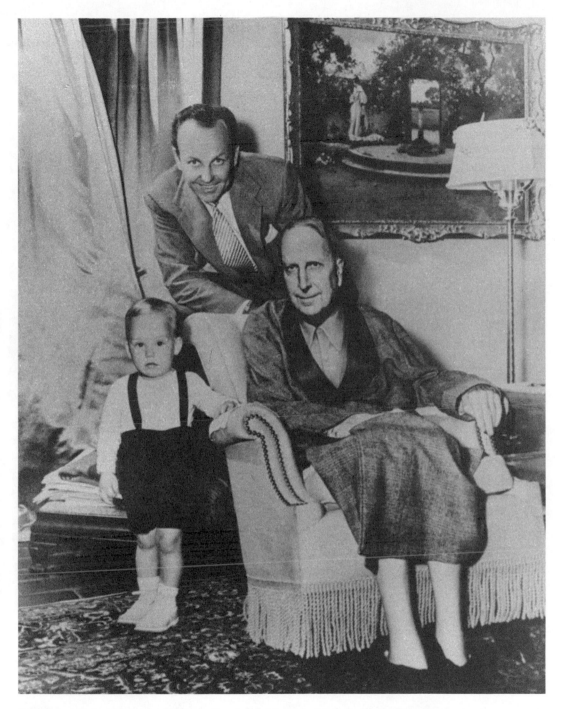

Taken just before the elder William Randolph Hearst's death in 1951, this photo shows three generations: William Randolph Hearst III (Will), Bill, and WRH.

ORIGINAL CARTOON FROM THE PITTSBURGH POST-GAZETTE
AUGUST-15-1951

This is the editorial cartoon that appeared in the Pittsburgh *Post-Gazette* on August 15, 1951, the day after Hearst Senior's death. "30" is how old reporters signed off their stories.

pensive, well-tailored suits. He would soon be back at Lindy's restaurant, his favorite midtown hangout, drinking coffee and picking up the latest gossip.

Damon started as a sportswriter and later wrote about everything from picking horses at the tracks to Broadway and murder. My father would use a good writer on any story. Pop thought the world of Damon as a writer and would not allow his copy to be touched. That was a rare tribute.

Runyon, Walter Winchell, and Mark Hellinger were the Big Three Broadway minstrels. There was often a lot of tension among them. Winchell wanted scoops. Hellinger followed with much of the same. But Runyon strove for good writing and character development. Damon wrote in the historical present tense, starting many of his columns and most of his fiction something like this: I am sitting in Lindy's and Hot Horse Herbie comes meandering in looking like he has just scored on the daily double. Runyon used to tell me that any story would soon be forgotten, but not its players.

Damon and Winchell, who had never been friends, drove around the city together in all-night excursions. It was like a pagan pilgrimage, watching fights, drunks, and robberies. I used to see them in the Stork Club, always at Winchell's Table 50, where they would hold court as the princes of Broadway. Both were a big boost to our circulation.

Runyon had two children by his wife, Ellen. She died, and he married a beautiful young showgirl, Patrice Amati. The pair spent every night, until dawn, prowling the city. That was the atmosphere of the times— live long now, die quick later.

Damon became as much a quintessential New Yorker as Jimmy Walker, a native. In fact, the two became very close friends. I never met two guys who so completely felt and moved with the pulse of a city. These two skeptical and often taciturn men exemplified the lively, lusty character of New York.

When the *Journal* and *American* merged in 1937, Runyon was shifted to our tabloid *Mirror*. He viewed the move as not much more than changing the paper in his typewriter. He used to say, "Mr. Hearst giveth and Mr. Hearst taketh away." Damon wrote for money, not sentiment. He made very big bucks and later lived big in fashionable penthouses and spent long winter vacations in Florida, where he played the ponies.

In the 1940s I was sorry to see Runyon move to Hollywood, where he adapted his short fiction to the movies. Damon was after the dough. I missed him. He continued to write a column for us, but it lacked the warmth and depth of his old Broadway stuff. He missed New York, and finally returned. But the news was bad. He had throat cancer.

Cancer ate Runyon alive. It ravaged his throat and body and he was in severe pain for several years. Mercifully Damon died on December 10, 1946. New York had more heart in those days. Captain Eddie Rickenbacker, a World War II ace and an old friend of Damon's, flew over Manhattan and sprinkled his ashes on the city. It would be nice to believe that some of them fell on Broadway, because no one personified the Big Street better than the little guy with the professorial glasses, smart suits, and gifted typewriter.

I was always after the old man for a raise. In 1936, after eight years of training in different jobs at the *American,* I finally got a fairly large one. My father named me publisher of the paper.

Edmond Coblentz, a kindly man and former editor of the *San Francisco Examiner,* had been running the *American* and took me under his wing. He was like a second father to me. But "Cobbie," as we called him, put all of his energies into supervising the editorial side of the *American* and other Hearst newspapers. He had neither the time nor the inclination to spend much effort on advertising and the needed revenues it brought in. So I took on that job. In effect I became the top advertising salesman. In those days Manhattan lived a lot by night. I became more of a night person—mixing with leading business owners and executives as well as high-powered advertising agency heads, at the best restaurants, Broadway shows, trendy nightclubs, and fashionable bars.

It was a crazy lifestyle because we were in the midst of the Depression, but it fit in perfectly with that of my wife. In the spring of 1933 I had married Lorelle McCarver in New York. She was a tall brunette, a former Follies girl and lots of fun. Lorelle was beautiful—but, a girl, mentally, not a woman. She loved cavorting under the bright lights around town, seeing and being seen. Lorelle was still living in the Roaring Twenties.

The whole thing seemed especially nutty because our whole organization was in financial crisis. Pop finally cut back on all salaries, including his own. Good men were still jumping off buildings even though the crash had occurred long ago. Others drowned themselves in alcohol and became faceless, forgotten men in the Bowery. Bread lines stretched from one neighborhood to another. Long lines formed when signs were posted for even the lowest-paying jobs.

The Hearst organization then began fighting for its life. In 1937 Pop merged the morning *American* and afternoon *Journal* to stabilize our New York operation. I became the publisher of both papers. The consolidation was painful for Pop, but he had long since learned that it had become necessary for survival and growth. He later explained his decision to *Editor & Publisher,* the newspaper trade magazine:

> Unsuccessful newspapers are a luxury which cannot be afforded and which one has no RIGHT to afford indefinitely.
>
> If by consolidation a loser can be eliminated, adding immensely to the circulation and influence and power and profit of the two remaining newspapers. . . to do so is, as I see it, a definite duty.
>
> It is strong papers that increase the need for employees, not weak ones.

The illustration is important because that was the way Pop used to write and talk with all his sons when we went to work. The last two paragraphs of his letter underscore how he wished us to conduct ourselves in the news business:

> The question of favoritism and sentimentality, therefore, does not enter into the situation.
>
> The questions primarily to be considered are those of sound business procedure and efficient service to the public.

Pop did not always put those principles into practice. He could be as sentimental as the next fellow, especially when it came to loyalty to longtime employees. However, he did carry out his word when it came to mergers. During the Depression he also consolidated Hearst newspapers in Boston, Pittsburgh, Baltimore, Chicago, Los Angeles, and San Francisco.

My job as publisher of the *Journal-American* was to show the flag while our troops fought to survive. So Lorelle and I hung on the night-life merry-go-round, where we hobnobbed with the big advertising spenders to increase the paper's lineage.

Some of the word around town was that "Young Bill" Hearst was becoming a playboy. Lorelle and I hopped from bar to restaurant to nightclub almost every night. Under the circumstances, the conclusion seemed justified. Let me kid no one: it was great fun. But the frolicking had to show bottom-line results. I was to increase our advertising lineage. Or else. The old man may have been sitting in San Simeon, but he was constantly looking over my shoulder.

If you had a job and money in those days, Broadway and midtown Manhattan offered great restaurants, theater, and nightclubs. With safe streets and no television, the best of these places were often packed until well after midnight.

Booze was big then. In Spain the great matadors faced the brave bull; in New York and across America men proved they were big and brave by how much sauce they could swallow and still appear to be sober. It was nothing for a guy to have four or five martinis or Scotches for lunch. Sure, he returned to the office tanked, but the trick was to act like it was an afternoon breeze. After work, before grabbing a cab or subway home— or often the train or bus to New Jersey or Connecticut—guys would have three or four more drinks. It was a hail-and-slap-me-on-the-back era in which liquor seemed to be the oil that greased much of Manhattan business and society.

I met Paul "Mac" McNamara in the heyday of these happy-go-lucky times. Mac headed public relations for our magazines. We hit it off immediately and became very close friends. Mac was a gregarious Irishman with the three qualities that I looked for in a friend: loyalty, a gift for storytelling, and a good sense of humor. His public relations work was closely tied to advertising. Many Madison Avenue agencies performed both services. So our meeting and relationship were a natural.

No promotional escapade was too crazy for Mac. He once went to Carmel Snow, who became world-famous as editor of *Harper's Bazaar,* and suggested a real dilly. McNamara wanted to laminate one of the monthly magazine's covers, and have Carmel speak from it as on a record disk. She would describe the latest Paris fashion collections. Richard E. Berlin, who was then vice-president of the Hearst magazines, refused, unless the magazine could find an advertiser to share in the cost by laminating the back cover.

Mac, who had an eye for good-looking gals, knew just the beauty who could pull it off. He used his charm on an old flame, Anita Colby, who was working for the magazine. Anita, known around the office as "The Face," later went on to modeling, acting, and television fame.

Mac put her in contact with a Mr. Hill, who called the advertising shots for the American Tobacco Company. Hill listened and leaped—at the idea, of course. Carmel described the Paris collections on the front-cover disc, while the back cover played a record from the Hit Parade and advertised Lucky Strike cigarettes. The idea was, indeed, a lucky strike. Calls of congratulations almost blew a fuse at American Tobacco and the sales of Luckies went up in profitable smoke.

Mac had a new idea the very next day. He wanted Carmel, who was game, to broadcast daily interviews with the leading couturiers from the famous Paris fashion shows. However, this was not technically possible in 1936. So Mac told Carmel to pre-record interviews with the couturiers in their Paris workshops and other natural settings. That would make listeners feel they were hearing transatlantic radiocasts. The tapes were shipped by plane to New York, where they would be broadcast each day of the fashion showings to stations in major American cities. Local advertisers bought the time. Only there was a hitch. Most of the French and Italian couturiers, unfortunately, could not be understood on much of the tapes.

Time was short, and it seemed that Mac may have outfoxed himself. Suddenly he found the answer. Mac hired actors and actresses to dub in the voices of the couturiers—after *Bazaar* secretaries painstakingly listened and wrote out their fractured English. The stations responded with thunderous approval. Buyers and wholesalers loved it. As one buyer told Mac, "Yes, that was good ol' Coco. I'd know her voice anywhere."

Mac later went looking for pigeons. The following year he arranged to have Carmel make the first fashion broadcast ever reported from Paris. To publicize this, he hired messengers to carry cages of carrier pigeons and deliver them to manufacturers, retailers, and advertisers around New York. Their message simply gave the time of Carmel's broadcasts. When the messengers arrived carrying the cages atop coolie poles, work stopped in every one of these offices. But the pigeons were not needed for any return messages, and none of the buyers or advertisers knew what to do with them. As Mac put it, "That was their problem, not mine!"

Marcus Jewelry had an idea, however. As a gimmick, they affixed one of their "diamond" rings—an "engagement" ring for *Bazaar*—to a pigeon and sent him on his way. Needless to say, Mac and Marcus Jewelry were in cahoots. *Bazaar* reported that the diamond-studded pigeon never arrived. This caused a crazy diamond hunt all over New York. Pigeons were running for their lives, especially in the Bowery, where the bums were looking for a killing.

Mac had to end it. Two little black boys from Harlem "found" the diamond and were rewarded by Carmel when she returned from Paris. Of course, McNamara was still milking the story by setting up the shot for photographers and again splashing Carmel and the magazine across the newspapers.

Mac and I agreed: New York was the greatest city in the world. We continued to make the rounds—swapping stories, jokes, and strategy on how to better our newspaper and magazine businesses. It was a warm, wonderful friendship that has endured for a half-century. Mac left New York to take a job as the top PR man for movie mogul David O. Selznik in Hollywood. He has now retired and lives in Beverly Hills. We still meet out in California and swap stories. These days he cannot drink more than a glass of soda. My strongest libation is usually a non-alcoholic beer.

My enduring friendship with Paul reflected a pattern in my life. If I ever made a friend, that person was my pal, come what may, until he died. The years and miles never separated us. Loyal friendship was a bond that was never to be broken. I cannot recall a single male friendship in my life that was ever untied. Unfortunately, I can't say the same for female friends. That bond was severed in my first two marriages. But my third was true love—the happiest friendship of my life.

Looking back today on the 1920s and 1930s in New York, the town rolled between two extremes: the poor, on relief, and biggies constantly chasing bigger bucks. When Prohibition started in January of 1920, New Yorkers soon saw that it would never work. The Eighteenth Amendment spawned local illegal breweries and distilleries, bootleggers and speakeasies, hijackers, corrupt cops and judges, and machine-gun murders among rival gangs. I saw it as a breakdown of law and order. Many called it the Flapper Age, but the times reflected a lot more than the dolls dancing up and down Broadway. A sexual revolution had begun in daring dress and flamboyant public romances. A devil-may-care attitude characterized both the East and West coasts.

New York tabloids reflected an American society that was busting out of its old ways. Old and new morals contrasted sharply. These changes were at the center of sweeping social conflict. The tabloids, half the size of regular newspapers, swept up readers with big photos and boisterous headlines about these social hijinx. The tabs, which had originated in England, attracted millions of readers. However, the tabloids caused the newspaper business to compete with itself. Joseph Patterson's *New York Daily News* and my father's *Daily Mirror,* begun in 1924, further segmented advertising. The battle for ad dollars was fierce.

The nation was beginning to move into a more urban, technical, consumer age. Cars multiplied amid better roads. Airlines began to open up the skies to travel. Railroads expanded. Radio flooded the public with music, news, and other programming. However, Wall Street crashed on Black Thursday, October 24, 1929. The newspaper industry continued strong for a while, despite the Depression. Documentary films and newsreels—Pop began his own company—became very popular. In the first years of the thirties, about 50 million people viewed newsreels and lengthy news features each week.

In the twenties Americans chose among four sources of news—papers, radio, newsreels and film documentaries, as well as weekly magazines. Newspapers became more innovative editorially, stressing interpretation of events, as film took people to the actual scene of world happenings, but only in a cursory, headline form. Magazines offered deeper interpretation of events than the papers, but on a less timely basis.

Newspapers began to stress news interpretation. The signed political column made its appearance in New York and began to develop across the nation. (Arthur Brisbane preceded the others by writing a general column in our *American* for decades.) Heywood Broun began a political column for the *New York World* in 1921. Walter Lippmann started his column for the *Herald Tribune* in 1931 and, within a half-dozen years, was syndicated to more than 150 papers across the nation. Others followed.

There was also a new emphasis on election polling. Voter sampling had been around since 1912, but there were many questions about its methods and accuracy. As chagrined political pundits and pollsters well know, polling took a terrific beating as late as 1948, when virtually every commentator and major poll in the nation predicted that Thomas Dewey would defeat Harry Truman. Polling has obviously become much more sophisticated and accurate since.

Women advanced in the media during the twenties, but in the thirties their leaps into newspaper city rooms almost halted. That was because they were seen as second-income earners. Papers gave jobs to men who needed to support families. The average reporter earned about thirty dollars per week in 1933. The American Newspaper Guild was organized in a bid to raise salaries.

The thirties and forties became the golden age of radio. Networks hired their own news staffs and started their own news programs. The sale of commercial time began competing with newspaper advertising lineage. President Franklin D. Roosevelt did much to help radio news by explaining new government policies in his "Fireside Chats." Roosevelt turned official Washington upside down during his first hundred days of change. The Depression dragged on until World War II, but the working man survived through public works and other federal expenditures.

Manhattan became more of a night town than ever. Forty-second Street, from Times Square to Eighth Avenue, was an arcade of theaters showing musical reviews. These ranged from big, flashy extravaganzas by George White and Flo Ziegfeld to Minsky's rip-roaring burlesque house. George M. Cohan and his family would wave to people who recognized them. Al Jolson walked down the street followed by a bevy of beautiful chorus girls. Jimmy Durante would buy himself a hot dog and eat it while dancing along. On Broadway, Katherine Cornell, Helen Hayes, the Barrymore family, Lunt and Fontanne, and others starred in the best drama.

The nearby streets of Tin Pan Alley—on Twenty-eighth Street between Fifth and Sixth Avenues—were studded with big musical names like Irving Berlin, Jerome Kern, Cole Porter, and George Gershwin. Also Rogers and Hammerstein, Victor Herbert, Sigmund Romberg, as well as Rogers and Hart. And Sammy Cahn, Jimmy McHugh, and Jimmy Van Heusen. The big music houses later moved uptown.

I loved the old midtown Palace, which was the queen of vaudeville. The featured acts—from dogs to magicians and dance troupes—were the best in the country. And comedians like Joe E. Lewis, Henny Youngman, and Milton Berle. If a comedian had an off day, some of the more boisterous customers would approach the stage and begin heckling. I liked the put-down line that many used, "Excuse me, I thought I was doing a single." After the show, pals and I would walk over to Jack Dempsey's restaurant on Eighth Avenue for a pastrami sandwich or some lamb chops. Jack was a good friend of mine.

Every once in a while, I would wander down to Greenwich Village. The bohemian restaurants, the coffee houses, ale gatherings hopscotched across

the narrow streets where you got your fortune told or listened to Dixie-
land or Eddie Condon's jazz. Some folks were very trendy and would hop
up to Harlem to hear Ethel Waters, Duke Ellington, Fats Waller, or Cab
Calloway at the Cotton Club.

Prohibition was king when I came to town. Eastside mansions had long
been converted to plush speak-easies. The day after Prohibition became
the law of the land—on January 16, 1920—the "50-50" Club was
opened on West Fiftieth Street. Scores of other such clubs and hundreds
of little dives mushroomed all over town. New York's most prominent
and fashionable citizens frequented the better spots. At least a dozen of
these were located in the ritzy pads of Park Avenue. It was chic to go to
the better clubs, which used passwords and other gimmicks, such as entry
keys. One joint used "Carrie Nation" as passwords.

Some of the best restaurateurs in town—then and since—operated
speak-easies. There were Jack Kriendler and Charley Berns at "21," John
Perona at El Morocco, Sherman Billingsley at the Stork Club, Big Jim
Moriarty at the Marlborough House, John Steinberg at the 5 o'Clock
Club, as well as Leon Enken and Eddie Davis at Leon & Eddie's. Texas
Guinan, a sharp-witted, wisecracking gal who really did hail from Texas,
was easily the queen of the speak-easies. It was she who, surrounded by
her high-stepping dancing girls, coined the phrase, "Hello, Sucker!"

The speak-easies died in April of 1933, but the town didn't skip a beat.
I can't recall a single tear shed. The better joints became legal and competed with restaurants and new legit places. Toots Shor introduced the
new era of earlier drinking by saying, "If a guy can't get loaded by
midnight, he ain't even half tryin'."

This snapshot of those years was the background for the dizzy days—
and nights—when Lorelle and I began our merry whirls on the New York
social-business circuit. It was quite common in those days to attend the
opening nights of new plays, and then catch dinner and a show after the
theater. There were the Stork Club, Toots Shor's, "21," the Latin Quarter, Diamond Horseshoe, El Morocco, and Texas Guinan's bawdy place.
New Yorkers club-hopped by night. Nobody went home after the curtain.
At least nobody we knew.

Virtually all the department store heads and many others did considerable business socially—making contacts, buying and selling ideas, trading industry gossip, hiring, and sometimes even firing when somebody had
one drink too many. You were largely in or out in New York by the

people you knew—not only the business biggies but headwaiters, bartenders, and hangers-on who knew what was happening around town.

My favorite joints were the Stork Club's Cub Room in early evening and El Morocco late at night. "Twenty-One" was best for lunch, but I sometimes went there in early evening. They were my three favorites because all were friendly. I never liked places that were more interested in who you were than what you were, or joints that catered to big spenders. That is why I liked the Kriendlers at "21" and Perona at El Morocco so much. Later, Toots Shor. All were regular guys who sold their booze and told their stories straight. Of course, to Toots everybody was a bum. Unless he did not like you; then he would say, "That gentleman over there." The description was so out of character that I would look at him quizzically. He would catch the question in my expression, pull my suit lapels to his, and whisper, "I mean that no good sonofabitch over there." And we would both laugh.

I would usually take Lorelle dancing when Eddie Duchin brought his band to the Persian Room. We would invite one of the older department store executives and his wife, and usually wind up talking advertising. I liked Eddie's piano and bubbly style of music. And I liked Duchin because he was another straight talker. He would chat with couples as they passed his tinkling piano at the edge of the dance floor.

After a night on the town (we would sometimes not get to bed until two or three in the morning), my first assignment of the day as publisher was usually a business lunch with an important advertiser. These ranged across the city's leading executives: Adam Gimbel at Saks Fifth Avenue and his cousin, Bernie, at Gimbel's. Andy Goodman at Bergdorf Goodman, Jack Strauss at Macy's, John Wood at B. Altman, Walter Hoving and Dorothy Shaver at Lord & Taylor, Sky Kudner and Albert Lasker, who headed their own advertising agencies, and many others.

Pop continued to ride my back to raise advertising revenues. I still have many of the letters I wrote him. Excerpts from one of those letters, July 15, 1937, will indicate some of the pressures he used and how I responded:

Dear Pop:

Joe [Willicombe, his secretary] said the other day that you were critical of our advertising showing last week.

Please don't misconstrue what I am going to say as an alibi because I am positive that we won't need one.

Since the merger [of the *Journal* and *American*], I have been devoting all of my time to getting expenses down. We have been handicapped in many instances by existing contracts, both in the advertising and editorial departments. Furthermore, it was our endeavor, as expressed in your statement, to maintain the highest possible degree of employment. As a consequence, the first two weeks P & L's [profits and losses] do not reflect the extent to which we can go and will be forced to go.

Now, to turn to our selling activities. Please keep in mind, Pop, that we are in the middle of summer; that we are not yet through with our economies; that we have just begun to touch the increased revenue potentialities for this paper.

Despite the Depression, the advertising industry grew considerably from the 1920s to the beginning of the war. The sale of consumer products not only often rose in proportion to advertising but was instrumental in distinguishing between competitive name brands. Promotion became more professional, it created the new phenomenon of national advertising: crossing the country with one ad.

As advertising developed, business and marketing strategies became more sophisticated. Advertising followed the new leads. Newspapers hired a new breed of advertising salesman, more educated and innovative. Major advertisers began employing their own copywriters to handle their large volume of ads. Large department stores began bypassing agencies and dealing directly with newspapers and radio outlets for their local advertising. As a matter of survival, newspaper publishers closely followed these developments.

While big circulation meant more advertising dollars, it became more essential to know the make-up of audiences within that readership. For example, the number of upper-class women readers and what ad techniques attracted them to a particular brand of soap or spaghetti. A great many demographic factors began to be incorporated into ads. All this is basic today, but was not in those times. The demographic segmentation of markets was then a trend-setting idea. We grappled hard to understand these developments, and they became crucial to ad salesmanship.

During those years I sat across from Cobbie Coblentz in the *Journal-American* publisher's office. He could not have been a better mentor or friend. We became devoted to one another. I would listen carefully to this balding, bespectacled little man as he would say, "Now, listen, Bill. I want you to follow closely everything that I do. You can hear exactly what I say and just how we solve many of our problems. Any time you wish to contribute something, just say so." He might not have looked like a tall, brave knight in shining armor, but Cobbie was a prince of a man. He was smart but self-effacing; a gentle man who made tough editorial decisions; a man educated in the college of hard knocks who comported himself like a studious professor.

Pop, while still riding me, would often send an encouraging message. This telegram arrived on my thirty-first birthday in 1939:

HAPPY BIRTHDAY. GET GOOD AND PIE-EYED AND VISIT ALL THE NIGHTCLUBS IN NEW YORK. I WISH I COULD BE WITH YOU. MUCH LOVE FROM YOUR AGED PARENT, SLIGHTLY BATTERED BUT STILL IN THE RING. POP.

I couldn't get pie-eyed since my ulcers would have boomeranged. But I made the bars and nightclubs to drum up more advertising with the movers and shakers because Pop had put the fear of God into me. I often suffered the torment of wondering what my father really thought of my professional performance. But he would soon write or say something, or an incident would happen, that would restore my faith and put me back on track with him.

I remember an unforgettable yarn along those lines. A bunch of fellows from the *Chicago Herald and Examiner* came to New York on a visit. Chicago was a notoriously tough newspaper town, and our Windy City men were seasoned street fighters. Some did not just talk tough; they were as hard and fast as baseball bats. We were having a few drinks and one of them asked me what happened to my spotted calf. I vaguely recalled a calf that had arrived many years before at my grandmother's hacienda as a present from Pop. The fellow inquired as to whether I knew the story of the calf. I confessed that all I knew was that Pop had given it to me as a youngster. This is the tale I was told. Having known a good many Chicago reporters, I believe it.

*

My father was headed to the West Coast by train and stopped in Chicago to meet with the paper's editor, Walter Howey. I was ten years old at the time and accompanied him. Howey filled Pop in on details of the editorial and business sides of the *Herald* and *Examiner*. At the close of the meeting the editor put us on the train to California.

A day later Howey received a telegram, signed by W. R. Hearst, Sr., from Dodge City, Kansas. It read: "IN A BOXCAR NEAR A WATER TANK ABOUT A MILE WEST OF KANSAS CITY IS A BAWLING BLACK-AND-WHITE SPOTTED CALF. BILL WANTS THE DARN THING."

Howey finally located a calf resembling the description, after burning up the long-distance telephone lines. Bill Bliss, a Kansas City reporter who worked for the Hearst newspapers as a stringer, reported he could buy the calf for twenty dollars. Howey told Bliss to hold it while he telegraphed the money. The editor then dispatched James Clarkson, a veteran Hearst reporter, to Kansas City to arrange for the calf's train trip to my grandmother's place. Clarkson met Bliss, and the pair proceeded to put a snootful of drinks and a big dinner on the newspaper's swindle sheet. The two agreed to ship the calf west by train the following day.

After dinner they made the rounds of several Kansas City nightspots. They wound up three days later in a place best known for its painted ladies. The madam claimed they had partaken of her best girls, steak, and champagne, and owed her $200. Clarkson was momentarily stricken with trepidation, since he had no money. However, true to the tough-it-out Chicago newspaper code, he sent a masterful telegram to Howey. The reporter claimed that, while the calf was still alive, it was suffering from croup. It had nearly frozen as Bliss looked for a place to board it. Veterinarians told him they feared the croup might turn into pneumonia.

Clarkson said he and Bliss had not slept for three days and nights as they watched over the stricken animal. They were concerned about Howey's relationship with Mr. Hearst if anything went wrong.

The calf's fever finally broke. Clarkson needed money to pay for the veterinarians, the calf's shelter and feed, and to ship the animal west. He asked for $300 in expense money.

Howey considered the telegram a swindling masterpiece and forwarded the funds with a knowing smile. He then tacked it on his wall as a classic. For the moment, however, the editor told no one that he recognized the address from a time when he had enjoyed the house's hospitality.

Meanwhile, Clarkson returned to his hotel and went to bed. When he awakened, the masterful urge was still in him. He phoned Howey and explained that the calf, with its illness and all, might need someone to accompany it to the West Coast. This time, Howey hit the roof: "You put that damn calf—or one that looks reasonably like it—on a train to California. Get a receipt. Then get your big fat ass in this office soonest. If you're not back by tomorrow night, don't bother showing your face around here again."

Clarkson phoned Bliss at home to get the address of the livery stable where the calf was being kept. He got Mrs. Bliss, who gave him an earful about keeping her husband out for three days. She hung up in a huff. Clarkson rushed to Bliss's home to get the address, but the family was gone. The wife had left a note for the milkman saying they had gone on vacation.

Clarkson then raced by cab to the stockyards, and inquired at dozens of nearby stables about a newsman who might have boarded a calf there. The Chicago reporter, now desperate, met a kindly cattleman and retold his sorrowful tale.

The cattleman asked the height and color of the calf. Clarkson said he was about as high as his belt and was spotted black and white. The cattleman asked for two dollars. He then walked to a stockyards clerk and requested a receipt for a Holstein bull calf, eight weeks old, to be shipped collect to California. He asked that the yard's San Francisco representative deliver such a calf to a Hearst representative when he came to pay and pick it up. The cattleman gave Clarkson a receipt with the name and address of the cattle company and its San Francisco office. He told the reporter to wire the information to the Hearst people there and mail them the receipt. Then he asked Clarkson to buy him a drink.

Clarkson gladly bought him a double bourbon. The newsman wasn't drinking at the moment. The cattleman lifted his glass and toasted: "One Holstein calf looks almost the same as another."

*

I often entertained out-of-town guests in New York. Most of these businessmen, vice-presidents of advertising, and directors of advertising agencies enjoyed a few days on the town. They loved to meet and swap information with Manhattan business and industry biggies. We also in-

troduced many to the sports and entertainment crowd in Manhattan—
from Jack Dempsey and Joe DiMaggio to Helen Hayes and Bing Crosby.
They returned home with a pocketful of stories.

Underneath and unspoken, however, many of these folks from Detroit,
Chicago, and the West Coast were suspicious and sometimes resentful of
New York's brashness and flamboyance. Henry Ford once said that New
York was a "different country." He suggested that perhaps it ought to
have a separate government. Ford concluded, "Everybody thinks differ-
ently, acts differently. They just don't know what the hell the rest of the
United States is." I like the description of Groucho Marx best: "When
it's 9:30 in New York, it's 1937 in Los Angeles."

The island is only twelve and a half miles at its longest, and two and
a half at its widest part. Five million people pour into the city every work
day by subway, bus, train, and car. They come across and under water
by way of twenty bridges, eighteen tunnels, and seventeen ferries—to say
nothing of planes and helicopters. There are three major airports in the
area. Sirens shriek and whistles wail all day and every night. Ship traffic
groans in and out of berths with loads of people and various wares.

I have often wondered if man was meant to inhabit this concrete,
howling, nerve-grating, littered place. In the rush of people and traffic,
the city seems like a mad, abstract blur of lights and shadows swallowed
up by great masses of concrete and glass. The throat of Manhattan often
seems to be strangling on car and bus fumes. It lives in a torrent of noise
and pent-up emotion. New York is the stress capital of the globe, the
alarm bell that says: This is the edge of humanity, the precipice beyond
which no civilization may go.

Yet this is my town. There is nothing more to say. I was born here.
I will probably die here if not at San Simeon. New York is in my bones.

VI
OFF TO WAR

On the chill morning of December 7, 1941, I hopped a cab to "21" in midtown Manhattan. The four Kriendler brothers, who owned the club, were hosting a Sunday buffet before the big pro football game. The New York Giants were playing the old Brooklyn Dodgers up at the Polo Grounds. The crosstown rivalry was terrific. The stadium was sold out, with more than 55,000 fans expected. The Kriendlers had somehow gotten good mezzanine tickets from the Mara family, which owned the Giants. The club rented a bus to take about sixty of us to the game. Many of the big hitters in town were at the buffet.

When I arrived, Pete Kriendler hollered, "Here he comes—the peace-maker—the only guy in the joint who's for both teams." Pete was ribbing me. We had a private agreement. If any of my four brothers—or any friend of mine—ever got in trouble at "21," Pete or one of his brothers would step in. I would later pay them any tab, ante up for anyone's cab ride home, and would personally apologize to any injured or insulted party.

I've been going to "21" for more than sixty years. The place has been sold, but Pete still hangs around there. My friends and I are now too old to get into trouble, but I recall that pledge vividly. The only accolade I ever cared about was that I was a fair and peaceful person.

The buffet spread covered two giant tables—from caviar to carved roast beef and chocolate cake. We ate like kids at Thanksgiving. They fortified us with Bloody Marys in large punch bowls. (I don't think they were actually called Bloody Marys until some years later.) The more we ate, the more we drank. A lot of guys got on the bus with half a load on. Two waiters served more drinks and sandwiches as we traveled to the game. The whole show was so damned elegant, it was unbelievable.

At the game I sat next to two close friends, Bob Considine and Paul McNamara. Bob, the star reporter of International News Service, was a good pal of mine. In fact, he was one of the finest gentlemen I had ever met. And Paul, who was the public relations man for our magazines, was among the funniest.

Bob noticed it first, then Paul. The public address announcer called out several names of military men and told them to contact their units. Both were intrigued because all those summoned were high-ranking officers. Then a call came for all enlisted men to go to their headquarters or barracks immediately. Finally, an official announcement was made. The Japanese had attacked Pearl Harbor. That meant war, and everybody knew it.

The game suddenly became meaningless to most of us. Brooklyn trounced the Giants, 21–7. It was a relief to return to the bus and ride back to "21," where all of us gathered around radios for more news. I've never seen the place so excited—before or since. "Twenty-one" was always low-key, class all the way. But guys were jumping up and down at almost every news spot. The radio blared nonstop and it was all war. I caught a cab home to do some thinking.

I had avoided violence all my life. If my father taught me anything, it was to be a gentleman. To be thoughtful, decent to others. The idea of war and killing contrasted with all I stood for and admired. "Good ol' Bill," my friends always said. "A pleasanter guy you couldn't meet. Good natured, a lively sense of humor, gracious even to people who don't like his old man." Then, someone would say curtly, "But he'll never be his old man, either. He's not tough enough. And he doesn't have his father's brains—or moxie. Just a friendly, democratic, down-to-earth guy."

I sat in the kitchen drinking coffee that evening, reviewing my life. I had lived a comfortable existence. My father was one of the wealthiest and most powerful men in America. Indeed, I had lived in the lap of luxury. I had never faced many of the harsh realities that confronted others. And now I was looking at the harshest fact of my life—going to war.

But would I go to war?

As publisher of the *Journal-American,* I was in an "essential" civilian category and deferred from the draft. I would be thirty-four in about two months, and there was some doubt about my passing a military physical. I had bad ears, ulcers, and jaundice. The ears and ulcers had been continuous problems. But, even with my medical background, I might be able to wrangle a spot somewhere as a military public information officer. Someone might say, however, that my father had pulled strings to get me in as an officer. It was a ticklish situation.

I went to see my mother. It would be best to see her first because Pop was still upset with the British. He believed they just wanted to use American boys to fight a European war. Mom was adamant: "You'll never forgive yourself if you don't see some kind of action. You'll hate yourself in later life. Go—somewhere—but go!"

I tried the Air Force because I was an experienced pilot. They turned me down for medical reasons. The Navy was next. No dice, same reason. In desperation, I went to Washington and spoke to a few friends. They could get me a desk job as a Navy officer in public information. I thought about that, but rejected the idea. I did not want to sit out the war in a cushy Washington job as a flack for the brass.

That took more than a year. Finally, I made up my mind and flew out to see Pop at San Simeon. He had already guessed what I was about to propose. I told him that I wanted to go to Europe as a war correspondent for our newspapers. No one could ever accuse me of running out on the fight. I would see plenty of battlefield action. Pop gave me his blessing but warned, "The English are very charming. Make sure they don't charm you out of your American heritage. You're an American first and always." After obtaining U.S. military accreditation and other clearances, I began covering the war in London during the summer of 1943. Despite my father's admonition, I soon became an admirer of British wartime courage and determination.

I flew to London, and Italian dictator Benito Mussolini bowed out about midnight on the very night I arrived. Early the following morning— too early—the British Ministry of Information phoned me at my hotel. I was staying at Claridge's, where our family was well known. The gentleman asked if I would like to hear British Prime Minister Winston Churchill address a joint session of Parliament in a few hours. Would I!

After a few moments of jubilation, I recalled Pop's warning: Do not let the English charm you. I concluded that, since my father and our newspapers had given them such a hard time, this was the Britishers' first move in a game of diplomatic manipulation. But I had a pleasant surprise. Churchill spoke in the smaller House of Lords because the old House of Commons had been virtually destroyed in the earlier German bombing blitz. I was ushered into the small gallery overhanging one end of the beautiful oak-paneled chamber. Such a ticket was about as rare in London as a Kansas City steak. At least I was still thinking like an American.

The speaker, dressed in black robes, sat directly below in what resembled a square jury box. The leaders of the two major political parties—the Tories and Labor—sat on either side of the speaker. Four rows of tiered benches lined the two long walls. The opposing parties sat on their respective sides. The room was about 100 feet long, some 50 feet wide, and 50 feet high. As I sat down, one of the Labor members was insisting on a full discussion of the conduct of the war. Foreign Minister Anthony Eden, in a black coat and gray trousers, replied from the front bench that there would be no such debate. Eden warned that he had the votes to back up his statement. The only purpose of the session was to hear the prime minister.

Churchill rose, portly and slow. He laid some notes on a table in front of the speaker's raised platform. It was a historic moment. A major enemy was starting to crumble after almost four years of war. Yet Churchill began softly, as if he were merely introducing some routine daily ritual. I was struck by the deliberate understatement of his speech. The gist of it was that, although Mussolini was now finished, the war up the boot would continue unabated unless the Italians surrendered unconditionally. There was not a single note of poignancy or emotion. It was clear that Churchill saw a long, tough war ahead, and he planned to let the Italians stew in their troubles.

There was no great applause during the speech, which lasted about a half hour, but members interrupted several times to shout approval: "Hear! Hear!" When finished, Churchill merely put his notes in a suit pocket and sat down. He had spoken extemporaneously, rarely referring to the notes. Members calmly rose and began exchanging views while strolling toward exits.

I sat in my seat for several minutes. In a quiet, deliberate way, Churchill had struck the right chord—for England and Italy. To both peoples he was saying there could be and would be no let-up in the fight. It was not a time for cheers but, rather, for calm relief at a milestone passed. But make no mistake: There were difficult times ahead. Deep in thought, I walked back to my hotel. The big unknown—the Allied invasion of the continent—was still ahead for millions of us who would make the leap.

In the following months I spent most of my time talking with the English and Americans fighting the war as well as with the ordinary Englishman on the street. I was trying to analyze the human factors that held the British together and whether they had the will to finish the job against Hitler. It did not take long to realize that, beneath their courtesy, the English had grit.

Americans were everywhere in London. Some Englishmen didn't take well to us. They were convinced that many Americans were braggarts, or at least big-mouthed. They detested overstatement and were past masters of the deliberate understatement—an art form that they much admire. I was particularly intrigued by English men's deference to women. Many called women "dear," whether they knew them or not, and treated the ladies with affectionate courtesy. This was actually a point of decorum, not affection. These good gentlemen conveyed the notion that they were really interested in the ladies, whether they were or not. That bit of intellectual gymnastics seemed to be a worthwhile feat. I have used the expression "dear" to ladies ever since.

Some Englishmen claimed there were more Americans, military and civilian, in London than in Washington—good for a laugh anytime. The British got a kick out of all the saluting of our military. The place seemed like the Pentagon at times. They would ask casually over a drink: How many salute casualties did you Yanks have today? And then laugh with an all-knowing look. I sometimes hoped some would roar with laughter and spill their drinks. But, alas, their reserve never allowed that to happen.

Just about every day, London newspapers quoted German papers concerning the latest rumors on Allied invasion targets across the channel. The Germans printed photos of large Nazi fortifications to scare us about the difficulty of an invasion and bolster confidence in their defenses at home.

Americans' morale was up. One reason, perhaps, was we did rather well on post-exchange rations. We were allowed seven packs of cigarettes a week. We also could buy soap, toothpaste, razor blades, shaving cream, fountain pens, chocolate, and cans of fruit juice. What a way to fight a war!

I went to Hyde Park many Sundays to listen to the soapbox speakers. Despite the war, and sometimes because of it, the freedom and range of subjects was astonishing. No one was immune from criticism. I particularly enjoyed one Sunday afternoon address by a Communist. This fellow was haranguing against Churchill and many of the Allied leaders. He stood amid a cluster of antiaircraft guns. I was with two old pals from the States, Paul Douglas and John McClain. The speaker was thoroughly rapping the Allies for not sending more war equipment to Stalin.

This guy got tougher and tougher, naming names and insisting that we were holding back fighting equipment from the Russians because they were Communists. My father was an arch anti-Communist and, at that point, Douglas leaned across McClain and whispered to me: "C'mon, let's get the hell out of here before this guy takes on your old man and we all get in a fight." I started laughing and the other two followed. The speaker soon noticed us. He thought we were laughing at him, and was ready to take aim at the disruptive trio. However, we quickly retreated and became merely three more Sunday strollers.

Along the famous shopping district around Bond Street, a black gentleman, carrying a dozen flags and dressed in blue silks with plumes in his turban, stopped us. He had spotted us as Americans. Leaning over, he said confidentially, "There'll be a hot time in the old town tonight. Come at seven." The three of us looked at one another and shook our heads. He glared and said sharply, "Seven sharp. Be there!" He squared his shoulders, lifted his turban, and marched off. Douglas asked, "I wonder if that's H-hour on D-day?" We started laughing again and couldn't stop. Other strollers probably thought we were happily floating home from a spirited afternoon party.

I found that Britishers didn't drink much during the war. There was too much serious work to do. The large hotels and restaurants closed their bars at midnight. After that a few "bottle clubs" opened. You joined and ordered a bottle of liquor to be held in your "locker." These places were very expensive, and required an almost impossible round-trip taxi ride in the blackout.

Despite the heavy bombing that had occurred, Londoners were calm. Indeed, the most raucous noises were arguments about the future of

Britain and Europe after the war. People constantly debated this—from the occupation of Germany to relations with the Soviet Union. It seemed to me that their dreams of war's end steeled the British against their present troubles and the coming bloody invasion of France.

For all its gentility, London was still a city of the unexpected. After some heavy German bombing, I was coming up from an air-raid shelter when a gentleman handed me a piece of paper. It was an anonymous poem. I put it in my coat pocket. On my return to Claridge's, I read it. The work was typical of British humor and understatement:

IF
(With apologies to Rudyard Kipling)

If you can keep yourself from going crackers,
At all the things that you are told to do,
When Hitler sends along his air attackers
With squibs and bombs to try and frighten you;
If you can bear the hellish Banshee warning
Without that sinking feeling in your breast;
If you can sleep in dug-outs 'till the morning
And never feel you ought to have more rest.
If you can laugh at every blackout stumble,
Nor murmur when you cannot find a pub;
If you can eat your rations and not grumble
About the wicked price you pay for grub;
If you can keep depression down to zero
And view it all as just a bit of fun,
Then, my dear sir, you'll be a bloody hero;
And, what is more, you'll be the only one.

Because of my earlier flying days, I haunted the camouflaged air fields in the English countryside that were used by the U.S. Eighth Air Force. Some seventy-five to eighty Flying Fortresses would take off from a single field to bomb Germany. They knew where to expect German antiaircraft fire, and when Nazi fighters would likely hit them. The attack force sometimes totaled 1,000 planes. They were escorted by British Spitfires, as well as American Thunderbolts and P-38 Lightnings at various stages. Many pilots kept a "death diary," recording the results of every mission they had flown. Most felt they were always riding with death. Even when they returned, the first sight to greet them was rows of ambulances lined up just off runways, waiting for the dead and wounded. I would later fly on some of these missions but, for the moment, it was essential to make contact with various military units, staffs, generals, and others running the show.

I met an old friend from California who had often come to my father's place at San Simeon. Captain Clark Gable, the actor, didn't have to join the U.S. Air Force. He was older now and could have sat out the war at home selling war bonds in uniform. Instead, he was at a bomber base north of London and flew five missions as a tail-gunner. Gable was patriotic and never believed, despite his movie fame and the Hollywood glamour that had surrounded his public life, that he was any different from the next guy. Both of us were earthy. We enjoyed talking about hunting, fishing, and flying.

Gable used to stay with me at Claridge's whenever he got a pass to London. If I wasn't there, I left word at the desk that he could use my room. On one occasion we got tickets to see a play. I cannot remember the name of the particular production or the theater, but that was only incidental. We arrived as the lights were dimming and enjoyed the first act. At intermission both of us stood to stretch our limbs. A buzz began in the audience and soon became a loud chorus of women. They descended on us with their programs to get Gable's autograph. Despite his many years of stardom, Clark was not only embarrassed but horrified by the scene.

He quickly urged, "Bill, let's get the hell out of here."

I said, "Naw, Clark, let's stay and see the rest of the play. Just sit down. I'll handle this."

He sat, and I waved them away. The moment the play finished, Gable bolted for an exit and I dashed after him. So much for the claim that all actors are hams—and most British are reserved.

I continued covering the air war until the spring of 1944. Then I went home for a brief rest before leaving for North Africa. That was the jump-off point for reporters joining American forces fighting in Italy. I boarded a Navy command ship at Norfolk, Virginia, in April. We landed at Casablanca, and I flew on to Allied headquarters in Algiers to prepare to cover the boot, from Naples up.

In late 1942 and the early part of 1943, U.S. and British forces had taken North Africa from Field Marshal Erwin Rommel's elite Afrika Corps. Patton commanded an All-American Task Force, part of an Anglo-American operation of more than 40,000 officers and men. They captured Morocco while British and American troops captured Tunisia and Algeria. All the Americans had sailed from U.S. bases. Never in history had such a massive invasion been launched from 3,000 miles away. Some 200 warships and another 300 transports took part in the operation.

Patton—already known as "Old Blood and Guts"—was itching to invade Sicily. Allied commander Dwight D. Eisenhower told George that this was a British show. He would have to play second fiddle to the two British commanders, Field Marshal Bernard Montgomery and Major General Kenneth A. N. Anderson. Patton did, within his limits. But an American fighting legend was being born and baptized in blood.

On July 10, 1943, more than 3,000 Allied ships—the largest armada of the war—anchored off southern Sicily. Nearly 500,000 Allied troops were ready to storm the beaches. About 350,000 German and Italian troops prepared to repulse them. Patton's Seventh Army was to grease the way and, according to Montgomery's battle plan, the Britisher would win the glory of capturing Palermo. The invasion actually touched off a race between the two to see who would take the Sicilian capital. Patton's troops, under General Geoffrey Keyes, captured Palermo on July 22. When Montgomery arrived in the capital, George greeted him with a big smile, his hands on his ivory-handled, silver-plated revolvers. The British field marshal was, to say it in the most polite terms, annoyed.

The Allies captured Sicily in just thirty-eight days. King Victor Emmanuel III, convinced by Marshal Pietro Badoglio that the war was lost, deposed Mussolini in the name of the monarchy on July 24. Badoglio was the king's chief military adviser.

On September 3, British and Canadian troops of the Eighth Army crossed the Straits of Messina and assaulted Calabria, the sole of the Italian boot. Meantime, the U.S. Fifth Army, under Major General Mark W. Clark, landed at Salerno, several miles south of Naples, on September 9. Under Major General John P. Lucas, they later assaulted Anzio below Rome, but were long pinned down on its beaches, suffering large losses.

Something generally unnoticed but very crucial happened in North Africa, Sicily, and the Italian Peninsula. It was the kind of significant development I sought most to find in reporting. The three men whom

General George C. Marshall, U.S. Army chief of staff, chose as his most crucial leaders of the war—Eisenhower, Bradley, and Patton—were molded into a team in those battles.

Patton was to fall in and out of favor. The worst incident, in Sicily, involved slapping a GI who was tied in mental knots and feared going into combat. Patton was later relieved of his command because of the incident, but Ike and Bradley still believed in him. On the other hand, many British officers despised Montgomery. They privately criticized what they saw as plans for self-glory at the professional expense of others. That divisive attitude never existed among Ike, Omar, and George.

After Sicily and the early Italian Peninsula campaign, I flew to Naples on April 23, 1944. I wanted to report on part of the Italian campaign, and then hoped to be able to return to London in time to cover the invasion of France.

Naples was a shambles. The retreating Germans had methodically destroyed the docks and many public buildings that might have been of any use. They left land mines and booby traps on many of the main streets. The Germans also regularly bombed Naples after fleeing the city. In fact, they hit it for an hour on the night before I arrived. Yet, despite the devastation in the city, the Bay of Naples was still as beautiful as in all the romantic songs.

The famous San Carlos Opera House still stood. Performances took place almost every afternoon. Prices ranged from forty cents to one dollar. Bars sold two fingers of Italian vermouth for fifteen cents a glass. A martini, with sugar around the rim of the glass, cost forty cents. The price of a bottle of 1940 Italian champagne climbed to four bucks. A haircut was more manageable: six cents.

I got a room in the Terminus Hotel, where our INS news bureau was located. Believe me, it was not Claridge's. The Germans had smashed down the walls of most rooms with sledgehammers. Our guys lived in this dilapidated downtown hotel, near the docks and railroad yards because it was only a brief walk to press headquarters. The INS gang called the hotel our "Little Home on the Range" because German planes regularly used it as a bombing range. Allied news briefings were held in the press building. Cable offices, censors, and military public-information offices were scattered through the structure. It seemed like a good marriage.

We also lived there because of First Lieutenant Evan J. MacIlraith, Jr., of Evansville, Indiana. MacIlraith was an ex-sports writer. He had never worked in a hotel in his life. So, of course, the Army put him in charge of the press hotel. Yet MacIlraith was an excellent choice. The booze flowed. The food was fine by available market standards. And the price was right. The head waiter, named Gallo (Italian for "Rooster") wore a tux at dinner. Every waiter wore a white jacket. A three-piece string orchestra played during lunch and dinner. Not only that, MacIlraith personally policed the place like Sherman Billingsley did at the Stork Club in midtown Manhattan.

I asked myself: This is war?

That is, until my first evening, when the German bombers returned and began unloading uncomfortably close to our domicile. I dove under a bed with Larry Newman, one of our INS correspondents, where we chatted for about an hour as bombs fell all around. Jimmy Kilgallen, our INS bureau chief, was nearby. Jimmy was as tough a news competitor as one would ever meet. He had earlier been the INS chief in Algiers. Jimmy's daughter, Dorothy, was to become one of our star reporters and columnists on the *New York Journal-American.*

I later learned that the safest place in the INS office was inside the bathtub. That was because flying shrapnel would not easily pierce it, and if the floor collapsed the bathtub made for a safer descent than a free fall. But somebody always seemed to beat me there.

I developed an affection for the Terminus. If you died under the command of Lieutenant MacIlraith, you did so clean-shaven and well-fed. Thank you, MacIlraith, wherever you may be.

On May 10 I went up by jeep, with Larry Newman, to the U.S. Fifth Army on the Garigliano front. The stone marker at the side of the road read 160 kilometers to Rome. We arrived at the town of Minturno, perched atop a hill overlooking the Gulf of Gaeta. Minturno was about 1,000 yards from German lines. The Germans were dug in trying to hold back the American advance. Fortunately, there was no fighting or shelling at the time, but our GIs were using machines to belch cottony, thick smoke across the hills. We could not see more than 200 yards ahead. They were apparently setting down the dense, white screen in preparation for an attack.

We held a village and the first ridge around Minturno. The Germans stood on higher ground on three sides beyond us. The GIs had dug shelters into the hillside. They also lined both sides of the road into the village and Minturno with slit trenches, surrounded by rocks and sandbags. To protect themselves from German shelling, they lived literally like animals in a cage.

I had a very eerie feeling watching the smoke thicken and envelop us. We left our jeep and climbed a road to a village below Minturno. Half the buildings in the village had been badly hit. Officers and troops occupied those that stood and appeared safe. Minturno rose above us. It had been shot to hell. The only thing standing was a big medieval castle that was heavily pockmarked from mortars and machine-gun fire.

We finally made it to the command post in the village. Lieutenant Colonel Raymond E. Kendall was in charge. With few words, he had us follow a staff officer outside, one by one, ten yards apart. We hugged the walls of buildings and headed up the hill. Finally, huffing and puffing, we arrived at our destination. We peered through slits in some walls and saw the German lines and their artillery. Suddenly I realized that we must have been under German observation for most of our walk up the hill.

We walked back to the CP, said our farewells, and trudged down the hill. We started our jeep and, as we began crossing the Garigliano River, the Germans and Americans started shelling one another. We gunned out of there. My heart was beating ninety-five miles an hour until we were well out of range.

Stars and Stripes had a story on Minturno the following day. It was headlined: "No Excitement at Minturno Front." It just goes to show that you can't believe anything you read in the papers.

A week later, *Journal-American* artist Burris Jenkins and I hooked up with the British Eighth Army on the Monte Cassino front. On the road to Cassino, we picked up a pleasant-looking U.S. Air Force lieutenant. We introduced ourselves, and he said his name was Blank—Jonas L., from Washington, D.C. Lieutenant Blank was a recent graduate of West Point, but found himself piloting Flying Fortresses. He had thirteen bombing missions to his credit. Blank had seen the war from a distance. Now, he told us, he wanted to see it firsthand on the ground.

We drove to the headquarters of Polish troops. They had advanced on our right flank. At that moment they were cutting around to the left on heights behind the monastery. A force of British troops had already crossed the Rapido River on our left flank. They were advancing up the Liri Valley. If the English were able to join up with the Poles on Highway 6 behind Cassino, the town would be encircled and all roads of retreat would be cut off to the German defenders.

We stopped our jeep on a high, winding, mountain road about three miles from Cassino. All of us were covered with dust, looking as if we were part of the road. Our hair felt like wire wool. Our noses, mouths, and lungs were parched. A ridge rose ahead. It was completely surrounded by flat land. A mountain, enveloped in thick dust and smoke, loomed beyond the ridge. The town of Cassino sat at the foot of the mountain. Monte Cassino itself is called Monastery Hill. Monte Trocchio is nearby.

British guns were barking below us like a pack of deep-throated animals closing in for the kill. The scene was bathed in haze—with dust and smoke spread like a light fog to cover the movement of troops below. Big guns boomed. From a distance, the scene was like some Hollywood spectacle rather than the grim reality of men at war.

We spent an hour with a battery of British artillerymen. They were firing their biggest guns—American 240-mm howitzers with extra-large powder charges. Other batteries were firing all around us: 105s, 155s, and English 25-pounders. Literally hundreds of guns of all sizes were roaring at the same time. The din was terrific and it wouldn't stop. Incoming German shells whistled from every direction. Our outgoing shells rent the air, creating a peculiar whirring noise as they began streaking toward Monte Cassino.

Burris Jenkins was busy sketching the artillery crews at work. Lieutenant Blank, grinning, was totally immersed in the action. I sat there with fingers in my ears, making mental notes for a story. Finally, our heads pounding, we turned our jeep around and drove back to a press billet so I could file my story and Burris could send his sketches to the *Journal-American*.

Believe me, I never returned to Cassino. I had the feeling that I might never hear again. My whole body was shaking from the screams of the shells. And, over and over again, I saw the grinning face of Lieutenant Blank.

The historic Benedictine abbey, dated from A.D. 529, was later demolished by Allied bombing. The British became convinced that the Germans had been using it as a base. General Clark had refused to shell or bomb the monastery. But British Field Marshal Sir Harold Alexander, in charge of the overall area, decided to bomb the abbey after U.S. General Ira Eaker flew over it in an observation plane and reported seeing German troops inside the monastery. Eaker was commander of Allied air forces. The Allies warned everyone inside the monastery to leave. Then 250 bombers dropped 600 tons of explosives on it. Eaker had been mistaken. There had been no German troops inside—but they quickly assumed defensive positions in the ruins of the abbey. After more prolonged violent combat on all sides, the Poles finally captured Monte Cassino on May 18 with the help of Indian mountain troops under the British. Despite the heavy bombing and shelling, most of the abbey's treasures were saved. Some had been evacuated earlier.

On June 4, 1944, the U.S. Fifth Army liberated Rome. I was sorry not to be there. I had flown back to London a couple of days earlier because of scuttlebutt that the Allied invasion of France was imminent. Two days later, on June 6, the invasion was launched. I was too late to be among the first correspondents ashore. Reporters had already been assigned to these units. However, I knew where I wanted to go—with Patton—and his Third Army had not yet kicked off.

The Allies had mustered nearly 2.9 million soldiers, sailors, and airmen for the momentous day. They had 11,000 aircraft and an armada of perhaps 7,000 to 8,000 vessels. These ranged from battleships and troop transports to landing craft and speedy patrol boats. On D-day, some 5,000 ships, 2,000 aircraft, and 23,000 paratroopers left for the French coast. Assault troops and commandos followed. About 175,000 men and 20,000 vehicles of all types landed during the first two days of the invasion.

On the big day, I was with the U.S. Ninth Troop Carrier Command in the English countryside. Two outer rows of transport planes were crammed with paratroopers. The inside rows were filled with gliders, which, in turn, were packed with more troops and equipment. The transports and planes towing scores of gliders took off in a deafening roar and soared out of sight. In a hushed tone a voice next to me said, "Goodbye, Johnny, take care of yourself." The planes had already melted into the silvery sky.

The Allies landed on or near five beaches. British airborne troops struck near the Orne River on the left, or east, flank. The Canadians hit on the second beach, named "Juno," about five miles west near the resort town of Courcelles. Somewhat farther west, in operation "Gold," the British landed near the small town of Arromanches. The Americans were to take "Omaha" beach to the right, near the French villages of Vierville and St. Laurent. Finally, the American paratroopers assaulted the western end of the invasion line at "Utah," near the town of Sainte-Mère-Église. Diversionary raids and airborne landings behind their lines caused the Germans considerable confusion.

Unfortunately, the gliders and their forces suffered heavy losses. The Germans had cut off trees, leaving stumps that tore the wings off many gliders, hurling them in sharp, deathly thrusts into the ground.

All the forces stormed ashore and secured their beaches except the U.S. First Division at Omaha. The first American assault waves were hit hard by German artillery and other fire. The Americans suffered heavy losses before a Ranger battalion climbed sheer cliffs and secured the point of the heaviest German firing. Some 2,000 Americans were killed or wounded, but the GIs held the beach and finally drove the Germans back. The Allies then began smashing ahead.

Three days later, I managed to catch a ride on a DC-3 medical evacuation plane that crossed the channel to pick up wounded. We landed near the town of Isigny. It was a few miles inland from Omaha beach, slightly east of the port of Cherbourg, near St. Lo. I spoke with as many officers and men as I could during the hour or so on the ground. Before takeoff, I interviewed French farmers and dairymen in the area. Despite the long German occupation, they seemed to be well off. As a matter of fact, I bought cheese from them to carry back to friends in England who were starved for the stuff.

I felt lucky because Patton and his Third Army were still sitting tight. Eisenhower was using him as a decoy because the Germans feared Patton more than any other Allied field commander. They expected him to lead the invasion. Ike and others felt that German spies may have been watching George's ivory-handled guns.

On June 13 Patton was still in England, so I went into the crowded briefing room of an American B-26 Marauder base that day. Around me were about 200 of what seemed to be the youngest American kids that I had seen in a long time. They were pilots, navigators, bombardiers, gunners, engineers, radiomen. And they needed to get all of us newsmen in the air, fight, and return.

The mission was to take us about sixty miles into France. The briefing officer reported low clouds. He said we would probably have to bomb from about 2,000 feet. The crews whistled in surprise. They were used to dropping their loads from 10,000 to 12,000 feet. One group of eighteen planes was to bomb the town—the name was censored, and I cannot recall it—while the other would strike a nearby railroad bridge. The briefing closed with pilots asking about German flak. The briefer had no information on it. He closed the meeting curtly, "You have six minutes to get to your planes."

Major Clayton Smith, one of the information officers, introduced me to Lieutenant Paul F. Cottingham, of Greenville, South Carolina. Smith said, "He's one of our veterans, with fifty-seven missions, and leading the high flight. You'll ride with him as co-pilot." I had already looped a Mae West life vest over my head. Then I climbed into the bulk harness of a parachute.

Cottingham wore a small, fur-lined cap beneath a GI helmet. He said nonchalantly, "There will be a flak suit for you on the plane." The flak suit is like a bulletproof vest, only bigger and bulkier. It slips over your head, comes down to the waist at the back, and extends down between the legs in front. It weighs about sixty pounds.

We jumped into a jeep and were whisked to the perimeter of the runway, where Lieutenant Cottingham's plane was waiting. We hopped out of the jeep. I was scared, but my mind raced ahead. I noticed the bomb bay door. If we got hit there before dropping our load, it would probably be curtains for all of us. If the bomber managed to remain airborne, some of us might be able to bail out. That would mean we would be prisoners of war for the rest of the conflict.

Other crew members were standing by the plane. No time for introductions. We climbed through the hole just aft of the nose. Cottingham and bombardier Lieutenant Thomas Shirley, of Louisville, Louisiana, got into the pilots' seats. The other crew got into their positions. I sat back in the radio compartment. The engines had already been warmed up. I put on the flak armor. Within two minutes we were churning down the runway. With the bomb load, the ship now weighed about 40,000 pounds. Somehow, since the takeoff seemed no different from any others I had ever made, I was no longer scared.

We lifted off and, for the next twenty minutes, circled the field to gain altitude and position ourselves in attack formation. Bombardier Shirley took his bombsight and crawled through the small door directly in front of the co-pilot's seat, into the nose. Cottingham motioned me to move in as co-pilot.

I noticed that the wings of the planes on either side of us were no more than thirty feet from ours. We were over the channel shortly. I was dumbstruck at the sight of hundreds of Allied ships coming and going from French ports. We flew over a long convoy of LSTs (Landing Ship Tanks) loaded with escorting destroyers and minesweepers. Their white wakes showed they were zigzagging. As we crossed the French coast, hundreds of additional ships were being unloaded at various ports. Red Cross tents seemed to be everywhere. The Cherbourg peninsula jutted out to our right. The town of Caen was off to our left. I spotted our guys constructing a new airfield.

We were soon over enemy territory. Friendly fighters flew overhead, looking for trouble. There was absolutely no traffic on the roads. The countryside looked like England except for the roofs of houses. Instead of being red or thatched, like the English, most French roofs were covered with blue stone or slate.

Thick clouds kept forcing us lower. We were now at only 2,500 feet. Cottingham told all of us to put on our helmets. I followed the flight formations above and ahead of us. Allied planes had three white and two black stripes painted around their bellies and across their wings. Finally, through the earphones, I heard the bombardier call out, "There it is, up ahead!"

A bolt of cool air suddenly swished through the ship. The bomb bay doors were open. Tracers streaked up at the bombers ahead. I stood up to get a better view. One of the planes in front suddenly turned from the formation. Cottingham said, "There goes Number Six. It has a hole through the wing." Number Six was still under control and would try to fly back to England.

I watched the B-26s ahead. They released their bombs over the town, and turned slowly away from the target. Shirley said over our intercom radio, "Hold her as she goes." Our ship suddenly jumped. Shirley spoke the fateful words, "Bombs away!" We banked steeply to the left behind our lead planes.

As we circled, I looked back at the town. Three columns of black smoke, one from each flight group, billowed up from its center. I found it hard to believe that we had just dropped tons of deathly bombs on humans living near our factory targets.

The bombardier's voice broke the silence. "I don't think all the bombs got away."

Cottingham asked, "How many are left?"

A voice said, "Four are still there."

Shirley suddenly said to the pilot, "Head a little to the right. I'll drop them on that bridge."

I kept watching the bombs in the bay until they dropped into space. The bomb doors creaked closed. We banked to the left and Cottingham gunned the engines so that we would catch up with our formation. Flak suddenly began exploding all around us. A bomber directly in front of us was hit, and its engine belched black smoke. But it was flyable. All of us returned safely to our English base.

As I got out of the plane I felt as if I had just climbed to the summit of a mountain. It was a kind of exhilaration that I had never felt in my life. I shook hands with the crew and said, "Let's do it again!"

They looked at me as if I were crazy.

On July 20 Burris Jenkins, Jr., the *Journal-American* artist, and I had the chance to fly across to Normandy and we took it. We landed in a Douglas transport at Isigny, the same airstrip where I had come just after D-day. Stretchers filled with wounded were already lined up so the injured could be placed quickly and more easily aboard the plane. A three-story house near the water's edge was being used as press billets, so we stowed our gear there. We finally found a dirty room under the roof and rustled up sleeping bags. Four newsmen were sleeping in each room. There was one bathroom in the place. If you wanted to shave, you got a helmutful of hot water from a large kettle over a wood fire in the garden. A shower? Forget it.

We got a jeep and set out for the city of Caen, which had fallen to the British the day before. Our first stop on the road was the historic town of Bayeux. It had somehow escaped the ravages of the fighting. The cathedral, one of the finest in France, was still standing. The famous Bayeux Tapestry, recording William the Conquerer's invasion of England, was preserved as beautifully as ever.

Caen is about fifteen miles from Bayeux. The road traffic was heavy, but thinned out as we got closer to the front. The wrecks of burnt tanks and other vehicles were scattered off the road. Artillery boomed over our heads. The front, parallel to the road, was off to our right. All the hangers at the big airdrome of Carpiquet, about a mile to our right, had been demolished. We reached the outskirts of Caen and were told the Germans were just across the river. We could proceed as far as the main square.

The town was pretty well banged up. Allied bombers had hit it on D-day and the RAF struck again later. The main square was oddly quiet. There were no military trucks or men there. Townsfolk walked about calmly. We parked our jeep in the square. I struck up a conversation with an English-speaking French youngster who was wearing a helmet painted white. He said that the last Germans had "run out yesterday."

We asked him about the Germans. He replied, "They are good soldiers but, oh, what thieves!"

He explained that, as their bug-out began, the Germans took everything they could carry, especially food and wine.The youngster pointed out that the Germans had occupied this area of France by simply walking in. They had not fired a shot. There was no damage or fighting until the Allies came. The boy's face had a quizzical look as he spoke. I was trying to read his thoughts. Then he spoke some of the most touching words I heard in the entire war, "But I want you to know that you are welcome."

We returned to Caen several times during our hops around the front. One time, we arrived shortly after the Germans had shelled St. Étienne Cathedral. Hundreds had taken shelter there. Eleven were killed.

Jenkins began drawing sketches of the utter confusion. A British loud-speaker told the populace to line up with all the belongings they could carry. They would be transported in trucks away from the city.

A lovely old lady came up to me and started speaking in English. Without any particular show of animosity, she said that her husband and daughter-in-law had been killed in the family home by a bomb from Allied planes on D-day. As she talked, German 88-mm shells began dropping on the outskirts of town. I nervously watched a dozen German planes circling the area.

We chatted a while longer about the misfortunes of war, and I began to leave. The old woman stood there, alone, with a suitcase and some bundles at her side. They were all she had left. She would go and live with a friend in Bayeux. We looked at one another. Without a word, I picked up her belongings and placed them in the back seat of the jeep, then took her hand and helped her inside. I drove her to Bayeux and said goodbye.

In the last week of July, Jenkins and I joined up with Patton and his Third Army at Nehou near the small Douve River. The area seemed little more than an apple orchard. The nearest city was St. Lo. Although Patton was now in the field, he and the Third were still under wraps. Patton had circled Avranches on his map as the spot for a breakout. It was a big, bold, red circle.

The general told his officers that they would strike fast. He wanted no complaints that anyone was being pushed too hard. Patton said the faster the troops moved, the more Germans they would kill—and fewer American soldiers would die. He then launched into some of his characteristic cussing that always made Bradley cringe. Some of Patton's staff later quoted him: "Some goddamn fool once said that flanks have got to be secure. Since then sonofabitches all over the globe have been guarding their flanks. I don't agree with that. My flanks are something for the enemy to worry about, not me. Before he finds out where my flanks are, I'll be cutting the bastard's throat."

Military historians now call it "The Breakout," though it was not known by that description then. But it did become the most lightning-fast Allied military advance of World War II. Ironically, perhaps only the Germans had a word that could adequately describe what Patton achieved: blitzkrieg.

We visited other American troops as fighting raged around St. Lo. GIs finally stormed into the city. We saw Americans interrogating German prisoners. Many were actually Polish, Russian, or Austrian. The Poles and Russians were apparently forced to serve the Nazis. These were kids; some seemed no more than fifteen. They claimed to be older, but that was clearly false. They kept saying how much better American K-rations were than their food.

We wanted to get some idea of how well the Allies were rebuilding French docks to supply their advancing troops. That was crucial because Patton planned to move rapidly. So we decided to visit the nearest large port, Cherbourg. Only we had no transportation; other newsmen had gotten their hands on our jeep. And that became a story in itself.

A friend told me of a little French car that the Germans had appropriated; it was now at an ordnance dump down the road from our billets. Burris and I hitchhiked there, explaining our predicament to the officer in charge. He turned "Nellie," as we christened her, over to us. Nellie was low-slung and well ventilated with bullet holes. The only piece of glass left in her was the windshield, which appeared ready to fall out of its shaky frame. The Germans had camouflaged her in faded colors. Some GI had painted white stars on the sides and hood.

Nellie was noisy and wobbly, and she certainly wasn't beautiful. We had to push her a half mile to get her started. But, once her engine turned over, she was gorgeous. The road to and from Cherbourg was filled with U.S. Army trucks. Children in the tiny French villages would give the V-for-victory sign to our truck drivers. Despite the new white stars, they recognized the car immediately and hissed derisively, "Boche!" (Germans!). It was a very uncomfortable ride, and I was happy to arrive in Cherbourg. I told Burris that if we used the car again we ought to paint it red, white, and blue.

The city itself was not much damaged, but the Germans had demolished several docks. Many Germans had surrendered. American GIs were now feverishly rebuilding the docks to accommodate more supply ships.

In late July the Germans launched a counterattack against St. Lo. Some forty to fifty Tiger tanks led the Nazi assault. They hoped to smash through to the sea and divide our forces. Burris and I went to the scene. Most of the German tanks were wiped out. Bodies of their men lay everywhere. We watched as U.S. Army trucks piled with dead Germans drove to makeshift graveyards.

I never got used to the war. It hardened my view of life and reality. Life became very basic—fear, courage, death, and perhaps a laugh or good time now and then. I never thought of money, my career, or something people called fame. Instead, I reflected mostly on decency and caring. The simplest virtues became the most important. I knew that I didn't want a slow, agonizing death. I wanted it quick if it came. When all was said and done, all I hoped for was that my father and family would say I had done my best.

We returned by plane to London. The U.S. military had to cut orders so that I would be formally assigned to Patton. It was terrible timing because the Third Army was made operational on August 1 and already had struck hard at the Germans. I was not able to get back to the front until August 13.

As Patton actually took command in the field, he was wearing three hats—commanding general of the Third Army, deputy commander of the First Army, and "supervisor" of VIII Corps, which was commanded by another general. Patton's troops immediately captured Avranches. The whole Third Army began squeezing through Avranches and fanning out across Brittany. Patton's rampaging forces struck east to take Rennes. GIs and their big tanks were storming unchecked toward Vannes. They were now on a mad dash across Brittany. Patton seemed to be everywhere. Hitler and the German high command still were unsure as to where Patton was precisely. Until he hit again somewhere else.

On my return to the front, I arrived at Patton headquarters in St. Lo. The city had been almost razed. I had not seen so much destruction since Cassino. Several correspondents teamed up and we got a jeep to drive up through the city of Rennes. We turned north there toward St. Malo. The Germans were still fighting there, so we advanced only to an artillery observation point in a four-story building. The town was engulfed in our shells and the Germans' return fire. GIs radioed back that they were on the outskirts of the city. Fighting was house to house and very tough. We turned back to file our stories, but stopped for a bite of dinner at Mont St. Michel.

The city was dominated by a 600-foot spire towering above beautiful Gothic churches. The only access to Mont St. Michel was by a narrow causeway that was inundated at high tide. We had a delicious French supper—vegetable soup, a fluffy omelette as only the French can make them, veal, mashed potatoes, string beans and, of course, wine. Regretfully, we had to rise from the table and drive back to press headquarters. After filing my story to New York, I got into my cold sleeping bag and dreamed about hot French food.

A few days later I met Patton. His command post was in a tent outside Vire, twenty-one miles from St. Lo, as elements of the Third Army battled for the town. It was one of the most memorable moments of my life. We simply shook hands, but I felt instinctively that this was a great man. He was the only individual I ever met in my life who reminded me of my father. There was an aura about him, a quiet poise, a self-confidence that radiated from his face and body. Yet we were very different men. I prized gentility—and that was a luxury Patton could not afford.

By August 19 the first units of Patton's Third Army had reached the Seine. That night his U.S. Seventy-ninth Division became the first Allied troops to cross the river below Paris. I was with Patton as his forces converged both north and south of the City of Light. The Allies had the city in a pincer movement.

I noticed that, perhaps indicative of their state of mind, the Germans took more and more to broadcasting their song, "Lilli Marlene." "Lilli

Marlene" seems to be a simple song, but it has a touch of deep irony in it. The first verse goes: "Underneath the lanterns, by the barracks square, I used to meet Marlene, and she was young and fair." All simple enough. The irony is, however, that the words following are quite cynical. Marlene first settles for the stripes of enlisted men. She moves up to the shoulder bars of officers. Finally, she is at the side of a brigadier general. The song rings of unrequited love. Any soldier of any army in the field understands its lonely lament. Frankly, I preferred the Australians' "Waltzing Matilda" or the Irish "Tipperary." The moody loneliness of "Lilli Marlene" seemed, however, to reflect a growing pessimism among the German military. I saw it as an omen of their impending disaster.

Another sign of things to come suddenly burst on the scene. General Charles de Gaulle, leader of the Free French resistance in England and later in North Africa, arrived in Ramboulliet, a small town about twenty miles southwest of Paris, on August 22. The choice of Ramboulliet was no accident. Its large château had become the customary country home of the French president.

Few newsmen covering the war believed the proud Frenchman would allow the advancing Americans or British to liberate Paris. He was determined, American correspondents were convinced, to lead a French Army march into the capital and hail the glory of France. I rushed from Patton and the Third Army, thirty miles from Paris at Mantes-la-jolie, to Ramboulliet.

I was lucky to get a room at the town's only hotel. The place was packed with other news correspondents from around the world. After checking in, I went to the bar to catch up on the latest scuttlebutt. Indeed, the Allies would march on Paris momentarily.

I had been there about twenty minutes when I glimpsed this GI courier out of the corner of my eye. The youngster, an Army private about nineteen years old, carried a message in his left hand. He stood perplexed at the door of the bar, looking cautiously around the room. The young man seemed lost, unsure about what to do or say. He suddenly discovered his voice: "Who's the officer in charge of this press billet?"

Hands lifted at the bar, but only those holding drinks. No one turned or answered. This was no press billet, although the hotel was crowded with war correspondents. I and other newsmen had left units because we believed de Gaulle would insist on capturing Paris, and we planned to accompany the French. Word was the operation would kick off the following day, August 24, 1944. It would be the biggest Allied victory since the Normandy invasion less than three months before.

A loud voice suddenly boomed, "I'm in charge!"

The private, a scared, skinny, straw-haired kid, walked up, saluted, and handed the bearded officer a sealed envelope. The officer signed for the message and the courier left.

Only the man was not an officer. He was dressed as one, but without the insignia of rank. He was actually a civilian war correspondent. Newsmen held a simulated rank of captain, primarily to be treated as such in the event they were taken prisoner. They also were treated as officers by the military to facilitate logistics—food, lodging, and travel. In real military terms, however, reporters had no rank. They were as much civilians as a Red Cross girl passing out coffee and doughnuts.

I walked over to the correspondent and quietly said, "You shouldn't have done that. You're not in charge."

He looked up from the message, glared at me, and replied loudly, "Who says I'm not?"

With that burst, the newsmen at the bar suddenly stopped talking and drinking. This man was the head rooster and everyone knew it. When he spoke people stood at attention. He was the Press Papa—Eisenhower, Bradley, Patton, and Montgomery rolled into one.

My voice was low. "You shouldn't because you could get that kid in trouble. He's a soldier, entrusted with a message. He clearly said it was for the officer in charge—which you ain't."

The correspondent's face reddened. He was irritated and asked again, "Who says I'm not?"

I replied, "I say you're not. You're a civilian. You're not an officer."

The big guy responded, "I AM in charge of this group. Do you want to see my credentials?"

"Yes," I said.

The correspondent was furious. Someone had challenged him. His fellow newsmen watched intently. I could see an angry fire rise in his eyes. He reached into the left breast pocket of his shirt with his right hand. My eyes were drawn there. Suddenly, like a lightning bolt, his left fist smashed into the bones of my right cheek. My head was on fire, and I fell to the floor.

I lay on the floor shaking my head. The room was spinning. I tried to rise, but the fire in my head had become a patch of smoke. I looked and saw Ernest Hemingway dimly above me. He folded the message from the courier, placed it in an inside pocket, slugged down the last of his drink, and swaggered out of the bar like a four-star general.

I was still shaking off the lightning left. I could hear a high-pitched question from a newsman at the bar: Was it a sucker punch? A babble of voices followed. A debate about the punch had begun. Correspondents called for more drinks to fortify the argument. Thoughts of conquering Paris were momentarily postponed.

None of us knew that Field Marshal Montgomery had been busy for some time behind the scenes. As commander of the forces merging on Paris, he noted to Bradley on August 20 that Patton was moving rapidly and irresistibly toward the capital. Montgomery further told Bradley that Patton should capture Paris when the Third Army commander felt it suitable. When I discovered this later, I swallowed all of the tough things that I had ever thought or said of Monty. He had promised Paris to Patton in a face-to-face talk they had had earlier, and he made good on his word.

At first Eisenhower wanted to bypass Paris. He did not wish to tie down a lot of troops in the city and have the responsibility of feeding so many civilians. But the Parisians and de Gaulle had other ideas.

Eisenhower was deeply cognizant of the diplomatic consequences of who entered Paris first, so he appeared to hesitate publicly on a decision. Actually, Ike had convinced Bradley days earlier that Patton should not take Paris; a French division would. Bradley was none too keen on either Patton or Montgomery. Indeed, Bradley and Monty were to split irrevocably during the German counteroffensive in the Ardennes during December. And Bradley was concerned about what Patton might do next.

Later, Bradley chose General Jacques Leclerc's (his real name was Jacques-Philippe de Hauteclocque) French Second Division to capture the city. Bradley quoted Ike when he conveyed the news to Patton on August 19 as George reached the Seine. Bitterly disappointed, because he knew and loved France more than any other British or American military leader, Patton nevertheless cooled his heels. He never divulged any of this to us. Despite what many have said of him, Patton was an honorable gentleman and a soldier who respected orders.

The French behaved miserably in much of this. It was astonishing because the Allies were pouring out their blood to win territory and a war that France had lost. It was the Allies who were winning the war, but the French wanted a big slice of the credit. The French military wanted to reclaim their honor, if only in appearance.

Leclerc, who was serving under Patton, wrote him an unsigned letter on August 15. He threatened to resign and cause a major diplomatic incident unless he was permitted to go to Paris at once. That evening, in a face-to-face meeting, Patton told the Frenchman that, as far as he was concerned, Leclerc would have the honor of liberating Paris.

Patton's staff and other American officers who witnessed the meeting were furious. The staff said Leclerc was loud, ill-tempered, and mean-spirited. The Americans considered Leclerc one of the most insubordinate officers they had ever met. The Frenchman was contemptuous of them and treated Patton little better. "Old Blood and Guts" paid Leclerc little mind. His aims were ever on the offensive and grand in scope.

At dawn on August 23 the French Second Armored Division began its parade toward the capital. In case the French had to fight, the U.S. Fourth Infantry Division accompanied Leclerc. The French general was in constant contact with de Gaulle. He sent the Free French leader two armored cars, draped with the Tricolor, for his triumphal entry into Paris. De Gaulle must not, at all costs, enter the capital in a foreign vehicle, although the relatively small French forces had nothing but American and British equipment.

The French underground continued fighting in the city. In a rage, Hitler ordered German General Dietrich von Choltitz to sack and burn Paris. The German commander ignored the order. On August 23 at 10:00 P.M., the first tank from the Second French Armored Division rumbled up to the Hôtel de Ville in Paris. American troops also had entered the city. Leclerc and his main force did not enter the capital until 7:15 the following morning.

The BBC announced from London that the U.S. Third Army had liberated Paris. Patton must have smiled.

The Tricolor finally flew from the top of the Eiffel Tower shortly after noon on August 24. It was also raised at the Arc de Triomphe, above the tomb of France's Unknown Soldier, about an hour and a half later. Choltitz formally surrendered Paris to Leclerc at 3:00 P.M. on August 25. It had been raining and gloomy the two previous days. Now Paris basked in bright sun and a pure blue sky.

De Gaulle arrived in Paris and met Leclerc about an hour after the German surrender. Some American correspondents had followed him in jeeps from Ramboulliet into the city. Others had gone with Leclerc and the Americans. Our group entered Paris from the south through the Port d'Orleans up the Avenue Orleans.

The Parisians lined the wide boulevard and flowed into the streets. They were going absolutely crazy. Our jeeps were swamped in human traffic and we were often forced to halt. Women were kissing us wildly. Men handed us bottles of wine. The most reserved kissed us on both cheeks. Kids shook hands, waved, and smiled deliriously. Some wept as they sang the "Marseillaise." We were being overwhelmed in a sea of joyous humanity.

We arrived at Luxembourg Gardens, the famous Latin Quarter. A street battle raged ahead. We got out of our jeeps to take a look. American tanks, manned by French crews, blazed into buildings with 75-mm howitzers at point-blank range. German army snipers fired from windows above while French civilians returned the shots. I climbed to a nearby roof and saw a half-dozen fires blazing in different parts of the city.

We jumped into our jeeps and drove as far as the Eiffel Tower, where the French army was collecting German prisoners. Shooting continued on all sides of us. The correspondents had no guns, so we felt rather naked. Next we raced to de Gaulle's headquarters. Just as we arrived, sedans carrying German high-ranking officers were descending the ramp. Their vehicles were draped in white flags. French officers told us they were fanning out with written orders for officers at German strongpoints to cease fire.

French mobs soon surrounded the vehicles and, were it not for American GIs waving them back with Tommy guns, they would have lynched the Germans on the spot. We ducked into a little bistro and lapped up some wonderfully cold beer. More girls were kissing us, and the drinks were on the house. War is really hell at times!

We were dog-tired and decided to move on to press headquarters at the Place de l'Opera. We crossed the Seine on the Alexandre Bridge, and passed between two beautiful buildings surrounded by lovely gardens. We halted in the middle of the Champs Élysées to have a good look at the Arc de Triomphe. I got a terrific bang out of that view.

We drove through the Place de la Concorde, past the Crillon hotel. The entire square was littered with chunks of masonry, barbed wire, barricades, burned vehicles, oil spills, and blood. Some 10,000 German troops had surrendered. The crowds were hysterical.

At last we arrived at press headquarters. The day had overwhelmed us. It seemed almost like a dream. We sat down in exhausted euphoria and wrote our stories. Then our group drove to the Scribe hotel, where American newsmen had taken over.

I walked into the bar for a Scotch before going to bed. Hemingway was holding court. He spotted me and sidled over. He said, "I hear you told some people about the other night."

I replied, "Yes, but what's your point?"

"Well," Hemingway explained, "I'm not particularly proud of that sneak punch."

I responded, "I wish you would have thought of that sooner."

That closed the chat. We met at various times later during the war and even shared a few drinks. I never felt any rancor against Hemingway, just disappointment. To me, neither the incident nor Hemingway himself ever fit the popular legend. My view was that Hemingway was a pompous stuffed shirt. I would have taken our INS guys—Jimmy Kilgallen, Larry Newman, Frank Conniff, or Bob Considine—any day. They were regular guys, and could hold a drink.

On the sunny afternoon of August 26 we followed General de Gaulle on his triumphant parade through Paris. He marched behind three tanks and was followed by three others, with French troops bringing up the rear. The general laid a wreath on the grave of France's Unknown Soldier. He and his entourage then marched down the Champs Élysées to city hall, where he picked up keys to the city. De Gaulle said a few words there about victory. Throngs of Frenchmen shouted wildly. The French leader then got into an open car for the ride to Nôtre Dame Cathedral and a Mass of Celebration. I jumped into a U.S. Army Signal Corps truck right behind him. It proved to be a front-row seat as great throngs of French went wild with joy.

The square in front of the cathedral was mobbed with civilians, police, and tanks. De Gaulle's car stopped, and he began to get out. All hell then broke loose. It appeared that snipers were firing on the crowd near the church. Some men, women, and children fainted and then were trampled as a stampede stormed away from the cathedral. De Gaulle dashed into the church. I took cover against the side of our truck. The shooting lasted for about fifteen minutes, then quieted down. Meantime, I sat among a group of disabled war veterans, figuring the snipers would not fire on them. The religious service finished calmly.

I switched hotels, moving with some of the correspondents to the Ritz at the Place Vendôme. I knew the Ritz, since my father had brought us there several times. I couldn't help but think how different it had been back then. In those days I listened to Pop's lectures on masterpieces in quiet museums, churches, and palaces. Gourmet lunches and dinners followed. Now my head was filled with loud shells and screaming sirens warning of German attack planes. Believe me, I slept as soundly at the Ritz as if I had been at home in bed. The next morning I went to Sunday mass at Nôtre Dame and prayed for everyone I could think of.

After lunch I went over to Gestapo headquarters. The Germans had systematically burned all their records and destroyed anything of value. I managed to collect a pair of German handcuffs, a leather-braided whip, and an Ellery Queen mystery. I felt as if I had stared into the face of evil. The experience was eerie and deeply unsettling.

The boulevards were crowded with smiling strollers. Some of them told me they had been smiling since the Allies had landed at Normandy. It drove the Germans nuts.

I stayed on in Paris to write a few more stories, then returned to London for an update on the war. Meantime, Patton was striking forward again. His troops penetrated the German Siegfried Line on September 6. To that point in the war, the Third Army had liberated 41,000 square miles of German-held territory. The Americans had killed nearly 30,000 enemy troops, wounded about 86,000 others, and taken nearly 95,000 prisoners. The Third Army's morale had never soared higher.

On September 10 I was back in the field with Patton at the Moselle River in the northeast corner of France. The U.S. First, Third, and Seventh Armies penetrated Germany near Aachen and Trier. I stepped onto German soil for the first time in the war on September 12, crossing from Luxembourg into Trier. For the first time I felt that German defeat was inevitable and the war was coming to an end. The exhilaration was indescribable. Still, the Germans shelled us heavily.

At Trier I had a long talk with Patton. We sat alone on collapsible chairs outside the tent serving as his living quarters. We looked out on flat farm fields as evening began to fall. The general talked about the roads. He said they were critical to an armored man like himself who used heavy tanks to do much of his fighting. The wrong road could slow down and even wreck an advance if tanks ruined the surface and bottled up other tanks and vehicles behind them. He had to know those roads better than Caesar or Napoleon had because his was heavier equipment.

Patton talked of reading Caesar's *Gallic Wars*. He said the Roman leader was a big road builder because he considered movement and communications critical. Of course Caesar used rivers and other natural means of movement, but he often built his own roads to ensure progress and good communication. Patton said Caesar constructed them, if possible, on high land along the top of a ridge, where it would drain. The general leaned back in his chair and reflected: "A simple thing. Most Americans would never think about it. After all, if you want to build a road from one town to another, you do it in the straightest line possible. But they're not at war with tanks." The sky was illuminated with bursts of orange and billows of a bright, fierce yellow. It seemed a garish mixture blazing against the twilight.

Patton talked of Alexander the Great, Hannibal, Napoleon. He seemed to become a mystical figure, harkening back centuries. He *was* Alexander. He *was* Hannibal. He *was* Napoleon. It was Patton who had crossed the Alps with thousands of elephants. Patton who led his men to such distant lands. Patton who had driven across Russia. He was marching back through history and living it himself. He was there. His incarnation. His military mind. He was the ancient warrior god. He was not talking history. He *was* history.

As he finished I noticed those two revolvers of his. Ivory-handled, not pearl. Patton noticed my glance and said, "Yes, it's true. I did say it. Only St. Louis pimps wear pearl-handled guns."

Patton had created his own image—a figure who would push his men forward, men angry at some of his forced-march orders—and then make them laugh and carry on with his salty salutations. He was one of them, yet held himself out as an imperial leader. "Old blood and guts," some GIs described Patton. "Our blood and his guts."

Sure he was grandstanding. But it took some of the fear out of the minds and hearts of his men. Yeah, he was a warrior-mandarin. But he was also there on the rough roads and on the battlefield with them. Above all he was an American—to the core. Ike knew it. Montgomery sure did. And Hitler as well. George Patton's mission, as he saw it, was to save America. That was his destiny.

We moved inside the tent and had dinner. We chatted pleasantly over a wide range of subjects. I finally took leave to return to my billet. In going to sleep, I saw my father in the face of Patton. Two Americans, two patriots, two men of destiny. I don't believe they ever met, although Patton grew up in Pasadena, California. I closed my eyes with a smile. Of course, they had met. It was in one of Patton's other lives.

By mid-April the Third Army had virtually cut the Reich in two. Patton's two great moments were saving the U.S. First Army at the Battle of Bastogne in Luxembourg during the Battle of the Bulge, and his astonishing blitz through Germany and crossing the Rhine River.

In one of the most famous staff meetings of the war, Patton had told Eisenhower on December 17, 1944, that his men would be in Bastogne by Christmas. Some Allied officers snickered at the boast. This time, some thought, Patton would eat crow. It was an incredible pledge at a time when Ike did not know if MacAuliffe could hold the city.

Bastogne, a little market town, was strategically one of the most critical battles of the entire war. It was the key to all western movement and all German supplies. General Anthony MacAuliffe, a deputy to General Maxwell Taylor of the 101st Airborne, had replied, "Nuts!" when the Germans demanded his surrender at Bastogne. But it was Patton's Fourth Armored Division that rescued MacAuliffe and his men, and made his historic battle cry of "Nuts!" stick. George arrived on December 26, one day late on his promise.

There was never a dull moment with Patton, and his crossing the Rhine was no exception. On March 22 the Third Army began fording the river at Oppenheim, some ten miles above Mainz. Patton disclosed no plans to cross, nor had he ordered laying down any artillery. His idea was to beat Montgomery across without the field marshal's knowing about it. He did. Then, as a climax, Patton walked across a narrow bridge and pissed into the Rhine to let the Germans know his feelings. A couple of GI photographers recorded the historic moment.

Patton died after a U.S. military truck hit his sedan in Germany following the end of the war in Europe. His wife, Beatrice, had flown across the Atlantic to be with him during those final December days. As he lay dying in a hospital bed, not long after his sixtieth birthday, Patton quoted Seneca, the great Roman philosopher of the Stoic school: "Nothing is lost. All has gone before!"

He had fulfilled his destiny. And now he had gone to Valhalla to meet again with his old friends—Alexander the Great, Hannibal, Caesar, Napoleon, and other legendary military leaders.

Larry Newman, who had covered Patton with our INS for most of the war, had carried in his wallet a $250,000 check made out to the general. My father had offered it to Patton for his memoirs. For a man who was often described as a glory hound, Patton proved remarkably humble. He had no plans to write about himself and the war, so he turned us down. Other generals wrote the books.

I began spending much of my time with General Pete Quesada's 9th Tactical Air Force Command and hopped around among various infantry units. I interviewed General Bradley and other American generals—from Eisenhower to Carl A. Spaatz, Mark W. Clark, Ira C. Eaker, Courtney Hodges, Sandy Patch, Walter Bedell Smith, Quesada, and perhaps a few others.

I had a farewell interview with Eisenhower in Paris. I asked him about his plans after the war, whether he had any party affiliation and whether he might run for the presidency. The interview began innocently. I do not think either of us contemplated the tremendous reaction his answers would cause at home and around the world.

Ike said he really was not affiliated with either party. He added that the Democrats seemed strongly in power and were tightly organized. Therefore he did not foresee joining them in any presidential bid. However, they had sent friends to ask whether he might run. Ike was not sure whether the Democrats were really interested in him as a candidate or were sounding him out to prepare against his running for the White House as a Republican.

Eisenhower indicated for the first time publicly that GOP leaders had privately said they might draft him as their presidential nominee. When the headlines hit, Dolly Schiff, publisher of the *New York Post*, tried to deny that Ike had ever made those statements. She was wrong, but this was a clear indication that the Democrats were afraid of the general. Dolly was a very liberal Democrat and the *Post* of those days reflected that. Ike himself proved her fears were justified when he ran on the GOP ticket and defeated Democratic nominee Adlai Stevenson for the White House in 1952 and in 1956.

It is often said that having one true friend is a treasure. I was very fortunate and made three of the finest friends of my life during the war: Frank Conniff, who was to become my editorial assistant; Bob Considine, who would become one of the greatest reporters in the history of American journalism; and Larry Newman, who worked for us in New York after the war. Coniff and Considine were close pals of mine until their deaths. Newman, who now lives in Massachusetts, is still going strong. I think of Conniff, Considine, and Newman even today. And, like Patton meeting Caesar and the others, I hope to join them one day and talk about the war and a lot of other stories we covered.

When the last gun sounded for me in Europe, I had changed as a person in two ways. First, new values pointed me in a different career direction. I now wanted to cover news instead of selling advertising and doing the administrative work of a publisher. I returned as publisher of the *Journal-American,* but it was never the same. My mind was made up. I would switch to reporting when the opportunity arose.

Second, I wanted to simplify my life and outlook. Physical violence and I had met on the same turf, and I had somehow survived. The average guy—the soldier, flyer, or sailor I had met at the front—had grown immensely in stature in my eyes. The big names and stars that had cast such large shadows over my earlier life dimmed in importance. I wanted to be a street version of a good GI Joe.

I returned to London, said goodbye to old friends, and flew home. Home was not only New York; it was also San Simeon, where my father now lived and worked in one of the most extraordinary lifestyles in the world.

VII
HOLLYWOOD: MARION
AND THE STARS

I had hardly shaken hands with Toots Shor, the wisecracking merchant of double martinis and other such lethal weapons, when Tokyo threw in the towel. Toots, the wet nurse to many New York newsfolk, threw a V-J night bash whose tremors are still felt among Manhattan gin mills. Reporters who had covered the war in Europe cheered: Tojo and Hirohito knew we were coming!

Pop had left his wartime headquarters up at Wyntoon, near the California-Oregon border, to return to his beloved home at San Simeon. I wanted to see him more than anyone in the world, so I flew out to San Francisco and drove down to the ranch.

It was a warm meeting. Pop said I had written some pretty good stuff. I had become a real newspaperman in his eyes. Nothing in the world was more important to me than the old man's approval. I told him about the big changes in my life—that I was happier reporting and writing. I hoped to make a switch gradually from the administrative work of a publisher to the news side. He seemed pleased.

I returned to work in New York but promised to come back for his next birthday party. (I did.) Pop was famous for his birthday parties, which were always superspectacular—100 to 300 guests in a costume extravaganza. The festivities featured fabulous foods, champagne, a big-name orchestra, humorous skits, Hollywood's brightest stars and celebrities, as well as personal friends and some of his top executives. Guests came by private train to San Luis Obispo and were met by chauffeur-driven cars that took them to San Simeon. To anyone motoring up the coastal highway after dark, the illuminated hilltop seemed like a distant fairyland.

Steve Zegar, a local fellow, transported guests from San Luis Obispo to the castle. He started out with one taxi and later added a second-hand Cadillac. Eventually, Steve owned a fleet of limousines that picked up guests at any hour of the day or night on the hill at San Simeon or the railroad station. He had chauffeurs on call—local carpenters, farmers, and school kids who would jump from their work clothes into a business suit at a moment's notice. Steve made a comfortable living out of his enterprise and investments. To me he was as bright a star in San Simeon as any actor from Hollywood.

Usually spring was at its height by the time of the April 29 birthday bash, meaning shirt-sleeves during the day and a dinner jacket or wrap in the evening. I flew out from New York for these and some weekend parties over a span of about twenty years. The weekend get-togethers would usually have a dozen to twenty guests—fifty would be invited on some special occasion—but these gatherings were relatively sedate compared to the birthday bashes.

On all occasions the Casa Grande and its three satellite houses were ready for the arriving guests. Maids and valets greeted them—about thirty staff people were on duty for birthday blowouts, with half that for weekend parties—even at late hours.

The birthday party would not begin until the following evening. The guests did as they pleased during the day. Dress was casual. Breakfast would be served on the terrace or in the Refectory, from about eight o'clock until noon. Then many of us went riding, played tennis, or swam in one of the pools. Others explored the gardens, the zoo, and the grounds. My father wanted people to enjoy themselves. If he heard that someone rode early, then played tennis and swam, he was delighted. He liked to have people feel at ease. However, I doubt that any but a few of us felt truly at home.

Pop was a good conversationalist. He dutifully obeyed the first law of good talk: to listen carefully. He was soft-spoken and reflective when he did converse. The old man enjoyed discussing almost anything—movies, art, the flowers in the garden, horses, travel, history, whatever interested his guests. No subject was out of bounds with him except music and smutty jokes. And he rarely discussed politics.

About one o'clock, Pop and Marion would appear at a buffet lunch, which usually lasted until about three or three-thirty. After brunch, the old man played along with the rest of us. He loved riding and tennis and was rather good at them. He often invited tennis greats as guests—Bill Tilden, Helen Wills Moody, Alice Marble, and Fred Perry. Pop was a very good swimmer as well and often swam laps in one of the pools. Marion did no exercise of any kind. She enjoyed jigsaw puzzles for entertainment.

Evenings would begin with cocktails before dinner—whether it was a weekend party or a big birthday gala. Guests usually limited themselves to one drink. Pop did not like hard liquor or heavy drinking. He put the word out that no guests were to bring their own booze to the place. But some did and got drunk. He would have someone ask them to leave, and they would be driven to the train station at San Luis Obispo.

I remember a notable exception to this. On Pop's seventy-fifth birthday, Marion and Connie Talmadge, her actress friend, became a little tipsy. As the evening wore on they were getting loud and pretty funny. I could see both were carrying a load, but couldn't figure out where they were getting the stuff. Finally, after talking with Connie for a while, I learned they had a couple of bottles of gin stashed in a ladies room, and made regular trips there. I don't know how the old man could have missed their tipsiness, but he never said anything. Nor did I.

My father has sometimes been described as a teetotaler. That wasn't true except for the last decade or so of his life. He enjoyed German draft beer and a glass of wine now and then. In fact, he had a special cooler installed in the Refectory kitchen to keep draft beer cool.

Dinners at most weekend get-togethers began at eight-thirty in the great tapestry-hung hall of the Assembly Room. Guests would have a cocktail there. Conversation would inevitably turn to the six Flemish tapestries hanging from the walls—four of the sixteenth century and two of the seventeenth. They ranged up to nearly fifteen feet in height and twenty-four feet in width. The earlier four commemorate the conquests of Scipio Africanus. One of the later period extols the triumph of religion, while the other honors Neptune and Venus. After drinks we moved into the Refectory for dinner, about nine o'clock. Pop sat opposite Marion at the center of the long tables seating as many as fifty guests. Visitors rotated if they were staying more than one night, so they could sit closer to the center.

Pop used no tablecloth and set out condiments in their original bottles at these weekend dinners—from ketchup to pickles and Worcestershire sauce. He sometimes, though not always, used paper napkins. The ketchup bottle seemed totally miscast amid the splendor of great tapestries and chandeliers, antique furniture and silver candlesticks. But the old man had a reason; it reminded him of those early days when we first came to Camp Hill and lived in tents. (When we boys had wanted hot dogs, we also wanted mustard—plenty and fast. And pickles, and relish, and anything else that spiced things up. We poured and scooped out of the factory bottles as fast as two hands could cover a sandwich. There were no tablecloths. With all the furor, we were lucky the rickety tables managed to stay upright.) The ketchup bottle was a sentimental gesture that Pop didn't care to explain.

Pop had special food flown in for weekend guests: salmon from Alaska, extra-large shrimp and Cajun dishes from New Orleans, oysters and terrapin from Maryland. For a birthday blast, there was no telling how far and wide he would go in search of gourmet dishes.

At normal weekend get-togethers, Pop showed a pre-release or new movie after dinner in his ornate, damask-hung private theater. He usually brought along one of his dachshunds, which would sit on his lap or at his feet.

As much as I enjoyed them, I was sometimes ill at ease at these gatherings. I would think of my mother, who loved parties, and feel guilty that she wasn't there. Here I was enjoying myself in California, while Mom could be alone in New York. All those years that I went to San Simeon, I missed my mother there, as I do even now.

The annual birthday fiesta would be held on the back patio of Casa Grande, the only arrangement that could accommodate the large number of guests. The terraces and gardens were lit by electrified alabaster lamps that cast a soft light on the marble gods, shadowy walls, palms, flowers, and clipped hedges. The food at these outdoor birthday parties was served buffet-style, with champagne and selected wines. There were toasts to Pop's health. A three-tiered cake was wheeled out just before coffee was served, and he would cut it amid rounds of good wishes. If it looked like rain, he would cover the patio with a giant tent. The old man planned everything himself—to the last detail. People would beg us to be invited.

Sometimes, even those who never came would brag about all the fun they had had.

Each birthday celebration was a wide-open affair—impromptu speeches and various skits, usually hilarious. Later, there was dance music until about midnight. Pop always wanted to shoot off a colorful explosion of fireworks, but the ground was usually dry at that time of year and he was concerned about possible fires. The birthday parties called for original costumes, and these created great informality and a lot of humorous make-believe. Skits made fun of anyone and everyone. There was an endless array of food, plenty of chatter and gossip, hours of dancing and flirting, all accompanied by a big band playing the latest popular song hits. It all seemed like some spectacular movie scene.

A lot of Hollywood pretense and considerable commotion were created by the costumes at Pop's birthday parties. The old man once came as James Madison and, another time, as a cowboy. Would you believe that Clark Gable came as a Boy Scout? And Joan Crawford as Shirley Temple? Clark was no Boy Scout, and Joan was certainly no smiling little innocent. Charlie Chaplin did a good job as Napoleon, but Gary Cooper never quite made it as Fu Manchu. Norma Shearer easily personified Marie Antoinette, but Harpo Marx would never be Rasputin. Bette Davis was perfect as a bearded lady.

At one such shindig, guests were asked to dress in circus costumes. Our oldest brother, George, came as a clown and the rest of us as weight lifters. I once came as a sailor from the *H.M.S. Pinafore*. I always had a heck of a good time and would invite close friends like George "Rosie" Rosenberg to join in the fun.

My friendship with Rosie said a lot about me as a person. He was an unpretentious natural, a loyal friend and decent man blessed with great humor. We met when I was just a young fellow hanging around Los Angeles. Rosie's father was a tailor. The family lived in East L.A. and life was a daily struggle. The lovable little guy talked and wisecracked his way into the movie business and soon became a top talent agent. But he was always Rosie—bursting with humor about the happenings around Los Angeles. Pop liked him so much that he took Rosie with us on two tours of Europe. Rosie never forgot his father's hard work. He had an immense pride in his old man. His example increased my respect and admiration for my own father. Some of the so-called big shots would say to me: "Why did you invite Rosie? The guy used to deliver the suits that his father pressed. Ya know, his old man was only a tailor. And he's only a press agent." I used to reply, "He's my pal. And, besides, he's awfully good company."

Rosie was my friend. But actors were actors. I had only two real friends in Hollywood—Gable and Bing Crosby, both regular guys.

As the Hollywood crowd came and went, so did Pop's birthday parties. The theme for one celebration was a kids' party. Another featured the circus. The costumes for the Civil War party were a big hit. Cowboys and Indians were another show-stopper. So were his merry-go-round, gambling casino, and balloon parties.

The old man's eightieth birthday remembrance in 1943 was in stark contrast to all that had preceded it. All of us sons, our wives, and a few friends gathered at Wyntoon, where he had headquartered during World War II. I remember there were not many guests because the occasion was muted by the war. And Pop had passed a major milestone. I felt a certain sense of foreboding—that perhaps Pop was finally getting tired and wanted to spend more of his time at peace and in quiet reflection.

We toasted him and had some cake, but the swarm of guests, the frenzied pace, and blaring bands of earlier birthdays had passed into memory. I remember feeling very nostalgic at the time, and became sad when Pop rose and spoke: "I shall not pretend that I'm very happy about being eighty. I would happily exchange that marker for two lifetimes at forty. Just as a woman reaching forty would gladly exchange that milestone for two at twenty. Yet I am thankful and grateful that I find so much in life that is fresh, stimulating, and dear to me."

Today, because of television, people are much less impressed with celebrities. Back then, though, an actor or actress could enjoy enormous popular attention. Fan magazines thrived on every detail of a star's life. A golden, other-world aura surrounded Hollywood, as if it were full of gods and goddesses. The average American was in awe of the place.

Marion was the star of Pop's spectacles because most of the guests worked in the movies and were friends of hers: Charlie Chaplin, Douglas Fairbanks, Sr., Norma Shearer, Irving Thalberg, Jean Harlow, Mary Pickford, Rudolph Valentino, Anita Loos, Lillian Gish, Joan Crawford, Tyrone Power, Clark Gable, Lady Sylvia Ashley Fairbanks, Ronald Colman, Carole Lombard, Dick Powell, Vernon and Irene Castle. Pop loved to dance with Irene. Both were very graceful. The two would remain on the floor for an entire set, and were disappointed when the band rested.

Now most Americans know few of these names, but they represented the *Who's Who* of filmland in the old days. All of them came to the parties: Norma and Constance Talmadge, Gloria Swanson, W. C. Fields, the Marx brothers, Spencer Tracy, Myrna Loy, Lionel and John Barrymore, Charles Laughton, Loretta Young. Loretta and her two sisters were lovely persons. They were a very close family, and I have enjoyed their company and friendship much of my life.

King Vidor, Mervyn Le Roy, Raoul Walsh, Louis B. Mayer, Sam Goldwyn, Flo Ziegfeld, Jack and Harry Warner, Louella Parsons, Joel McCrea, Sonja Henie, Joan and Constance Bennett, Claudette Colbert, Robert Montgomery, Dolores Del Rio, Ginger Rogers, Fred Astaire, Mary Astor, Leslie Howard, Errol Flynn, Bing Crosby, George Jessel, Merle Oberon, David Niven, Henry Fonda, Pat O'Brien, Jimmy Stewart, Ava Gardner, and Gary Cooper.

Cooper was a real character at times. He drove his own car to San Simeon and used to play games with the gate leading up to the complex. About twenty feet before a car came to the closed gate, its front wheels would hit a mechanical metal device and the gate would spring open. As the driver continued on, his front wheels would cross another device and the gate would roll closed.

Cooper would try to open the gate by backing up and rolling his rear wheels over the device. He tried it over and over during different visits, and couldn't figure out why the gate wouldn't swing back. He got so mad one day that he jumped out of his car, opened the trunk, pulled out a rifle, and began shooting at pelicans hundreds of yards down on the beach. He just kept pumping away and couldn't hit a damn thing. I told him the old man loved birds and would be pretty sore if he killed any. Cooper replied: "Hell, I'm not trying to kill anything. I'm a mechanical nut, and I'm so damn frustrated that I'm working up to shooting myself!"

I had seen and known so many Hollywood big shots that I made clear distinctions among them. Some, like Errol Flynn and John Barrymore, were in love with themselves. Others, such as Sonja Henie and Sylvia Ashley Fairbanks, were snobs. Still others, like Connie Talmadge and Constance Bennett, were beautiful bores. Since I wasn't in the movie business, I didn't have to cultivate a producer or director. I looked for people like Rosie and chose friends slowly and carefully. I've tried all my life to be faithful to friends. But I always asked two things in return—loyalty and truthfulness. I did my level best to maintain both.

I felt a special loyalty toward certain people in Hollywood. Crosby was one. When he died, I truly grieved. Bing may have been a big singer, but he was no show-off. He was a laid-back, quiet guy, more of an introvert. I was sitting in New York and asking myself: Is there anything I can do for Bing or his family now? I thought all day and finally came up with an idea. Bing loved sports, and what greater event was there than a World Series game? The series was being played up in the Bronx at Yankee Stadium. Why not play one of Bing's hits before a game? That was something he would have liked a lot. And many of us would have wanted to have that as a last memory of him.

I knew that Bing had recorded "God Bless America" some years before. So I searched around Manhattan and finally found the record. I called the Yankee brass and sent it up to the stadium. They played it before one of the games, and people were genuinely moved. I didn't want anyone to know I had anything to do with it, and was grateful that my name was never mentioned. Bing would have done the same kind of thing for another guy. He was a class act, and my friend—always.

Gable was a good friend because, off screen, he was such an unassuming guy. He liked animals, especially horses; loved the land and the outdoors, especially hunting, fishing, and camping. Clark preferred ranch clothes and an informal life. He was, by the way, a crack shot. Perhaps that was why he liked hunting so much. He would invite me out to his ranch, and we would go riding.

In Hollywood Gable was called "The King." Clark disliked the term and would cuss when he heard it: "What bullshit! Besides, I've got big ears!" By box office measurements, however, he stood taller in his heyday than anyone. He made about sixty movies, which reportedly grossed nearly $800 million in those years (that would be in the billions today). About 2 billion tickets to his movies were sold during his long reign, and many millions of new fans have now seen him in television and other reruns.

I remember Clark's wedding to Kay Spreckels. It was his fifth marriage, and he was still childless although headed for sixty. Kay, a lovely woman who had known Clark many years, became pregnant. Gable was so happy that he became a blessed but blooming idiot; he was busting out all over with pride and joy. But he never saw his son. Clark died on November

16, 1960. The death of perhaps no other entertainer—with the exceptions of Will Rogers and Rudolph Valentino—so stunned and moved the American people. His son, John, was born in March 1961. The happy occasion of the birth was one of the saddest days of my life. I have never been a formally religious person, but I said a private prayer for Clark that day. He would have preferred it that way because it was without pretense.

Of all the people I knew around Hollywood, more questions were asked me about Howard Hughes than anyone else. Is he a genius? Is he crazy? Is he a health nut? Is he really a recluse?

In those early days, when we were both new to Hollywood, Howard was far from the recluse he later became. I not only liked but admired Howard and don't care who knows it. We were car and airplane buffs together for many years. He owned various planes and I had a small Privateer and later an Aeronica. He was always a straight guy with me. He was shy and guarded his privacy, but a lot of Hollywood people did. With all the gossip in that town it was a prudent thing to do. In the final analysis, Howard was my friend, period.

I remember him not for all the scatterbrained starlets we took out together but for three amusing incidents—two of them in Palm Springs, California. The first occurred after we had flown down there to meet two gorgeous girls. We were staying in a motel that had just opened. Time was running late before our dinner date, but Howard remained in the shower for a long time. I called to him several times. I was getting only a few groans from him so I marched into the bathroom and hollered into the shower, "Howard, are you going or not?"

He stuck his head out the door and his head and face were covered with black, oily, gooey stuff. He looked like a character in a monster movie.

"What the hell is that?" I yelled.

He squinted and said, "It's oil. I turned on the water and got oil."

I started laughing and couldn't stop. Finally, I said, "Only you, Howard, you rich bastard, could look for water and strike oil!"

We later entertained the girls telling them how Howard struck oil.

Another time, I was to fly down to Palm Springs with a couple of girls and meet Howard. I was running late and so were the girls. We were several hours behind schedule, and Howard got antsy and phoned me at San Simeon. He asked for Mr. Hearst, who finally responded. Howard asked, "Where the hell are you? Do you have the girls?"

Of course Hughes didn't know that my father had picked up the phone. Pop, who enjoyed a joke, responded, "No, I don't have the girls."

"Goddammit, what happened and where are you?" Howard asked.

"I'm here at San Simeon," Pop replied.

"Well, Bill, why the hell didn't you phone me?" Hughes asked.

"I didn't know you wanted girls," Pop chuckled.

Hughes blew his stack until Pop said, "Mr. Hughes, this is Bill's father. You obviously have the wrong Mr. Hearst. Sit tight. Knowing Bill, I expect he'll be there with the girls shortly. I wish I could be there with you!"

The final incident occurred while I was staying at the Beverly Hills Hotel on a business trip. I left a message telling Howard that I was in town, in case he would like to get together for lunch or a drink. He phoned me on New Year's eve.

"What are you doing tonight?" he asked plaintively.

I told him that Mike Romanoff had invited me to the New Year's party at his plush restaurant. He asked if he could go too and I told him it was no problem. Then, in a hushed voice, Howard said: "I'll meet you about nine o'clock tonight. Get your car and park in front of the hotel. I'll come by, driving a dark Chevy. I'll flick my lights twice. If you see me, flick yours once. I'll keep going but you stay there. I'll drive around the block again to make sure no one is following me. I'll pass you again, but this time you follow me. I'll park a few blocks down, wherever I find a space. You wait behind me. I'll get out of my car and get in yours. As soon as I slip in, drive off. Got that?"

Of course I didn't have it. "What the hell is going on, Howard?" I asked.

He said, "I'll repeat the instructions." He did.

I thought I had it straight this time, but I was wondering if Howard was straight. It sounded more like he was losing his marbles.

Everything went according to plan. Howard hopped in my car and we drove over to Romanoff's, where the party was in full swing. I said to Hughes just before we went in, "Howard, are you okay?" He nodded. I took a deep breath and said, "Howard, let's keep it simple. I'll drive you home."

That was my first inkling that Howard was getting eccentric.

Howard began imagining dangers everywhere. I think it started with his deafness and physical pain from old plane crash injuries. He seemed to be hooked on prescription drugs and was only a ghost of his former six-foot four-inch frame. He lived in Beverly Hills, in a hideaway in the Bahamas, and later in a Las Vegas hotel penthouse surrounded by private guards.

He didn't communicate with me in the last years of his life. That was unlike him. I could count on Howard to pick up a phone at almost any hour or day and give me a jingle. We would shoot the breeze about old times and promise to get together. But he never did in those last stages of suffering. I presume he didn't care much about anything anymore. I would have liked to hear from him.

Howard died, an emaciated waste, on April 5, 1976, in a plane that was only some thirty minutes away from his old hometown of Houston. To me he was an introspective genius, a dreamer—the kid whose head was always in the clouds chasing rainbows. I was in New York when I heard the news. I remembered the words of Dorothy Parker at the death of F. Scott Fitzgerald: "The poor sonofabitch."

Hollywood was as full of different types as any city. Jack Warner was a fun guy. I liked him thoroughly. The studio chief could sit out on our castle terrace and zing humorous one-liners for an hour without ever repeating himself. One time we got on the subject of newspapermen and scriptwriters. Warner blurted, "They're all crazy egomaniacs still paying on their Underwoods!" At one of Pop's parties we were sitting back having a drink, eyeing the beautiful actresses. Suddenly, out of nowhere, Jack cracked, "Watch out for girls who wear sweaters!" Here he was, a top producer, yet Warner probably made more and funnier wisecracks than any comedian who worked for him. Jack was a natural comic.

So was Sam Goldwyn of MGM, although he didn't know it. I remember one time he had come to San Simeon by private yacht with his wife and a party of friends. He told me that they were going off on a trip somewhere. I mentioned this to my father, and we accompanied Goldwyn and his friends down to the pier where the yacht was tied up. As the boat began chugging away from shore, Sam waved and shouted back to us, "Bon voyage! Bon voyage!" Pop and I smiled at that one.

Actors Cary Grant and David Niven also had great senses of humor. Grant, who had visited San Simeon often, once told me, "I've slept in every bed in this place. Alone, of course, except for that bottle of booze that your father told me not to bring!"

Niven also was a castle old-timer. He made himself completely at home, "I love this place. It beats hell out of those bloodcurdling New York hotel prices!" No one was more enthralled with the art and beauty of San Simeon than Niven. He was constantly studying the paintings, tapestries, woodwork, and other art. David loved friends and good food. A lot of actresses, including Mae West, used to study Niven's proper English ways, making him very uncomfortable. When he reached the end of his patience, Niven would blurt, "And I eat all my veggies, too."

He came to stay with us for a weekend at San Simeon after Pop died. David enjoyed painting and did a large oil for us of San Simeon, looking from the pergola to the hilltop. It was reminiscent of the French Impressionists. Niven later said he did it with "French tongue in cheek." He signed it "de Niven." The painting still hangs in our library. David, a cherished friend, was without doubt the best storyteller I ever met.

No visit to the castle created greater Hollywood interest and commotion than the arrival of British playwright George Bernard Shaw in the spring of 1933. The old man invited the literary lion and his wife to San Simeon as soon as he heard of Shaw's plans to visit the United States. The cream of Hollywood came up on a private train with Shaw for the luncheon. Everyone seemed in awe of him. I wasn't there but was told the caustic writer proceeded to insult actress Ann Harding, who rushed out of the reception and burst into tears in a ladies room. It seems Harding had told Shaw that she had played in his *Androcles and the Lion.* He glared at her coldly and said it must have been a version that he didn't write. The playwright never apologized to Harding, however. To Shaw, she and other people didn't seem to exist. The Shaws seemed to like Marion and her vivaciousness, though. I believe Marion wrote to them in England as long as Shaw lived.

There was nothing quite like Hollywood in the old days, even though it was a small town. I remember Hollywood in 1939 well because I often went west then on business trips. Great movies had created an enormous entertainment appetite among the public—from Clark Gable and Vivien Leigh in *Gone with the Wind* to Judy Garland in *The Wizard of Oz* and Bette Davis in *Dark Victory* to Greta Garbo in *Ninotchka.* Other great films of the time included *Stagecoach, Wuthering Heights, The Women, Gunga Din, Mr. Smith Goes to Washington,* and *Babes in Arms.* It cost only twenty-five cents to go to the movies in those days. Some 85 million moviegoers—about two-thirds of the populace—saw a cartoon, newsreel, and double feature every week.

Hollywood was supreme. Very few films were shot on location, and the place became a fantasy factory. The Broadway theater sneered at what many easterners called Tinsel Town, but the great actors and directors were inexorably moving west. Surprisingly, only a few thousand people made the movie industry tick in those days. Few ever dreamed of having one home in Los Angeles and another in New York.

Marion Davies had long been an established Hollywood star by that time. She not only had starred in many pictures but was rated one of the most popular comediennes in Hollywood. Marion was a friendly, frivolous blonde who loved to have fun and particularly enjoyed parties. She was also sentimental and generous to anyone she knew in need. Pretty, except when she swore like a Brooklyn longshoreman, Marion was born in Flatbush in 1897. She was dancing on Broadway by the time she was eighteen. Her father was a neighborhood politician. Pop first saw her in the Ziegfeld Follies of 1917. Marion was not exactly an intellect, and she stuttered. But Pop was smitten with her, and she became his sex kitten. My father and Marion began seeing one another regularly in 1918 when he was fifty-five years old and she was twenty-one.

The affair became public only after Grandma passed away in 1919. Pop didn't flaunt Marion before that because it would have embarrassed and upset Phoebe. By then he had formed Cosmopolitan Productions. The film business was a natural outgrowth of his wide-ranging media empire, but he also made movies to raise Marion to national stardom.

As the years went on and we sons grew older, each of us became aware of Marion in his own way. It was not a subject we discussed much. I first realized that somebody named Marion was around when Pop took me and my brother Jack to a film studio he had opened up in the Bronx. It was 1918 and I was ten years old. I met Alma Rubens and Ricardo Cortez, big stars who were making a silent film for my father. (At the same time, Pop was filming *Little Old New York* with Marion.) I liked Rick Cortez. Years later he was to introduce me to Frank Conniff, a newspaperman who was to become my closest friend. Pop was also filming a very successful serial called *The Perils of Pauline*. It was full of cliff-hanging scenes, an early-day soap opera. These episodes were shown as shorts once a week before the feature film. Pop moved from this and similar shorts to full-length silent movies. One day someone asked the old man if there was any money in movies. With self-deprecating humor, he replied, "I don't know, but I've got several million dollars in them."

(In all that has been said about the old man, no one has mentioned the fact that he insisted on "family" entertainment. Pop never allowed any off-color or indecent scenes in any movie he ever made. He once mentioned to me that moving pictures would one day have greater public impact than newspapers. That was nearly seventy years ago. Not bad foresight.)

At that time, my brothers and I didn't know our father was having an affair. Pop continued to live at home in the Clarendon and was on very friendly terms with our mother. He kept a watchful eye over all of us. We sure knew it when our marks fell at school. He took Mom to many social and political functions around town. Pop also helped with her Milk Fund, a charitable organization that gave free milk to needy children. Mom was a very compassionate, dignified woman, and she never once showed the slightest irritation or disappointment with our father. In fact, she always told us: "Your father is a great man. The people who say otherwise don't know him."

I was very pleased at this because I was beginning to hear from school-mates and young friends that some people were publicly criticizing the old man for his editorial views. Frankly, because of my youth, I never understood many of the battles or issues. All I knew was somebody didn't like my father. Since Pop never discussed these attacks, Mom's words were a great reassurance that he was all right.

In the early 1920s my father began spending more and more time making movies with Marion in Hollywood. I wept when I began to understand what was going on. Because of the embarrassment to both of us, I never initiated the subject with my mother. She never complained about Pop or Marion to me.

The movie business was to occupy much of his time for the next twenty years. Pop wanted to make Marion happy because her beauty, humor, earthiness, and generosity were, for him, a delightful distraction. She was an expensive but relaxing ornament that brightened the darkness after a long and stressful day. Except for a trip to Europe with Mother, George, Jack, and me, the old man was spending most of his time on the West Coast. In 1925 Pop and Mom quietly agreed to live apart permanently. He spent much of that year in Hollywood and she remained in New York.

Pop continued to phone and write to Mom. He always provided well for her. She had an apartment on Park Avenue and a summer place out at Sands Point, Long Island. Mom later had a beautiful home at Southampton, Long Island, where she entertained frequently. I never believed that Pop completely lost his love for her. As far as I could tell, neither did she for him. However, she was proud, and I don't believe she ever asked him to return home. Nevertheless, even in his latest years, after living with Marion for three decades, my father would still drop a private note to Mom. Few people outside the family have ever known that.

Nineteen-twenty-five was the year in which Louella Parsons, who was to become one of the most powerful women in Hollywood, began her climb to the top as a movie columnist for the Hearst newspapers. She, my father, and Marion were to become longtime friends.

Pop joined his Cosmopolitan Productions in a working agreement with Metro-Goldwyn-Mayer and collaborated closely with MGM chief Louis B. Mayer. The old man built Marion a fourteen-room "bungalow" on the MGM lot in Culver City. Somebody told me it cost him about $700,000—millions of dollars by today's standards. He stayed at the Ambassador Hotel in Los Angeles with Helen, his favorite dachshund. Pop was devoted to dachshunds and loved them like personal friends.

Marion ultimately became one of the biggest stars in Hollywood, although she had her critics. In 1928 *Variety* listed her as one of MGM's six top stars. The list included Greta Garbo, Lillian Gish, Norma Shearer, Joan Crawford, and Marie Dressler, so she was in top company. A number of her movies lost money, but a few were big box office. I saw one of her films, *Going Hollywood,* with Bing Crosby, and thought she was very funny.

A lot of people said that Pop made her a star—with his money and by promoting her in his newspapers. There's certainly some truth to that. But Marion had talent, beauty, and a terrific sense of comedy. She was an excellent dancer and became a better actress. However, because of her stuttering, Marion developed an inferiority complex when talking pictures arrived with *The Jazz Singer* in 1927. She worked hard to overcome the problem but never did master it. When she got drunk, which became more and more frequent, she would sometimes stutter like a machine gun.

Pop's infatuation was now full-blown. He built her a $7 million beach house at Santa Monica—some $3 million for construction and another $4 million for furnishings. They began to throw the best parties in all of filmland. Pop hired Tommy Dorsey and other big-name bands, and often danced himself because he was excellent on the ballroom floor. Pop used such occasions to present Marion with expensive new jewelry; she ended up with one of the finest collections in the country. Marion had become more than a star. She was one of the richest and most important women in Hollywood.

Marion never became a filmland snob. She was warm to almost everyone, and was one of the softest touches in Hollywood. She would donate $10,000 to a children's clinic in Los Angeles, pay the doctors' bills of a stricken actor or actress, and give young people enough money to get married. She was elected four times as president of the Motion Picture Relief Fund, which helped those in the business who were down on their luck.

About 1933, however, Marion began to slip as an actress. She had been drinking heavily for several years. Her face and figure began to show it.

Marion disliked some of Pop's top executives. She was an excellent pantomimist, and would sometimes mimic their voices and gestures. She once told the old man that one was a crook and another a no-good bastard. (I never heard my father swear, but Marion's cussing seemed to increase with the years.) At one of her frequent parties, several of my father's news executives, who were guests, sensed that an explosion was about to erupt. Pop was deep in conversation with some of them when Marion's outburst hit. She had been sitting on a sofa, getting quietly splashed. Suddenly, she burst out, "H-H-Hey, y-y-you! H-H-Hey, y-y-you!"

No one was quite sure whom she meant. She shouted again, "H-H-Hey, y-y-you!"

My father, who was embarrassed, tried to end the outburst. He said, "Are you speaking to me?"

Marion hollered, "Y-Y-Yes! Come here!"

The men stood, shocked and mute. My father looked at them and said, "I suppose it would be best for me to go."

He walked slowly across the hushed room. I was told you could not hear a word spoken. My father asked Marion what she wished.

She stammered: "D-D-Do all that b-b-business stuff downtown—not at my party. My g-g-guests are waiting for drinks. Get them!"

The old man nodded and walked behind the bar. He invited one and all for refills.

The incident was never forgotten—or forgiven—by my father's associates. She had embarrassed a man who was simply doing his job—and them as well.

I heard the story in the New York office grapevine. I swallowed hard. By this time I had no illusions about the situation. This was not, after all, my father's first affair. Marion, despite her innocent smile, was a very worldly woman. And this was not the Victorian Age.

In the final stages of my father's life, he was losing his voice—it was barely audible at times. Marion would get on the phone to these same editors and issue various instructions, claiming her words were his orders. Some executives felt that Marion was trying to take over running the company, and they didn't like it because she was clearly not competent to do so. It was entirely out of character for the old man to give her any authority. He was very strict about that. You had to prove yourself professionally before Pop would trust you with any real responsibility.

I don't believe my father asked Marion to make some of these calls because his voice was so weak. While drinking, she may have decided to have a little fun with the boys she so disliked. But Pop never indicated to me or any of my brothers that Marion had any say whatsoever in how things were run. On the contrary, because of her heavy drinking, he was often shamed by her behavior.

Two things eventually came between them—her drinking and the fact that my father never married her. Perhaps Pop felt that Marion's heavy drinking—she became a hardened alcoholic—may have been his fault because he had not married her. This caused him much soul-searching and grief in his final years. It is a side of the old man that has never been revealed.

I was offended and, at times, deeply hurt by the relationship. That was because my mother, who had given Pop five sons, deserved her husband at her side. And so did my brothers and I. Nevertheless, I loved my father so much that nothing he could do would tear me from him. I wanted to contribute to society as he had. He was my hero, and I admired the old man to his last breath. My father was hardly a symbol of human perfection, but I have never believed in being the final judge of anyone. And certainly not of him, because he was a better man than I or any of my brothers. Neither I nor my brothers were seeing much of our father during that time. Since the affair caused misgivings, I didn't go to Hollywood or San Simeon for several years. The hurt was too deep.

Yet, in the beginning, Marion offered my father what he craved as he grew older—a sense of youth and energy. He was nearly thirty-five years older than Marion. He was giving her everything she had never known: money, fame, power, jewels, and luxuries. In a topsy-turvy world, they wanted and apparently needed each other.

I repeatedly regretted what was happening, but my father had his own life to lead. I told myself over and over that only God, not us mortals, judges men and women. I've never tried to justify my father's relationship with Marion. At the same time, I tried to analyze the circumstances.

There were many liaisons among rich men and beautiful women in those days. The long affair between Joseph Kennedy, father of the Massachusetts political clan, and actress Gloria Swanson was perhaps the most notable. The Vanderbilts and others were part of a long line of well-known and respected men who maintained mistresses on the side. The difference was that my father left our mother and consorted openly with Marion, while others lived a lie. Nevertheless, the nature of all these relationships was the same.

Many wealthy men in those days saw two kinds of women. Mothers and wives were put on a pedestal and idealized. Then there were "fun" girls, the sexy playthings. In earlier times, men and women were partners who worked and raised their families together. In my father's day, among the wealthy, marriage was much less a partnership. Today, modern husbands and wives are sometimes no more than good friends, not intimate souls. They are, on occasion, even in competition with one another.

These and similar thoughts have crossed my mind scores of times. I've even considered the possibility that Marion was the vivacious daughter my father never had, and he was the father figure she needed and missed.

Most of the time she was a pleasant distraction for him. All the heavy blows he took in politics as well as in newspapering caused the old man to seek the chatter and laughter he found in Marion. Despite repeated claims that my father sought the presidency up to 1925, Marion was one indisputable reason why that could never have been realized—at least after 1918, when the old man met her. Pop understood that well. Perhaps he had sought the White House in earlier years, but he never gave any indication of such ambition to me, my brothers, or our mother.

Some acquaintances of my mother have suggested that she may have had some fault in the breakup with Pop. They explain that Mom felt she could not safely have more children after the twins. As a Catholic, she did not wish to practice birth control. Therefore, she began to withdraw from my father. That view is sheer speculation.

My father moved full-time to San Simeon in the late 1920s, and transferred his news headquarters there. He set up a communications hub under Joe Willicombe, his longtime secretary. The castle and grounds had about eighty regular line telephones, and another three dozen radio phones were used on the ranch, at the zoo, and in distant areas. Three different systems were integrated into a central switchboard at a telephone office. One operator was on duty at all times. She also controlled the lights at our small airport.

Phones were installed on every floor of the Casa Grande and other structures as well as on the terraces, at the pools, and even in the gardens, where they were hidden in small boxes. That allowed Pop to take an important call almost anywhere. The veteran Willicombe short-stopped many calls, of course, and answered questions himself. That was because he knew the business mind of the Chief better than anyone. Pop didn't want to be bothered unless the call was urgent or it came from one of the family.

The old man had pencils and pads placed in all parts of the Casa Grande—on the terraces, at the outside pool, tennis courts, and other places on the grounds. He dashed off ideas until the very last days of his time at San Simeon.

Willicombe had a teletype machine in his office. This was adjacent to the telephone exchange. He also used a powerful shortwave radio whose call letters were W6GOU. This radio was used until 1939, when it was disconnected. By then, only teletype machines and phones were used. One teletype system connected him with all the papers, while another was used to send and receive Western Union and other messages. Pop had two complete electric generator systems, in case of any power failure and emergency.

For years people used to ask me how the old man ran a financial empire from that isolated spot. Easy. He had a detailed knowledge of each operation, whether it was a newspaper or a mine, and had regular reports sent to him. If he had questions, either he or Willicombe would phone, telegraph, or write those responsible. From time to time editors and publishers as well as other directors would fly to San Simeon and meet with him. Pop had more time to work at the castle because there were virtually no social obligations, except those he initiated, and few distractions. If he had been in New York, for example, he would have been spending a lot of time—and money—at art galleries. Pop continued to receive auction catalogs from all over the world and to buy art and antiques.

Frankly, I would have gone crazy living full time at San Simeon. I love to ride horses and gaze over the hillsides to the Pacific—but give me a lively New York restaurant at lunch and a lot of people doing business and socializing. I loved the action in Manhattan. It's not easy to talk to a teletype machine or a couple of cows eating grass. Although I love animals, after a few months of conversation with San Simeon buffalo, they are for the birds.

Yet Pop continued to keep tabs on all of us. These are excerpts from a letter he wrote me on July 18, 1932. It was typical of his thoughts and concern not only for me but also for my brothers and mother:

> Come on out to the Coast. It is almost too cool, but we expect to have some California weather before the month is out.
>
> I am worried about your eyes. Send me a little telegram and let me know when everything is all right again.
>
> I hope you got your mother something nice for her birthday.
>
> I suppose you have heard about George. He has had rather a hard time. He bumped into a drunken Mexican in an automobile, or the drunken Mexican bumped into him, or the Mexican bumped into— well anyhow, George got his shoulder broken and his knee badly cut.
>
> I have more trouble worrying about you kids than a hen has with a lot of chicks.
>
> You add to the excitement by getting your eye banged up.
>
> Now please take care of yourself and get in shape again, and as I say, send me a little telegram when everything is okay.

I thought it was more than interesting that, seven years after our father left home permanently, he was still writing me about Mom.

Marion and my mother never had anything to do with one another. Various publications have said that they met, but that's not true. Mother was too dignified for that, and Pop would never have put her through such distress.

Of course Marion came up in conversation at various times and places, but Mom usually refrained from comment. If she was forced to refer to Davies, she called her "the woman." Marion is said to have called Mom "The Black Widow" and apparently resented the fact that, while both were baptized Catholics, Mom went to church. Marion also was quoted as saying our mother had too many social pretensions and spent too much money. Most of my friends never brought up the subject, but if anyone ever did I simply said that Millicent was my father's wife and our mother. That truth spoke louder than anything else that could be said.

For a couple of years, after Pop and Marion began spending most of their time at San Simeon, my brothers and I didn't visit there. But my mother didn't wish us to be estranged from our father, and began encouraging us to see him. All of us waited, though. The reason was that none of us wanted to embarrass Mom or Pop—or ourselves. Also, as of 1925, none of us had been introduced to Marion and we weren't sure it was a good idea. Anyway, after some time as a reporter in New York, I decided to break the ice. Merrill "Babe" Meigs, publisher of our Chicago paper, a good friend and World War I pilot, was going to fly up from Los Angeles to San Simeon in his puddle-jumper. He asked me to go with him.

I had no intention of imposing myself on Pop and Marion. When we arrived at the castle, they were having lunch with a few friends and business associates. Babe and I sat down in the pantry area off the kitchen and grabbed a bite. Someone told my father that we were there, and he came back to see us. Pop was brusque. "What's the matter, aren't my guests good enough for you?"

I explained that their lunch had begun before we arrived, and we didn't want to interrupt him and the guests. I added quietly, "Also, I haven't been introduced to anyone there."

He immediately knew, of course, that I was referring to Marion. I didn't want to intrude if he didn't wish to make the introduction. The old man said, "Come out when you've finished here, and I'll introduce you."

We did, and I met Marion for the first time. I was very casual about it. So was she. One might have thought we had met before. I later talked business with Pop, but we didn't discuss Marion or my mother. I concluded the visit saying I missed seeing him and hoped we might get together more often. He was glad to see me, and we promised to remain in closer contact.

I believe my father was relieved that the ice was broken and Marion had finally met one of his sons. My brother George and his wife visited San Simeon later. He and Marion became friends. George made no bones about the fact that he enjoyed Marion's humor and company. Both liked to drink and they were to see a lot of one another. I and the rest of my brothers generally kept our distance from Marion. We nicknamed her Daisy.

As the years passed, the age difference between my father and most of Marion's Hollywood crowd became more evident. Yet Pop could keep up with the best of them in swimming, riding, and tennis. He put on weight and turned gray, but the youthful spark was still there. He loved humorous stories and Marion seemed to know all the latest.

When any of us had seen the old man, Mom would tactfully ask whether he was well and happy. I simply related the facts—that we had had dinner, talked business, and that Marion had been present. All of us were involved in a delicate balancing act that, in my opinion, was never comfortable. We simply made the best of it.

Pop and Marion were calmer than most of us when the 1937 financial crisis struck the company. I was very concerned as publisher of the merged *New York Journal-American.* Many of our newspapers were losing money as a result of the Depression, and a good number of Pop's properties were heavily mortgaged. But the old man didn't want to surrender a single paper. For the next decade, a committee of executives fought to save as much of the organization as it could.

Marion sold much of her real estate, stocks, and jewelry as the battle of survival heated up. She lent Pop $1 million, and that gave us breathing room to meet additional debts. She was paid back in full when business got better. I mentioned this crisis earlier, but want to point out here that Marion did not hesitate to help. Sure, everything that she turned over to my father came from what he had already given her. But I privately respected and admired her spontaneous generosity.

Orson Welles and Herman Mankiewicz were far less generous to my father. They wrote and produced the movie *Citizen Kane,* which was a thinly concealed takeoff on the old man's life. The picture caused one of the greatest storms of controversy in the history of the film business, although Pop shrugged off the movie and never saw it. He did not, as some claimed, slip into a San Francisco movie house with Marion to see it on the sly.

I have never seen *Citizen Kane*, out of principle and deference to the old man. However, our lawyers and others who dissected it scene by scene filled me in on the details. I feel as if I've viewed every frame.

The film portrays a wealthy but tyrannically ambitious man who seeks political power. In the failed process, he dies a lonely death in a ghoulish castle. There are many brazen references to my father, portraying him as an arrogant, megalomaniacal newspaper publisher drained of human compassion. His character is framed in one scene of doom after another. The moral is: Having gained the world, he loses his soul.

The film opened in New York on May 1, 1941 at the Palace Theater. Fifty years later, on May 1, 1991, *Citizen Kane* was rereleased at two Manhattan movie theaters. The *New York Times* described those openings as "the movie event of the year, one of the two most glorious achievements of American black-and-white cinema." The other was D. W. Griffith's *The Birth of a Nation*.

Many respected industry greats and movie critics view the film as an artistic classic. In particular, cameraman Gregg Toland apparently shot magnificent deep-focus scenes, a technique allowing audiences to see objects far and near with equal clarity in the same frame. This is especially effective since the four major movements of the film are flashback recollections. I don't consider myself a movie critic and see no reason to challenge these long-time experts.

However, there is a critical difference between artistic and moral stature. A film can be cinematically outstanding but morally reprehensible. Essentially, I believe that to be the case concerning *Citizen Kane*.

The movie is presented as a type of docudrama. But even Welles has admitted that the final scene, with Welles himself playing Charles Foster Kane, is a "gimmick." Kane's last word is "rosebud," a bleak, obscure reference to something in his childhood—perhaps recognition of a lost youthful innocence. Welles described it as "rather dollar-book Freud." That was no cinematic artistry speaking. It was box-office bucks. Welles dismissed the staged scene as a Freudian subtext of a poor, little, rich boy who never recovered from the loss of his mother. All of this is set in place as part of a moral judgment of my father. It is an inaccurate debasement of his person.

Welles and Mankiewicz targeted my father because his life was big box office. I have been told that, at the time, *Citizen Kane* didn't make money.

The film got our company lawyers and Louella Parsons, our influential movie writer, excited. Louella raised all kinds of hell when she and a couple of our attorneys viewed a private screening before the movie was released in May of 1941. Welles apparently was present to get her reaction, but she reportedly stormed out of the showing without speaking to him.

There are some strange sidelights to this mess. A lifetime friend of mine, Robin "Curley" Harris, blames much of it on Louella. He recalls that she gave the film glowing plugs and "went overboard" for the movie while it was being made. However, in the closing weeks of shooting, Louella learned that Kane was presumably not merely any mean-spirited tycoon but, in reality, her old friend and chief, William Randolph Hearst. Harris, who has written for us over many decades and still does, told me, "Louella really went wild." I never wanted to become involved in the battle, because I didn't believe it served any useful purpose. Yet, Louella was, in reality, giving the film a lot of ink and creating a larger audience for it.

The hullabaloo raised a question about Louella's power. Was it limitless? If not, at what stage should my father or one of his top assistants have stepped in and told her to cool it? The same question was asked many times about Walter Winchell, whose columns sometimes reflected personal vendettas. For decades, the old man believed that a columnist should have complete freedom to report and write. Speculation that he ordered Louella or Winchell to "get" people was nonsense. Any vendettas they engaged in were their own.

RKO Studios, which financed and was about to release the film, realized they had a real fight on their hands. Louella could make or break any film, director, writer, or actor in her columns. She also could spell trouble in the future. Louella was, in the eyes of many, the most powerful woman in Hollywood. Her column was carried throughout this country and abroad.

Contrary to many claims, my father told me that he never made any effort to stop the film, but he asked his newspapers not to ignore it completely. Louella tossed barbs against the film every chance she got. It seems the whole country began talking about the picture and, of course, most people became curious. Many wanted to see it to find out what the uproar was about.

In a bid to make the picture more acceptable, RKO held private screenings in several big cities. The studio invited famous people to see it, in the hope of winning support for the film. Curley attended the New York showing. Sitting near him were Henry and Clare Boothe Luce and Sarah Delano Roosevelt, mother of Franklin D. Roosevelt. Welles was present and tried to get Mrs. Roosevelt to publicize the picture. She said, "It was a very good picture, but it should never have been released while William Randolph Hearst is alive."

Louella managed to get the film blackballed by most of the big theater chains. She masterminded attacks on almost everyone connected with it. For example, Mankiewicz was involved in some minor auto accident in Hollywood, but, to hear Louella tell it, his car ran over half an orphan asylum.

My basic problem with *Citizen Kane* was that its portrait of my father was untruthful and unfair. Kane was depicted as a harsh, loud, imperious braggart. Unquestionably, my father was not that. Pop was also portrayed as a man without conviction. Even his bitterest newspaper competitors would never claim that.

Kane's closest friend ended their long relationship by calling him a "swine," a characterization that may say more about the Welles and Mankiewicz movie-writing than about my father.

Kane was disappointed in the world and built his own. Pop never kept San Simeon to himself. He shared it with thousands of guests who were made fully welcome. In the end, the castle and gardens were given to the state of California and they are now enjoyed by millions of Americans.

Kane strikes his wife. I am certain that my father never imagined such a contemptible act.

Kane's girlfriend had no singing talent. Marion Davies became a popular Hollywood actress with good credits. However, Mankiewicz is said to have told friends that the singing failure made for a better plot. That was the one aspect of the film, relayed to the old man, that apparently caused him real pain.

Kane went into rages: smashing his round snow glass as a child, throwing suitcases as an adult. Neither was true of my father.

The portrayal of Kane as my father was completely out of character, as his family, friends, and colleagues would testify. Pop was a soft-spoken man who seldom showed emotion—and certainly never rage.

Neither Welles nor Mankiewicz ever rose to the heights that apparently were expected of them. The two quarrelled over who should get what credit for the film. At the end, the careers of both men appeared as superficial as the treatment they had given my father.

I thought that Vincent Canby, in a *New York Times* article of April 28, 1991, summed up *Citizen Kane* better than anyone: "brilliant effrontery."

In the aftermath of all this Louella Parsons became an even more powerful voice in Hollywood. Nobody wanted to tangle with her, for any reason.

I liked Louella, personally. She had cutting wit and a great gift of gab. However, I never wanted to cross her—no, sir—and just about everyone in Hollywood came to the same conclusion. She was one tough lady.

Louella had been a small-town girl, raised in Dixon, Illinois. Her reporting first caught Pop's eye while she was a movie columnist for the old *Chicago Record-Herald*. She later came to New York with the *Morning-Telegraph*. Finally, the old man hired Louella and sent her to Hollywood for us. And she became a star in her own right.

Louella, who had one daughter, Harriet, saw herself as Hollywood's mother. Actresses who were trying to break off affairs would consult her. She would tell about an actor coming to ask her forgiveness for doing wrong to someone. Louella would patch it all up—in print. Stars would ask her if they should have a baby. Of course many of them were buttering her up for a line or two in her column. That was okay because it was a curtsy to the queen. But woe to that soul who lied or misled her. Her vengeance was legendary.

Louella's own life had a few interesting tidbits. One was that she was married to Dr. Harry Martin, a physician, who was an old-fashioned, two-fisted drinker. He would stagger to his feet at the end of an evening and announce, "It's time for me to leave. I have brain surgery to perform in the morning." I often wondered how he and Louella got home.

She closed out her long career somewhat disenchanted with Hollywood. Louella told me in the mid-1960s that she was fed up with the amount of filth in films. She said that what was passing as "art" in Hollywood was simply another word for "money."

The war came along and Pop and Marion moved to Wyntoon, his property near Mount Shasta on the McCloud River. The uproar over *Citizen Kane* subsided, and the old man was more out of the limelight. Because the retreat was quite a distance from Hollywood, there were fewer guests. As usual, Pop began to plan on expanding Wyntoon.

The two moved back to San Simeon in 1944. Slowly, imperceptibly, Marion and Pop were drawing apart. The old man began thinking more of the family. He wrote us more often, and obviously wanted to see me and my brothers. Pop was about to receive an unexpected blessing, which he was to enjoy immensely.

John Hearst, Jr., son of my brother Jack and better known as Bunky, had spent the summer of 1946 at San Simeon and loved it. My father enjoyed his grandson's company so much that he prevailed on Jack to allow Bunky to stay with him for the school year. The gregarious young fellow, who was about thirteen at the time, went to eighth grade at the San Simeon elementary school and put in one year at the public high school in nearby Cambria. He later went to high school in Beverly Hills, when his grandfather moved there in 1947 to be near his cardiac specialists. In all, Bunky lived with his grandfather and Marion for nearly four years.

The spunky youngster had his own room in the three-story, stucco villa that was located on eight acres along fashionable Beverly Drive. Of course Marion was happy to be back in the film capital and spending more time with the Hollywood crowd. She evidently had had her fill of San Simeon.

Bunky and the old man really hit it off. The youngster played all kinds of pranks. I guess he reminded the old man of himself when he was a kid. Bunky, always completely himself, would say almost anything to his grandfather. The old man enjoyed the banter immensely. Pop had to dress Bunky down on a few occasions, when his mischief got out of hand, but it was usually over quickly.

The two talked newspapering a lot. Bunky said that if he learned one thing from the old man, it was the power of newspapers. He recalls some poignant moments, one in particular:

We had a birthday party for Grandpop. I guess he was about eighty-three at the time. Some of his editors and publishers got together and came up for the afternoon. They found a copy of a San Francisco paper that was published on the day he was born. It was a thoughtful gift and they presented it to him with real affection.

Grandpop removed the wrappings and cover and began reading the paper. Most of the news covered the Civil War. He quietly thanked them but said little else. After they had gone, he put the paper down and never looked at it again. Newspapers had power—even over him.

I instinctively knew what he was thinking. That he was no longer invincible. Age was making him vulnerable. Time was catching up with him. And newspapering is, when you get down to the guts of it, a young man's game.

Grandpop was a tough guy. He didn't lie to himself. The years were running out.

Pop's irregular heartbeat didn't go away. His condition had been diagnosed as auricular fibrillation. He was under the care of specialists, who told him that he would never be fully healthy again. Yet he had to confront another continuing problem. Bunky recalls:

Marion had become a real lush. When they invited guests, he kept her upstairs for as long as he could during the cocktail hour. Otherwise, she would be soused by the time they got to dinner, and embarrass herself and him.

Marion was drinking during the day. She was sometimes pretty well lit by early afternoon. Grandpop asked me to find out where she was hiding the stuff. I did. She put most of it—several different bottles of gin—in toilet tanks. Grandpop told me to get rid of them. I did. But her supply was endless. She had someone buy more, and simply replaced what I tossed out.

Pop had lost the battle against Marion's alcoholism. She was pouring down gin like it was lemonade. It distressed him terribly, and the old man lost a lot of heart because of it.

Rumors began to circulate that my father had palsy. That wasn't true. He was getting old and fretful at Marion's drunken binges. She was harming herself—and killing him. For the first time in his life, my father suffered depression. For a man who lived and breathed the concept of limitless horizons, that was real agony.

I wasn't present when Pop left San Simeon for the last time in 1947. Marion later recounted it to me and some of her friends. I can see the scene almost as clearly as if I had been there on that fading afternoon.

He and Marion entered his car. The driver slid into the front seat. The Pacific was clearly visible below, lapping against the shoreline. The driver motored cautiously because of the old man's concern about the zoo animals and the grazing cattle. The gates opened slowly. Marion fully understood the drama under way. She was silent but watched the old man's face as the car wound hesitantly down the five-mile course of the hill. There were no signs of emotion at first. Then tears welled up in his eyes and began trickling down his face. They would not stop. He made no move to wipe them away. Marion took a handkerchief from her purse and wiped his face. He did not see or feel her. His senses were now overwhelmed by the recognition of his own mortality.

The car swung onto the dirt road toward our mile-long private airstrip. My father's plane waited. The two got out of the car. For the first time, the old man lifted his head and turned to see the twin towers of the Casa Grande. They seemed to be only shadows in the distance of the Enchanted Hill. The bells atop the castle were silent.

The two climbed into Pop's private plane. Neither spoke as the aircraft rose and headed south to Los Angeles.

The gulls along the coastline circled above the rolling surface of the Pacific as if to bid farewell. The light was fading as the sun slipped slowly into the sea.

The old man asked Marion what time it was, but he didn't listen for her answer. He knew it was running out for him. Pop would have only four more years. He knew he would never return to San Simeon. His ever-boundless horizons were now limited by human frailty.

VIII
THE BEST AND
THE BRIGHTEST

Some of the world's most famous writers, editors, artists, and editorial cartoonists worked for us—gifted, colorful, intrepid, visionary men and women. And a few skunks. They came from all parts of the United States and abroad. Dignified, disciplined, gentle, gracious people and prima donnas with poison personalities. Wild, wonderful characters and paranoid pens. All managed to stay within tolerable limits of human behavior, but sometimes needed a prayer or two to do so. All these stars shared one attribute: success through popular acceptance.

Winston Churchill and Jack London. Mark Twain, Charles Russell, and Arthur Brisbane. (My father carried Brisbane's column on the front page of our newspapers for about forty years; to my knowledge, no publisher in the history of U.S. journalism has so featured a columnist over such a span of time.) James Creelman, Damon Runyon, Edmond Coblentz, Burris Jenkins, Jr., Walter Winchell, Louella Parsons, Bugs Baer, Adela Rogers St. Johns, and Karl Von Wiegand. Walter Howey, Jack Lait, and Harry Romanoff. Westbrook Pegler and Bob Considine. Jimmy and Dorothy Kilgallen. Joseph Kingsbury-Smith, Frank Conniff, Inez Robb, and Phyllis Battelle. Barry Faris and Bill Corum. Jack Kennedy and Jack O'Brien. Richard Deems, Carmel Snow, John Mack Carter, Helen Gurley Brown, and others.

These were our big byliners and editors. I knew most of them, of course, but let no one believe I ever dared to choose one above another.

I will leave that for anyone crazy enough to try it. But if I had to pick our ten most memorable men and women reporters and editors over the past six decades, these would be my choices:

Jimmy Kilgallen and his daughter Dorothy. Jimmy because he saw and covered so much of America and the world. Dorothy because much of her career, and her life and death, were so dramatic.

Walter Howey, Jack Lait, Harry Romanoff, and all the crowd at the old rip-roaring *Chicago Herald-American*. A wild, nutty bunch who not only were the characters in the famous newspaper play *The Front Page* but a breed apart in the legendary flamboyant world of earlier newspapering. I loved to go to Chicago and share their exploits.

Carmel Snow, who may have been the greatest—and most feared— fashion editor and writer of all time. I still never fail to think of her on glancing at a fashion section.

Bob Considine, who was probably the most prolific reporter-writer of this century. As fine a gentleman as one would ever meet. Raconteur, humorist, and sage of Toots Shor's and other esteemed bistros. I still miss him, more than fifteen years after his passing.

Walter Winchell, undoubtedly the greatest gossip columnist since the English and others began telling old wives' tales. Our last chats perhaps made up for all our previous differences.

Westbrook Pegler, one of the most controversial political columnists in U.S. history. A man who knew the English language as well as anyone who ever cracked a Webster's dictionary. Yet I never understood Peg and still don't.

Jack O'Brien, who understood New York's entertainment beat better than anyone who ever covered it. A great legman who made being a street reporter an art form.

Joseph Kingsbury-Smith, who not only scored the greatest scoops on the Soviet Union in this century but was the essence of a diplomat in his long, worldwide reporting and management career. We still write and travel together on reporting trips.

Frank Conniff, my closest pal, who not only had the gift of Irish eloquence but the smile and loyalty to go with it. I miss his laughter and wonderful stories.

Three great newswomen, whom I knew well, could easily be on the list instead of Dorothy Kilgallen. Louella Parsons was certainly more experienced and powerful in her field. Adela Rogers St. Johns, a truly fine reporter. And Inez Robb, a regal lady of impeccable manners who may well have been a better reporter and news analyst than any of the three. But Dorothy got a lot of breaks and made the most of them. Yet there could hardly be a greater contrast between the young Dorothy, student of the good nuns, and the beleaguered soul who died in anguish.

I would list a pinch hitter on this roster—my wife, Austine. She had been a columnist for the *Washington Times-Herald* and knew a lot about the newspaper business. For many years she was a helping hand in much of what I and others reported and wrote. Without her encouragement and sharp mind, some of us would have faltered along the way.

One who never faltered, morally or mentally, was Jimmy Kilgallen. In more than sixty years of knowing him, I never met anyone who did not like Jimmy. As a newspaperman, he was the ace of diamonds. As a family man, the ace of hearts.

We met when I was a young reporter starting out on the *American*. He was already a star with our International News Service. Jimmy always had a kind word, a whimsical smile that covered his bad eye, and a calm but knowing air. Damon Runyon once confided to me that Jimmy kept a suitcase packed next to his bed in the event he had to rush out of town to cover a story. Damon added, "He's an editor's dream of a reporter."

Jimmy told me he started selling newspapers near the Chicago stockyards when he was twelve years old. He also hung around local telegraphers and a Western Union office. When Jimmy graduated from grade school at thirteen, he went to work as a Western Union messenger and studied telegraphy in his spare time. He became a telegrapher for the *Chicago Daily Farmers and Drovers Journal* at fifteen, and picked up a part-time job as a news stringer for the *Chicago Tribune*. He soon became a reporter on the *Trib*.

I remember talking with him one afternoon about thirty years ago in my office. We were telling lies about how great the old-time reporters were compared to the ambitious young lions of today. I could see Jimmy's eyes going misty. His mind was wandering far back through the years. His five-foot five-inch frame hunched over like a priest in the confessional as he spoke: "I remember covering my first story. I wasn't even a reporter. I was standing on a street corner in the stockyards district one day and heard the clack of telegraph keys in a Western Union office. The clicks said a nearby bank was in financial trouble. I walked to the bank, identified myself as a reporter with the *Trib,* and asked to see the president. When I started asking him questions, they threw me out."

The bank made the mistake of calling the *Tribune* to complain about Jimmy's penetrating inquiry. Walter Howey, the *Trib*'s assistant city editor, who later became a legend with us, smelled a big story. He questioned the bank official himself and broke the story about its difficulties. Howey then gave Jimmy a job as a full-time reporter.

Kilgallen later joined our INS in New York. Some of the big stories Jimmy covered are still remembered today: interviews with Al Capone and Thomas Alva Edison, the Bruno Richard Hauptmann trial, the *Morro Castle* disaster, the blowup of the dirigible *Hindenburg* over New Jersey, all of World War II (including the discovery of the Dachau prison camp in Germany and the agreement to end the war), the Count de Marigny trial in Nassau, the two Alger Hiss trials, the Rosenberg spy case, various Communist trials, and the McCarthy hearings.

Perhaps the greatest story that Jimmy ever covered would be unknown to most newspaper readers today. It was the most sensational scoop of its time: the Samuel Insull case of the Roaring Twenties. Insull was head of the Mid-West Utilities empire in Chicago. Thousands of investors had lost millions of dollars in Sam's network of firms—their life savings in some instances—amid charges that Insull was involved in financial skullduggery. Sam skipped the country, but was found and put under house arrest in Athens. The U.S. government moved to extradite him to face trial in Chicago. Insull dyed his gray hair and mustache a pepper-colored black. Slipping away from police guarding his apartment, he hired a Greek ship that sailed quietly into the Mediterranean.

Kilgallen was reporting from our INS Rome bureau at the time. He received a cable from Barry Faris, the head of INS New York, with instructions to find Insull regardless of cost.

Jimmy flew to Athens. He soon got a tip about a ship called the *Maotis.* He was told that it was anchored at Istanbul and Insull had hidden himself aboard. Kilgallen hired an amphibious plane and landed in the waters of the Dardanelles near Insull's ship. Jimmy sneaked aboard the boat and found Insull, who clammed up, saying he never talked with reporters. The Turks also discovered Insull and put him in jail for two weeks while they tried to decide whether to extradite him to the United States. Meantime, Jimmy was happily abiding by his instructions and spending expense money like we owned Fort Knox. He had purchased tipsters in the police department, the government, the courts, at Greek newspapers, and every place where he could buy a drink or another news source.

Istanbul was now crawling with American newsmen trying to get to Insull. The Turks decided to extradite him, and their police secretly drove the beleaguered executive to Smyrna harbor, where they put him aboard the American Export Line's *Exilona* for the voyage to America. Thanks to his ongoing largesse, Jimmy was aboard a few minutes after Insull.

It was to be a twenty-day voyage, so Kilgallen decided not to press Insull. In fact, he did not go near the utility chief for several days. He noticed, however, that Insull sat in the same deck chair every day, so one afternoon Jimmy quietly took a seat next to him. Insull could be very crotchety, and of course recognized Jimmy from their earlier meeting. He still did not want to talk. Gradually the two began to discuss Chicago, where both had lived. Even then Insull insisted that every word was off the record.

Bit by bit Jimmy began to win over the industrialist. He said he could not show up in New York and tell his bosses he had learned nothing. He had to write something. Insull finally began to budge. He said he was innocent of all charges. He had gypped nobody. On and on, he talked by the hour. After each session Jimmy would return to his room and bang out all he could remember on his typewriter. Finally he took one of the biggest gambles of his career. He showed Insull his typewritten notes. The old guy eyed Kilgallen suspiciously and began to read—and read. Down to the last word. He turned and said to Jimmy, "It's O.K." Jimmy asked him to sign the last page, showing that the notes were accurate. Insull did.

The scoop catapulted Kilgallen to national attention. Insull was eventually tried in a Chicago court and found innocent. He left the United States and died, a lonely man, in Paris.

I asked Jimmy about the scoop one day and he replied, "Hell, Bill, we were just two guys from Chicago. But I'll tell you one thing. I put in an expense account that would have done justice to Insull!"

In 1965, after more than sixty-five years of marriage, his beloved wife, Mae, died. Jimmy said to me, "I was married to the newspaper business but in love with Mae." She was survived by not only Jimmy but their two daughters, Dorothy and Eleanor. Jimmy lived to be ninety-four and worked for us, in one capacity or another, almost until he passed away.

Jimmy had been ill for more than a year, so I had the Hearst Corporation pick up the tab for his stay in the Mary Manning Walsh Rest Home in upper Manhattan. It was no big deal. I just did not want the guy who may have been a better financial jockey than Sam Insull to die broke.

To his last breath, Jimmy delighted in and defended his daughter Dorothy. He used to tell me that the greatest thrill of his journalistic career came when he covered her take-off on an eighteeen-day, round-the-world trip aboard the dirigible *Hindenburg*. That was a bit of Irish blarney based on fatherly pride.

Dorothy had three trademarks: a keen mind, a tailored exterior, and a steel rod as backbone. She was more than a sob sister. Dorothy was life and death. She reached to the precipices of people's emotions, in both her writing and her personal confrontations with her own existence. She went all the way in the line of duty and in her private life.

Dorothy wanted a career that would fly high and fast like Lindbergh, Amelia Earhart, Wiley Post, and Howard Hughes. The *Evening Journal*'s notion in the mid-1930s to send a reporter around the world in record-breaking time was nothing new. But for Dorothy, who landed the assignment, it was not so much a race against time as against male chauvinism. She knew it. Women all over America and the world cheered her on.

The publicity attached to the race was fantastic. Dorothy returned a darling of pre-war New York and café society. She became "The Voice of Broadway" for our *Journal-American* and wrote a column about the real and tinsel jewelry of the New York smart set. Her career skyrocketed. Jimmy's little girl was tired of dolls and pussycats and wanted the big lights, fame, and wealth.

Press agents, restaurants, and nightclubs showered her with champagne, perfume, magnificent cigarette cases, free dinners, and all the vodka she could pour down. And she got to like the stuff.

Dorothy became a celebrity at the Stork Club, Fefe's Monte Carlo, La Conga, and a dozen other joints that dazzled with rich debutantes, models, actors and actresses, wealthy playboys, and other performing seals and society swingers. She was dating and dancing with everyone from big-name authors to lounge lizards who were hanging on for the ride. People began to call her the female Walter Winchell. By Broadway measurements, Dorothy was its comet. Walter Winchell was still the Big Street's star, since he got most of the juiciest gossip. But Dorothy's trail of sparks also lit up the sky.

Broadway had screwy ways to say somebody was shining. One sign came from Reuben's, a top theatrical hangout. They named a sandwich after Dorothy. That's a crazy symbol for making it, but Broadway was outrageous. I can't remember what was in the sandwich, but Reuben's charged more than a buck for it—a hefty price in those days.

In her travels along the Great White Way, Dorothy married Richard Kollmar. He came from suburban New Jersey. Dick dabbled in various aspects of theater. The two launched a radio show in the 1940s called "Breakfast with Dorothy and Dick." They broadcast live from their home, discussing happenings in and around New York and Washington. The Kollmars were soon seven: Dorothy and Dick, three children— Dickie, Julius, and Jill—as well as their butler and their canary, Yasha. It seemed that all New York knew the comings and goings of each of them.

In the 1950s Dorothy's career soared into the social stratosphere. She became a panelist on television's highly popular "What's My Line?" The panelists were blindfolded and then tried to guess the professions or jobs of guests by questioning them. Dorothy's name began to span the midwest farm belt to Hollywood and the West Coast. Her writing was becoming much more daring, featuring highly candid impressions of people and unexpected, cliff-hanger conclusions about events. She became one of the most talked-about reporters of the era.

In 1954 we sent her to Cleveland for the *Journal-American* to cover the most sensational trial of the times. Dr. Sam Sheppard—a handsome, one-time football star and prosperous professional living in the lakefront suburb of Bay Village—was accused of killing his pregnant wife, Marilyn, who was blond, comely, and well-liked.

Sheppard contended he was sleeping on a downstairs couch, when Marilyn began screaming. He rushed upstairs, struggled with a "white form," but was knocked out. The physician claimed that when he regained consciousness, he saw that Marilyn was dead, and then chased a bushy-haired man along the beach. The two struggled, but he was knocked unconscious again. He finally revived, returned home, and phoned the police. Many felt Sheppard's account was too fanciful to be real. They asked: Can a physician get away with murder because he is a doctor? The case attracted phenomenal national interest.

In covering the trial, Dorothy attracted almost as much attention as Sheppard. Judge Edward Blythin, of Cleveland's Common Pleas Court, wanted to meet her. She obliged. Dorothy told some of our rewrite men at the *Journal* that Blythin, who was seventy years old, asked her to sit on his knee in his chambers. The scuttlebutt around the office was that she did. Sheppard himself sent her a message through his brother that he liked her stories. *Time* magazine said, "It becomes increasingly difficult to tell the reporter from the principals."

Sheppard finally was found guilty and sentenced to life in prison. Dorothy was furious and assailed the jury. Our headline, which appeared above the *Journal-American* masthead, roared: DOROTHY KILGALLEN ASTOUNDED BY VERDICT. That is how famous Dorothy had become. She was bigger than the story.

For all her glory, Dorothy was still running—and playing—hard. Her vodka and tonics flowed more freely. There was the perennial nightlife gossip about romances. Family and friends protected her.

I always liked Dorothy and would see her from time to time. If both of us had a few minutes, we would have a drink and talk newspapering. She was enthusiastic, open, full of life.

Dorothy was good—very good for us. Her flashy gossip column had many buying our *Journal-American*. She mixed the aristocratic crowd, café society, and show biz into one big heady cocktail. It was a glamour stinger. Because of her high profile—the name-dropping from 5:00 P.M. to sometimes 5:00 A.M.—Dorothy became café royalty. As any historian will confirm, royalty had the power to chop off your name or even your head. And everybody in New York knew Dorothy had that power.

Suddenly, in 1965, it was all over. The biggest story in Dorothy's long career had dropped in her lap, but she would not cover it. Dorothy died under circumstances that shocked unshockable New Yorkers and many in the rest of the country. She was discovered dead in her bed. The New York medical examiner's office issued a certificate stating death was caused by "acute ethanol and barbiturate intoxication—circumstances undetermined." Simply put, she died as a result of too many pills and too much booze. The inevitable question: Was it suicide? I don't believe the question was ever adequately answered. Her enemies suggested it was a deliberate overdose. Friends said Dorothy had simply made a mistake.

As hard as I tried, I could not dwell on Dorothy when she died. I thought of her father. My God, I prayed, take care of Jimmy. His lovely little girl had crashed in her race for it all. I put my head in my hands and my heart ached for a long time.

If New York, as a news town, had heroes and heart, Chicago reveled in underworld shenanigans, shootouts, and political spice. Shortly after the turn of the century, Pop founded the *Chicago American.* This paper became the *Chicago Evening American,* the *Chicago Herald-American,* and finally ended with its original name. Some of its top editors and reporters became newspaper legends.

We leased several buildings, but finally settled in a large, old, five-story structure at 215 West Madison Street. The third-floor newsroom was massive—10,000 square feet with no partitions. The shouting and tumult soon became 400-point type on the paper's front page. We had nine daily editions and, let me tell you, none was dull.

Our confidential payroll was spread out like a map and *Who's Who* of the city: dozens of chief operators at the phone company; more phone operators at hospitals, hotels, and other large public places; police and firemen; judges and court reporters; doctors and lawyers; politicians; and many others.

We brought in our own roughhouse boys to fight the circulation crews of other newspapers. All sides battled with brass knuckles, blackjacks, and even guns. We had a tough time simply getting our feet on street corners to sell papers. The *Chicago Tribune,* with cousins Bertie McCormick and Joe Patterson at the top, fought a no-holds-barred war against all comers. As I was told: This is the way we do business in Chicago.

Our papers' two most famous editors were Walker Howey and Harry Romanoff, known among his colleagues as Romy. Howey was with us for many years and Romy for more than a half-century. There were others, like Frank Carson. But this pair defied gravity. With them, our papers never seemed to come down to earth.

I knew both men, of course—from a distance. We had met on my various trips to the Windy City, but they flew well above my cruising altitude. The newsroom seemed to be in constant panic. It was bark and bite like a lost dog on the South Side, shout and cry like a newsboy hawking papers at State and Madison, roar and whine like the creaky, old elevated trains above Wabash Avenue.

Howey's antics were personified as the character Walter Burns in *The Front Page.* He was as enterprising as a big-time bank robber, as imaginative as any scientist at the University of Chicago, and as inspirational as any of the city's long line of distinguished Catholic cardinals.

I remember talking with Howey one day about his rules for good reporting. He recounted his ABCs with a brief example. A good-looking doll is rubbed out by her jealous lover. First you get the story. Then you get several good pictures of the doll. Finally you find her diary telling everything.

One time, Howey's reporters kidnapped a good-looking gun moll. She had gotten herself involved in some underworld caper. She was shanghaied to the office, grilled by newsmen, photographed from every angle, and then hidden in a hotel to keep other papers from finding her. Each day Howey would release more of her interview and new photos until he had milked the story. Then he paid her hotel bill and she hit the streets.

Howey was a thin, little guy with neatly combed light-brown hair and knotted, polka-dot ties. He looked like a small-town minister about to lead a prayer meeting. His left eye was glass but his right could cut down a lying judge or penetrate the rocklike oath of a phony preacher.

Romanoff was an actor, changing roles with every story. He would phone a gangster, saying he was an FBI agent ready to make a deal. He was a judge, monsignor, rabbi, physician, and, in real crisis, an undertaker. Romy never wrote stories. He was a phone editor who broke stories. And what breaks. He not only solved some of Chicago's biggest crimes but got the bad guys to confess to him personally. Romanoff was as daring as Howey. On the phone he impersonated, among others, the Chicago police commissioner and the Illinois director of public safety.

This is the story of one Romanoff hunch. He zeroed in on a neighborhood handyman who knew a missing child and her family. The police were about to release the worker after fruitless questioning. They were convinced he was innocent. Romy, who had real power when he wanted to use it, asked the police to hold the man until he arrived at the station. The police thought he had more information. On the way to the station, Romanoff purchased a very large doll. On arrival Romy told officers he needed some time alone with the man before he could tell them what he knew. It was pure bluff, but the police didn't know that and they agreed. Left alone with the handyman, Romanoff pulled out his hearts-and-flowers routine and the child's "beloved doll." He figuratively shoved that doll down the guy's throat for nearly an hour. The handyman couldn't take another moment with Romy and confessed to murdering the girl. The flamboyant editor was on Page One again, big. The killer was later hanged.

Howey and Romanoff worked together on one of the paper's most sensational scoops. And I mean sensational. All Chicago wept at "The Case of the Ragged Stranger."

Carl Wanderer's pregnant wife and her unborn baby had been shot to death by a "ragged stranger" as they returned home to the lobby of their darkened apartment building. Wanderer was carrying a pistol. He and the attacker exchanged fourteen shots. Carl was found weeping over the body of his slain spouse. The killer escaped, leaving his gun behind. Wanderer was so distraught at the deaths of his wife and unborn child that he tried to throw himself into the grave at their burial. He was hailed as a hero. Tens of thousands shed tears for the family.

This time Howey had a hunch. The two guns in the battle looked too much alike—both well-oiled and cleaned, as if by the same person. The editor put his bulldog, Romanoff, on the scent. After considerable sleuthing, Romy traced the stranger's pistol, through its serial number, to a cousin of Wanderer's. Grilled by Romanoff, the cousin admitted lending the gun to Wanderer the evening before the murder. Romy called the police and all confronted Wanderer, who claimed that two similar guns might have been mixed up in the excitement. Romanoff and the police backed off.

Romanoff had a police pal, Lieutenant Mike Loftus. The pair plotted. They called on Wanderer's mother-in-law, with whom the couple lived. While the lieutenant engaged the woman in conversation, Romy pretended he had to phone his office. He searched the apartment and found several love letters to Wanderer from a girl named Julia, as well as photos of the two together. Romy and the lieutenant departed, telling the woman nothing of their discovery.

Romanoff did not have Julia's family name and could not locate her. Finally he devised another plan. He went to Wanderer and told him that Julia had sent him a note. She was coming to see Wanderer. Romy could phone her and head her off. Stunned and bewildered, Wanderer gave him Julia's phone number. Romy found Julia, and she told him Wanderer had said he was single and had proposed marriage. Confronted with Julia's story, Wanderer confessed to Romy that he had murdered his wife.

Howey and Romy were on the front page again.

But we didn't win them all in Chicago. We were once soundly trounced by a saint.

Harry Reutlinger, a reporter on the *American*, was assigned to get a photo of a man who had shot and killed his wife in a suicide pact—only he chickened out after killing her. The man was hauled to Chicago's

Columbus Hospital for observation. He took all the family photos with him.

Reutlinger entered the hospital looking for the man. After wandering around without luck, he was stopped by a small nun carrying a large scrub bucket and wet mop. The nun asked him whom he wanted to see. Reutlinger dismissed her, saying he was there to see Mother Frances Cabrini. Suspicious, the sister asked the reporter if he knew where to find her and whether he would recognize her face. Reutlinger dismissed her again, saying he was all right and she could go about doing God's work. With that, the nun demanded to see his identity. Reutlinger thought he would blow her away by presenting his impressive Chicago press card. Instead, the tiny figure immediately ordered him from the building, saying he was probably there to bother one of the patients.

Reutlinger pretended to leave but later climbed the fire escape to the fifth floor of the hospital. He was looking for a room with a police guard. Suddenly he slipped and fell in the soapy water on the marble floor and slid down the corridor. When Reutlinger stopped he was at the feet of the same little nun. Mother Cabrini swung the soapy mop at him and chased Reutlinger up the corridor and out of the hospital.

Mother Cabrini, though born in Italy, was named by the Catholic Church as its first North American saint shortly after World War II. We ran a big story in Chicago. I was sorry that we didn't include a sidebar about Reutlinger and the wet mop. But it was nice to know that we sometimes moved in saintly circles.

I heard about Romanoff's retirement party, but it was too late to attend. I would have gone just for the education. Some of the guys who were there told me about it.

The setting was fitting, a Chicago bar. A lot of old-timers sat around having a few belts with him. Romanoff was asked the secret of his scoops. He answered in one word: psychology. Romy spun a long tale of those scoops. Let me recall one, my favorite: the story of Sammy Samootz Amatuna.

Sammy was five feet two inches tall. He loved music, especially opera, and carried his violin case with him wherever he went. Sammy worked mostly for Al Capone. He also did odd jobs for Diamond Jim Brady. He was paid $50 to make music when he started his career. Later, little

Sammy and his violin case commanded $5,000 a gig. You see, he made music with a machine gun. Those big jobs meant more opera tickets for Sammy and his friends.

Romy was having a drink in a downtown bar late one night. Sammy came over and said he had heard a lot about Romanoff. He asked if Romy would join him at his table for a drink so they might get acquainted. Romy agreed, and they had a belt and a pleasant chat about opera.

Romanoff was at his work desk listening to the police radio one evening a few months later. In laconic, flat tones, a report said a killing had taken place at a nearby barbershop. A lone killer had entered the shop and sprayed a customer with bullets. Romy rushed to the scene. Sammy was dead, his chest covered with blood. He sat in the barber chair, his face still lathered for a shave. Romy noticed that Sammy's violin case lay in a distant corner. Sammy also had something in his blood-soaked shirt pocket. Romy carefully reached in. He pulled out a small envelope. It contained six unsullied front-row tickets for that evening's opera.

After finishing the story, Romanoff said that was his last recollection of the evening. He raised his right hand for silence and looked around the room. When everyone was silent he spoke, "I want all of you to know this. If you ever wind up in jail or get in any trouble, call me. I'll take care of you. Don't forget. That's a promise from Romanoff."

No one doubted him. It was time to go. The old-timers shook hands with Romy and drifted into the night. Romanoff concluded his retirement party with these words: "In fifty years I never had a byline."

Carmel Snow was born in Dublin, Ireland, with a mind of penetrating insight and a soul of sweeping effervescence. The slim, little lady with the searching, steel eyes became world-famous as the editor of *Harper's Bazaar*. Her career and life reflect the high fashion of this century. Her own wardrobe created a vogue of its own.

Carmel's deep-throated but delightful Dublin accent echoed through the houses of Paris, Rome, and other salons of Europe like the commands of a goddess. She would accept nothing less than top quality—not only in fashion but in *Bazaar*. And, as a devoted wife and mother in her own family. Her intuition and intelligence, romance and adventure, extraordinary eye for detail and vitality all created an editor with an uncommon, unrivaled touch. In her own sphere she was the ultimate professional, America's queen of fashion.

Carmel's brother, Tom White, was general manager of the Hearst newspapers. I saw her most often through my pal Paul McNamara. The two often had their Irish heads together plotting some publicity scheme for the magazine. She seemed so casual, elegantly simple in dress and demeanor. Yet there was absolutely nothing casual or simple about her. Her blue-white hair crowned a regal bearing. She never looked like a model or anyone else. She was always Carmel Snow.

Pop asked Dick Berlin to get her from *Vogue*. *Bazaar* became the fashion bible under Carmel. She proceeded to give early publishing breaks to such writers as Eudora Welty, Truman Capote, Jessamyn West, and Jean Stafford. Under Carmel the magazine published Sean O'Casey, Anne Morrow Lindbergh, Rebecca West, Dylan Thomas, Frank O'Connor, E. E. Cummings, Marianne Moore, Edith Sitwell, and other famous writers. *Bazaar* was class from cover to cover.

But Paris and fashion were Carmel's true loves. She once told me that going to the Paris shows was like attending a royal wedding. Paris and fashion were the epitome of grace and elegance, the very essence of quality, boasting workmanship and fabrics that were one of the world's most perfect marriages. Even when American and other designers began to challenge Paris after World War II, Carmel was unwilling to concede their equality with the French. She was as Parisian as Charles de Gaulle and, with slight exaggeration may I add, as French as Joan of Arc. I say that because Carmel was as mystical about fashion as she was about her Catholic devotions.

To the American woman, who was then becoming fashion-conscious, Carmel was the Queen of Rags, as we used to joke at Toots Shor's. We would speak of her in such endearing terms, because she could belt down a martini with the best of us. Her shrewd judgments not only made and broke new collections but captured the complete attention of international buyers and others in the trade. There was rarely any doubt about where Carmel stood, good or bad. And she always seemed to be ahead of everyone on fashion trends.

I happened to see Carmel one day after she retired. She told me she was flying to Paris. I asked her if the trip was a vacation. She replied, "No, it's work." She was going to review the latest collections—for no one but herself.

Carmel died in 1961. I reminded myself that it was about the time of the Paris spring showings.

I will always remember Bob Considine with a typewriter on his knees writing a news story, column, magazine article, or his latest book—while waiting for a plane, train, or bus to take him to his next assignment. Bob also worked in radio, television, the movies, and was constantly in demand for speeches all over the country. He wore a half-dozen hats at all times—and a beat-up favorite of his own.

I don't believe—and virtually all newsmen who knew Bob share this conviction—that any newspaperman in history ever typed faster than Considine. He learned to type as a young clerk-typist in the U.S. State Department, and his mind moved as fast as his touch system. Shirley Povich, the longtime sports editor of the *Washington Post,* once told me that he watched Bob bat out a column of 600 words on the St. Louis Cardinals in exactly nine minutes. It was during the 1942 World Series. Only Bob was not sitting down in the relative calm of the press box; he was standing on a train platform in St. Louis with his typewriter perched atop baggage that was piled high on a loading cart. It was the only place Bob could find to type.

Hundreds of passengers, porters, and trainmen—all talking, shouting, and rushing somewhere—poured past Considine and the baggage. As Bob's nimble fingers played a tune on his portable, the conductor of his train began calling, "All aboard!" As the train began to pull out, Bob yanked the copy from his typewriter and handed it to a waiting Western Union messenger. He hopped on the train and invited Povich for a drink. Shirley said, "I was a little concerned that you might miss the train." Considine replied, "Hell, I was worried that a porter was going to start moving the baggage!"

There is another famous story about Considine writing in an unorthodox position. Bob, Frank Conniff, and I flew to Rome in 1958 to cover the death of Pope Pius XII and the election of Pope John XXIII. Bob and Jack Casserly, our Rome bureau chief, drove out to Castelgandolfo, where Eugenio Pacelli had died at his summer residence. Shortly after arriving at the town square, they met a Vatican monsignor who asked, "Would you like to see His Holiness?"

It was the chance of a lifetime. No one outside his personal and papal family had seen the dead pontiff. Bob and Jack, hardly able to contain their enthusiasm at a big scoop, accepted the invitation. The monsignor led them inside the imposing gate and up the villa stairs into the pope's bedroom. Pius lay in his papal raiments waiting to be transported to the Vatican. Bob and Jack were Catholic, and knelt at the bedside of His Holiness out of respect. They also were trying to memorize every detail about Pacelli and the room. Before leaving, both kissed the hands of the pontiff.

The two set their portables on rickety tables outside a café at the edge of the square and began to write. Jack wrote a news story based on details the monsignor had given them about the pope's return to the Vatican. Bob wrote a column about their emotional moments alone with His Holiness. When they finished, Jack began reading Bob's column, which was date-lined CASTELGANDOLFO, ITALY. He quietly suggested that Considine change it to: AT THE BEDSIDE OF THE POPE—CASTELGAN-DOLFO, ITALY. Bob did, and the column received not only sensational play in the United States but won numerous journalistic prizes, including the Overseas Press Club award for foreign reporting.

Red Smith—one of the greatest sportswriters who ever lived, and a friend of Considine's—was at Toots Shor's for Bob's return to New York. Red was a Catholic and a gentleman but he had a journalistic bone to pick with Considine. "Okay, Bob, you were at the bedside of the pope. Where the hell was your typewriter—on the pope's bed?" "No, Red," Bob answered. "On the floor in front of my knees. I was praying."

Publisher Cissy Patterson, of the old *Washington Herald,* and Povich, of the *Washington Post,* gave Bob his first jobs. He started out in 1930 at thirty-five dollars a week writing sports. My father brought Bob up to New York in 1936 as a sportswriter on the *Mirror.* Considine rose to the top of the game, earning several hundred thousand dollars a year reporting and writing.

Bob always remained a gentleman. I never met a finer human being. He was a loving father to three sons and a daughter, and a faithful, devoted husband to Millie, his wife of forty-four years.

Bob loved self-deprecating humor. After reaching newspaper stardom, he often told of an incident in his hometown of Washington, D.C. He had just come out of the *Washington Times-Herald* and hailed a taxi. The cabbie asked, "Do you know that fellow, Considine?" "Yeah," Bob

Bill as publisher of the *New York Journal-American* at his office in 1939. A photo of his father as a young man is in the background.

The Hearst Corporation, from the boardroom to the newsroom. Shown above at
Hearst headquarters in New York are the five Hearst brothers: seated are Bill, George,
and John; Randy and David stand behind them. The photo below shows the *New York
Journal-American* city room in 1937.

Above: Ever the sports fan, Bill Hearst joins Babe Ruth for an interview on New York radio station WINS in the 1930s. *Below:* The *Journal-American*'s own "team" in the 1950s—before the Brooklyn Dodgers left for Los Angeles. Bill is in the back row with columnist Westbrook Pegler (to his left, holding baseball); Dorothy Kilgallen sits at center, with Frank Conniff to her right and sportswriters Bill Corum and Max Kase to her left.

Bill as a war correspondent for the Hearst papers in France, September 21, 1944.

Above: Cartoon by Burris Jenkins, Jr., of the *New York Journal-American,* showing Bill Hearst in a bunker on the Italian front in 1944. *Below:* Bill (at right on bike) riding along the Champs Elysees following the liberation of Paris. Riding bikes at left are INS correspondent Dick Tregaskis and AP reporter Frank Scherschel. An unidentified GI and three French women pull them along in a jeep.

Above: Bill welcomes General Douglas MacArthur to New York on April 21, 1951, during the Far East commander's tumultuous reception following his unpopular removal from command in Korea by President Truman. *Below:* Bill in South Korea on April 7, 1956 with General D.D. White, commander of the U.S. Eighth Army, and General Chong, chief of staff of the South Korean Army.

Above: Bill, Bob Considine, and Frank Conniff—the Hearst Task Force—at Hearst headquarters in New York in the 1960s. *Below:* Hearst, Considine, and Conniff at U.S. positions in Vietnam in 1963.

Facing page: Joseph Kingsbury-Smith, Bill Hearst, and Frank Conniff stand before the Kremlin during their Pulitzer Prize-winning trip to Moscow in 1956. *Above:* A year later, Bill again sits across the table from Nikita Khrushchev for a follow-up discussion. To Bill's right are Bob Considine and Frank Conniff.

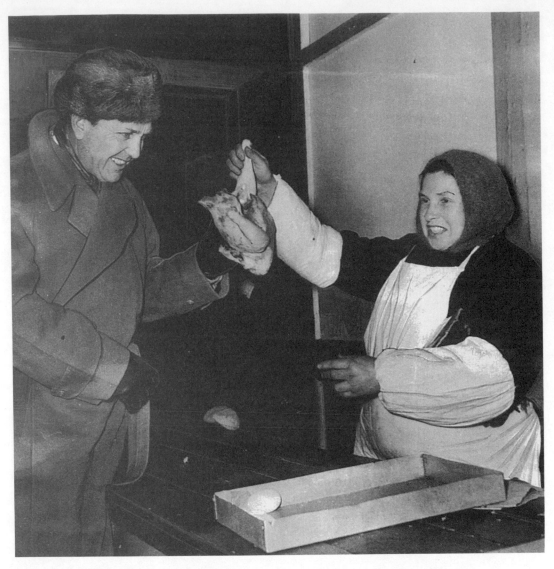

The missions to Moscow provided Bill Hearst with rare first-hand glimpses of Soviet life, as the photos on these two pages illustrate.

Bill, famed *Chicago American* editor Walter Howey, and Howard Hughes chat at La Guardia Airport in 1946 before flying to California.

Above: Bing Crosby sent this photo to Bill with the inscription: "Just want you to know I read the right papers—upside down!" Crosby, shown here at his hotel during a visit to New York in the 1940s, was a life-long friend of Bill Hearst. *Below:* Elsa Maxwell, longtime Hearst society writer and gossip columnist, makes a point to her publisher.

Above: Bill visits pal John Wayne on the set of *The Alamo. Below:* At a dinner honoring actor Ed Wynn in New York in 1966, Bill is joined by comedian George Jessel, Roddy McDowell, Bette Davis, and Bert Lahr.

Bill greets the Duke of Windsor at a New York Luncheon.

Bill Hearst and Joseph Kingsbury-Smith in front of the Elysée Palace in Paris after a 1988 interview with French President Francois Mitterand.

Above: Longtime Hearst reporter Jimmy Kilgallen and his wife, Mae, with Bill Hearst on the occasion of Jimmy's retirement party at New York's Overseas Press Club. Jimmy retired at ninety. *Below:* A party to celebrate Bill Curley's fiftieth anniversary with the Hearst organization. Left to right: Austine Hearst; J.D. Gortatowsky, Hearst General Manager; Bill; Curley and his wife Mary. Curley was one of the great editors of the Hearst newspapers.

Above: Bill, Joseph Kingsbury-Smith, and Frank Conniff with former President Harry Truman at the 1956 Democratic convention in Chicago. *Below:* Bill interviews Indian Prime Minister Nehru in India in 1963.

Above: Bill Hearst with President Eisenhower during a Washington reception in the mid-1950s. Herbert Hoover is at center. *Below:* Frank Conniff and Bill meet West German Chancellor Konrad Adenauer in Bonn after interview in 1954.

Bill greets Vice President Nixon during a New York reception.

Above: The author compares globe-hopping with Nixon in 1956. *Below:* GOP Presidential candidate Barry Goldwater and comedian Harry Hirshfield with Bill at the 1964 March of Dimes dinner in New York.

Above: The author greets Chiang Kai-shek before a 1956 interview in Taiwan. *Below:*
Eamon de Valera, who served Ireland as Prime Minister and President for thirty-five
years, stands with the author outside Aras an Uachtarain in Dublin in June, 1963. Bill
Hearst found this great leader of the Irish "deeply religious, charitable, and forgiving
. . . a studious, Old World gentleman." Courtesy Irish Press Group, Dublin.

Above: Bill and President John F. Kennedy. the inscription at center reads: "For Bill Hearst—the shoe off his foot and the shirt off his back. With best regards from his friend Jack Kennedy." *Below:* With President Johnson in the Oval Office.

Above: The author with President Jimmy Carter following an interview. *Below:* Bill and Joseph Kingsbury-Smith thank Egyptian President Anwar Sadat for an interview in Cairo in 1975.

Above: With Deng Xiaoping before an interview in 1980. "I left Beijing convinced that the brutal rule of terror instituted by Mao had been buried with the late dictator. History shows how wrong I was." *Below:* President Reagan listens to a question during a White House reception in June 1981.

The author at U.N. headquarters at Flushing Meadows, Long Island in 1949 with his longtime friend Carlos P. Romulo, Philippine Ambassador to the U.N.

answered uneasily. The driver chuckled and said, "I knew that bum when he didn't have shoes."

Bob treated all women like saints and Scotch whiskey like holy water. He always went out of his way to be kind to women and double Scotches. But the only one I ever saw him make a pass at was booze. Yet I never saw him drunk, or even tipsy.

Considine covered the biggest stories in the world for INS and our papers for more than three decades. The extraordinary range of his work—especially under the incredible pressure of so many deadlines—demonstrated his greatness. From the Joe Louis-Max Schmelling fight to the World Series. From World War II and our atomic bomb blasts to presidents. From Korea to the Middle East and, as a member of the Hearst Task Force, interviews with Soviet leaders. From news stories to columns, from books to movies, from radio to television, he was everywhere. Bob's column "On the Line" was syndicated to hundreds of newspapers across the country.

He also wrote many bestselling books: *The Babe Ruth Story, Thirty Seconds Over Tokyo* (the story of Jimmy Doolittle's raid with Captain Ted Lawson), *MacArthur the Magnificent, The Rape of Poland, The Brinks Robbery, The Irish in America,* and a dozen others. But probably only a few read his book, *Matt Talbot, Alcoholic,* a reverent account of the saintly Irish drunk who finally defeated the bottle. I think that Bob loved Talbot and, although Considine never quit drinking himself, he was very close to Talbot.

One of Bob's finest pieces was "A Newspaperman's Prayer." Part of it reads:

Dear God, may I be fair, Circumstances and dumb luck have placed in my thumby paws a degree of authority which I may not fully comprehend. Let me not profane it.

Give me the drive that will make me check and countercheck the facts. Guide me when, lost for want of a rudder or a lead, I stumble through the jungle of speculation.

The twenty-six sharp-edged tools we call our alphabet can do what other tools do: build or destroy. Let me build. But let me know clearly, also, what should be destroyed, what darkness, what bigotry, what evil, what curse, what ignorance.

This tall, broad-shouldered, smiling soul went home to God in 1975. He died of a stroke in New York Medical Center at sixty-eight. A lot of newspapermen in New York and around America and the world got drunk remembering him that evening. When they sobered up, many—Catholic, Protestant, Jew, and atheist—got on their knees for the funeral mass at St. Patrick's Cathedral. No eulogy could ever sufficiently capture his life. We all put it the way he would have done: "So long, Bob. See ya in Rome, Paris, Tokyo, Buenos Aires, New York, Washington, and heaven." I remember taking a cab instead of walking back to my office on Eighth Avenue after the funeral mass. It was raining—tears.

Bob's wife, Millie, came to see me. She said she had no money to meet Bob's burial and other costs. Like a lot of reporters, Bob had turned the family budget over to his wife. Millie had lived high and never quite managed to save. The company paid for the funeral and other bills. Millie, who was usually seen lunching at "21" most days, seemed to disappear. She passed away still in grief over Bob. Bob would have written the ending that way, however painful it might have been, because truth was his game.

I have thought of him often since he went away. I cannot go into a New York restaurant or saloon without seeing his big Irish kisser at the bar. He orders us both a drink and says, "Bill, excuse me a few minutes. I've got a column to finish."

Walter Winchell was cut from different cloth. He could be a real bastard—and often was.

Walter was a self-centered egomaniac who was small-time in my book. Pop allowed him too much power. When Walter went after a dame, he took her clothes off in print. And he cut the gizzards out of many a man. He was a mean-spirited SOB if you ever got in his way.

I saw a lot of Walter in the Cub Room of the Stork Club and around town, but I never had much use for him. He sat at Table 50 and nobody ever dared go near it, day or night, without saluting with a big hello as you walked by. Otherwise, he would say loud enough to be heard a dozen tables away, "What a prick that guy is!" So I always gave him the big hello, and Walter would nod like Casey Stengel to a rookie trying to make the Yankees.

One late night in the 1950s I bumped into my nephew, Bunky Hearst, a news photographer for the *Mirror,* at a restaurant. He said:

I just left that crazy sonofabitch, Winchell. The guy has a police radio in his Cadillac, and he's responding to the same calls I do.

I get this signal 1013. Shots fired. There's a prowler up on this apartment building along Eighth Avenue. Two or three cops are ahead of me up the stairs. They have their guns drawn. I am lugging my camera and want to be the first to get the hell out of there in case somebody starts shooting. But somebody is right behind me and blocking my retreat. It's Winchell and he has a gun out, a small .25 caliber. The sergeant ahead of me sees Winchell's piece and shouts down the stairs, "Put that fuckin' gun away or I'll come down there and shove it up your ass."

Well, nobody talks that way to Walter. Nobody. He's screaming back at the sergeant, "Fuck you. And that goes double!"

They are really pissed off at one another. Anyway, the cops catch the prowler and haul him down to the sidewalk, where they cuff him. I'm trying to get the picture, but Walter is in my way, bitching at the sergeant, "Well, Sarge, maybe you were right but, by God, I'm Walter Winchell. Do you hear me? Winchell!"

The sergeant won't budge. He tells Winchell that he's not a trained cop, that he should butt out. And don't pull a gun again or he'll run his ass in.

Winchell is turning purple. He's spitting over and over, "I'm Winchell, you can't talk to me like that!"

The Sarge says, "The hell I can't."

It's a standoff.

Winchell was at his height in the late 1940s and early 1950s. His column probably had 10 to 12 million readers (he claimed 50 million) and was syndicated in more than 1,000 papers. Another 30 million listened to him on radio.

Nobody knew Winchell better than Robin "Curley" Harris, who was one of our reporters. They had been friends for many years. Curley also was a good pal of mine and I asked him about Winchell one day at lunch. He told me that Walter was born of immigrant Russian parents in Harlem. His real name was Velvella Vincelski. Curley related a story of Winchell's boyhood:

Walter was going to a public grade school in South Harlem. He told me that when he was in the fifth grade, his teacher said he was so "hopelessly bad" in English that he would have to repeat the grade.

Walter was so disgusted that he decided then and there to quit school. He joined a vaudeville troupe as a hoofer. Later he became a single, singing and dancing.

In his early twenties he began posting tidbits about his vaudeville and other entertainer friends on a theatrical bulletin board. It became very popular and he was hired by *Vaudeville News* and later the *Daily Graphic* to write the same kind of stuff. He changed his byline and the rest is history.

I remember when Pop hired Winchell as a Broadway columnist for the *Mirror*. It was because of his terse dot-and-dash staccato style. He married June Magee, a Mississippi beauty who had been part of a song and dance team. They had a two-room apartment on Forty-sixth Street, and later had two children.

Walter introduced "slanguage"—street talk that was all his own. He created a new lexicon among the New York smart set with phrases like, "He went phffft" and "She was makin' whoopee!" Winchell seemed to know more about what was happening on Broadway and around town than anyone. His column soared and *Mirror* circulation skyrocketed.

Alexander Woolcott, the writing darling of the smart set, was asked by an interviewer which newspapers he preferred to read. Woolcott said he never read any newspapers because he did not have the time. However, he kept up on important news by reading "the two Walters." When asked who that might be, Woolcott replied: Lippmann and Winchell. Winchell carried the news clipping around for months and would show it to us, saying it was the greatest compliment of his life. He was right up there with Walter Lippmann. And Winchell believed it!

Yet Walter was not without some big-name enemies. One of the most outspoken was comedian George Jessel, who was famous for delivering, of all things, funeral eulogies. People privately chuckled all over town when Jessel said, "I can't wait to speak at Winchell's funeral." Walter never forgave him.

Winchell was a good friend of FBI director J. Edgar Hoover's. He also ingratiated himself with President Roosevelt. Walter began sending Harry Truman private notes when the Missourian became president. He wrote of his personal contact with FDR and hoped to continue such a rapport with Truman. The president never responded to his letters. Winchell began knocking Truman in his column and never stopped.

At the same time, Walter was palsy-walsy with Owney Madden, Lucky Luciano, Frank Costello, and other New York mobsters. He once told me, "I learned to respect racketeers when I was a kid and never lost it." I never understood why Winchell admired these thugs. Perhaps it was the attention they got. To Walter, the limelight was synonymous with success.

One of the most sensational scoops in Winchell's mercurial career was the night that Lepke Buchalter, chief of Murder, Inc., and wanted for murder, surrendered to him near Madison Square Garden. Walter, who was going bananas with his great beat, called the *Mirror* before he turned Buchalter over to J. Edgar Hoover. He wanted a big splash with his byline on Page One. The editors said no. Furious, Winchell demanded to know why. They replied that Germany had just invaded Poland. Their headline was: WAR IN EUROPE. Walter had been scooped by Hitler.

Lepke was eventually tried for murder and sentenced to the electric chair. Until his death in Sing Sing prison, Lepke screamed his surrender was part of a deal, that he had been double-crossed by Winchell, Governor Thomas E. Dewey, Hoover, and anyone else within a thousand miles of his voice.

Walter was then making more than $800,000 a year. No individual in the history of American journalism had achieved such notoriety and power. He had become a national figure.

Once he hit the big time, Winchell probably never picked up a tab at the Stork Club or anywhere else in New York—and a lot of other places. Yet he could be generous. When Curley Harris became ill and faced heavy doctors' bills, Walter offered him $1,000 to help out. Curley declined. When Winchell received $55,000 in reward money for the capture of Buchalter, he gave it all to the Damon Runyon Cancer Fund. The two had been good friends in Damon's final years.

Winchell would broadcast his big radio show on Sunday evenings. He talked like a missile firing into outer space, about 235 words a minute: "Good evening, Mr. and Mrs. America and all the ships at sea. Let's go to press!"

That was Walter. He sizzled, crackled, ripped, and zapped. Much of what he reported was a mad dash of trivia, but Winchell never bored. He was show biz shot out of a cannon.

Walter would rush over to the Stork Club after each broadcast to get his reviews, like an actor. One time, actress Tallulah Bankhead was perched at Table 50, and drawled, "Sensational, daaahh-lin'." (I was not in the Cub Room at the time, but the happening became a Stork Club legend.) Winchell responded to Tallulah's accolade by kissing her on the cheek and patting her ass. Tallulah was no Girl Scout, and Walter loved to pat girls' asses.

People stopped by, congratulating Walter on the broadcast. Winchell loved the adoring drivel, but Tallulah was getting annoyed at the interruptions. Walter kept introducing her to all these jerks she didn't know, and didn't care to know. Some guy came along and Winchell introduced him to Tallulah, who was juiced to her bitchy eyeballs by this time. The actress replied in her throatiest stage voice, "Nice to meet you, Herman— or whatever your name is. Now go fuck yourself!" Winchell, who was quick on the draw, gave the guy a split-second smile and said, "She only speaks French."

The curtain began falling for Walter in the mid-1950s. He had been acquainted with Roy Cohn, who was Senator Joseph McCarthy's right-hand man. Cohn was slipping material to Winchell about Communists in government and elsewhere. Walter swallowed the whole hook. He wrote a lot of questionable stuff.

Actually, I began raising questions about Winchell as early as March 22, 1938, when I wrote to my father:

We may as well face it. We no longer have a first-rate Broadway columnist in Winchell. His main interests apparently lie in international, social, and religious problems. He is, so I am told, getting increasingly hard to handle, and continually threatening to quit. I assure you that I am not alone in realizing and commenting on this.

A few weeks later, Pop returned my letter with this note attached to it: "Dear Bill, I agree with you entirely about Winchell. In fact, the next time he wants to quit, please let me know so we can accept the resignation." Winchell's threats to quit quieted down. So did some of his vitriol. But other hates and zany wars with new people surfaced. This rose to a new pitch in the mid-1950s, when Walter attacked James A. Wechsler, editor of the *New York Post*, and others concerning alleged Communist connections. A lot of his stuff was not only harsh but, more important, never washed. The ABC network and we issued a retraction on some of the material that Winchell broadcast and wrote about Wechsler. My father had been concerned about Walter and had warned our editors about

his copy long before Pop passed away in 1951. He told them to edit
Winchell "very carefully" and "leave out any dangerous paragraphs."

In the late 1950s and early sixties, a steady stream of papers dropped
Winchell's column. The *Mirror* folded in 1963 after a long printers'
strike, so Walter moved to the *Journal-American*. I reduced his column
to three times a week and cut its length. When the *Journal-American*
closed in 1965 and the combined *New York World-Journal-Tribune* ended
in 1966 after another prolonged printers' walkout, Winchell himself began looking for papers that would use his stuff.

Dismayed at his crumbling column, Walter announced his retirement
in February of 1968. Later that year, at Christmas, Winchell's son and
namesake shot himself to death at his home in California, leaving a
widow and two children. Winchell's wife passed away shortly afterward.
And Walter himself was not well.

I saw and talked with Walter several times over the next few years.
Despite all the misgivings I had about his braggadocio and vengeful style,
no reporter in American history raised personal journalism to such popularity. That is not all bad, friend. We still need the eyewitness, the
human touch to newspapers, magazines, radio, and television.

Winchell had lost considerable weight and his voice had become only
a whisper. He was dying of cancer, and we talked about Runyon and his
battle against it. Our last conversation was shrouded in death. Walter
finally placed the cover over his typewriter in 1972, and was buried next
to his wife in Phoenix, Arizona. I was told that only a rabbi and a single
mourner—his daughter, Walda—were present. I would have made it there
if I had known about it in time. I would have gone not so much to bury
Walter as to pray for him. Vengeance is a rotten game.

Winchell was never nastier than toward Westbrook Pegler, one of our
longtime columnists who also practiced the poison pen. The two clashed
not only over Winchell's treatment of President Truman, not necessarily
a friend of Pegler's, but also Secretary of Defense James Forrestal, who
committed suicide.

The language on all sides was unpardonable. Pegler accused Winchell
of being guilty of "grossly vulgar and often malicious and untruthful
gents'-room journalism." Walter seethed over that for days in the Cub
Room. He called Pegler a "presstitute" in print and a "prick" in private.
Winchell finally called off the war because he feared Pegler's ability at

word-slinging. That was the highest accolade that Walter could pay anyone.

Winchell was right. I never met anyone with Peg's command of words. Perhaps he learned some of that from his father, who had been a reporter and worked on our Chicago paper for years. Peg wrote for us over a tumultuous eighteen-year span, starting with King Features in 1944. This followed a dozen as a columnist with Scripps-Howard and many years as a sportswriter and reporter with United Press. Pegler was perhaps the most controversial and outrageous columnist in the world. His way with words in "As Pegler Sees It" also made him one of the most influential.

Pegler was a midwesterner. He stood six feet one inch; approached the world with aristocratic bearing and manner; was a devoted husband to his wife, Julie, who was a cardiac cripple; and was very interested in his Catholic faith. Yet Peg was one of the most cantankerous, colossally cussed men I ever met.

Communism, from when he first came in contact with it in the 1930s, was his top target for the next thirty-five years. There were also plenty of others, particularly organized labor and its internal scandals. There seemed to be only three people in the world he wouldn't attack: his wife; Dr. Sara Jordan, who treated him for ulcers at Boston's Lahey Clinic; and the pope. Everybody else was fair game, including me and our company. This attack on President Truman is a typical example of Peg's stuff: "This Truman is thin-lipped, a hater, and not above offering you his hand to yank you off balance and work you over with a chair leg, pool cue, or something out of his pocket."

Pegler had a knock-down verbal brawl with his erstwhile good friend and fellow writer, Quentin Reynolds. The *New York Herald Tribune* had asked Reynolds to review a biography on the life of Heywood Broun, a top New York columnist and writer. The book was written by Dale Kramer, a literary historian. Kramer recounted in the biography a savage attack by Pegler on his one-time friend, Broun. Peg had alleged that Communists had infiltrated the Newspaper Guild. Broun was a Guild founder and leader.

Kramer, in the book's final scene, reported that Broun was so shocked at the harshness of Pegler's attack on him and the Guild that he retreated to bed. Reynolds related that Broun found it virtually impossible to relax and sleep. He lay mentally paralyzed and finally died. Although neither Kramer nor Reynolds had accused Pegler of causing Broun's death, they clearly implied that Peg could have been more merciful toward his old pal.

In turn, Pegler unleashed on Reynolds perhaps the most vitriolic attack of his long, cantankerous career. In a series of columns he accused Reynolds of being a moral degenerate, of displaying his "mangy hide" naked on Connecticut roads. Pegler also claimed that Reynolds had been a war profiteer, that he faked stories as a news correspondent, and was a notorious coward with no guts. As if that were not enough, Pegler asserted that Reynolds had proposed marriage to Connie, Broun's widow, while accompanying her to the funeral and burial. Reynolds sued Pegler and the Hearst Corporation for libel.

People have long asked me how anything like this could have occurred. Here is what actually happened. The top men at King Features Syndicate and the Hearst papers had been concerned about Pegler's increasingly vituperative attacks for some time. A corporation lawyer and a KFS editor were assigned to clear all his columns. They flagged Pegler's columns on Reynolds and questioned him. Could he prove his accusations? Of course, Pegler boomed. He had confirmed every charge.

The human factor then assumed control. The lawyer and editor believed, wrongly in this case, that Pegler had greater clout in the company than they did. They felt he was vindictive and could get them fired. This fear obscured the reason they were assigned to the job—to protect the company and, indeed, Pegler himself.

Second, both men were aware that Hearst didn't censor its columnists. It gave them complete freedom to report and write. That is what attracted many top writers to us. Aware of this tradition and Pegler's perceived clout, the lawyer and editor backed off and let the columnist fire.

Finally—and this was a point of strong disagreement between us—I believe my father allowed big-name writers like Pegler, Winchell, and Parsons too much power. In all three instances, power went to their heads. All believed that normal journalistic rules of behavior were for others, not them. They were larger than life, living on some far-off planet. I felt all of them needed a regular kick in the butt so they would be more objective.

The company and Pegler lost the case. The corporation paid Reynolds $175,000 in punitive damages.

After the trial, Pegler began to view me as a personal enemy. As publisher of the *Journal-American* I removed his column from up front, cut its length, and placed it deep in the paper. My father was then dead, but

I believe he would have agreed with me. I told our editors to remove any potentially libelous copy from Peg's columns. I suggested they apply the old rule: When in doubt, leave it out. They applied my order scrupulously. The editing took some—and, at times, much—of the bite out of Pegler's columns. However, I was not about to be blindsided by another Reynolds case.

Pegler saw it differently. He complained about the cuts, saying his entire career had been built on "my courageous disclosure of facts which other journalists will not tackle." That is not accurate. Pegler's career had been built on one concept: attack. That was Peg to the core.

He soon drew a bead on Mrs. Eleanor Roosevelt. He called her "La Boca Grande" (The Big Mouth). We allowed that because she had a reputation for giving a lot of speeches and expressing herself on innumerable subjects. Later, Peg got very personal. In 1959 he wrote a column comparing the former first lady to Medusa, a snake-haired mythological creature with huge teeth. He sarcastically noted that Medusa's followers saw her as "The First Lady of all Creation, a roaring or forensic being who roamed widely on unexplained errands."

Pegler defended the piece, saying Mrs. Roosevelt did have big teeth, and she was a perennial globe-trotter on any and all missions. The column wasn't libelous, but some of the wordage was of very questionable taste. I told our people that Peg was overstepping decency and we ought to think about ending the relationship. However, at that time in 1961, Pegler's contract with KFS still had three years to run.

Meanwhile, company people still dealing with Peg were convinced he had become paranoid. Some thought he was nuts.

In late 1962 Pegler addressed the Anti-Communist Christian Crusade in Tulsa, Oklahoma. In a blast of invective, he accused me and our editors of censoring his criticism of the Kennedy administration. Among the complaints, Peg said he was forced to suppress a column assailing Pulitzer Prize procedures. He added that I had started a "petulant yowl of a spoiled brat for a Pulitzer Prize" and killed that column so that I and my "baby sitters," Joseph Kingsbury-Smith and Conniff, could win the prize. The truth is I was abroad and never saw or heard of the column.

On August 4, 1962, the company announced that KFS would no longer carry Pegler's column nor would it appear in the Hearst newspapers. I was busy elsewhere and had no part in the decision, although I would have voted for it.

Peg returned to Tuscon, Arizona, where he became involved with various far-right-wing groups. He was not well. Doctors removed a cancerous section of stomach. A similar operation followed. He died in the spring of 1969 and was buried beside his wife's unmarked grave.

Some said that, after his wife died, Peg talked only to God. I am glad that God will judge him, not men of lesser talent like myself, or editors, or some of our readers. I believe that Peg loved and respected God, because he sure quieted down on his many visits to churches. But the old devil wanted his talent badly and fought hard for Peg. I don't know who won, but, in my heart, I am pulling for Peg. Forgiveness is a gallant virtue.

I met Jack O'Brien for the first time more than forty years ago. Morton Downey, the late singer and a good friend of mine, was playing Shea's Theater in Buffalo, New York. Morton introduced me to a priest and young Jack, a local reporter who assisted the priest on a weekly radio program.

O'Brien later moved up to New York with the Associated Press, where he became their drama and movie critic as well as Broadway columnist. After several years with the AP, Bill Curley, editor of the *Journal-American,* hired Jack to work for us. We often met at the paper, and as Jack made the rounds of New York shows and nightlife we became friends.

Jack became a pal of Runyon's, Louis Sobol's, and others who covered Broadway. And he became very close to Winchell. In fact, his two children called WW "Uncle Walter." But I believe that Jack knew more people on and around Broadway than Runyon or Winchell. I mean the little as well as the big people—cashiers, newsboys, waiters, cab drivers, cops, ushers, bartenders, vaudeville performers, doormen, petty crooks. He knew absolutely everything that was going down, from the jazz joints to both Lindy's restaurants on Broadway.

One night Downey and O'Brien invited me out to dinner in Manhattan. We had a good steak and wound up in a joint whose name is best forgotten. Morton was one of those Irishmen who never drank. Jack and I started ribbing him about not having a few belts. He shot at us, "You bastards. You're all alike. You think it's a trick to drink. Well, it's not. The trick is *not* to drink!"

With that, Morton ordered a whiskey and soda and poured it down like mother's milk. Another and another. Suddenly, he threw up all over our table. He tripped a waiter who was carrying a large tray of about a hundred clean napkins. Then he tripped another waiter carrying a big tray of dirty dishes. He insulted the manager and threatened to bounce the bouncer. We were thrown out of the place. I never again asked Morton to have a drink.

The marvelous thing about O'Brien was that he knew the history of midtown Manhattan upside down and sideways, from people to buildings and the theater. Only Jack would recall a figure like this: In 1927 there were 264 legitimate Broadway productions; of those, 53 were musicals. Jack and I agree that Broadway has lost a lot of its glamour—today's nightclubs couldn't make the top twenty of four decades ago—but not its soul. It still attracts some great talent in plays on and off the Big Street. But the really big crowds, the consistent volume, isn't there anymore. The answers are obvious: television, crime, cost, and so many people moving to the suburbs.

My wife and I now go out at night only infrequently. And never to nightclubs or other joints. O'Brien and his wife still do. They are night people. But Runyon, Winchell, Hellinger, Sobol, and Kilgallen are gone. And nobody really covers the beat well anymore. I wonder whether we will ever again produce any Broadway historians.

Joseph Kingsbury-Smith was a different cut of historian. He served twice as an INS Washington correspondent, and was a foreign correspondent as well as Paris bureau chief and European manager for nearly twenty years. Joe has spent almost another four decades on special international news assignments and top management posts for us. Joe, Conniff, and I won the Pulitzer Prize in 1956 for a series of exclusive interviews the previous year with Soviet Premier Nikita Khrushchev and other Kremlin leaders.

Joe was sixteen years old when he started with us in 1924. Barry Faris, then chief of INS, hired him in New York as a copy boy at fourteen dollars a week. Joe went to night school to learn typing and shorthand. He was hired away by United Press in 1925. A very intelligent, diligent young fellow, Joe was hired back by Faris, who made him a foreign correspondent in London at the age of nineteen. He later returned to Washington to cover the State Department and get experience on the U.S. view of foreign affairs. Joe got a lot of scoops there. Faris sent him back to London in 1936 as bureau chief. After a Canadian military officer who had drunk too much drove their jeep over an embankment in 1938, Joe spent about two years in Southampton, London, and New York hospitals recovering from injuries.

In 1940 Joe returned to work on the INS foreign desk in New York and went to Washington to cover the State Department from 1941 to April 1944. Cordell Hull was secretary of state during those years, and, when Faris assigned Joe to London as European manager, Hull wrote a letter about him to John G. Winant, the U.S. ambassador there. It concluded: "I have always found him to be a man of high intelligence, discreet, and in every way a worthy representative of his profession. He is a man of character and integrity, and my close association with him here has not only been most enjoyable, but it has at all times redounded to public benefit."

Joe did a magnificent job organizing our coverage of D-day and other stories. After the war, Joe found himself in Paris as European director of International News Service. Joe and I have often talked about those days, especially his world-shaking scoops with Josef Stalin. Few people know the details. They are fascinating.

Joe had sent news questionnaires to Stalin on previous occasions, but the Soviet leader never replied. In 1949, during a prolonged Soviet blockade of Berlin, General Walter Bedell Smith, the U.S. ambassador to Moscow, stopped off in Paris on his return to Washington for consultations. Since April of 1948, the three Western Allies had been forced to supply Berlin by air, since the Soviets had cut off ground access to the divided city. Joe, who knew the general from his London and Washington reporting days, phoned Bedell Smith at his hotel and asked to see him. The general agreed.

Joe asked Bedell Smith if he thought there was any hope for a solution to the Berlin crisis. The ambassador said, "Well, there is nothing definite. I have a feeling Stalin wants to get off the hook, but doesn't know how to do it without losing face."

After Joe returned to his office, he began thinking about the ambassador's assessment. He then sat down at his typewriter and began composing questions that Stalin might answer to extricate himself. Essentially, the three were: Did he wish to improve relations with the United States? Would a solution to the Berlin blockade issue be in keeping with improving such relations? Would Stalin be willing to meet with President Truman to facilitate positive action?

INS had a Russian woman in Moscow who covered basic news announcements for us. Joe sent her the questions by French post office telegram. He then phoned Moscow and asked her to translate the questions into Russian. She was to place them with his name and Paris bureau address in an envelope addressed to Stalin. She herself was to drop the questionnaire into the Kremlin mailbox. If she thought of a better way to get the questions to Stalin, she should use it.

Some forty-eight hours later, on January 30, to his utter astonishment, Joe received a telegram from Stalin. In essence, the Soviet leader said he was ready to meet Truman and solve the Berlin crisis. Joe had scooped the world. His story was played in banner headlines from Washington to Moscow and beyond.

As soon as Joe cabled his first story to INS New York, he rushed another questionnaire to Stalin. This time he sent an urgent and official telegram, via the French post office, directly to the Soviet leader in the Kremlin. It asked when and where he would be willing to meet Truman. Within twenty-four hours Stalin replied, "official and urgent," via the French post office. Stalin told Smith he would be willing to meet Truman in Vienna, Warsaw, or Moscow. He could not meet him in Washington because his physicians had advised him not to fly that long a distance. Both telegrams were signed: "Respectfully, J. Stalin." Joe had another world scoop.

For the next three months the U.S. and Soviet ambassadors to the United Nations met secretly in New York to negotiate terms for lifting the Berlin blockade. An accord was finally reached and it was ratified at a four-power foreign ministers' meeting later, in Paris. It was certainly fitting that Joe covered the Paris finale.

Joe was to score many more scoops—exclusive interviews with many of France's postwar leaders: Germany's Adenauer, Yugoslavia's Tito, Egypt's Nasser, various Israeli leaders, and other major figures on the world scene. He always did it in a calm, self-effacing manner. Perhaps the secret of his greatness as a reporter was that so many statesmen recognized that Joe himself was a fine diplomat.

Today, after his more than sixty years with the company and our many trips around the world together, he is the last old friend at my side. Joe is a vice-president, director, and trustee of the corporation, and our national news editor. He is blessed with a lovely wife, Eileen, and two daughters.

Our friendship has withstood time. That is one of the real joys of my life.

Shortly after Pop died, in 1951, I appointed Frank Conniff my editorial assistant. Our friendship had matured slowly but surely since World War II. Frank was a very funny guy. He also was smart, loyal, and a wonderful conversationalist.

Frank, born in 1914 in Danbury, Connecticut, was a third-generation Irish Catholic. He wore his ancestry and religion on his sleeve. His father was an Associated Press wire operator and his mother became "the grand old lady of Democratic politics" in Connecticut.

Frank went to the University of Virginia for a year, but left because he and his family ran out of money during the Depression. He became a sports columnist and, later, sports editor on the *Danbury News-Times*. He joined the *Journal-American* in 1936 and subsequently became a city hall reporter, feature writer, and rewrite man. He later wrote a column called "East Side, West Side," on local happenings, and another on events around the nation and world.

Frank covered World War II for INS and the *Journal*. We met at various times in Africa, Italy, and Germany and became friends. But it wasn't until after the war that we really got to know one another. I liked Frank because of his good humor, savvy judgments of people and situations, and the genuine friendship he gave me. I was certain that I could trust him, and that he would remain my friend for as long as we both lived.

Conniff was a guy who always had a smile on his face, a good story on the tip of his tongue, and time to listen. Frank was a terrific reader. He must have read three or four books a week, especially history. That is where he got many of his stories.

Frank became my assistant in 1952 after coming home from two tours of covering the Korean War. He was too old to cover wars any more, had turned prematurely gray, and wanted to settle down. Frank married Mary Elizabeth Murray, of Southampton, Long Island. She was one of the most beautiful and kindest women I ever met. They had five children.

Frank protected my back. As publisher of the *Journal-American*, I needed that. He warned me about Richard E. Berlin, president of the Hearst Corporation. Berlin was saying around town that he had inherited the mantle of my father, that I was just a kid, and that he treated me as such. Our battle with Berlin was later to consume much of our time and energy.

Austine and I were of different minds about Frank. She used to say, "Sure, Frank is witty, well read, and good company. But he eats too much and drinks too much. He's disorganized and forgetful. Frank is also very much a politician."

Frank always pretended to know a lot about wine. Austine, who accompanied us on many of our foreign trips, never believed him. Conniff somehow got wind of this. One evening, at a restaurant in Paris, Frank chose the most expensive wine listed. In effect, he was saying to Austine: OK, top that choice! Austine kicked me under the table and pointed to a superior wine at a much lower price. I ordered that but Frank did not notice. Throughout dinner he lavished praise on the selection. As we walked to our hotel room that night, Austine remarked dryly, "Don't say I never told you so."

Despite Austine's skeptical eye, my friendship with Frank developed. We became like brothers. We would go to lunch at "21" or Toots Shor's and start tossing quips around at one end of the bar. Our happy talk was contagious. Guys would come over and ask, "What's so funny?" We would say, "The news business." They would invariably reply, "I'm in the wrong business."

We were in love with news and saw beyond the robberies and murders to the humorous and happy endings. We argued politics a lot. I used to call Frank our "house Democrat." Although an Independent, I have tended to vote Republican. Our jousts were healthy fun, but neither gave an inch. The exchanges always ended in a laugh.

Frank began to take a dark view of change in America. He seemed to yearn for the sureness and serenity of his youth in Danbury. I first noticed this change of attitude in discussing a very simple subject: jazz. Conniff was a jazz nut. He became quite upset because bebop was creating a new direction in jazz. That was heresy to Frank. There was only one jazz: swing. Bebop never existed.

Frank exhibited this same unchangeable attitude on many subjects. I finally concluded that, in many ways, Frank had never left Danbury. He had the unquestioning religious faith of a schoolboy and an unquenchable belief in the rightness of America. He used to tell me, "Americans are different, Bill. They believe in heroes. They believe in freedom. And they are sentimental about both."

I believed in the same Christian principles and was imbued with considerable patriotism. However, I was more flexible. My principles did not change, but I listened and carefully considered other views. Frank often did not.

Yet Frank was a street-wise, self-made man. He could be as tough as the next guy. And on the subject of communism, he was a street fighter. He started throwing punches in his columns and speeches. To him, communism was a nightmare attempting to replace the American Dream.

Frank saw his religious and American values threatened. He thus began a war with communism that lasted until his death. He became a strong supporter of Senator Joseph McCarthy's campaign against communism. Conniff reached back to his early years as he wrote: "People like my father instinctively know that McCarthy is fighting their fight."

Frank hated Soviet Communists for their teachery and aggression. He was obsessed with the threat of communism at home, and never understood how any American could sympathize with the Communists. He was disturbed that a good number did. Many leading liberals despised my father for his anticommunism, although his view was primarily based on strong patriotism. In Frank's case, it was hate.

I agreed with Frank's premise—that communism was our deadly enemy. However, I was disturbed at the intensity of his feelings. They became almost violent. Communism had become a red flag in his face. Frank went to Korea because of the Communist threat. He also went to Vietnam four times, starting in 1956, because he saw communism as our implacable enemy. He traveled through Poland, Hungary, Czechoslovakia, and Romania to get a closer look at the Communist apparatus. To Frank this was good versus evil, a life and death struggle. Frank never understood why we didn't fight to win in Korea and Vietnam. It haunted him until his death. He would say to me in anger at the Vietnam antiwar protestors: "American boys are fighting. Don't these people know that? And don't they know that we are lucky to be Americans?"

The boy from Danbury wanted to rescue the Democratic party from sacrilege. It had opposed war. He ran for Congress in 1964 and lost.

When the *World-Journal-Tribune* was formed of the *World Telegram, Journal,* and *Tribune* in 1966, Frank was named its editor. When "Widget," as many of us called the paper, later folded after a printers' strike, Conniff died as well. I wrote a column about Frank's passing. It read in part:

It's hell to lose your best friend. This grievous, deeply personal wound came to me this week with the passing of Frank Conniff, who died at 57 in what should have been the prime of his life.

Frank was, quite simply, one of the finest newspapermen and finest human beings I have ever known. I visited him for the last time just a week ago. With great effort, he managed to say three words: "I'm going home."

It was, I told myself at the time, an appropriate parting. Frank was not only going home to God but also to Danbury, where he would finally be at peace.

I cannot mention Conniff, Considine, Kingsbury-Smith, and the others without including my wife. Austine knew all of these colleagues and accompanied us on many stories across the country and abroad. She never completely left the news business. Marrying Austine was the wisest and happiest decision I ever made.

We first met casually at a party in Washington during World War II. Her friends called her Bootsie then, a nickname given her as a child by her mother. Austine told me later that she thought I was a "fun and entertaining fellow," but she wasn't especially impressed.

After the war, when I had returned home for good and my second marriage had gone sour, I went up to San Francisco from San Simeon to witness the founding of the United Nations. It was a busman's holiday, since I was on vacation and staying with my father at San Simeon. Austine was covering the story as a columnist for Cissy Patterson and the *Washington Times-Herald*. I mention Cissy, the newspaper's publisher, because as a good friend of my father's, she did all she could to edge us closer together. She was convinced it was a good match.

When I bumped into Austine in San Francisco, I was surprised and pleased. She was as thin and wispy as ever and retained her fresh look and beautiful smile. She had established herself as a first-rate columnist, writing about everything from people to politics to Washington parties. Austine was among the first to blow the whistle on Alger Hiss, a member of the American diplomatic delegation at the U.N.'s founding. Hiss was later convicted of perjury in connection with Communist associations.

The VIPs were staying at the St. Francis, the Fairmont, and the Mark Hopkins. Most of the media were at the Palace. Austine happened to be waiting for an elevator to go to her Palace room one day when a sloppy-looking, tousle-haired young man gave her a big smile. Austine recalls that his suit was unpressed and his necktie was askew.

The two began chatting. The young man said his name was Kennedy and he was working for the Hearst newspapers. He mentioned that his father, Joe, had asked Hearst senior to give him a reporting job. Both men thought the work would cheer him up. He was still recovering from wounds suffered in the Navy during the war in the Pacific. Of course the young man was Jack Kennedy.

After being repeatedly pressed by Kennedy for a date, Austine relented, and they arranged to have dinner. Only she phoned and asked me to come along. It was a delightful occasion. If Kennedy was disappointed when he saw me, he didn't show it. We had a lot of fun in the old newspaper game of dissecting the diplomatic maneuvers. Austine got back to her room in a good state at a decent hour.

Austine and Jack came to know one another better at news conferences and other events. Kennedy was constantly asking Austine for a date. She explained that she was married to Igor Cassini, a society columnist on the *Journal-American*.

I would see Austine from time to time. Gradually, it was becoming clear that both of our marriages were going downhill. There was some attraction, but no romance.

In 1947 the lavish Greenbrier Hotel in West Virginia was rebuilt, refurnished, and reopened. There we met again. I was then divorced and Austine was in the process. The swells came from New York, Palm Beach, and as far away as London. There was one party and dinner after another. Austine was not only beautiful, I concluded, but she had a brain inside the beauty. I was beginning to fall.

Austine would come to New York regularly as a panelist on a television show called "Leave It to the Girls." The panelists answered all types of questions from women throughout the country. I would see her, but she had other beaus. It wasn't until late 1947 that we began to get serious. Finally, one lonely evening in New York I picked up the phone and proposed to her in Washington. I was so excited that I can't recall the words. It doesn't matter. She accepted.

We were married in July of 1948 at her parents' home in Warrenton, Virginia, where Austine had grown up. It was the heart of Virginia's horse and hunt country. The wedding was a simple candlelight ceremony.

Of course there was a wedding crisis. Virginia, unlike most of the country that summer, refused to go on Daylight Savings Time. In the confusion, half the guests invited for dinner were about an hour early and the others an hour late. It was memorable, though: a moonlit night, outdoor supper in an old Virginia boxwood garden strung with lanterns, and it didn't rain.

Austine's father, Austin McDonnell, was a retired Army major who lived as a country gentleman. Both her parents' families traced their lineage back to the English who fought to have King John sign the Magna Carta. Their descendants came to Maryland and Virginia in the seventeenth century as early colonists. They served as officers in the Revolutionary War.

In the first several years, we had somewhat of a long-distance marriage. Austine continued to work as a Washington columnist and held a huge, weekly fashion-show luncheon for political wives. We bought a house on Decatur Place in the capital. I would go to Washington on Friday and return to New York on Monday. Austine would come up to New York for three days at midweek. This arrangement sometimes changed, depending on our work schedules. In 1953, after I became editor-in-chief of our newspapers, Austine left reporting and came permanently to New York.

We have had two fine sons—William Randolph Hearst III and Austin. If Austine taught me one thing, it was the importance and love of family. Looking back through more than forty years of marriage, perhaps that is what I most admire about her—her untiring, unbending, unquenchable love and devotion to family. I had missed much in not seeing my father for many years while growing up. Once our boys were born—and I was ecstatic at both births—nothing was more vital or more important. I was carrying on my father's name and I wanted my legacy to be a good one.

Austine and my father are the two most important persons I have known in my life. Both were blessed with keen minds, strong wills, and even temperaments. Both believed in public spirit and giving. Both openly expressed love and devotion to country. Austine has spent years helping the Girl Scouts of America, the Colonial Dames of the American Revolution, and other patriotic organizations.

After these four decades of marriage to Austine, I have come full circle. I see my grandmother, Phoebe Apperson Hearst, in her. Austine brings me back to those wonderful days at Grandma's hacienda when I was young, carefree, and full of life.

These have been treasured memories for an old duffer like me. It has been wonderful to relive such happy times. Perhaps that is why I like to return to our cottage at San Simeon so often. I sit on our porch in the afternoon sun and see two faces—Phoebe and Austine—the past and present at the same time. Our whole family passes in review. Pop and Mom are there, my brothers, early playmates, and, finally, my own children. For better or worse, it's a snapshot of four generations of Hearsts. Like Frank Conniff returning to Danbury, I am home on that porch. It's a full and blessed feeling.

IX
FAREWELL TO POP

The death in 1948 of Joe Willicombe, my father's longtime secretary and aide-de-camp, was an enormous loss to the old man. The two men had worked side by side for more than thirty years. Willicombe knew Pop's mind to the core on innumerable subjects. At times Willicombe became the alter ego of my father by simply responding to letters and queries himself rather than bothering the Chief with details. Joe wielded extraordinary power within the organization. The reason went beyond his long service. Willicombe had two qualities that served everyone well: He was completely loyal to the old man and did not suffer fools gladly.

The closeness of the two became increasingly important as age and illness took its toll on my father. The Chief, long known for his quick, tough professional judgments, became more and more nostalgic when he hit eighty. Joe was Pop's pipeline to the past, since he knew all the old faces, places, and people. Willicombe's passing was all the more painful because it compounded other recent tremors in my father's life—his own heart problems and an abiding, deep emptiness caused by leaving San Simeon.

Willicombe managed to so submerge his own presence that few in the organization knew much about his personal life. Joe was married, with seven children. He was a native New Yorker who came to my father's attention when he was a reporter on the old *New York American*. Perhaps the proudest moment of his life came when he was made a lieutenant colonel in the Army reserves as a result of his intelligence work in World War I. In formal correspondence and in meeting with people he didn't know, Joe preferred to be addressed as "Colonel." Willicombe died of a heart attack at seventy-four in Carmel Valley, California.

I was among the first to notice the effect of Joe's departure, because Pop communicated with me so often about the *Journal-American*. Slowly, a communications gap began to develop between my father and his editors and publishers. Actually, Willicombe had gone into semiretirement in 1947, two years after Pop and Marion returned to San Simeon from Wyntoon. H. O. "Bill" Hunter, who had been secretary to the publisher of the *Los Angeles Examiner,* succeeded Willicombe, but he never completely took Joe's place. Willicombe continued to work part-time, and came to the rescue whenever Pop or Hunter needed him. Pop had trusted Joe so completely that Willicombe knew virtually everything about the business.

I noticed not only that answers to letters and memos had slowed but instructions were less sharply defined. Pop said little about losing Willicombe, but that was his way when he was painfully hurt—to withdraw quietly. Yet Pop's withdrawal was the one thing the organization could not tolerate. That was because the old man was the one person who dominated it on a daily basis.

My father was an extraordinary leader. He would turn from one problem to another and make major decisions in seconds—from what to do about retail advertising in Boston to how to get better sports pictures in Milwaukee. He knew perfectly what he wanted done and exactly how to do it.

After Joe's death, Pop took to the phone himself for nearly two years because he felt there was a lack of clarity and a time lag in his instructions. Despite his weakening health, he tried not to slow down. It wasn't easy for him to speak—his voice was high-pitched—but he forced himself for the sake of the company. The old man had a tremendous sense of obligation to the employees. He told me that all his life. Pop said that being the Chief meant one had more responsibility to assure that the boss himself, the company, and its employees remained vibrant. He never separated the three.

Work became my father's last, lonely passion, inexorably lessening his closeness to Marion. However, his remembrances of San Simeon and his attachment to his art collection remained strong. His working hours became later and later. Some of his calls to executives came at ungodly hours. He sometimes phoned me and other publishers long after we had gone home and to bed. These calls extended far beyond the time difference between the East and West coasts. Since his voice had weakened, Pop didn't repeat instructions. So editors and publishers had to snap out of their slumber quickly; several kept notebooks beside their phones. We feared missing any instructions because the old man would surely recall them.

For the last year of my father's life, Marion made some of these late-night calls for him. The old man was simply too weak to use the phone so often. She was merely to relay messages, but she sometimes went beyond that. Marion continued her feud with news executives. All of them were aware of her outspoken view: "All they care about is their g-g-g-goddammed circulation."

In some of her more exuberant moments she suggested that, with her Hearst stock holdings, she might one day have a role in running the organization. Her calls were a source of concern to many editors and publishers. They wondered how much my father's health might be sliding downhill, and whether Marion could possibly be speaking for my father in answering their questions. Was she exaggerating her role to intimidate them and put them down? Was she in the midst of a palace coup to control the company? (Despite all that has been published about her holdings, Marion never owned any stock outright in the corporation.)

My father, who never liked confrontation or unpleasantness, was facing the greatest confrontation of his long life as 1951 began. He didn't have the strength to continue much longer, and all the family knew it. For the first time he began to take orders. His heart fibrillation increased markedly at times. Dr. Myron Prinzmetal, a Beverly Hills heart specialist who was attending my father, allowed the old man to work—but only for limited times, when he felt strong. This meant Pop worked at odd hours of the day and night. He required considerable rest, with few visitors and no excitement.

Richard Stanley, who was quick at shorthand, became Pop's new secretary. The old man apparently scared hell out of him when he asked Stanley whether he could sleep in a guesthouse and be available at all hours. Pop told me that Stanley agreed, saying he was still single and had few friends. My father liked his frankness and, with uncharacteristic directness toward someone he didn't know, said, "When you die, Mr. Stanley, if you have as many friends as the fingers on your two hands, you'll be very fortunate." This again dispelled the notion that the old man would never speak or hear of death. This encounter became, in fact, the clearest indication to me that death was near and on his mind.

I would visit Pop whenever I could. It was always painful for both of us. He had lost weight (down to 128 pounds) but would talk about getting down to "fighting trim." He was nostalgic about the old days and often talked about Adela Rogers St. Johns and other old-time reporters and editors. I saw he was drawing closer to death, and these visits became almost unbearable.

Pop enjoyed dinner downstairs but could barely walk to the elevator, and he later used a wheelchair. Marion was often soused, and this would ruin his meager meal of vegetables and fruit. If there were guests—old friends like New York executive J. D. Gortatowsky, Louis B. Mayer, or Louella Parsons—he would suffer Marion's boisterous imbibing as long as he could. Then Pop would excuse himself and return upstairs. If he was well he would ring for Stanley and work. If not—and usually not, in these cases—he would quietly nap until the urge to work returned. He once told me that he often tried to imagine what it would be like to go back to San Simeon for a few days. Sometimes his mind would return to the hill briefly, but he would suddenly wake up to find himself staring blankly around his sterile room.

My father never practiced a formal religious creed. He believed in the immortality of the soul as the only logical explanation for truth and life. He believed in the will of God—that our Maker would act in His own good time. His own inspirational poem, "Song of the River," reflected his belief in a divine presence:

> So don't ask why we live or die,
> Or whither or when we go,
> Or wonder about the mysteries,
> Which only God may know.

In his final years Pop turned more and more to Mom, my brothers, and me. He phoned all of us, despite his weak voice, and sometimes had long conversations with our mother. My father's separation from Mom was different from the way biographers, gossip columnists, and others described it. Mom and Pop wrote and phoned one another from the time they formally separated in 1925 to my father's death in 1951. Not all these letters reflected agreement, but they were generally loving and caring. Also, my mother expressed continuing affection for Pop.

Millicent Willson was sixteen when she met my father. She and her sister, Anita, were Gibson Girls dancing in *Merry Maidens* on Broadway. Their father was an old vaudevillian. Millicent had a very pretty, smiling, open face with beautiful, clear skin. She was about five feet four inches tall, with chestnut hair and light-hazel eyes. Mother had a great sense of humor and a good, strong laugh. She liked attractive clothes and was always well groomed. In her later years she had a tendency to gain weight, but fought it and remained about 140 pounds. All of us called her Mamalee, because one of the grandchildren couldn't say grandmother or Millicent and called her by that name. She loved having people over for tea and thoroughly enjoyed lively company and funny jokes. She wanted everyone to have a good time.

Mom told me that Pop had appeared like a Prince Charming one evening backstage at the theater. She agreed to a date if Anita could accompany them. The two were closely supervised. And what a date it was! Pop took the two to dinner, but then hailed a carriage to rush them downtown to the *Journal*. The sisters didn't have the foggiest notion of what was happening, except that they were climbing over boards and walking on rough planks in evening slippers. Mom said:

> He took us inside a dirty, noisy newspaper office, asked us to be seated, rolled up his sleeves, and began making all kinds of marks on sheets of print. This was no Prince Charming. We told ourselves this fellow was a late-night printer!
>
> By asking questions, we finally learned that he owned the *Journal*, but we weren't sure of that until the second date. He seemed very modest to me, but Anita had the idea he might be one of those big western braggarts. She said we shouldn't believe anything until he proved it. Well, he proved everything to me when he proposed a couple of weeks later. I said yes without so much as a deep breath. I was head over heels in love.

The two wed five years later in 1903. They were married at Grace Episcopal Church in Manhattan in a simple ceremony. The honeymoon was more in Pop's style. He took his bride, as well as some of her family and friends, on a trip through Britain and other parts of Europe. They then went to Mexico and toured his ranches and other property, before traveling up to California to meet his mother. Phoebe had declined to attend the New York wedding. She had reservations about stage girls, but graciously received the new bride at her home in Pleasanton. As already stated, Grandma would bide her time to decide on the bride.

Less than a year later, Phoebe felt better about the marriage. On April 10, 1904, Millicent gave birth to a healthy George Randolph Hearst. Pop was ecstatic. He went out and bought a half-dozen electric fans after Mom became concerned about the sultry heat in their Lexington Avenue apartment and little George's ensuing baby rash. They moved to a hotel that was cooler. And then, in 1905, Pop bought the thirty-room place in the Clarendon Apartments, at the corner of Eighty-sixth and Riverside Drive, overlooking the Hudson River.

In 1906 Pop won New York's Democratic gubernatorial nomination when the Tammany crowd decided they had no candidate who could win, and so finally supported him in an attempt to make peace. My father then swept our mother up in the political whirl. She was rarely, if ever, home at night, attending political rallies and later accompanying Pop to the *Journal* while he checked the morning front-page layout. The old man was ultimately defeated by Republican Charles Evans Hughes, who later became famous as a U.S. Supreme Court justice.

The family grew to five sons in a decade, but Mom continued to ride her nonstop merry-go-round at the top of the newspaper world and politics. Meantime, Phoebe was delighted with her grandchildren. Her relationship with mother changed from a distant "How is your husband?" to "My dear Millie." They wrote to one another regularly. We were one big happy family. Or so it seemed.

Mom began complaining of physical exhaustion. Phoebe was concerned and comforted her. But Pop seemed oblivious to the situation because he was so tied up in politics and newspapering. Mom always seemed to be either pregnant or regaining her strength from the last birth, yet Pop insisted she remain on the road with him. My father's energy was unbelievable. Mom wrote in desperation to Grandma that she felt her life was one long train ride.

Grandma was very proud of the Hearst name. She had a right to be, considering her extraordinary charitable and other social work. So Phoebe was pleased that Mom placed so much emphasis on the family and improving our social status. Grandma's goal was not celebrity but undertaking civic responsibilities—contributing time, effort, and money to various public causes. She was attempting to bless the new generation with her life's creed: community service. Nothing could have brought Mom and Phoebe closer than my mother's willingness to share us with Grandma. As I've mentioned, we spent our summers with Phoebe in California, where she showered us with attention.

Some have said that Phoebe became upset with Pop because he was spending too much time in politics and newspapering, to the detriment of his family. That wasn't the case. Grandma had poured out millions of dollars to support Pop at the paper, and she wanted his full attention to that work. She also wrote out checks of $10,000 a month to cover our living expenses, so that our father could better concentrate on his job and not be worried about finances. However, Phoebe also wanted Pop to spend time in politics so he could be of public service. After all, she had been a senator's wife and tried to accomplish all she could in that position. She expected her son to be a dynamo like herself. But Phoebe wanted the opposite for the mother of her five grandchildren—that Mom be taken off the road and spend more time with the family. And that's what our mother wished too.

Mom wanted our father to drop politics for two reasons: It was too time-consuming and exhausting for everyone, and was too crooked. She felt that being a politician meant not only robbing the public till in one way or another but also issuing political payoffs and broken promises. In Pop's case she was concerned about broken promises. Mom knew that her husband would never become involved in any form of stealing public funds, but she was very concerned about the political double cross. It was simply unthinkable for our father to break his word—or deal with others who did so. In that respect Mother thought Pop was naïve. She had seen too much of New York politics and considered it rotten to the core. Political promises were made to be broken. She told Pop over and over that he would become bitterly disillusioned with politics—above all, that he wouldn't be able to control those in his own party, even those close to him. She was right.

Of course my father has been criticized for breaking the most important promise of his life: faithfulness to his wife. He was unfaithful. However, as the record clearly demonstrates, the old man was unassailable on every other promise he ever made. In his own fashion, he attempted to be true to both his wife and his mistress throughout his life, particularly in his final years. That may seem like the view of a libertine, but I am trying to deal with the facts as they were, not as I wanted them to be.

Mother and the whole family had, of course, heard and read all the rumors that Marion wanted to marry my father and that he had promised her to seek a divorce. Marion would tell this to some of her film colony friends, and each new tidbit would quickly make the rounds of Hollywood gossips. These rumors have, for decades, filled pages in biographies and articles about the old man. Indeed, detailed scenes are narrated with Marion requesting that my father get a divorce and marry her, and he promising to do so. All of this is false. My father never asked my mother for a divorce. Not a word. Never.

Mom told Austine the facts. The two were very close, like mother and daughter, and regularly confided in one another. Not only had her husband never asked for a divorce, Mother said, but she would have agreed if he had requested it. She told Austine, "I never had any desire to see him or her unhappy. I loved him too much for that kind of personal pettiness. I would have given him a divorce if he asked me, but he never did." As a Catholic, Mother could have agreed to the divorce as long as she never remarried. But she never had any intention of doing so.

When Austine related the conversation to me, I wasn't surprised. Mom was always a gracious person. I don't believe she ever wished anyone harm in her life. In her calm, quiet, and even humorous way, she merited all the love that my father ever gave her. It was a pity he didn't offer her more, because she loved him until the day she died. My mother's devotion to our father is a dimension of our family history that not even my brothers and I fully comprehended until her later years. Although Grandma was no longer around by then, she certainly would have been proud of the girl who danced into all our lives.

There were obviously reasons why my father never asked for a divorce. One was his wife's impeccable reputation; she led a thoroughly good life that reflected well on him and the family. Also, a divorce could cause considerable financial and legal problems for my father and the company. California community property laws could have become a serious problem for him. And he didn't want more children, since a second family could complicate his estate.

Pop didn't wish to cause my mother or us new personal embarrassment. He also wanted to avoid alienating any of us. Critics never seemed to get it through their noodles that the old man loved us, and we cared about him. That was the bottom line.

My mother was not entirely blameless in the breakup. I thought she made a big mistake when she first heard about Marion. Pop came home one evening, and she confronted him with the fact that she knew he was seeing another woman. Mother was very upset and my father tried to calm her. Suddenly she took off her wedding band and threw it on the floor, declaring, "If this is all you think of our marriage, keep it!" She stomped out of the room and remained secluded for several days. When Mom returned, she was wearing her ring. She and Pop pretended the incident never took place, but apparently he never forgot it.

Later, all of us went to San Simeon. Pop said he had to go to Los Angeles on business, but someone told Mom that he had seen Marion. When he returned, she had packed and left for New York. That was another mistake. He intensely disliked unpleasantness and even indirect confrontations, as I've mentioned, and he strongly wished to avoid them. Mother had openly challenged him twice. She then forced him to make a choice: Marion or her. It was an ultimatum. My father then knew he couldn't have what he wanted—his wife and family, and Marion too.

Yet my mother's demand need not have been immediate or perhaps even necessary. Pop might have eventually left Marion, as later became evident. Despite the fact that my father was attracted to the actress, he made no commitments to her. They had not yet decided to live together. It was still possible that Mother could have prevailed. But she would have had to be patient and plan her feminine strategy carefully, with no personal threats or outbursts. Mom's strategy was simply unwise.

Mom loved her native New York. She enjoyed society parties and continued to attend many of them. This made Pop uncomfortable. He detested these occasions because they seemed a waste of time when he was under so many business and political pressures. As the years went by, the city and its leaders became less attractive to our father. Pop never entirely left the West. As his news organization became national and his eastern political battles rose in intensity, his love for San Simeon and California began calling him back. Mom liked California, but she never envisioned living there full time.

I've reflected on the reasons for my parents' separation for more than a half-century and have finally concluded that our father wanted to preserve the family name and tradition above any and all considerations. So did our mother. That was his major motivation, because it had been so important in his own mother's life. He knew that family service and good will were at the heart of all Phoebe did and, in the end, she won. Pop loved and respected his mother, perhaps as he did no other woman. He may have hidden Marion from her, but my father could not and would not go against Phoebe's bequest that no one and nothing was ultimately above the family lineage.

Since Marion had become a wedge between my mother and father, Mom sought refuge in her sister and parents. She poured out every detail to them. As I've already said, from the time my father began seeing Marion steadily in 1919, to his separation from Mother in 1925, our parents continued to live under the same roof. But Marion was always in the shadows. My parents finally agreed to separate, amicably.

My mother's outlook took two different roads—disappointment and a surge of personal pride. She began to spend money lavishly and sought a new life as a matron of New York society.

Mom had already become prominent for her charity work, particularly her pet project, the Free Milk Fund for Babies, Inc. For many years she had led fund-raising campaigns so that poor infants and the needy children of New York could receive free milk. There was no federal welfare like our modern children's-lunch programs in those days. So Mother's program was truly needed.

Later, during World War II, Mother organized New York canteens where American soldiers could get snacks, cigarettes, and entertainment. She was very good at lining up big-name stars to sing and take part in various free shows. Our mother had organized similar canteens during World War I.

Despite the fact that Pop began spending all his time with Marion, there was hardly a week that he didn't write a letter, send a telegram, or speak with Mother on the phone. Even when Mom went on vacation to Europe in 1927, the two exchanged cables of good wishes. Before Mother sailed, Pop had insisted that she take vaccines. On her return aboard the *Leviathan,* Pop, as well as Commissioner Grover Whalen and other city officials, met her to announce that Mother had been appointed honorary deputy commissioner of correction. Mom joked that it sounded like a full-time job.

Mom was spending big and sending Pop the bills. On August 24, 1927, he wrote her: "I have a bill from Urban [florists] for decorations at the birthday party in the Ritz for over three thousand dollars. I think it is wasting money to pay that amount of money for mere temporary decoration. If it were something to go into the house, of permanent value, it would be all right. But for something that is gone in an evening, I think it is wasteful, and I wish you would talk to me before doing anything like this again."

In one 1927 telegram, Pop advised Mother to hold on to her oil stock and perhaps buy more. He was concerned that she wasn't paying sufficient attention to her financial future. At the same time, he was asking her to send him some family photos.

Two years later Mother telegraphed him about her pending arrival at San Simeon. My father, in turn, asked her to invite some additional friends along. There were numerous communications at the time about me and my brothers.

On May 19, 1930, five years after he left home, Pop sent a telegram to Mother about many magnificent tapestries, as well as sixteenth-century cabinets and bureaus that he was sending her, to furnish a large summer home that he had purchased for her at Sands Point, Long Island. On October 8, 1930, Mother and Father entertained at a formal dinner marking the opening of the house. The guests included former President and Mrs. Calvin Coolidge. Seven years after he left home, on May 3, 1932, my father sent Mother a beautifully worded message about Mother's Day, in which he addressed all us boys directly. Four sentences struck me:

Make the most of these years [with one's mother], my young friends, both for her pleasure and your own benefit. Realize that no one will ever love you as your mother does. No one will ever give you such sincere and unselfish guidance. You will benefit not only yourselves but all those whom you influence in your way through the world.

As 1932 closed, Pop telegraphed Mother his congratulations on her various public recognitions for work in behalf of the Milk Fund. He noted, significantly: "Your kindness to me personally is a matter of added gratitude. I appreciate very deeply this expression of your personal friendship."

The two continued to exchange birthday and wedding anniversary presents through the years.

Mom decided to move from her apartment at the Clarendon in 1936. She asked Pop to help find her a suitable place. He did, buying her a beautiful apartment at 300 Park Avenue. In a long letter to Mother on December 9, 1936, Pop noted that he had "not only strictly lived up to the provisions of our [separation] agreement, but had gone far beyond them."

The two continued to have some financial differences, especially in 1941, when she requested $25,000 to meet a bank note on her Sands Point place. She apparently had used the money for other purposes. Mother also asked that her monthly allowance be increased by $1,000.

In 1942, although we were now grown and working for the company, Mother still wrote to the old man about promoting us and other aspects of our lives. She concluded: "I do not care about myself, but I do care about the boys."

In all of these communications, then and in the years ahead, the two were helpful and gracious to one another. In the last decade of his life, because of his isolation at Wyntoon during the war and his subsequent illness, Pop communicated with Mother less in writing. But he did phone her to the very last days of his life.

Pop would have preferred a European arrangement, keeping wife and mistress. That was not to be, so he threw back the curtain on his life, contrary to his private nature, and accepted the consequences. His enemies dealt it to him in spades. As far as I or any of our family knew, my father was faithful to Marion, although Hollywood gossip was less kind to her in that respect. He lived with our mother for twenty-two years and was involved with Marion for thirty-two. My father knew that divorce would have saved him from public attack. He chose to accept the blame attached to his life and spare the family.

It's important to make a more accurate assessment of my father's attitude toward money and knowledge of economics than has been presented by others. His astuteness is reflected not only in his business and personal finances but in his final will. Company records indicate that many observers misread the will and misunderstood his personal finances. Specifically, Pop has been accused of having little comprehension of money or finance, of spending wildly without consideration of his own and the company's limits, and not knowing much about the actual financial status of most of his newspapers and magazines. The record demonstrates otherwise. The old man devoted detailed personal attention to both on a systematic basis.

My father wrote a memorandum in January of 1920 as to how the organization carried on its business through various corporations. He pointed out that the "fullest measure of unified control is not afforded under the present organization." He broke down the company into its components and concluded:

> It will be the function of this corporation to provide a system for keeping constantly in touch with the financial condition and require-ments of the organization as a whole and of each of its component parts; of marshaling the cash and other resources of the organization so that they may be employed to the best advantage; of anticipating the financial needs of the entire organization and its individual members; and of devising and executing plans for the development of the organization through the extension and enlargement of activities of existing enterprises and through the acquisition of new enterprises.

He separated this legalese into functions, including this specific request, "It should provide for the periodical requirements of Mr. Hearst."

Pop was saying, of course, that he was well aware of the fact that he was spending—and would continue to spend—large sums of money on art. The corporation should be aware of that as well. As its owner, he expected the organization to have sufficient funds on hand to meet these notes, and not wait up to six months to pay such bills.

I chose at random records covering a decade of my father's life—1918 through 1927—to see how closely he followed the company's and his own accounts. Each week he received a typewritten profit-and-loss statement from each newspaper. This included the latest seven-day period, the pre-vious week, and the same week during the previous year. My father made comments or asked questions in the margins; for example, for the week ending January 14, 1923, he asked why the *Los Angeles Examiner* was making less money than the previous year, while the *Los Angeles Herald* was earning more. These P&L statements are filled with questions about the earnings in specific types of advertising.

My father followed financial developments at each magazine just as closely. As early as 1918 he wrote to Joseph A. Moore, general business manager of the Hearst magazines, a letter on magazine earnings. He said: "Mr. Moore, we must make money out of these magazines. I am not conducting them merely for an artistic success. I do not think any business is successful that does not pay and pay well."

My father noted that such earnings would be less than forecast for 1918, and he called a meeting to increase revenues. In doing so, the Chief wrote candidly and, I'm sure, with a touch of humor: "As Mrs. Hearst and I will have a good deal of our personal income out of the magazines, I am naturally taking a lively and immediate interest in this proposition."

As soon as it could be done after December 31, the Chief was given a financial breakdown on annual advertising revenues at each publication. This prompted congratulations as well as some corporate storms.

It's clear that the old man knew from memory, within $1,000, the weekly and annual P&L of each paper, magazine, or other business. On January 23, 1923, he wrote a detailed letter about each of the newspapers—what was good and bad about each editorially and financially, how future profits and circulation could rise or fall (he offered solutions to financial problems), and what executive changes were needed.

Some have said my father ignored the coming of the Depression. This is part of a letter he wrote to me at the *New York American* on February 7, 1932: "Every business in America is radically reducing expenses. Our business must do the same. We have reduced expenses on the Pacific Coast's three morning papers over two million dollars per year without injury to the papers."

Pop said he was sending two of his top financial men to New York to reduce our expenses, adding: "We must not only have the required reduction of one million dollars, but must have it promptly. Let us get busy and do the work, and let us realize that it can be done because it has been done in our business and is being done in every business."

He also was regularly advised of his personal notes due. For example, five bills due the Duveen Gallery on Fifth Avenue went as follows in 1925 and 1926: Two notes on October 28, 1925—each for $100,000. Another on November 28 for $100,000. And two more $100,000 bills on January 28 and April 28, 1926.

The old man well knew what he was doing as he spent about $15 million per year (critics said "wildly") on personal projects, from politics to new planes and San Simeon. He spent money as a matter of personal choice. He understood the financial impact on the company and himself when he continued pouring millions into San Simeon. It's true that he may have paid excessive prices for some antiques and other art collections. That's because, to him, the price was worth it. And it was his money, his company, his life, and his future.

I recall in 1990 when Malcolm Forbes threw a million-dollar birthday bash and invited scores of guests to Morocco for fun and feasting. Forbes and his guests apparently had a great time. He was immediately assailed for squandering the money on extravagance. However, on reflection, the critics finally came to understand that this was his money and he had a right to spend it as he chose. As a matter of fact, Forbes showed some foresight: He died not long after the party. Knowing Malcolm, he would have cherished that.

As I look back now on San Simeon, the old man's critics appear clearly shortsighted. The estate has become a national public treasure. Such a place will probably never rise again. I believe the important thing is not that my father expended a lot of money but how he spent it. And these were his own bucks.

The campaign of General Douglas MacArthur to win the Korean War, and his homecoming after being fired by President Truman, were my father's last hurrah. Some called it a "crusade," but I would hardly term it that. You go into a crusade to win. In the final episode of MacArthur's career, Pop just wanted to fire one last broadside in bidding goodbye to an old soldier. In so doing, he was also saying farewell to his own career.

Both of us had long admired the five-star general—from his brilliant campaigns against the Japanese during World War II to his post as supreme commander of allied forces in Japan after its surrender. Finally, we supported him in Korea when he wanted to win that conflict, but he was then fired after calling for an attack on Communist forces in a sanctuary beyond the Yalu River in North Korea. Truman feared the Chinese would enter the war, which they did anyway.

My first and most memorable meeting with MacArthur occurred in the summer of 1945. My father sent Barry Faris, the editor of INS, and me to Tokyo, to ask the general if he would write an account of his World War II experiences for our newspapers. We carried a check in his name for $500,000. The general was living in the U.S. embassy, one of the new buildings in Tokyo that appeared to show no damage. His military headquarters was located in the shambles of downtown in a large office building.

When we arrived at his office, I was bedecked in an Eisenhower battle jacket. It was strung with all the ribbons I could muster, from battles covered to divisions and squadrons. To my horror, the general greeted us with his shirt open at the neck—and not a single decoration except the five stars on his collar. I explained the splash of ribbons, saying that war correspondents always tried to show that they had been around. MacArthur got a big kick out of the decorations and became quite friendly. I took my jacket off.

Unhappily for us, the general declined Pop's offer for his memoirs. MacArthur said he did not believe he should write anything while still in uniform. He also felt his recollections, if he ever wrote them, would be too long for newspaper serialization. Nearly twenty years later, Henry Luce of Time-Life reportedly paid MacArthur $1 million for his story.

When MacArthur was hauled home by Truman in 1951, my father pulled out all the editorial stops. Our newspapers hailed him as a hero, and a presidential boomlet began—but it was to fade because of bad timing and other factors. The crowds greeting the general were enormous. I thought his farewell address before Congress was one of the finest speeches in American history. A lot of people agreed.

I remained in contact with the general and his wife for many years. He died in 1964. I was taken aback at the vehemence of his critics, who attempted to deflate his supposed ego and reputation. I remember one sentence in particular from a commentary: "MacArthur was an unscrupulous, self-serving soldier whose manipulation of image and good fortune gave him a largely undeserved reputation for effective military leadership and allowed him to hide repeated efforts to win the presidency."

I recall shaking my head and reflecting: The old man is in good company. If we removed one word—"military"—the critics could be saying the same thing of my father.

As MacArthur faded, so too did Pop. He was descending to the first floor for dinner less and less as 1951 progressed. He dressed mostly in bathrobe and slippers. At times his voice was barely audible. As summer lengthened it seemed apparent that my father would last only a few more months.

Dick Berlin, president of the corporation, and I met to make plans for the eventual death and burial. They didn't include Marion Davies. We were certainly not going to embarrass my mother by inviting both women. If there had been a divorce, I could understand inviting both, but not under the circumstances, particularly because Marion had been drinking so much.

As the first week in August ended, Pop became very weak and remained in bed. Berlin and I flew out to the coast to be present in the event of death. I stayed in the guesthouse part of the time and with my old friend, Paul McNamara, who lived a short distance away on North Beverly Drive.

In these private visits with my father he would generally not say much. He wanted to touch and look at me. I used to rub the back of his neck and head. It seemed to relieve him a great deal; he would smile when I did that and close his eyes. I did it because my mother had rubbed him the same way in their younger days as a sign of tenderness. I remembered those happier times as I sat there by the side of his bed and watched him slipping away.

As I was leaving one afternoon, one of the nurses stopped me and led me to a closet. She opened the door and inside were all the presents that I and the family had sent Pop the previous Christmas. I have not often been genuinely shocked in my life, but was dumbstruck as I looked at our names on the gifts.

"Miss Davies?" I asked the nurse. She nodded affirmatively.

I closed the door and began to walk away. The nurse followed me. She said, "She comes running into the room and calls him vulgar names. 'You old bastard' and phrases like that. One day, she had a scissors in her hand and shouted, "I'm going to cut your balls off."

I was speechless, but finally managed, "Miss Davies?"

The nurse nodded yes. I asked if Marion had been drunk. The nurse nodded again and said, "I was upset and turned to your father and said, 'Get her out. You don't have to put up with this, for heaven's sake. Put her out.' He responded, 'Oh, I would, but think of the scandal it would make.' "

I left my father's room and walked over to see my old friend McNamara. The sadness of it all made me feel like I needed a drink. Paul was the perfect companion. As I walked along the street in the fading sun, everything seemed so incongruous. Nothing was making sense. My father had taken Marion into his heart and house, and defied the mores of

American society in having an open relationship with her when he was married. And now he felt it would be a scandal to break with her. It was a moment of supreme irony. As I reached McNamara's home, I opened the garden gate. I was upset, and hesitated. My mind kept saying: Pop made his bed and now has to sleep in it. I closed the gate and walked back to the guesthouse, because not even Paul could ease the pain that ached in my heart.

I went to see my father the following afternoon. Marion was sitting alone in the first-floor living room. She had a drink in her hand. She appeared to have been in the bottle for some time. Marion became vulgar when she was drunk. She would also flirt, which she did even with me and my brothers.

She was swearing and not making much sense. A bottle of Scotch stood at the side of her couch. She had switched from her usual gin. She didn't like Dick Berlin and demanded, "What's that crook doing around here? Does he think he's the new chief? Well, I've got news for that bastard. He's not half as smart as Pops, and I may kick his ass out." Marion started laughing and I rose to leave. "Have a drink," she urged. "Let's be friendly. After all, we're all one big happy family!" I told her that I was going up to see my father in his bedroom.

I stayed with Pop for a long time, rubbing the back of his neck and head. I could hear Marion and several of her friends downstairs. They were drinking and talking loudly. I told my father that everything was going to be all right. He would soon be firing off new instructions to me and others. Of course we both knew otherwise. He could glimpse it in my eyes, and I could see the end in his. Pop kept thanking me for rubbing his head and neck. I had no thoughts of his placing his leadership mantle on my shoulders. We were simply father and son. He began to grow very sleepy, so I stopped rubbing, stood, and took one last glance at him. Then I quietly left the room. Marion was nowhere to be seen. I slipped out the back door of the house and returned to the guest quarters.

I ached all over and was emotionally drained, but I couldn't put the incongruity of what was happening out of my mind. I saw two Marions— the young, beguiling, fun girl and now the embarrassing, throw-up drunk. Lying there, I recalled that Bunky and I had had dinner with her and the old man not long before, and she was stinking drunk at the table. Pop never referred to the situation, nor did we. Suddenly Marion got up and rushed into a bathroom, where she vomited her dinner. Pop never invited either Bunky or me to dine there again—nor many other people.

I went to dinner that evening with my two old pals, McNamara and George "Rosie" Rosenberg, leaving word that I could be reached at Mike Romanoff's restaurant. McNamara, who knew Dick Berlin well because the two had worked together for years at our magazines, warned me, "Don't trust this guy, Bill. He's a shit. An office politician. An intriguer. An in-fighter. He wants to run everything and everyone. He's going to announce that he's the new chief. Mark my words, Bill. This guy is big trouble."

I heard McNamara, but the warning went over my head. Losing the old man, which could come at any moment, was knocking me for a loop. God, I prayed, let him die calmly and quietly. I returned to the guesthouse and went to bed.

Shortly before ten o'clock the following morning, there was a knock at my door. Henry Monaghan, my father's Irish valet, stood there and said, "Your father has passed away." It was August 14, 1951. After all the waiting, I thought that I would not be surprised when the time came. But I was thunderstruck. I wept.

I dressed and met my brother David. We went up to Pop's room. Berlin, Gortatowsky, and Huberth arrived from the guesthouse about the same time. The nurse told me that she had checked my father's pulse about 9:45 and found none. She knew he was dead, and immediately summoned Henry. The valet phoned Dr. Prinzmetal and Dr. Elliot Corday and then awakened all of us. The physicians officially confirmed the death. Marion was still asleep. She had gotten drunk and been sedated by her doctor.

Much has been written and said about what happened next. Marion claimed the body was rushed out of the house so that she could not pay her last respects to my father. She was quoted as saying, "His body was gone, whoosh, like that. The boys were gone. Do you know what they did? They stole a possession of mine. He belonged to me. I loved him for thirty-two years and now he's gone. I didn't even get to say goodbye."

Her claim that the body was rushed out of the house is inaccurate. Pierce Brothers Undertakers in Beverly Hills were phoned to come for the body. Berlin and I agreed on that earlier. We didn't tell them to hurry. As a matter of fact, they didn't arrive for an hour or more.

Marion also was later quoted as saying that Dr. Corday, who was her own physician, had injected her with a sedative while she was stooped over picking up a telegram from the floor. Some of her friends suggested there was a conspiracy on the part of our family and company executives to get her out of the way as quickly as possible once my father had died. There was no such plan, although some expressed concern about her drinking and conduct. No one knew what she would do or say. I certainly didn't want to see her drunk in a face-to-face confrontation with our mother. Nor did Mother.

Frankly, I don't know when Marion woke up or how she learned of my father's death. She rarely got up before noon. In any case, all that we had decided was openly discussed in front of the doctors and servants as well as the undertakers. They also heard our phone calls to family, friends, company colleagues, and those professionals involved in the funeral and burial. And who could have missed Berlin! He was running around, shouting, and telling just about everyone what do to. McNamara's warning about him came back to me, but I dismissed it as trivial at a time like that.

If Marion had walked into any of the numerous rooms we were using, she would have heard everything. She didn't. That was clearly because she had been sedated, was exhausted, and was hung over. Our plane to San Francisco didn't take off until about four o'clock, some six hours after my father passed away.

The body was embalmed. That took about four hours. It was placed in a bronze casket and driven out to Lockheed Air Terminal in Burbank. We chartered a plane, and four of the old man's sons—George, David, Randy, and I—accompanied his body to San Francisco for the church service and burial. I asked the pilot to fly over San Simeon and dip his wings there. He did. My mother and my brother Jack, as well as Austine, met us in San Francisco.

I have written all of this with reluctance. No one wishes to wash family laundry in public. But many false reports surrounding my father's death have gone unchallenged for three decades. Since I and my brother Randy are the last persons with detailed knowledge of the facts, it seems incumbent on one of us to speak out now to bring some sort of balance into the reporting of these events. As every newspaper reporter comes to know, however, denial rarely, if ever, undoes the damage done by original falsehoods. Nevertheless, in the long run—perhaps a century from now, when a history is written of these times and American journalism—some harsh judgments of my father and our family will be viewed in fuller light.

Austine broke the news of Father's death to my mother. Mom quietly responded: "He's mine now. He's finally mine." My mother repeated that to me and her other sons as we awaited the funeral.

Marion and others have claimed that I phoned her from San Francisco and indicated she was unwelcome at the funeral. That is also untrue. I never had a phone conversation with Marion during that time. Therefore I could not have refused, as she asserted, to give her the time and place of the funeral. The truth is, it was published in many California papers.

Friends and associates came from around the United States to pay their last respects to my father at the Chapel of Grace in Grace Episcopal Cathedral on Nob Hill. Roses covered the sides and base of the casket. My father had been born, had lived, and had gone to school nearby. The *San Francisco Examiner* also was near. Many flags around the city were at half-staff in remembrance of a well-known native son.

For a day and a half my father lay in state, wearing a dark-blue suit with a blue tie over a monogrammed shirt and cuff links. Hundreds passed the bier. Some 300 floral arrangements overflowed the chapel. Honorary pallbearers included California governor Earl Warren, San Francisco mayor Elmer E. Robinson, Herbert Hoover, General Douglas MacArthur, Arthur Hays Sulzberger, Bernard Baruch, Roy Howard, Colonel Robert McCormick, John N. Garner, and Mrs. Ogden Reid.

About 1,500 people filled the cathedral on the day of the funeral. Several hundred more stood outside. Those in attendance included old-time executives and editors like Gortatowsky and Howey; writers such as Gene Fowler, Louella Parsons, and Adela Rogers St. Johns; and dignitaries and friends like Louis B. Mayer; Hugh Baillie, president of United Press; A. P. Giannini, president of the Bank of America; and Robert G. Sproul, president of the University of California.

The half-hour service was from the Book of Common Prayer. There was no eulogy or homily. The Right Reverend Karl M. Block, Episcopal bishop of California, chose to read the lesson from the fifteenth chapter of the First Epistle of St. Paul to the Corinthians. It spoke of the resurrection of triumphant souls: "O death, where is thy sting? O grave, where is thy victory?"

The organist played Bach and César Franck. The men's chorus sang Malotte's "Lord's Prayer." A full chorus then sung Dvořák's arrangement of the Twenty-third Psalm. In keeping with the liturgy, my father's name wasn't mentioned at the service.

The cortège of about two dozen limousines then journeyed down the peninsula about ten miles to Cyprus Lawn Cemetery in Colma. It halted at the Grecian mausoleum where George and Phoebe Hearst were buried. Japanese plums and Australian silk oaks, planted by Pop, surrounded the grave site. As was his wish, my father was entombed with his parents as Bishop Block read the brief Episcopal committal ceremony, and then closed by reading my father's poem, "Song of the River." It included these lines:

> For life was born on the lofty heights
> And flows in a laughing stream
> To the river below
> Whose onward flow
> Ends in a peaceful dream.

I walked down from atop the grassy knoll with my mother, wife, and brothers. Mom had cried at times during the past several days, but she bore up well during the services. As we walked to our car, she said, "I very much hope he's in heaven. I'm going to pray for him."

Our mother lived for another twenty-three years. In that long span I never heard her say a disparaging word about my father. We had many happy times together. She continued with her charities and retained great interest in each son and his family. To the close of her life, Mom remained quick with her quips, even about Pop. Austine once asked her if she was ever called "Chief" like her husband. "No," she replied, "I was never on the reservation long enough!" Mom passed away in 1974 at the age of ninety-three.

I plan to have the same service and burial as my father, with one addition: to have more of "Song of the River" read, particularly the section mentioning God.

The obituaries on my father were long and many. Virtually every large newspaper in the nation ran not only a lengthy obit but also an editorial on his career. The *New York Times* printed a summary of his life that ran an extraordinary 20,000 words.

The *Los Angeles Times* called the old man "a force of nature" that could only be summed up "as a physicist describes some phenomenon of the universe."

Most newspapers and editorial writers refrained from making a conclusive assessment of his career and life. The *New York Herald-Tribune,* a longtime critic of the old man, seemed to sum up the reaction of most: "One cannot assess [his] final influence."

I was personally interested in what the *San Francisco Chronicle* would say about my father, since the two battled for about six decades. It said: "We would not try to outguess history and offer any final appraisal of William Randolph Hearst. But we know that he came into American journalism with both fists swinging, that American journalism will never be the same as it was before it felt his hurtling impact, and that the era has been a more colorful, more zestful time to live for his having been part of it." It summed up the old man in two words: "Tremendous voltage."

Pop never dodged a fight or an issue, yet some observers challenged his integrity. Others claimed he had a few principles, yet he spoke, wrote, and acted all his life on the basis of principles. Some challenged his beliefs and concluded he held no rocklike truths. Yet he was one of the most fearless fighters against social injustice and communism in the history of this country, as well as a staunch, outspoken supporter of hundreds of decent causes.

The fact is, many were upset because he was such a rich, free spirit who, at one time or another, took on just about every special and political interest in the country and beat many of them. In the process, he was in the direct line of fire.

In my own judgment, it appears historically and professionally superficial to dismiss my father as a mere news sensationalist. The characterization doesn't seem to stand up in the context of the massive contributions that he made not only to journalism but to the basic concept of free ideas—the now often-invoked First Amendment. The old man didn't fit into any mold, any formula, any traditional frame of reference. For that, one biographer dismissed him as eccentric and a failure. This was an individual who never met or exchanged a single thought with my father.

For all the criticism of my father while he lived, his journalistic epitaph was remarkably free of the rancor hurled at him by the same newspapers when he was alive and competing with them. I said it then and repeat it today: Newspapermen instinctively knew that they had lost one of their own. They could slam him and damn him for his news judgment and views, but he remained a newspaperman—one who had never sold out to any establishment and least of all to any herd journalism. He was an individualist, one of those wild western mustangs that refused to be broken and saddled. Let us put our trust in the test of time.

Several hours after my father died, company lawyers filed his 125-page will for probate in San Francisco Superior Court. This was done expeditiously, so the organization would continue functioning normally.

The will set up three trusts. The first granted our mother $6 million in Hearst Corporation preferred stock. It included an additional bequest of $1.5 million in cash to cover taxes that would have to be paid on the stock.

My brothers and I were the beneficiaries of the second trust. It contained sufficient parent corporation preferred stock to ensure each of us an annual income of $30,000. Also, we were bequeathed a hundred shares of corporation common stock, a controlling interest.

The third was a residuary trust for charitable and educational purposes. It went to benefit the Los Angeles Museum, which had already received more than $3 million-worth of art from my father; the University of California; and other institutions, to be chosen by a Hearst Foundation representative. My father also directed that a memorial to his mother be built and be open to the public; it would contain some of his art treasures. My brothers and I were named trustees of all three trusts.

The executors of the will were a mix of company executives and attorneys: Martin Huberth and Richard E. Berlin of New York, Harold G. Kern of Boston, William M. Baskerville of Baltimore, and Richard A. Carrington, Jr., and Henry S. McKay, Jr., both of Los Angeles. In addition to his five sons, the trustees at my father's death included all the executors as well as two of our newspaper executives, William A. Curley and Walter Howey—a total of thirteen.

The old man made certain that his will was carefully conceived, securely structured, and meticulously worded so that, when he died, the corporation would not have to be broken up in order to pay the inheritance taxes. About the time of my father's death, many other family businesses and fortunes had to be sold in order to meet these taxes. The law has since been changed so that a family business may spread out and pay inheritance taxes out of earnings. The will was actually written not only to preserve what my father had built but to make sure it was inherited by his sons.

Little attention was paid to what I considered the most important aspect of the will: the future of our publications. My father said: "I request my executors and trustees not to part with the ownership or control of any newspaper, magazine, feature service, news service, photographic service or periodical, either directly or by sale, or by exchange of the capital stock unless it shall, in their opinion, be necessary or prudent to do so." I was to invoke those words again and again as Dick Berlin later began selling many of our newspapers and dismantling other news operations.

There was public speculation that my mother, brothers, and I met secretly in San Francisco about the time of the funeral to discuss the will and plan family strategy concerning it. There were no such meetings because, for some time, we had known the precise contents of the will. And, even if we had wished to, we couldn't have changed it. However, Marion was later to surprise us.

Marion received no bequest in the will. She was to have, in a trust fund dated nearly a year before my father passed away, a lifetime income from a block of 30,000 shares of Hearst Corporation preferred. This stock was to revert to my brothers and me on her death.

However, several days later, Marion's lawyers startled all of us by presenting the executors with an agreement by which my father combined her 30,000 shares with his own 170,000 shares, giving her sole voting power in the corporation. Thus, she had known what she was talking about when she suggested to editors and publishers in some of her phone calls that she might one day hold power in the company. Nevertheless, to suggest that my father actually wanted her to run the corporation was contrary to all his previous policy. Company executives were experienced men who had grown into their responsibilities only after years of steady performance.

My father was aware of the personal and professional dislike between Marion and most of the executives. I believe he acted on the feeling that she might suffer in some way as his estate was implemented. Yet he himself had named these executives to all the executor posts except that of his personal attorney. He knew the editors and publishers would never accept her as the new chief. In death the old man had left us a dilemma: his concern for Marion, balanced by his responsibility to the company.

Attorneys for both sides met for a couple of days and finally worked out an agreement whereby Marion relinquished all rights she may have had to act as a voting trustee of the corporation. She was named an advisor to management at a salary of one dollar per year. She apparently wanted to create the public appearance that she had been and would continue to be one of the brains of the company.

On October 31, about two and a half months after my father's death, Marion was married in Las Vegas to Captain Horace G. Brown, Jr., a Merchant Marine captain. News reports indicated both were pleasantly splashed at the quickie ceremony. A few months later, I happened to be in Romanoff's restaurant when Brown sent a waiter to ask me if I would have a drink with him and Marion. I declined, telling the waiter that I was just leaving. Brown followed me outside, and asked if I thought I was too good to have a drink with him and his bride. There was no sense in making a scene and I told him I had to go. He began cursing and then threw a righthand punch. I ducked, decked him with a right, and walked away. It was the last time I saw either him or Marion.

Shortly after my father's death, voting control of the entire corporation was placed in the hands of thirteen trustees—the five sons plus Berlin and other executives.

A few months earlier, Harold G. Kern, publisher of our Boston papers, had succeeded Gortatowsky as general manager of all the newspapers. And Richard E. Deems was promoted to executive vice-president in charge of our magazines. Deems is, by the way, still with us in an advisory capacity and now has more than fifty years with the company.

In September 1955, I became editor-in-chief of the Hearst newspapers—a post my father had held for about a half-century. After nearly twenty years as publisher of the *Journal-American,* I moved to corporate headquarters at Fifty-seventh Street and Eighth Avenue. Berlin and I now had the two most public roles in the company. (Dick had been president of the organization since 1943.) I said at the time that I felt like Harry Truman when President Roosevelt passed away—that the stars, moon, and all the planets had fallen on me.

Assets of the corporation then totaled about $235 million. Net profits after taxes averaged about $11 million a year. *Time* magazine pointed to "the emergence of Bill Hearst, who looks strikingly like his father, as the organization's most powerful figure." They added that "the modest son is different from his imperious father." I had reason to be modest. The old man had always been far ahead of me in every aspect of the craft.

I chose Conniff as my editorial assistant, and formed what I called the Hearst Task Force, which was comprised of Joseph Kingsbury-Smith, Conniff, and myself. The idea was to cover major news developments around the world and interview international leaders. I also began writing a weekly editorial column that continues to this day. And, to assure that we would have a good working relationship, I took trips to meet with all our editors and publishers around the country. They liked the fact that I asked them to call me Bill. My father would never have said that. I felt the new informal style was more relaxed, and they approved.

Seymour Berkson, head of INS, was named to succeed me at the *Journal-American* and remained there until his death in 1959. Joseph Kingsbury-Smith, European general manager of INS, returned from his post in Paris to take Berkson's place as head of the wire service. Bob Considine took Kingsbury-Smith's place on our reporting team, because Joe was tied up with numerous problems at INS and, later, with the *Journal-American.* (In 1959 Joe succeeded Berkson and remained as the *Journal-American's* publisher until the paper merged with the *Herald Tribune* and *World Telegram & Sun* in 1966. Conniff was appointed national editor of Hearst Headline Service after INS merged with UP in 1958, but he continued on the Task Force.)

Meantime, Berlin was moving behind the scenes to consolidate and increase his power. He was sixty-one years old in 1955, and had been with the company for thirty-six years. I was forty-seven and felt we would make a good team.

Berlin had actually joined the company through my mother. She met him at one of her New York canteens when he was a young Navy lieutenant during World War I. After the war, she helped get him a job as an advertising salesman with our *Motorboating & Sailing* magazine. He was a good salesman and was later promoted to business manager, executive vice-president, and general manager of the Hearst magazines. Shortly afterward, he was appointed president of the company's magazine division.

I had gotten along well with Berlin. He worked hard and had a sharp business sense. However, after my father's death the relationship changed.

Friends and associates mentioned to Conniff and me that Berlin was privately putting me and my brothers down. He referred to us as "the kids" and said he "threw us a bone now and then." In essence he was saying: Forget the family. I'm in charge.

But this was no time for internal bickering. We were a family company and had to keep our own peace. Besides, Conniff, Kingsbury-Smith, and I had a date with destiny, so I dismissed these reports. I was about to meet some of the toughest guys in the world.

X
MISSION TO MOSCOW

I n February of 1955 Moscow was an iceberg in the globe's glacial politics. Most of the world shivered amid the gusty political winds of the Cold War. My family and friends compared the Soviet Union to the far side of the moon.

Georgi Malenkov, a question mark after Stalin, was the Soviet premier. Nikita Khrushchev, a rambunctious redneck from the Ukraine, had leapfrogged his comrades to become first secretary of the Communist party. "Old Iron Pants," V. M. Molotov, was the stone-faced foreign minister who wouldn't budge on an issue unless Stalin rose from his icy grave and growled. Defense Minister Nikolai Bulganin, long known as a hatchet man who betrayed close friends in his climb up to the Kremlin hierarchy, deceptively appeared to be a smiling sideliner. Many Westerners believed Bulganin was overshadowed by Marshal Georgi Zhukov, first deputy minister of defense and commander of the Soviet forces that had captured Berlin. But that view was a misinterpretation of the real muscle in the Soviet capital: the Communist party.

Moscow was a city ruled by fear and the Soviet Union a country dominated by these and a few other men. This fear and domination were more than the far side of the moon. They were the black side of human existence—a society of silent assassination, soundless banishment, and the fatal stillness of Siberian slavery. Why would any sane individual think of walking down the labyrinthine ways of this political and social back alley? I was about to find out.

In December of 1954 David Sentner had invited me for a drink at the Washington National Press Club. We slipped away from a crowd of colleagues and sauntered over to the bar. Sentner was the longtime bureau chief of the Hearst newspapers in the nation's capital. We had a few minutes before sitting down at the annual Gridiron Dinner, a reporters' roast of Washington bigwigs.

Dave said, "Bill, I think you can break the silence of the Iron Curtain for the first time since Stalin's death." Stalin had died the previous year.

The unexpected remark set me back on my heels. I said, "Dave, one of us needs another drink."

Sentner smiled, but I could see that he was serious. "I have a hunch. Your father campaigned against the global threat of communism ever since the first days of the Bolshevik Revolution. The fact that he was anathema to the Commies might be a very good reason for Moscow to give you a visa. Bill, I think they're hurting and want to get more of their views out to the West. I believe you may get a visa."

The words hit me like a blast of Moscow winter wind. "But, Dave, they're not issuing any visas. I understand that Cy Sulzberger (the *New York Times* correspondent) has had a request on file for about seven years. No visas to any Western reporters. Besides, they censor most of the best stuff. Dave, with the anti-Communist record of our newspapers, if the Russians did give me a visa, they'd probably hold me for ransom." Both of us laughed, but the idea intrigued me. "I sure would like to get inside and see for myself. If I could get in, I might also bring some fresh ideas from the West to Soviet leaders. Dave, send me a memo with all your thoughts and let me think about it before we try to get a visa."

In the following days I sounded out my wife, colleagues, and friends. Virtually all were adamantly against the idea. Austine saw nothing but trouble. The Kremlin leaders were a bunch of cutthroats. Dick Berlin felt the Russians would dream something up and throw me in jail. He reminded me that my father had attacked the Communists with all guns blazing. They had never forgiven him. The Soviets had been waiting years for just this opportunity. E. D. "Cobbie" Coblentz, who had virtually raised me at the *Journal-American,* quietly begged Frank Conniff not to let me go. He said the Russians would slip some beautiful ballerina into bed with me and bingo—Siberia! J. D. Gortatowsky, who was now ultimately responsible for all our newspapers, had had a bad dream: Conniff and I had gotten splashed on a bottle of Russian vodka and were caught red-handed burning the Soviet flag outside the Kremlin walls. My mother began to sob that she would never see me again. They all ganged up on me, and it sounded like at least twenty-five years in the Gulag.

A few days before Christmas I wrote Dave a brief note, asking that he explore the possibility of a trip to the Soviet Union. I told him the idea was just too good to pass up. However, I hedged my bet. I wanted to bring Frank Conniff and Joseph Kingsbury-Smith, our INS European general manager in Paris, with me. Later we were to call this dauntless trio the Hearst Task Force.

Since Christmas isn't a Communist holiday, K. G. Fedoseev, who was in charge of the Soviet embassy while the ambassador was away, invited Sentner for a drink in the National Press Club. Only one other person was present—the bartender. Dave was quick and blunt, since a Christmas roast was waiting: "Bill Hearst wants to go to Russia and report on the changes there since Stalin's death. News since then has been meager. There are reports the new regime is shaky. Have things changed enough that Mr. Hearst could get a visa? He wants to talk with the Russian people and possibly the new Kremlin leadership. The world will believe him because of the strong anti-Communist stand of our newspapers."

Fedoseev slowly put down his glass and said matter-of-factly, "I don't see why not. I think it could be arranged."

However, Fedoseev seemed less sure of Kingsbury-Smith and Conniff. He asked that Sentner provide their backgrounds. Several lunches soon followed at the Mayflower Hotel. The Soviet counselor was meticulous about paying his half of each bill.

Dave sensed that each meeting was becoming more positive. None of us knew, of course, that Nikita Khrushchev, a name not well known outside the Soviet Union, was calling the shots. He was going to make big news and wanted us there.

Fedoseev engaged in a series of questions and potential obstacles at each lunch. The tactic was consistent with virtually all Soviet bargaining. Move methodically; get as much information as possible.

Fedoseev phoned and, on January 4, 1955, Sentner was ushered into the reception room of the Soviet embassy. A bottle of vodka and a bowl of caviar sat on a small marble table. Fedoseev entered and immediately announced, "I have good news for you. Everything is approved, and I think it deserves a drink." At that moment, Ambassador G. N. Zaroubin entered and joined them in toasts.

The Russians suggested that mid-February was a good time for the trip. Visas would be granted to all three men for three or four weeks. Interviews with Soviet leaders would be discussed after we arrived in Moscow. Mr. Hearst could stay at any hotel he wished. The Hearst and Conniff visas would be ready as soon as their passports were presented at the Soviet embassy in Washington. Kingsbury-Smith's visa was waiting at their embassy in Paris.

Conniff and I later visited the Washington embassy to pick up our visas. Ambassador Zaroubin broke out vodka and caviar. As we drank and nibbled, I wondered aloud about what Pop would have thought of such a chummy meeting beneath a huge picture of a smiling Stalin. The ambassador grunted to the effect that my father would have approved of such a mission. He might have, but we nevertheless touched base with the State Department.

A week later, as we were about to board a Pan American flight to Paris, Ambassador Zaroubin popped up. He too was headed to Moscow. After landing in Paris we learned from Kingsbury-Smith that Soviet ambassadors from around the world were being summoned home. He surmised that something big was under way.

On our way to Moscow we boarded a Soviet airliner in East Berlin. It was one of the worst plane rides I have ever had in my life. A group of Indians from New Delhi sat a few seats behind us and farted from East Berlin to the Soviet capital. I gagged much of the way and was never so happy to get off a plane. Soviet customs officials couldn't understand why this American was so pleased to be in their country.

To shake the experience I mentioned to Joe and Frank that another Hearst had preceded me and lived to tell about it—Grandma Phoebe. Some seventy years earlier, braving the rugged travel of the Russian railroad system and fears of the czarist police, she had ventured to St. Petersburg to view the Hermitage collections, palaces, and galleries, before touring Moscow.

We checked into the National Hotel, which faces Red Square. They gave us a suite on the first floor with a fine view of the square. It had a balcony in case anyone wanted to catch a numbing chill and perhaps a case of pneumonia. The suite had high ceilings and long, red drapes circling much of each room.

We soon heard our first of the many rumors that floated around Moscow in those days. Western diplomats were picking up hints that the Soviets might be returning to the harsh decades of Stalinism. The brooding Moscow winter had turned cold and melancholy. I began to understand why the Russians drank so much vodka.

Joseph Kingsbury-Smith, our longtime foreign hand, took over. He hired a Russian secretary who spoke English. She would type the letters that we planned to send to the top Soviet leaders: Malenkov, Khrushchev, Molotov, Zhukov, and others. The letters were simple and direct. They said we had come to Moscow in hopes of serving some useful purpose, especially toward improving the relations between our two countries. We would welcome the opportunity of an interview. We walked over and dropped them in the Kremlin mailbox.

Nothing happened for almost three weeks. I began to lose hope. Nevertheless, we spent part of each day honing our possible interviews. From the start, I suggested we hold these sessions in a bathroom with the water running so no "bugs" could eavesdrop. Joe and Frank agreed.

Joe and Frank were more optimistic than I was. They remembered what U.S. Ambassador Charles "Chip" Bohlen had told us shortly after our arrival: "Your visit will be significant. Your arrival was reported in *Pravda* today. They never put anything in *Pravda* unless it means something. I think you'll have success."

Kingsbury-Smith suggested that we divide the questions among us. We should ask each question immediately after we thought we had the crux of an answer to the previous one. That would help cut off long-winded propaganda speeches. Each of us had ten to twelve questions for each leader, so we were ready to start.

I got even more edgy. What the hell were they waiting for? If we were getting the stiff arm, we should pack up. I sounded out the other guys, and we went into our think tank—the bathroom—for a decisive session. Joe and Frank made an unusual suggestion, and we implemented it immediately. The two walked around the sitting room addressing the drapes, chandeliers, and anything else we thought might be hiding a bug. For much of the next two days, Joe or Frank spoke variations on the following theme: "Now, Mr. Hearst, the president said you could give your message only to the premier or one of the top Soviet leaders. Yes, Mr. Hearst, you must deliver it personally—that's what the president said—personally to Premier Malenkov. Or another Soviet leader. But the premier and the others don't seem to be available, so perhaps we should prepare to leave."

On the third day the Kremlin took the bait. Our phone jingled. It was the foreign minister's office. Molotov would receive us the following morning. Be ready for a ministry car at 10:45 A.M.

Relations between Moscow and Washington were tense. The U.S. Congress had just passed a resolution pledging support to Formosa. The U.S. Sixth Fleet was on the scene. A sense of concern seemed to permeate Molotov's office as we sat down.

One of our first questions to Molotov related to the crisis in the Formosa Straits. General Chiang Kai-shek, who had retreated from China to what is now Taiwan, had maintained a considerable number of troops on two islands—Quemoy and Matsu—just off the Chinese mainland. They had been under heavy artillery fire from Communist forces on the mainland and were suffering many casualties. We knew that President Eisenhower was willing to have the U.S. Sixth Fleet evacuate Chiang's forces and take them to Formosa. However, the president was fearful that our ships would be fired on, and he hesitated to order the evacuation. We therefore asked Molotov if he thought the Sixth Fleet could evacuate the Chinese Nationalist troops on the offshore islands without being fired on. Molotov replied affirmatively. We then asked him whether he would obtain such assurances from the Chinese Communist government. He said, in effect, that was none of his business.

Our interview with Molotov was published the next day in the Soviet press. Shortly thereafter, President Eisenhower risked ordering the Sixth Fleet to evacuate the Chinese Nationalists on Quemoy and Matsu. Not a shot was fired. It was obvious the Soviets favored a reduction of tension in the Formosa Straits, and Molotov was advising the Chinese Communists accordingly. That single aspect of our story not only captured global headlines but managed to contribute to international stability.

There was much more. In the midst of the eighty-minute interview, Molotov began to accuse the United States of encircling the Soviet Union with military bases and threatening its security. He said these bases should be withdrawn. Kingsbury-Smith suggested that a start could be made if the Soviets would be willing to withdraw their troops from the Soviet area of occupation in Austria. (The Big Four—the United States, Britain, France, and the Soviet Union—then maintained occupation forces in individual zones within Austria.) Molotov hesitated before responding and then asked, "Would that be contagious?"

We replied that, as journalists, none of us was authorized to give any such assurances. However, Soviet withdrawal from Austria might be a first step in the withdrawal of military bases by both sides. We pointed out that such moves would create a favorable atmosphere for coexistence. Molotov made no further comment on the issue, but he left us with the impression that the door to Soviet military withdrawal from Austria might open. And a peace treaty might eventually be worked out.

After our interview was published, the Austrian ambassador to Moscow arranged to see Molotov. As a result, negotiations were soon held in Vienna. The four major powers agreed just four months later, in May of 1955, to a peace treaty and evacuation of Austria. Chancellor Julius Raab credited our interview with paving the way for Austrian independence.

We had hardly written our Molotov story when our phone rang again. A car would arrive at eleven the following morning to take us to Communist party headquarters, where we would meet Comrade Khrushchev.

The rumors were already rife. Khrushchev, the strongest adversary of Malenkov in the presidium of the Central Committee, might purge the premier. *Pravda* and *Izvestia* had been publishing attacks by Khrushchev on Malenkov and some of his associates. The criticism assailed those who believed consumer goods could be produced without slowing the manufacture of heavy goods. Heavy goods usually meant military hardware.

As we walked into his long, narrow office, Khrushchev made little impression sitting casually behind his desk. He gave the appearance of a short, portly man who was anchored down by his own weight. Doctors had not yet put the party leader on a strict diet, which included limiting his reportedly prodigious intake of vodka.

No impression could have been further from reality. The squat man with the round, bald head and peasant face bounded forward and gave us a toothy grin and a full, firm handshake. After a few minutes of jocular sparring, there was no doubt in any of our minds who ran the Soviet Union. Khrushchev would take all questions on any subject. His telephone interrupted his response to one of our first queries. The party chief was clearly annoyed. He quickly signaled with his stubby fingers that he was taking no calls. We were never disturbed again. (On our way home, Conniff said that proved that Khrushchev was the head man. Everyone else we had met kept their phone ready.)

We seesawed back and forth for three hours. Khrushchev was direct, blunt, threatening, shrewd, boisterous, and humorous. He seldom paused. Yes, indeed, based on his authoritative answers and manner, this was the real leader of the Soviet Union. However, we didn't let him get away with some of his stormy political diatribes about communism ultimately prevailing over capitalism. The interview often became a wide-open debate.

Despite all of Khrushchev's bluster, one ringing phrase came through clearly: peaceful coexistence. He echoed it again and again. The party leader was talking peace and better relations with the United States, not a return to Stalinism. He repeatedly stressed that there must not be a nuclear war between the United States and Soviet Union because both would be destroyed. At one point he leaned over the table and patted my arm, saying, "You're a capitalist, but we're having a peaceful talk here. If we can coexist around this table, I think we can coexist around the globe." Khrushchev's blue eyes flashed and he broke into a broad grin.

The party secretary was soon calling me his "capitalist friend," and I returned the gesture by referring to him as "my Communist friend." By this symbolism, Khrushchev was stressing the significance of what he was saying about peaceful coexistence. I well understood what he meant.

Khrushchev suddenly blurted that Americans were afraid to visit the Soviet Union. He said pointedly, "You're free to go anywhere you want in Russia except our military installations. Anywhere. I'd like our people to go to the States, but they wouldn't be allowed in."

We suggested maybe he could start in some way. Perhaps the Soviet government could offer to send top Soviet artists, ballet performers, musicians, and others to the United States. America would send some of its best performers to Russia, and we would begin a cultural exchange. Khrushchev was delighted at the idea. Of course, he said, the Soviet Union would be pleased—but the U.S. government would never agree to it. (That was one of the first things we mentioned to President Eisenhower when we returned to the States. Ike thought it was a great idea, and later spoke to the State Department in favor of it. Our Kremlin visit thus led to the first cultural exchange between Moscow and Washington.)

The Khrushchev interview touched on virtually every area of the world: Eastern and Western Europe, the Far East and Middle East, Latin America, and elsewhere. The subjects ranged from communism's atheism to Russian proverbs and the openness of the American people. But nothing was more powerful than those two words: peaceful coexistence.

As we rose to leave, Khrushchev stood and put his arm around my shoulder and said, "When you get home, you may be summoned before the [House] Un-American Activities Committee for coming over here and having this conversation with me. If you do, I'll come over and tell them how you defended your government's policies."

It was a light parting touch and Khrushchev added another. He said we could meet any people we wished. I mentioned viewing the Bolshoi ballet, meeting some of their top performers, and seeing other Soviet artists, musicians, poets. Khrushchev smiled, but said nothing. He simply nodded to his interpreter that he understood.

After we returned to our hotel, Kingsbury-Smith, who had taken notes in shorthand, began banging out on his typewriter a transcription of what Khrushchev had said. Frank and I alerted Barry Faris at INS New York and the *Journal-American* that we had the Khrushchev interview and would soon be filing a long story. Of course everyone was quite excited.

We phoned the story to the INS London bureau, bypassing the Soviet postal-telegraph system, which could be unreliable, and Russian censors who were even more unpredictable. It was understood from the start that we wouldn't be censored, but we didn't want to test our luck. Chuck Klensch, our INS Moscow bureau chief, phoned it paragraph by paragraph as Kingsbury-Smith typed and all three of us agreed on each sentence. It was a priority call and we paid the higher phone rate. The telephone line became very scratchy, and Klensch often had to repeat and even spell words. He was exhausted, and Joe took over the call after he had finished typing our story. Soviet operators obviously listened but did not interrupt. We were home free!

The story was quickly cabled from London to INS New York. It was immediately put on the INS wires around the nation and the world. Within an hour we were receiving congratulatory phone calls from Dick Berlin, various publishers, and many friends. Everybody seemed to use the same word: "Sensational!"

I couldn't help thinking of Pop. He would have been so pleased and proud.

Over the next few days, rumors of a Kremlin shake-up persisted. The Soviets suggested we might wish to interview Nikolai Bulganin, another Soviet leader. We decided Bulganin would make little news and politely passed on the offer.

On the eve of the crucial meeting of the Supreme Soviet, we were received by Marshal Zhukov. Zhukov was relaxed and friendly, with a keen sense of humor. Eight rows of medals stretched across his broad chest, but he was a plain-spoken, unpretentious man who was at peace with himself. He wanted to be remembered to Ike.

Conniff asked the marshal an old but intriguing question: What were Hitler's greatest strategical and tactical mistakes in invading Russia? Zhukov said Hitler's greatest strategical error was the initial decision to march into the Soviet Union. He simply never had the necessary war machine to capture the country. The German leader's biggest tactical mistake was his heavy dependence on aircraft instead of using more artillery. Planes often were grounded in Russia's bitterly cold and gray weather, but artillery could always function. Zhukov said he had made powerful use of Soviet artillery.

The marshal echoed the peace line of Khrushchev and Molotov. He didn't understand how the United States could accuse Moscow of warlike intentions while it took no postwar advantage of other nations. I quietly demurred and mentioned that the U.S. monopoly on atomic bombs might have been a deterrent to even greater expansion. Zhukov shrugged, "You had only three." I asked him how he knew that, since Americans didn't. He shrugged again. (When I met with Prime Minister Churchill in London on the way home, Churchill corrected Zhukov. He said the United States had sixteen atomic bombs when the war ended in 1945.)

After the Zhukov interview, we learned that Khrushchev was a man of his word. We could see anyone. Soviet notables suddenly appeared from nowhere. We saw Dmitri Shostakovich, the distinguished composer, for an hour at the Moscow Conservatory of Music. Shostakovich was quite nervous and smoked constantly as a government bureaucrat watched and listened. When the flustered composer faltered in any answer, the bureaucrat prodded him. Shostakovich openly reproached himself: "When a comrade gets off the correct path, it's only right that his comrades should help straighten him out."

Shostakovich seemed to be under such distress that we took pity and quietly ended the interview. He left the room miserable and emotionally exhausted. This was a great man, but the system had reduced him to a human cipher. I later learned he had been summoned from Leningrad to meet us, and endured an uncomfortable night-long train trip. The bully boys on top had spoken.

Svetlana Stalin seemed a similarly pathetic figure. She lived in a gray, grimy ten-floor structure with stone stairways lit by dim lights. A squeaky elevator carried passengers up, but not down. It descended empty when a button was pushed on the ground floor. Svetlana opened the apartment door herself. She looked frightened as we entered her cramped quarters. The daughter of the recently deceased dictator offered us her hand. She was slender and fair-complexioned, with red hair; she wore a beige pullover with a brownish tweed skirt. All that faded behind the strained look on her gaunt face. Her cheeks were taut and eyes tense. She led us into a living-dining room off the entrance. It was a very small room. I remember a lace-covered table.

We exchanged pleasantries. Svetlana was married, with two children, and teaching Soviet literature at the Moscow Academy of Social Science. I mentioned her brother, Vassily. She froze. Foreign diplomats had heard rumors that the onetime high-ranking Soviet Air Force officer had been executed as a result of repeated drunkenness and other fast living. Tears came into her eyes. She didn't speak. She seemed agitated when her father was mentioned, but avoided discussing him by inviting us into a tiny nearby room. A large poster, not a photograph, of her father stood above it. She looked at it but made no comment.

I asked if her father had done any writing. Svetlana said he had been too busy to write any memoirs. She spoke softly, matter-of-factly. Stalin's private views—she seemed to be referring to him not as a father but as a head of state—were exactly the same as his public speeches. In his last years, he spent a lot of time reading and puttering around the garden of his country home just outside Moscow. Stalin worked nights and also read late into the night. Unlike Roosevelt and Churchill, he preferred historical books, not detective stories.

I studied her. This was possibly the only human being whom Stalin had cared about in his last years. Yet what an uneasy life he had bequeathed her. The commonest Russian peasants lived under less emotional strain.

There was one proud, happy moment. Before we left, Svetlana introduced us to her young son and daughter. I'll never forget her standing alone in the doorway as we departed. Her words seemed to echo in my footsteps as we walked down the stone steps, "No, my father wrote no memoirs.'' What a pity, I told myself. He would have written his own tormented version, but it would have been one helluva history book.

In her book, written after she married an American and was living in the States, Svetlana disclosed that Molotov had phoned and ordered her to see us. He told her to be courteous but to say practically nothing. She made her home in Arizona for several years, went back to Moscow, returned to the States again, and seems to have dropped out of sight. She was perhaps the most tragic figure I have ever met.

We met others, including the acting chief monk at the famous monastery of St. Sergei, seat of the Russian Orthodox Church. Father Sergei said the church wasn't allowed to teach religion to children, but, he smiled, people still believed in God. Before leaving Moscow, I saw Patriarch Alexei there. I mentioned the regime's atheism, and Alexei replied, "I think perhaps there are times when they do believe in God."

I mentioned God in various discussions simply because religion and communism were so diametrically opposed—as were freedom and communism. Frankly, I've always believed that freedom and religion would be the West's two strongest weapons against the totalitarian state.

The Soviet regime was gathered before us. We sat listening to Malenkov addressing 1,300 delegates at the long-awaited first session of the Supreme Soviet. Suddenly, our translator began choking on the premier's words. Then, the man became speechless. He began to shake.

Kingsbury-Smith seized him by the shoulder. "Speak up, man, what's happening down there? Tell us!"

The man could only croak, "It's sensational! Sensational!"

Joe shook him again. The translator finally blurted, "Malenkov just quit!"

The meeting was adjourned after it was announced that a new premier would be named in about two and a half hours. The speculation among diplomats and newsmen was all Khrushchev. We were delighted, since he had spoken with us only three days before. Our interview would now have even greater significance.

However, like most guesses around the Kremlin in those days, the speculation proved wrong. Khrushchev rose and proposed Bulganin as the new premier. The words were barely out of Khrushchev's mouth when 1,300 hands rose in approval.

We then understood the significance of the early government offer to interview Bulganin—but only after the meeting of the Supreme Soviet. Our Soviet hosts had offered us a world scoop and we had passed it by.

We returned to the National Hotel in low spirits. INS chief Faris had already cabled us from New York: Please try to interview the new premier. We dutifully dropped another interview request in the Kremlin mailbox, but weren't optimistic because of our schedule. We were leaving for Leningrad the following day and flying to Helsinki in two days.

Yet we hadn't done badly—interviews with Molotov, Khrushchev, Zhukov, Shostakovich, Svetlana Stalin, the religious leaders, and meetings with many Western diplomats. The interviews were carried not only around the world but in *Pravda, Izvestia,* and other Soviet newspapers, and broadcast on radio.

Chip Bohlen had his U.S. embassy staff check what was printed in the Soviet press and compared it to our reports. Nothing that we or the Soviet leaders said had been censored. The ambassador considered that highly significant. Most interviews with foreign journalists were censored or not published at all in the Soviet press. (Two years later, in the interview that Conniff, Considine, and I had with Khrushchev, we had some tough exchanges, and the text of the interview published in the Soviet press was censored. It failed to give a complete account of what was said. Kingsbury-Smith didn't participate in that interview because he had become head of our INS and couldn't get away.)

Before leaving Moscow, we tried to say thanks in typical American fashion: an evening cocktail party in our suite. The hotel had vodka and caviar, but I still don't know how we rounded up Scotch and other booze. That may have come from the U.S. and other Western embassies. Our Ambassador Bohlen and his wife came, of course, as did Great Britain's suave envoy Sir William Hayter; French Ambassador Leon Joxe; the longtime dean of the diplomatic corps, Sweden's Rolf Sohlman; and many others. It was a noisy shindig because of the day's sensational change of leadership. Diplomats almost leaped from one group to the next, anxiously picking up the latest rumors about the reasons for the switch to Bulganin.

Suddenly the noise and chatter slowed and then almost stopped. The door had opened and there stood Galina Ulanova in the flesh. The celebrated prima ballerina of the Bolshoi, renowned throughout the world, had lived her entire life and even become a grandmother without once coming in contact with a Westerner. At least that was the story around Moscow. In ballet, Ulanova was almost worshiped as a legend. However, her lithe figure halted at the footlights. So did foreigners who wished to meet her.

I didn't say anything about it to anyone, but in fact we had met Ulanova a few evenings before. After seeing her dance at the Bolshoi, we were informed that she was waiting backstage. Of course we had heard the story about her not seeing foreigners, so I thought there might be some misunderstanding. But we were taken into Ulanova's dressing room.

She wore Western clothes—a skirt and cashmere sweater. There was no comparison between the housewife sitting in front of us and the vision on the stage. Ulanova said little, but a half-dozen other ballet people came in and introduced themselves. I invited them to our cocktail party. Maya Plisetskaya, the beautiful heiress apparent to the prima ballerina, walked in next. Yuri Zhdanov, male dancer of the Moscow ballet, and Nicolai Fadeyechen, another top performer, followed the acclaimed twosome.

Ulanova was gracious but still talked very little. However, behind her elegant air and the facade of her makeup, she projected a strong self-discipline. Some of the younger diplomats surrounded the lovely Plisetskaya. One Britisher seemed to think he had just seen a goddess; he couldn't take his eyes off her and followed the ballerina wherever she went.

Bohlen understood the meaning of the visit. Soviet leaders were signaling that they wanted friendlier relations with the West. There had been virtually no socializing, except at formal functions, among Moscovites and Westerners for a full decade. That was a political decision and so was the presence of Ulanova and the others. Bohlen smiled and told me to come back anytime.

We spent a day touring Leningrad and were about to board our plane from there to Helsinki. An airport official suddenly announced that our aircraft had engine trouble and would be delayed. Kingsbury-Smith engaged our guide and translator in a chess game while I began to write my column. Conniff had been stricken with his longtime bugaboo, gout, and sat in pain.

Ten minutes before the final announcement to board the aircraft, an attendant rushed up and said we had an urgent phone call. It was Klensch, our INS bureau chief. He was panting: "Premier Bulganin will see you tomorrow or the next day. You've got to get back to Moscow as soon as possible."

We just managed to catch the Moscow train. Cold and hungry, we found only heavy sandwiches to eat. Kingsbury-Smith grimaced when he saw cold slices of fat between the bread. He turned away and went to sleep. I nibbled at the edge of the bread but felt my insides rising and quickly quit. Conniff was feeling better and kidded our guide after several bites of his sandwich: "This is great. We ought to have this in America. It beats hell out of pizza." Frank began humming "The Star-Spangled Banner." I thought he might have been nipping at a martini flask but saw none. I went to sleep. This world-scoop stuff wasn't all steak and smiles!

But Bulganin was all smiles. He didn't say much, however, and the interview was somewhat of an anticlimax. He stressed, as Khrushchev had, "peaceful coexistence," and said the Soviet government wanted to lessen world tension. The new Soviet leader also hoped for a rapprochement with the United States. The interview was again splashed in international headlines.

I couldn't help contrasting Bulganin and Khrushchev as the new premier spoke with us. Bulganin chatted in professorial, cultured tones. He polished that soft image by wearing conservative clothes. On the other hand, the freewheeling, sometimes boisterous and contentious Khrushchev was far from a portrait of sweet reasonableness. He appeared rumpled, and his temper seemed to fit his sartorial appearance. If what we learned about both was accurate, the two shared a common trait: ruthlessness. Bulganin was simply an old smoothie. Khrushchev was an upfront slugger.

The interview was headlined on Fleet Street as we arrived in London. The *London Daily Mail,* which had a circulation of about 2,250,000, wrote of me and our trip: "No Western journalist—in fact no Western minister or ambassador—has talked with so many top figures on both sides of the Cold War front in so short a time. No man has been granted such an insight into high places in both Eastern and Western policies." The newspaper concluded that our reporting trip to Moscow was "the most remarkable mission in postwar journalistic history."

I phoned for an appointment to see Churchill and visited with him for about an hour. He would see only me alone.

The British leader had a wonderful way of putting visitors at ease. He always came forward with a big smile and extended his hand many steps before actually shaking hands. He ordered a whiskey-and-soda and started puffing on one of his famous cigars almost as soon as I arrived.

I told him that Khrushchev and the other Soviet leaders were willing to act as an intermediary in the China-West dispute over Formosa. The British leader said that China might one day drive the Soviet Union toward the West. Not today, he explained, but in twenty to fifty years. He added pointedly, "We should be ready to receive her."

Khrushchev's phrase "peaceful coexistence" had caught the world's fancy, but I pointed out to Churchill that he had used a similar phrase that impressed me more. That was "competitive coexistence," with greater emphasis on competitive economies. The latter phrase was to become almost as popular as the first.

I told him that Khrushchev came across as genuinely concerned about nuclear war. Churchill puffed on his cigar and pointed to a small, brass-plated coal pot near his fireplace. He said, "Now look at that little pot. Filled with a nuclear bomb, it would be enough to destroy the entire British Isles. That's why we can't have a nuclear war."

After our chat I introduced Churchill to Joe and Frank, who waited in an anteroom. He was profuse in his congratulations on the Soviet interviews, saying, "It was not only a fine journalistic job but a diplomatic achievement. You greatly served the interests of the West."

Those were heady words because Churchill often professed disgust for and distrust of the press. He was fond of saying one couldn't believe anything he read in newspapers; nevertheless, he took them seriously. I was honored that he received us.

We arrived back in New York and were soon off on a speaking tour of our newspaper cities, with stops from Manhattan all the way to Los Angeles and San Francisco. I called for a cultural exchange program with the Soviets, from ballet to sports, but urged the continuation of our national defense build-up. Meantime, news clippings still poured in from around the world.

On a cold February night in 1956, Khrushchev stood before the Twentieth Congress of the Communist party in the Kremlin. He then delivered one of the most astonishing addresses of the twentieth century—a seven-hour, 30,000-word denunciation of Stalin as a tyrannical despot. It was all the more savage and unusual, because the late dictator had been Khrushchev's mentor and the party secretary one of Stalin's foremost hatchet men.

No anti-Communist writer in the West had ever matched the harsh language and horrendous charges that Khrushchev fired at Stalin that night. The party chief accused the dictator of having run a regime of unspeakable terror and persecution. Many Soviets had been unjustly shot and murdered while others had been unlawfully imprisoned. He summed it all up by decrying Stalin for introducing a false "cult of the personality" instead of exhibiting collective leadership.

The purpose of the speech was to reconcile differences at home and among the Soviet satellites. It also was another peaceful overture to the United States and the West. Khrushchev implied that by destroying the myth of Stalin's greatness, Moscow was abandoning its belligerent foreign policy. He subsequently crushed the Hungarian uprising and used threats to keep other nations of the Eastern bloc in line. As premier, he was as bellicose as ever.

In late November of 1957, we interviewed Khrushchev in Moscow again for more than three and a half hours. Bob Considine took Kingsbury-Smith's place because of Joe's INS duties. The party secretary sized up Considine and said, "He's bigger than Smith, but is he as good?" Everyone laughed.

It was a long, blunt exchange. Khrushchev said the Soviets had won the arms race, and the next war would be fought on American soil. He declared that the U.S. "monopolists" wanted war. He pounded his desk and said Moscow had made many concessions in disarmament talks, but the United States had not. The party chief boasted of the Soviet Sputnik, and claimed the Russians could launch twenty space satellites the following day. Finally, after more bluster and bombast, Khrushchev said we should stop discussing weapons and talk trade. He concluded on economics, "We'll outstrip the United States. We'll win."

Almost as an afterthought I got into a boisterous argument with him about God. He unleashed a long outburst, denouncing priests and proclaiming atheism. I responded that no great civilization existed without recognition of a Supreme Being. The party leader shrugged and said, "It doesn't prevent us from coexisting." Once again, the interview captured world attention.

We made our third trip to the Soviet Union in 1959 as members of the press corps covering the visit of Vice-President Richard Nixon. Before leaving, Nixon invited us to lunch in Washington. He wanted some reporters' views of Khrushchev. We suggested he bone up on American proverbs because Khrushchev would have a Soviet maxim for almost every subject. Also, to know his statistics—from the arms race to trade and agriculture. He would have plenty ready.

For unexplained reasons, the Soviets created a lot of problems for Nixon and the press before finally approving the trip. And in Moscow, Khrushchev and the Soviets did just about everything they could to show up Nixon.

It began by Khrushchev snubbing Nixon on arrival. He landed from Warsaw only minutes before the Vice-President's plane touched down, but didn't greet him. A local newspaper completely distorted Nixon's unscheduled but friendly visit to a Moscow open market. And the first thing Khrushchev did when Nixon entered his office was to hold up a sphere the size of a baseball. Nixon asked what it was and the party chief boasted: "Our Sputnik!"

It was bush, but pure Khrushchev.

As for what was then called the Kitchen Debate between the two men, it was actually a series of confrontations that lasted for most of the visit. Khrushchev simply wouldn't let up on Nixon in public. The party leader was rude, loud, and generally obnoxious. He wanted to show the world he was the better man.

The Vice-President finally had enough and poked Khrushchev in the chest with his finger. He told Khrushchev that the party chief was constantly filibustering, that he was tired of his ultimatums, and concluded, "You don't know everything!"

Khrushchev blustered, claiming he wasn't giving ultimatums, and Nixon shot back through his interpreter, "Tell him I've been insulted by experts."

Khrushchev wanted to know if the entire exchange would be on U.S. television. Nixon said it would. Khrushchev claimed it would be edited to his disadvantage. Nixon said it would play in full; he was certain the networks would carry all the fireworks. The Vice-President challenged Khrushchev about putting the entire discussion on Soviet TV. The party leader promised to show everything if all of it was televised in America, adding, "But you suppress!" Nixon nailed him good, saying: "Listen, for every word you print in your newspapers from a speech by our President, we print a hundred words of your speeches."

The climax of the Kitchen Debate took place later near the kitchen of a model American home on display at an exhibit. Khrushchev began filibustering again. Nixon said that no major power should try to "dictate" to any other nation believing it was speaking from a position of greater strength. Khrushchev became very angry because he thought Nixon had called him a dictator. He shouted, "We will answer your threats with threats. We have means at our disposal which can have very bad consequences for you." Nixon poked Khrushchev in the chest again, saying, "We have, too."

I was standing next to Considine, and we smiled as some of our fellow newsmen and several Americans applauded. (The Soviets clapped earlier when they thought Khrushchev had made a point.) The hot exchange continued for almost another hour. The day ended with Khrushchev shouting something in Russian as Nixon spoke in front of the U.S. exhibit. The Vice-President shot back, "I have the floor. You can speak when your time comes."

Looking back on the encounter more than thirty years later, it's obvious what Khrushchev had tried to do. This was the highest-ranking American official he had ever met. The party leader would test and push him to the wall right here in his own back yard, where he couldn't lose. Khrushchev was wrong. He had never before come up against a politician who was forced to debate the opposition almost every day. That was the test of a free society. It was Khrushchev who was at a disadvantage. He had never seen a democratic government or society in action.

The visit closed when Nixon addressed the Soviet people on TV. It was a warm, appealingly human address. And if Mr. K saw it, which I believe he did, he knew that he had met a politician.

Our Task Force flew to Czechoslovakia and Poland, where we tried to get a feel for what was happening by talking with ordinary people and a few diplomats. The Communists had the lid on. People became fearful when you said you were an American. They couldn't help but be somewhat friendly because they generally liked Americans; but most were guarded because Big Brother was watching and they could wind up in trouble.

Khrushchev later visited the United States—pounding his shoe on a desk to make a point at the United Nations, pinching open tomatoes at a supermarket, touring Iowa to say the Soviets grew taller corn, and visiting Hollywood, where he proved he was a consummate actor. Then he was to test President John F. Kennedy with tough talk in Vienna at their first meeting. But the Soviet leader was ultimately forced to back down in 1962, when the U.S. Navy confronted Soviet ships on their way to Cuba in the nuclear missile crisis. The Russians halted and returned home. It was a great international embarrassment for Khrushchev and Moscow.

That was the beginning of the end for the premier. There was another reason why his colleagues dumped Khrushchev. Though it was given much less attention, I believe it was highly significant. Khrushchev's comrades viewed the premier's outgoing personal style as his own cult: his waving to Soviets from his car and trains, cracking jokes and jesting in public, his public drinking, and numerous incidents like his pounding his shoe at the U.N. In my own case, I was startled when he put his arm around my shoulder. This was not collective leadership, as his comrades saw it; it was a popularity game, like that played by Western politicians. So they booted him out in 1964. Characteristically, they gave him the hook in secret.

Since Khrushchev's departure I've spoken with some Soviets about the shoe incident. They viewed Khrushchev's behavior as boorish. One explained that shoes in Russian culture are filthy because, in peasant society, they were always dirty. Dirt meant more than mere mud. It also indicated you walked in pig swill and everything else that stinks in farmyards. An educated Russian, for example, would never place a briefcase on the floor, because it's a culturally dirty action. He would never, like American youngsters often do, put his feet up on the seat of a bus or train. It's simply uncultured. Khrushchev might have thought he was playing to the U.N. gallery, but he looked like a yokel to the Russians. They were mightily embarrassed.

Fear of Khrushchev was another reason why he was ousted. A private source told me this startling story. Bits of it have leaked, but not the party chief's actual words and role. It occurred in 1953, shortly after Stalin's death, when Khrushchev was jockeying for leadership with Lavrenti Beria, chief of the secret police. Beria was making moves that indicated he might try to take over the government and oust Khrushchev from party leadership. The tough, rotund Ukrainian secretly sounded out his Politburo colleagues about what they thought of Beria. It became obvious that all were terrified of him.

Khrushchev asked Premier Malenkov to call a Kremlin meeting. Malenkov was fearful, but did so. Everyone but the secret police chief himself seems to have known that Khrushchev was going to make a move on Beria. Each of them, particularly Malenkov, was extremely apprehensive about what the party chief would say and how Beria would react. They believed that, if threatened and angered, Beria might have them all arrested and thrown out of office, if not worse.

When everyone was assembled, Malenkov introduced Khrushchev. The party chief rose, pointed to Beria, and roared: "You son of a bitch, you're under arrest!" With that, Soviet army troops entered the room and took Beria away to prison. He was later executed as "an enemy of the state." Zhukov obviously helped Khrushchev. The marshal was later ousted by Khrushchev. This was the Stalin legacy—little or no loyalty to one's comrades. Their paranoid machinations were to continue until the coming of Mikhail Gorbachev. And even today.

I believe that Khrushchev will go down in history as the Soviets' first reformer, the man who opened the door for Gorbachev. Khrushchev was very courageous to stand before party leaders and denounce Stalin. It was also remarkably brave of him to remove Stalin's body from its honored mausoleum in the Kremlin and bury him elsewhere. But I don't know of anyone who belived Khrushchev was a good manager. He kept changing the administrative structure of the Soviet economic apparatus. It was often said by Soviet administrators that he never left any change in place long enough to see if it would work. Also, he was inefficient.

Yet he had a spontaneity about him that was attractive. I remember a story some U.S. diplomats told me about Khrushchev meeting Gabriel Reiner of the long-established Cosmos Travel Agency. The two bumped into one another at a July Fourth party at the U.S. embassy in Moscow. Reiner said to the Soviet leader, "Why don't you open up your doors to tourists? You'll make a lot of money." Khrushchev decided then and there to do it. Intourist opened the country to tours, and the Soviets have been pulling in a lot of dough ever since.

In an odd way I liked Khrushchev. He was not only spontaneous and lively but he had a great sense of humor. Being a Ukrainian, there was a lot of the Russian people in him. And I liked the Russians—not as much as the Chinese, who smiled more and were much more outgoing—but the ordinary Soviet citizens were quite friendly. I found this remarkable in view of all the anti-American Communist propaganda in those days.

Kingsbury-Smith, Conniff, and I won the 1956 Pulitzer Prize in international reporting for our interviews with Soviet leaders the previous year in Moscow. The prize had a very special significance for me. I'm sure it did for my Pop and old Joe Pulitzer too. The Hearst-Pulitzer war was finally over.

Columbia University professor John Hohenberg, administrator of the prizes, related some background on the event. The panel of jurors, selected by Hohenberg for their expertise and impartiality, met in advance of the award—in mid-March of 1956. They spent three full days reading and judging about fifty entries. Our Moscow mission was their first recommendation. It met no challenges. As was customary, they listed second- and third-place choices.

The Pulitzer Board met at Columbia the following month under chairman Joseph Pulitzer, Jr., editor and publisher of the *St. Louis Post-Dispatch* and son of Pop's nemesis. There were fourteen board members, and all, except Columbia president Grayson Kirk, were associated with journalism. Pulitzer and the others didn't have anyone in their organizations contending for the prize.

Hohenberg recalled there was no discussion of entries at the meeting. On a single motion, the board unanimously accepted the recommendation of the jurors that we win the prize. Joe Pulitzer leaned back in his chair and smiled reflectively.

Hohenberg said that in his twenty-two years as administrator of the prizes and secretary of the Pulitzer board, there had been many stormy disagreements among jurors, board members, and trustees. Yet the trustees approved the board decision on us that May with no objections. We were awarded the prize in May after being unopposed by the selectees throughout the voting process.

Over the past several years, unbelievable changes have taken place in the Soviet Union and Eastern Europe. It is now abundantly clear that we reporters and diplomats missed most of the signs of these coming changes. Indeed, they burst across the world in a series of political, economic, and social shock waves. No one foresaw the swift fall of the Communist party and the rise of democracy in Poland, Hungary, Czechoslovakia, Romania, and Bulgaria. Nor did we reporters or diplomats offer any clear indications of the extraordinary developments that were to occur inside the Soviet Union—from the openness of glasnost to the restructuring of Soviet society through perestroika. Not only were the Communists to surrender some of their monopoly of power to other parties but the first signs of private property and a free market began to penetrate the Soviet system. Nor did we anticipate the Russian Reformation—a new dawn of religious liberty.

No one foresaw that Lithuania, Estonia, Latvia, and other Soviet republics would proclaim, in one measure or another, their independence from Moscow. Nor did we recognize the undercurrent of the nationality movements in the republics of Georgia, Russia, Armenia, Azerbaijan, and elsewhere.

We reporters and diplomats conveyed the impression that communism was monolithic and immutable. Others had described the same changelessness in more colorful terms. Churchill called the Soviet Union a "riddle wrapped in a mystery inside an enigma." Former U.S. ambassador George Kennan, one of America's foremost experts on the Soviet Union, assailed its constant "terrible, cynical, demeaning contempt for the truth."

For me, all of this came to a climax on February 11, 1990, when I wrote in my Sunday column that approval of a multiparty system by the Soviet Communist Party Central Committee was "one of the great reform victories in world history."

I've been surprised at the democracy movements from the Baltic to the China Sea, and from Berlin to Beijing. Even if some failed, they are still alive and will ultimately triumph.

The reason that I mention these changes is, of course, to recall that my father predicted them more than a half-century ago. My life has gone in a constant circle, always returning to the old man. Perhaps some people may consider that somewhat sentimental. Yet it is the truth. I like to think that he helped me light that single candle on the far side of the moon.

XI
THE LAUGHTER
AND THE TEARS

I lived and died the *New York Journal-American*. We were a family. Reporters, advertising salesmen, secretaries—we had worked there most of our lives. We cared for and helped one another. We cried when a pal was in trouble. No one had more fun covering the heartache and happy times of the city. That was because most of us were native New Yorkers. We were a wild and often sentimental bunch who loved New York because it was our town. We wrote about it with affection, anger, and despair—as one would chronicle the lives of fathers and mothers, brothers and sisters. There was perhaps never more camaraderie on any metropolitan newspaper in the United States.

No one covered New York as well as we did in the 1950s and first half of the 1960s—not the *Times*, not the *Herald-Tribune*, not the *World-Telegram & Sun, Daily Mirror, Daily News*, or the *Post*. In those days you competed hard for millions of subway riders. Counting the *Brooklyn Eagle* and Long Island papers in the early 1950s, we had ten papers scrapping with one another on the streets. (There are now only four: the *Times, News, Post* and *Newsday*. The *News* and *Post* are in trouble.) New York was then the most exciting city in the world.

If you don't believe we covered New York better than anyone else, just ask those who worked on the paper at the time. Ask our competition. Ask the man on the street. We were good. At times, magnificent. Many reporters were debonair dandies with Ivy League degrees; others were high-school dropouts with college degrees in street smarts. We had our share of flamboyant drunks, and a few normal souls who did not shout or swear.

The physical plant and offices were like a scene from an old-time movie. The yellowing sandstone, square-block building on South Street faced a long row of abandoned docks on the waterfront. American eagles were carved into the sandstone, but they had become grimy with soot. Smelly fish markets, notorious bars, and decaying tenements surrounded the place. This was the real Lower East Side.

The building, constructed in 1926-27, was originally one of Arthur Brisbane's real estate ventures. He sold it to my father on the theory that Pop could save a lot of money by towing newsprint down the East River on barges. The old man reportedly took one look at the building on an inspection tour and said, "Arthur, you've done it to me again!" He meant that Brisbane had dropped another lemon in his lap.

My father is said to have gotten in his car and never returned. The old man did, of course, move his news operation to San Simeon in 1925, but he retained an office at the paper. And, even though the place was a formidable hulk, the old man always flew an American flag above the central tower.

Dirty marble and semidarkness created a foreboding mood in our small, drab lobby. The elevators creaked on the way up and moaned on the way down. I used to joke that someday its rubber bands would break. When I first went to work there, the *American* was on the fifth floor and the *Journal* on the sixth. The operators used to stop at these floors with a jerk, which could somersault your stomach onto the roof. If one of those gentlemen had imbibed too much rye that day (one always carried a pint of Four Roses on his hip), you'd have to leap up or jump down to land on your floor.

The city room had a wooden floor. When women in high heels walked on it, the wood squished like the sound of wet galoshes on marble. All the wooden filing cabinets were chipped and burned by cigarette butts. Several of these looked more like orange crates. They rarely matched in height. The other furniture didn't match, either. The reporters and rewrite men used industrial-steel desks on a connecting rim. Other furniture was of solid oak, worth a lot of money today. The copy boys sat on three old desks pushed together and put their feet on the lower drawers. They would leap off when someone hollered for them.

The executive offices, along narrow corridors, were the only walled areas on the floor. The rest was one huge room, sectioned off into departments: sports, society, Sunday, and so forth. The photo department was located at the back of the building.

I often walked into the city room and shot the breeze with anyone available. None of us stood on ceremony or rank, and we could say almost anything to one another. Well, almost anything. It didn't make any difference if it was an executive, copy boy, or cleaning lady. We were each other's people—friends. One guy was the *Journal-American* as much as the next gal.

We weren't going to change the world. We were going to make New York laugh and cry—but most of all look at itself in the mirror every day. Perhaps even make it a little better.

Let me tell you about some of our people.

*

Florence "Flossie" Wessels had been a chorus girl. One look at her and you knew she was even more than that in her day. Flossie was what would now be called a media event. She was a long-stemmed, beautiful dyed-blonde with milk-white skin and a whiny voice, perfect for what she was: a reporter who wouldn't take no for an answer. When she came to us, Flossie had never taken a journalism class or covered a story in her life. But she wanted to be a reporter more than eat, and nothing would stop her. That's how she got the job—undeniable persistence.

Flossie once followed Edward R. Murrow into the men's room of the Waldorf-Astoria Hotel. Murrow was the god of television news in those days. He was anchoring "See It Now," a spectacular series of CBS TV news documentaries around the world. He was also doing interviews of famous people on "Person to Person." Both programs had a vast television audience.

Murrow was the epitome of the suave, sophisticated intellectual. He came across on TV not as a regular guy but as a scholar on Mount Olympus reading the world's great books. But Flossie was unimpressed.

She tailed Murrow right into the men's room and confronted him when he was in no position to escape: "Mr. Murrow, I think you're deliberately avoiding me. I'm a reporter with the *Journal-American,* and have been assigned to interview you. We've got to talk. Here and now or someplace in the next day or two." That was "Person to Person" as Murrow had never seen it. Flossie got the interview—later.

*

Samuel Crowther III was an erudite Harvard man from a distinguished family. He worked for years on rewrite for us and prided himself on his literary background and tastes. Sam was also well known for his taste for the sauce. He had a large, flaming-red, bulbous nose.

Late one morning Eddie Mahar, the gruff city editor, called across to Crowther on the rewrite rim. Mahar barked that a wire service just reported an escaped convict had taken an entire family hostage. The armed gunman threatened to kill the parents and their five children unless the police dispersed and allowed him to escape from the house. I can't recall the precise location, but believe it was somewhere in Rhode Island. Anyway, Mahar tossed the wire story to a copy boy, who handed it to Crowther. The city editor asked Sam to get a telephone interview with the convict. There were no if's or maybe's when Mahar talked.

Crowther obtained the family's name from the story, then got its phone number from a long-distance operator. About twenty minutes later, Sam rushed over to Mahar and said, "Eddie, would you believe it, the convict himself answered the phone and talked with me. He told me that if the police don't get out of there and give him a chance to escape, he's going to kill the family one by one."

Mahar was ecstatic. He shouted: "That's fantastic! Great work, Sam, terrific!"

The interview was splashed in headlines across the next edition. Everyone in the city room was excited because this was Old School journalism, five and six press runs of fierce rivalry. The adrenalin was always pumping. We had soundly trounced the other New York papers. This was what the news business was all about. We were champs for a day. Everybody offered to buy Sam a drink when he got off work. And Crowther was one drinker who measured up to all offers.

About an hour after our story hit the streets, bulletin bells sounded in the wire room. The police had closed in, crashed through the doors of the hostages' home, and shot the convict to death. He was identified as so-and-so—a deaf mute.

You could hear Mahar all the way to the Grand Canyon: "CROOOWWTHER! COOOOOMME HERE!"

Sam got up from rewrite. His face was flush red but that was normal. He walked straight and erect, as he always did to prove he was sober, to the city desk. Mahar handed him the latest wire story and said slowly, "Read that."

Crowther read the story, looked up, but didn't speak. Mahar stared at Sam, his eyes as cold as blue steel. Finally Crowther spoke, but his distinguished training completely failed him, "Gee, Eddie, the guy never told me that!"

Wherever *Journal-American* veterans gather today, twenty-five years after the paper died, they tell that crazy story.

*

Eddie Mahar was a story in himself. There are so many yarns about him it seems like Eddie must have been the city editor forever. Mahar was a tough-talking sweetheart who loved his reporters but liked a good story more. He was about six feet tall, some 200 pounds, with a shock of white hair and a big, white mustache. Eddie had a ruddy face and always seemed to have a cigarette dangling from his lips. The smoke and nicotine stained much of his mustache. He was a Queens Irishman who called for the help of the Blessed Virgin one moment and swore at reporters with a long stream of curses the next. That included women. But Margaret "Maggie" Farnsworth, a staff veteran, stood up and put him in his place many a time. He began treating her more like a nun.

Eddie was the last of a breed, a flamboyant figure who ran the city room like he was at war. The entire sixth-floor newsroom was one big screaming madhouse until the last edition was put to bed about four-thirty in the afternoon.

Mahar would arrive early every morning and immediately get a fistful of paper towels. He would water them down and wipe the top of his desk until it glistened. His desk, the nearby rewrite rim, and all the typewriters were covered with soot from the night before. The "black plague," as some called it, came from incinerators and other smokestacks on the East River. The opaque windows were always left open during the summer because we had no air conditioning. Some remained unclosed even in winter, to clear out the cigarette smoke and dank air from the musty offices. And we could always use more sunlight.

Paul Schoenstein, who succeeded Sam Day as managing editor, did the same thing—only he used a bright-blue glass cleaner. Schoenstein was a real cleanliness nut. He wiped his desk all day long.

Eddie may have had a clean desk top, but he used to spit on the floor. There were spittoons beneath the rewrite rim, but he never took one for himself. Mahar never quit spitting. The sweepers used to clean it up with sawdust.

Mahar sat in the middle of this bedlam. Being city editor was his life. Eddie had once been a hard drinker, but gave up the booze to move from deputy into the city editor's slot. Mahar really ran the paper from one edition to another. Schoenstein slipped into the background because his office was not in the city room. And he didn't know the city and its sources like Mahar. And Eddie made split-second decisions. Schoenstein could deliberate interminably while cleaning off his desk.

Schoenstein had won the Pulitzer Prize for distinguished reporting in 1943 by deploying seven reporters to go out and find some penicillin to save a two-year-old girl's life. The drug was rare then because it was difficult to manufacture and was being used to aid wounded U.S. troops. Some of our staff believed that the reporters who actually found the drug should have been awarded the prize but, unfortunately, that was not to be. I believe that if Mahar had won the Pulitzer, he would have insisted on sharing it with his reporters.

Some reporters said they hated Mahar, that he was a tyrant. But they were unanimous that he chased stories better than any newsman in New York. And Eddie was a superb teacher. Martin Steadman, a fine reporter, recalled recently:

> I made the mistake one time of letting my opinion slip into a story. He loudly called me over to his desk.
>
> "What is this?" He had put his finger on the questionable phrase.
>
> I knew immediately what the mistake was.
>
> "Mr. Hearst wouldn't like that," he said. "He doesn't want your opinion. I don't want your opinion. Nobody wants your opinion. This

is not my paper and not your paper. It's Mr. Hearst's paper. And he keeps his opinions on the editorial page. Don't forget that."

I was furious because he had embarrassed me before the staff. I went back to my desk, typed out my resignation, and handed it to Mahar. He tore it up in my face and told me to get back to work. I didn't know what the hell to do, so I went back to my desk and started making calls on another story.

Eddie Mahar was the greatest teacher I ever met. And there was something else about him. He was kind to the paper's drunks. He covered up for them and a lot of other people. To my knowledge, he never fired anyone. I think that, behind all the bluster, Eddie had a soft heart.

Nevertheless, Mahar didn't win all the souls he sought to save. One rewrite man was getting smashed every day. Eddie watched him closely but couldn't figure out where he was getting the booze. So he assigned a copy boy to watch the guy. "You're not to leave him for an instant. If he goes to the bathroom, you go with him. If he walks to a window for fresh air, you get fresh air. If he gets drunk, I'm going to kill you."

The copy boy arrived early the following day and stood by the rewrite man's side throughout the morning. He never took his eyes off the man— only the rewrite man was so blasted by noon that he could barely stand up.

"You went someplace," Mahar angrily accused the copy boy.

"No, I didn't," the young man insisted.

So the two went through the rewrite man's entire desk, his suit coat, and raincoat. Nothing was found until Eddie frisked him.

It turned out that, under his shirt, the man had taped a surgical bag to his chest. A tube ran down his arm and came up through the strap on his wrist watch. He would take a swallow of booze while pretending to look at the time. Mahar turned, looked at the copy boy, and said, "I'm asking for divine help on this one."

A few days later, Eddie was back at war and screaming at Morty Feldman. There was no arguing with Mahar. He would outshout anybody—and for longer. There had been a plane crash at Idlewild (now John F. Kennedy) International Airport. Feldman was our reporter on the scene. Morty was calling in his story from one of our new radiophone cars. Mahar was listening and he didn't like what Feldman was saying. The whole newsroom was watching and listening. Eddie stopped Feldman with a stream of swearing. Mahar wanted the reporter to return to the scene of the crash and get answers to a long list of questions. Feldman started to argue, but immediately knew he couldn't win. So he bluffed: "I'm sorry, Eddie, I can't hear you. Something happened to the radio. These damn new gadgets."

Mahar interrupted with more questions and commands. Feldman replied, "Would you please repeat that, Eddie? I'm not getting you completely."

Reporters in the city room recognized that Morty was pulling Mahar's chain and they started laughing. Eddie kept trying to reach Feldman, who, every twenty or thirty seconds, would say, "I'm sorry, Eddie, but . . ."

By this time the newsmen were splitting their sides laughing. In frustration and anger, Mahar finally slammed down the receiver.

One day dozens of people were killed in a plane crash at Idlewild. One of those who died turned out to have had a Park Avenue address. Eddie sent reporter Marvin Sleeper to the home, telling him the dead person was probably a wealthy big shot and to get his photo from the family.

Sleeper was uneasy about the assignment. He didn't know if the family had been notified of the death, and whether the fatality was a father or mother, son or daughter. It could be dreadful if he were the first person to tell a family about a death. Marvin was concerned about invading the family's privacy. But Mahar had spoken and he was not about to argue with Moses.

The father came to the door. Marvin told him of his city editor's assignment. The man shouted, "That sonofabitch. That vulture. I ought to punch the shit out of both of you. Get the hell out of here."

Marvin phoned Eddie and told him what the father said. Mahar replied, "Go back and tell him he can't talk that way to me."

The story became a Mahar classic.

Eddie did get the shit kicked out of him one day. As reporter Harry Manis put it:

Mahar was on my ass every day. He was always saying, "I can't do this for you. I can't do that for you. I can't do everything for you."

But I was working my ass off, and couldn't take it anymore. So I told Mahar, if he had the guts, to come up on the roof and we'd settle this thing once and for all. He did and I beat the crap out of him. I never told him that I'd been a college boxer at Syracuse.

But Eddie never fired me. He took it like a man. Eddie still hollered—though a little less.

*

Dorothy Kilgallen was no screamer although she could be quite temperamental. One day in 1962 she marched into the city room draped in a mink coat with singer Johnny Ray on her arm. She also was towing a couple of fancy dogs. Dorothy turned every head, including Mahar's. Which, of course, made Eddie think of a story for her to cover.

John Glenn had circled the earth in space, becoming the nation's first astronaut. New York would honor him with a hero's tickertape parade in a few days. Mahar told Kilgallen that she would cover Glenn's welcome and ride in a car in his caravan. Dorothy insisted that her car be a Rolls Royce. Mahar looked at her and thought better of what he was about to say. Of course it would be a Rolls Royce.

He yelled for somebody to get her a Rolls, and then bellowed for reporter Don Sheard. He told Sheard to arrange for Kilgallen's Rolls to enter the caravan as close to Glenn's car as he could. Don wasn't too happy about the assignment, but he took it with grace and went to see Johnny King. King was the assistant police chief in charge of traffic. King told Sheard, "Are you nuts? Forget about it. I'm telling you to forget about it, and I'm advising your boss to forget about it."

Sheard consulted Martin Steadman, who also was assigned to the Glenn coverage. Don told Marty that he didn't have the nerve to tell Mahar what happened. Steadman did. Mahar said in exasperation, "Look, the parade starts tomorrow morning in Battery Park. Go down there and do anything you can to help Kilgallen. Her story's leading the paper."

Steadman saw Sheard again. He told him to find some way with the cops to get Kilgallen's car into the official caravan. Sheard shook his head and walked off. Marty was worried. Sheard was an outstanding reporter, but when things went wrong he could disappear into a bottle of booze. He prayed that wouldn't happen the following morning.

When Steadman arrived in the Battery, Kilgallen was already standing there, impatiently tapping her toe, in high heels and a party dress. Kilgallen had no coat although it was a chill March morning. Marty had never met her. My God, he told himself, what am I going to say? There was no Sheard and no Rolls. She's going to freeze to death. Steadman introduced himself amid the bedlam. Dorothy said he was a nice man and all this was thrilling, but where was her Rolls? And whose car would it follow in the parade?

Steadman told Kilgallen he would phone the office for information. He called Mahar and said all the plans had blown away in the March winds. "Terrrrific!" Mahar said sarcastically. "Just go back and ask her to give you a few lines so we can combine everybody's story into one for the front page."

By this time the parade had started. Steadman relayed Mahar's question. Kilgallen said, "Just tell him I saw Annie Glenn. She's adorable in a pillbox hat."

Steadman decided he couldn't call that in to rewrite. They'd think he was nuts. Was Don drunk somewhere? But wait. There was the pool press car. And of all people, there was Sheard sitting on the righthand front seat like he was the mayor or police chief. Marty ran to the press car and yanked open the righthand door. He yelled at Sheard, "Get out, you SOB! That seat is for Kilgallen."

The press car stopped and Marty yanked Sheard from the seat. He pushed Kilgallen in and slammed the door shut. For the next two minutes Marty gave Sheard the Mahar treatment.

Steadman grabbed a cab for the Waldorf-Astoria, where there would be an official luncheon for the Glenns. Marty would try to get some color for the paper.

The *Journal-American* had one ticket for the lunch, and Dorothy had it. She showed up with the official party but didn't go to the luncheon. Instead, she went off to a bar where members of Glenn's Marine Corps Honor Guard were drinking. She regaled the Marines with stories about the celebrities she knew, and pretty soon they were all great pals.

This is a dumb dame, Steadman concluded. Very dumb. She's going to miss the speeches and other stuff at the luncheon. He rushed to cover that scene, standing in the back of the room.

When the first edition of the *Journal-American* hit the streets the following morning, Marty discovered that Dorothy was not so dumb. Kilgallen's story led the paper with an eight-column, front-page headline: WHAT MAKES JOHN GLENN TICK?

Dorothy had prevailed on the Marines to take her upstairs to the Glenn suite, where she interviewed not only the Marine Corps hero but his and his wife's parents. Steadman later said, "Dorothy Kilgallen was a shrewd piece of work."

*

The *Journal-American*'s finest hour came on January 21, 1957. After one of the longest and most desperate manhunts in New York history, police finally captured the "Mad Bomber" as a result of our enterprise. The unknown culprit had placed numerous bombs in New York movie theaters, train stations, and other public places, injuring about three dozen people, and had eluded capture for some sixteen years. But George Metesky was finally seized at his home in Waterbury, Connecticut.

Metesky had begun the bombings in the early 1940s, after being injured in an accident at a subsidiary of what was to become Con Edison. Metesky contracted tuberculosis as a result of the injury, but couldn't get compensation from the company. He moved to Arizona, halting the bombings for about a decade. Metesky had made a meager living in Arizona, but returned to the East in 1953. He was still determined to get even, because society had wronged him.

Metesky began by manufacturing pipe bombs in a garage at the back of his old home in Waterbury. He launched a four-year rampage of explosions, planting bombs in such crowded places as the New York Public Library on Forty-second Street, Radio City Music Hall in midtown, and the Paramount Theater on Broadway in Times Square. His biggest bomb blasted the Brooklyn Paramount, causing numerous injuries among moviegoers.

We covered these explosions but were frustrated at the lack of leads on the bomber. Finally, Seymour Berkson, then the *Journal-American* publisher, suggested we write an open letter to the bomber, asking him to surrender for the good of the community. It read in part: "The *New York Journal-American* guarantees that you will be protected from any illegal action, and you will get a fair trial. This newspaper is willing to help you in two other ways: It will publish all the essential parts of your story as you may choose to make public. It will give you full chance to air any grievances you may have as the motive for your acts. We urge you to accept this offer now not only for your own sake but that of the community."

The appeal listed the city editor's phone number. It was published on the front page of the *Journal-American* on December 26, 1956. An accompanying story reported that the bomber had set his thirty-second explosion at the Forty-second Street Public Library on Christmas Eve. It said the full force of New York's 20,000 policemen was now on the case. Shortly after the letter appeared, Metesky left another pipe bomb in Grand Central Station, but it didn't go off. Other bombs were planted. All of us involved with the paper were disappointed at the silence following our appeal.

Then, in mid-January, we and the police got our break. In a long anonymous letter to the *Journal-American,* the bomber explained his motivation—that he had been permanently disabled as a result of an accident at a Consolidated Edison electric plant. He mentioned receiving no company assistance and having to fight for his life. He offered one clue after another as to his identity: over the years, hearings on his case had been closed four times; he had written Governor Herbert Lehman for help several times; the assistant governor answered him; he was still waiting for help after twenty years.

The letter arrived about five o'clock one afternoon. The fellows on the city desk noticed the block lettering on the thick envelope and suspected it might be from the bomber. They opened it with tweezers so as not to destroy any fingerprints.

We notified police after photographing the contents. Police Commissioner Stephen Kennedy sent a team of detectives to pick up the letter and bring it to headquarters. By examining Con Ed records, officers quickly traced the writer. Detectives notified Waterbury police, and the two forces arrested Metesky at his home. They found pipe-bomb materials in his garage.

The *Journal-American* broke the story in banner headlines. All New York breathed a sigh of relief. It was among the finest community services that the Hearst newspapers ever performed. Pop would have danced a jig in the office if he'd been there.

Metesky was found unfit to stand trial. He was sentenced to Matawan, a state hospital for the criminally insane in Duchess County. Metesky served sixteen years before being released in 1973. George Carpozi, Jr., who had written many of our stories about the Mad Bomber, was present when Metesky was freed. He was working for another paper, since, by then, the *Journal-American* had passed into history. The bomber asked if any old-timers from the *Journal* were still around. Someone motioned to Carpozi. Metesky walked over to George and said, "I want to thank you fellows for what you did. You probably saved lives. I'm glad you did it."

Metesky returned to Waterbury and I never heard of him again.

*

We never won the Pulitzer for our work on that case, although many people thought we deserved it. Instead, the guys and gals went over to Moochie's saloon and got some pretty good loads on. This one-time longshoremens' dive was located on the docks across the street at Market Slip and South Street. It was a *Journal* hangout.

Moochie's was a bucket of blood straight out of Eugene O'Neill's or central casting's waterfront. Inside the seedy entrance, dirty sawdust covered the cracked tile floor, and the smell of stale beer mixed with that of musty walls, creating a sour odor.

The longshoremen had moved on after the piers had been abandoned, so our *Journal* staff staked out the bar every day. The place was divided mostly between pressmen, dirty with the grease and grime of newsprint and the pressroom, and reporters who were tired and sweaty. Secretaries, fashion columnists, and other women staffers at the paper rarely ventured into the place, even if someone offered to accompany them.

Customers walked up to the wooden bar to order. Initials and other knife-markings were carved across its face from one end to the other. Hard-boiled eggs were lumped in bowls before high wooden stools. The eggs, once a nickel, had risen to a dime each. Most guys ordered boilermakers—a glass of beer with a shot of booze on the side. Both were forty cents or so.

The menu was not from "21." Moochie had greasy hamburgers and ham-and-cheese, club, and meatball sandwiches. The hamburgers were almost inedible but the ham-and-cheese wasn't bad. I never had the nerve to try the meatballs. They looked like badly scuffed minibaseballs hit out of the park by Murderers Row.

Bent silverware accompanied the orders. As the utensils were placed on the soiled, greasy table tops, customers grabbed them fast. They wiped off the scarred knives, forks, and spoons with paper napkins, then put them carefully atop the same napkins. Most of the ashtrays overflowed onto the wooden tables and chairs. The chairs were rickety and regular customers always tested them before sitting down.

Sometimes, if one of the reporters or pressmen had had too much to drink, he would wander back to the paper and sleep on top of the giant rolls of newsprint. Some slumbered in the locker room on the third floor. They were sure of making it to work on time.

At night, when the bosses had gone home, the guys on rewrite would send a copy boy to Moochie's for a tall, white container of draft beer. These cost ninety cents each. Sometimes, when the humidity rose on hot summer nights, they would send out for a second container. There was no air conditioning, of course, and the cold beer was refreshing. Once in a while the evidence would be forgotten and left behind. Mahar or Schoenstein would see it and raise hell when he arrived for work. But these rewrite men were good—very good—and fast. No rewrite men in the city were better on a breaking story. We kicked hell out of every other paper on a regular basis.

I've thought a lot about those days and our people as well as those on other papers. If you worked for the *Times* or *Wall Street Journal* your colleagues inquired as to what university you had attended. If you worked for us your buddies asked whether you grew up in the Bronx, Brooklyn, or Queens. If you were a real New Yorker you read the *Journal-American*. If you commuted from the suburbs you read the *Times, Trib,* or *Wall Street Journal.*

Gus Engelman, who worked on the *Journal* for many years as a reporter, put it this way: "I used to feel sorry for the guys on the *Times.* Here we were, living in the most exciting city in the world, and they weren't really covering it. The *Times* guy wanted to be a dignified foreign correspondent covering the Court of St. James. We wanted to cover city hall, the police stations, the people on the streets. The *Times* buried good local stories and we put them on the front page. The *Times* had little, if any, local color; I never met a *Journal* reporter who wanted to work there. It was a stodgy newspaper with an antiseptic atmosphere. I loved the *Journal* because I loved New York."

Frank Conniff was one of us. He fell for the city after leaving his Connecticut birthplace. After his five kids were born, he moved from Manhattan to suburban Westchester County so they would go to better schools. Frank couldn't bring himself to buy a round-trip train ticket at his home station. He had a psychological hang-up about the city—that every time he came he was going to stay.

For some—bachelors, boozers, those from broken marriages—we were their only family. For others, those who came to the paper in their teens and remained until they were gray, the *Journal* was the only workplace they ever knew. It became a surrogate family. The paper was like a neighborhood club or town hall—down-to-earth, boisterous, feisty, sharing, caring—where people laughed, cried, lived, and died together.

*

Dick Berlin was the antithesis of the people at the *Journal-American*— and of my father and me. He cared little about the editorial content of the *Journal* or any of our papers. He knew no reporters, advertising people, or pressmen. Berlin liked to say, "I'm a magazine man."

Actually, he wasn't that. He had been an advertising salesman and, later, a business executive for the magazines, but he knew little about the guts of publishing them. Ultimately, for him as company president, each newspaper's monthly profit-and-loss statement was the whole story.

Eleanor Lambert, a fashion expert and the wife of Seymour Berkson, who had been publisher of the *Journal-American*, explained what happened to our papers under Berlin as well as anyone: "After Mr. Hearst died, the organization's colorful figures began disappearing—publishers, editors, reporters. No one looked for or had the talent to find the great ones anymore. The old man was a genius for spotting gifted people."

Eleanor recalled an evening at home with her husband a few months after my father passed away. Berkson had the blues and began musing aloud. He had been with the company since he was a young reporter. Berkson lamented to his wife that the old camaraderie was gone. Eleanor remembered that her husband said the company had become a corporation.

Berkson felt Berlin had assumed the role of my father without the old man's spirit, genius, or foresight. He added that I was too generous of spirit, too easy going. I would have to battle Berlin to keep INS and some of the papers alive. Dick would put nothing into them—not talent, not money, not direction. Berlin was going to dismantle much of what the old man had built.

No one in our company believed Berlin had the rounded leadership to take my father's place. I wanted our eighteen big-city newspapers to be highly competitive—only with less rigid control from the top. I aimed to work closely with our publishers and editors, but give them more local autonomy. Berlin kept remarking that I just wanted to be one of the boys, not the boss. He seemed to want me gone from the organization.

My brothers and I were told a hundred times by our colleagues in the company that Berlin's greatest disappointment was that he was not born a Hearst. After my father died, Berlin had the company issue a news release, which he had prepared, showing that by title and experience he was now the chief. Later, after Lyndon Johnson became president, Berlin met LBJ and spent the time impressing on him that he was the man who made all the decisions at the company. No one else counted. This was reported to me by some of our Washington newsmen.

In 1955, as Berlin and I jockeyed for position, the company's trustees voted me the newspapers' editor-in-chief. As the organization's owner and leader, my father had always held this post. The decision that I fill that role was made after Frank Conniff, Joseph Kingsbury-Smith, and I returned from our Moscow interviews with Khrushchev and other Soviet leaders. The decision apparently surprised and upset Berlin, because he thought he could always control executive choices through the trustees. It also indicated that he didn't completely control the company itself.

Friends warned me that Berlin was headed on a collision course with me. Berlin didn't want to share power with anyone. Feedback from other company executives told me that Berlin often knocked me. As yet, I had had no major quarrel with Berlin and felt we could get along together. I had never aspired to run the business side of the corporation. Not only did I lack the financial and other management background but I was happy on the news side.

I later learned that Berlin was also upset because I gave John Hancs, the Wall Street banker and former undersecretary of the treasury, much of the credit for saving the company. Hanes had been brought in by my father when the organization was in financial crisis. Hanes drew up virtually the entire financial plan that was instituted, but Berlin flew to the West Coast and presented the strategy to my father as his own. All of us knew that Dick wasn't the architect of the plan, and were taken aback when we learned what he had done. Hanes was a brilliant man with a much better educational and financial background than Berlin. Dick was a high-school graduate. Ultimately, Berlin forced John to leave the company. Other executives told me that Berlin feared Hanes might take his job.

This is not to suggest that Berlin didn't help the company during our crisis of the Depression years. He managed to secure for my father an $8 million loan from A. P. Giannini, president of the Bank of America, to help our magazines. Berlin also convinced Morris Wilson, president of the Royal Bank of Canada, to intercede on a nearly $10 million debt that we owed to Canadian paper manufacturers in 1940. That allowed the company a one-year moratorium on repaying the debt, on the condition that my father pay cash for all future newsprint purchases.

Berlin deserved considerable credit for that work, but he was careful never to invite another Hanes into the company. He was cautious about having any impressive men around him. Dick also suggested to various executives that they were his choice to succeed him. He wanted yes men. That helped him to influence the board of trustees in an attempt to overrule anything our family might request. This caused a rift, never to be bridged, between Berlin and our family. For years Dick talked vaguely of naming a successor, thereby hoping to control anyone on the board who might wish to take his place. In his own mind he never planned to retire and, eventually, had to be removed from office for health reasons.

Berlin and I disagreed strongly as he began to sell or merge our newspapers. I believed we should have made more of a fight to keep some of the papers. Yet, with the emergence of TV news and drive-time radio in the mid-1950s, newspaper advertising lineage began to fall. So did readership in many papers, especially afternooners. So we and other newspaper chains found ourselves in a financial bind. Berlin's answer was to sell or merge. I always felt that we could have saved some of those papers through better financial and editorial management. But Dick never understood how to strengthen a newspaper—nor, apparently, did he care to learn.

In 1959 Berlin combined our afternoon *San Francisco Call-Bulletin* with the Scripps-Howard *News*. In 1960 our *Pittsburgh Sun-Telegraph* was sold to the morning *Post-Gazette*. Several months later, Berlin sold our *Detroit Times* to the *News*. A year later he merged our *Boston Daily Record* with the *American*. Then he merged our two Los Angeles papers into the *Herald-Examiner*. The morning *Milwaukee Sentinel* was sold to the *Milwaukee Journal*. In 1963, after a 114-day New York newspaper strike, Berlin closed the *New York Mirror,* which had the second-highest circulation in the country. He axed, one way or another, eleven of our eighteen papers.

Berlin insisted it was necessary to slash our newspaper holdings. I was much less sure, especially when he used the money to invest in magazines, which also were suffering financially. He created the impression that the Hearst newspapers were in an uncontrollable nose dive but that the magazines could be saved.

By 1963 Berlin had been president for twenty years. Though he tolerated me and others, neither I nor any of my brothers knew much about office politics. Berlin seemed to be a past master at it. Many people maintained that he was a naturally competitive and combative go-getter. One thing was certain: Dick wasn't particularly sensitive to the feelings and aspirations of most people in the company—and that was certainly not following in the footsteps of my father. Paul McNamara, who had worked with Berlin for many years, had already warned me of this. Conniff and my wife reinforced McNamara's conviction. For many years Austine had said: "Berlin is a street fighter. In office parlance, he's a wheeler-dealer. Neither you nor your father ever became an office politician, stabbing people behind their backs. He's a bully with little culture. He tries to compensate for what he lacks in educational background with glib blather. But, basically, Berlin resents you and your brothers. He thinks he worked hard and the Hearst sons didn't. His idea of corporate management is back-room connivance and street smarts. He always looks at things as 'them against me.' Berlin's got about as much class as a sidewalk brawler. He's pushing only one product—Richard E. Berlin."

I used to relate some of Austine's impressions to McNamara in phone conversations. Paul and I remained close, despite the fact that he was working in Hollywood. He listened to me this particular day and finally said: "Bill, let me offer you one little glimpse of Dick Berlin as I worked with him. I would go in to see him to discuss our magazine promotions. He would pull out a brush from his top desk drawer and brush back his hair. It was thinning, so he did it slowly and carefully. Brush, brush, brush. Back, back, back. He drove me crazy because I was trying to make some very important points. I couldn't help but stop and stare at him. But he kept brushing, oblivious to what it looked like to me or anyone else. That was Berlin—virtually detached from a lot of important business. This guy was in love with himself. There was often nobody else, nothing else. Just him and his thoughts."

Conniff was as tough on Berlin as Austine and Paul—only Frank fought him. He'd have a drink with a pal on a magazine or some other publication and say things like, "Bill is really taking over the helm of the newspapers. . . . Bill has some good ideas to strengthen the papers. Bill wants us to get more eyewitness stories." Conniff played down Berlin's importance on the editorial side, and he apparently drove Dick nuts. I never suggested to Frank that he do this. Conniff knew, however, that I'd never meet Berlin on his back-room terms. So Frank took it upon himself to be the family's street fighter.

*   *

In 1958 Berlin merged our INS wire service with United Press. I reluctantly agreed, after prolonged discussion within the company. Since the old man started it in 1909, INS had been our window on the world. For nearly fifty years, we had sent men and women to the far corners of the globe to report back on wars, uprisings, government downfalls, coronations, earthquakes, plagues, heroes, international scoundrels, and medical miracles. We walked the Halls of Montezuma and the shores of Tripoli. I never wanted to go through the pain of an INS folding again. The reasons were as plain as the wonderful people who worked for us.

For fifteen years, the greatest wire-service man of all time—Bob Considine—wrote for INS. He was a matchless reporter-writer with priceless integrity. Our Washington bureau, run by bureau chief Bill Hutchinson and chief editor Art Herman, was superb. Bill Theis, Bill Umstead, Al Spivak, and others ranked among the finest reporters in the country. Hutchinson simply went home and died when the merger with UP was announced.

Our New York editor-in-chief, Barry Faris, was a news legend. Editors like Milt Kaplan, Phil Reed, Paul Allerup, Freeman Fulbright, and others took second place to no one in the business. Lawton Carver and Charley Einstein were brilliant sportswriters. Phyllis Battelle and Olga Curtis easily matched the top women reporters in the country. The best was probably our own Inez Robb. Louella Parsons not only scooped all of

Hollywood for years but was a major influence in shaping some growth in clean film entertainment.

Our undermanned staff kicked hell out of the other wire services covering the Korean War. And, in a final coup de grace, INS correspondent Jack Casserly broke the story on the agreement in principle of the United Nations and the Communists to end the three-year conflict. INS had won a clean, hours-long, world beat.

We had terrific people who covered for us at the front in both world wars and in Korea: Floyd Gibbons, Dick Tregaskis, Bob Brumby, Pat Robinson, Lee Van Atta, Pierre Huss, Mike Chinigo, Lee Ferrero, Howard Handleman, Marvin Stone, Cecil Brownlow, Don Schanche, Ray Steinberg, Bob Schakne, Irving R. Levine, John Rich, Bob Horiguchi, Don Dixon, Ed Hymoff, and so many others. All went on to much bigger jobs in newspapering, magazines, radio-TV reporting, and writing books.

It's hard to mention the fellows who were killed, because the pain is still there. Guys like John Cashman, who was blown away when the carrier *Wasp* was torpedoed, and Jack Singer, slain by the Japanese in World War II. Our Ray Richards was the first correspondent killed in the Korean War. Three of our men died in the same plane crash during that conflict: Frank Emery, Charley Rosecrans, and Ken Inouye.

Time magazine was merciless toward us when INS and UP merged on May 24, 1958. It described our reporting as "slap-and-dash" and said we interviewed "the barmaid across the way" from where the action was. It was a despicable slap in the face to good men and women. Considine answered *Time* and its poison pen for us in his column "On the Line": "The men and women who sat in our silenced newsrooms and read that farewell nose-thumbing felt more than anger. Many of them were seasoned at their trade when you, in all probability, were making your first little jabs at a typewriter. Their anger was tempered by a pity for you; a pity born of the sadness that one feels in the face of flippant ignorance."

Considine wrote of our men and women with the tenderness of a father over the grave of a son. He recalled our heroics on the battlefields of places like Sicily, Guadalcanal, and New Guinea. Of Jimmy Young, rotting in a Japanese prison. And Alfred Tyrnauer, dumped into one of Hitler's death cells in Vienna for writing the truth.

Considine concluded his eulogy: "Someday, son, venture out of doors and ask a couple of good men like Frank Bartholomew and Alan Gould [editors of AP and UP] what kind of a time they used to have when they had even an undermanned team of INS reporters competing against them on a big, fast-moving story. Someday, son, if you improve, you'll be good enough to change the ribbons on their beat-up mills."

Two footnotes, long after the passing of INS:

Phyllis Battelle, who wrote for both INS and our King Features Syndicate for about forty years, dropped us a note on February 14, 1989. She recalled how, long before other major news organizations, Hearst gave women a chance at top reporting jobs. I smiled when I read this line: "Hearst was chivalrous toward women."

Bob Schakne wrote us on December 21, 1988. After his INS stint in Korea and Tokyo, he had gone on to become a fine correspondent for CBS News for more than thirty years. Bob was dying of cancer as he wrote these words: "There is one other recollection of INS that may be worth mentioning. It was the only news agency at the time [early 1950s] that did not discriminate against Jews in its hiring policies. . . . We were there on our merits, whatever they were. That says something for Mr. Hearst [referring to both my father and me]." Bob passed away in 1989.

With the merger of INS, a good outfit had passed into the history of our organization and the news business. The hurt was not easy to swallow. And I have never forgotten it.

In 1964 the *Journal-American* began to leak red ink. Berlin started to hedge about the paper's future. Without my knowledge, he spoke with Walter Thayer, publisher of the *New York Herald-Tribune,* about a merger. Nothing materialized.

But I got wind of it of course, and was shocked. This was our flagship paper, our biggest voice in the country, the old man's triumph against impossible odds. The paper was more than that to me—it was my heart and soul.

I was determined not to have more anguish shoved down my throat at the *Journal-American.* I explained to Berlin that some of our newspaper mergers had not gone well, particularly the joint ownership of the *San Francisco News-Call Bulletin* with Scripps-Howard. Also, we would have nothing left of what my father had built if he kept dumping papers. Berlin continued to talk merger. He said half a paper was better than none.

Reluctantly, I talked with Jack Howard, publisher of the *New York World-Telegram & Sun.* He was ready to merge. Then, Walter Thayer, acting for John Hay "Jock" Whitney, owner of the *Herald-Tribune,* wanted to make it a three-way deal. Whitney had been attempting to rid himself gracefully of the failing *Trib* for more than two years. Our former ambassador to Britain had purchased the paper in 1958 as a favor to fellow Republicans who wanted a liberal GOP voice in New York. The paper was losing about $3 million a year when Thayer approached us in mid-1965. He had already failed to cut a deal with the *New York Times*.

The complex negotiations continued for months. Whitney kept insisting that the trio form a company whereby the *Trib* would continue as a morning paper, with the *Journal* and *Telly* merged into an afternooner. We wouldn't buy it. Finally, Whitney agreed to indemnify Scripps-Howard and us if the *Trib* caused the new company any financial losses over a two-year span. The World Journal Tribune, Inc., was formed.

Most people called the new company "Widget," because it sounded like the WJT letters of the coming enterprise. The new operation looked good on paper to our corporate board: circulation of more than 500,000 at the *Journal*, 400,000 at the *Telly*, and 300,000 at the *Trib*. And the new paper's staff would be much smaller than the three current operations.

I foresaw trouble and said so. The three papers combined had about 5,750 employees. The *Journal* alone had more than 2,300. More than a third would lose their jobs. This put not only us but the unions in a very tough position. The three companies and ten unions involved haggled for months over who and how many employees would be let go, the amount of severance, and other issues.

The *Journal-American*'s final edition was published on Sunday, April 24, 1966. Employees had been notified of the *Journal-Telly-Trib* merger a month earlier on March 21. But they weren't advised of the date of the *Journal*'s last edition until several days before our actual demise. Notices were posted in the newsroom and other departments. No one in management had the stomach to make a speech. The occasion was simply too tragic.

On the day the notices announced the last official edition, our distraught city-room staff resembled a grieving family. These heartsick men and women had struggled together for many, many years. No one was unprepared, but the end still seemed unreal. Up until these very last hours, hoping against hope, they had nourished a truth that just couldn't hold up: This is the Hearst flagship. It can't possibly sink.

Formal portrait of Austine Hearst, wearing a Charles James creation. She was famous for modelling his designs.

Bill and Austine's wedding photo on July 29, 1948, in Virginia.

Austine and William Randolph Hearst, III, get to know Austin.

Bill and Austine at the Taj Mahal in India.

Millicent Hearst continued her work with the Milk Fund for Babies well into the 1950s. Helping to promote the Fund in 1957 was actress Marilyn Monroe, shown here with Millicent before a benefit performance of the film *The Prince and the Showgirl*.

Austine and Bill at Southampton, Long Island with sons Austin and Will.

Above: Austine and Bill riding at San Simeon in the late 1950s. *Below:* The author's son, William Randolph Hearst, III, publisher of the *San Francisco Examiner* with his two children, Addie and William Randolph Hearst, IV. The setting is again San Simeon.

Bill at work at San Simeon.

The author on his favorite Arabian stallion, Zamal, near the family cottage at San Simeon. The saddle belonged to his father.

Patty Hearst poses beneath a portrait of great-grandmother Phoebe in this photo taken shortly before her kidnapping by the Symbionese Liberation Army.

Bill, Randy, and David (all seated, lower right) gather with their families for a group photo in 1984.

The author in 1984.

William Randolph Hearst, III.

Bill Hearst and his assistant, Jack Casserly, in a recent photograph.

Gus Engelman stood numb in the middle of the city room. The phones were ringing off their hooks with queries from other local newsmen. No one was picking them up. Gus recalled, "The elevator doors opened and there was Gabe Pressman of WNBC-TV News followed by a film crew. Gabe was known around town as a news undertaker, the Number One bearer of gloom. I took one look at Pressman's face, and that was the end." Gus began to weep.

Stan Bair, who worked on the Brooklyn section of the paper, walked over and put his arms on Engelman's shoulder. He too started to cry. Stan said, "Well, buddy, this is it!" With that, Bair broke down completely. He had come to the paper when he was seventeen years old and now, near forty, he would have to leave his familiar waterfront moorings and put out to sea.

Tears flowed through the city room. The hard-bitten edges of the reporters washed away as they embraced in sorrow. Marvin Sleeper said, "It's been my life and it's all gone."

Bottles suddenly appeared and booze began to flow among the desks like a river. Some reporters couldn't take looking at the dead city room and slipped out quietly to Moochie's. It was all like an Irish wake— sentimental talk and nostalgic jokes as the gang got drunk.

I caught a cab from our headquarters over to Toots Shor's. Considine was waiting for me. We had quite a few drinks to drown the sorrow, then lunch and more booze. I got loaded. I had never seen anyone cry at Toot's, but as the empty void of the *Journal*'s death overwhelmed every part of my body, I wept. I told Bob, "I failed the old man, Bob. I should have kept the paper alive. I failed."

Considine remonstrated with me. "I and a lot of other people don't see it that way, Bill. You did your best. You were just out-voted."

Toots came over, but I didn't have the heart to exchange a word. When it was time to go he walked us to the door and hailed a cab. Toots was silent. It was completely unlike him, but he knew I was dying inside. I appreciated his understanding.

We slumped into the taxi and Bob dropped me off at home. I went to bed, my face still wet with tears.

On the following day, the reporters at the *Journal* wore black arm bands.

The *World Journal Tribune* failed to begin publishing as scheduled on April 25, 1966. The publishers and unions were deadlocked over their differences. Picket lines formed around all three papers. Berlin and some of our other leaders believed Jock Whitney was deliberately dragging his feet in settling with the unions. They concluded that he hoped to dump the $5 million in *Trib* severance costs on the *Journal* and *Telly* by suspending his paper's publication. Ultimately, the *Trib* would drop out of the new enterprise. I was heartsick and never really accepted the merger. It was a dreadful compromise.

Hearst and Scripps-Howard raced to make a quick settlement with the unions. They had come to agreement with nine of the ten groups, when Whitney closed the *Trib,* blaming the decision on the unions. The *Trib* was dead, but Whitney was still contractually part of Widget. It was then decided that a single afternoon paper would be published. I went along with the deal on the basis of Conniff's becoming its editor. He was later named to the job.

Despite formidable obstacles, some 900,000 copies of the *World Journal Tribune* rolled off the presses in September of 1966. However, Widget had rough sailing early, including much less advertising than had been anticipated and endless production problems. Plus, the editorial staffs of the *Journal, Telly,* and *Trib* never even began to approach the family atmosphere that we had had at the *Journal.* They had fractured into office factions that would never come together. All would remain *Journal, Telly* or *Trib* people. Yet, from a reader's standpoint, it was the best buy in newspaper history. The paper combined the finest columnists, cartoonists, comics, and fashion, food, and sports writers from three highly featured newspapers. Some experts said its editorial mix would appeal to both the sober suburbanites and scampering subway riders.

Whitney and his advisors soon gave up on Widget. The paper was losing money, and Whitney refused to put up any more cash to keep it going. He gave up his stock in the company, opening the way for Hearst or Scripps-Howard to buy the other out and take complete control of the operation. In the meantime, new negotiations with the unions were starting.

The paper began to collapse. Berlin called a crisis meeting at his office on Sunday afternoon, April 30, 1967. The paper had been losing $700,000 a month. The unions had forced some 250 employees on Widget that the paper neither needed nor wanted. This cost us $2.5 million a year in added payroll, on top of $7 million in severance pay that the three papers had paid those employees for whom there were no jobs. At that point all the owners of Widget threw in the towel. The paper couldn't match the wage settlement and other details of the unions' new contract with the *Daily News*. To do so would have cost us $10.5 million over a three-year contract. Widget ceased publication on May 5, 1967. I was devastated.

The year after Widget folded was the most emotional of my life. Much had boiled over behind the scenes—my heightened differences with Berlin, the trials of closing the *Journal,* and Conniff's battle to save Widget.

Berlin had not kept our family adequately informed about what he had been doing. Yet we owned the company. It was very painful to be consulted only at moments of crisis. His attitude was that he understood the business practices of my father better than any or all of his five sons. He ridiculed us as inept.

Berlin was right in that my brothers should have worked harder and paid more attention to the business. However, I did work hard and did pay attention to these functions. So he had to contend with me. But Dick told me as little as possible about what was going on. Austine constantly referred to Berlin as "Machiavellian." I very much regretted that we didn't have a healthy working relationship. Berlin became one of the few individuals in my life for whom I had little respect.

The five-month strike that had delayed the birth of the *World Journal Tribune* until September 12, 1966, changed Frank Conniff's life. One of the greatest blows came when Dorothy Schiff, owner and publisher of the *Post,* broke her word to the other papers and began publishing. During those agonizing months, Frank worked about sixteen hours a day to see if he could somehow help win over the unions and repair factions among the reporters. Finally, and perhaps worst of all for an experienced newsman like Conniff, he never had the time in its brief eight months of life to give Widget its own editorial personality.

Conniff would often sleep at a hotel in town instead of going home, awaken in the middle of the night, and return to his office. If only they could solve the union's featherbedding, Frank told himself, everything else would fall into line. They would have to get into automated printing. And they would have to stipulate that printers couldn't be guaranteed lifetime jobs. There would be trade-offs on salaries and other issues. Ultimately, a strong paper would emerge.

Frank's wife, Liz, said that when he did go home, he sometimes wouldn't even speak. Her husband would collapse in bed with all his clothes on. Frank was obsessed with the problems at Widget and didn't seem to care about her, their five kids, or anything else.

Conniff was drinking heavily and was steadily losing weight. His wife noticed he held one of his hands in an odd, limp position. He began to drag one leg slightly. She warned Frank to slow down and suggested he see a physician. He did and the doctor told him to quit drinking. He found another doctor who said it was all right to drink a few martinis every night. In those days, Frank counted a few as a fistful.

Conniff hung on as long as he could. He explained everything to his wife in these words: "Being editor of this newspaper is the job I've dreamed of all my life."

When Widget collapsed Conniff quickly suffered a series of strokes. He was hospitalized and later bed-ridden at home. I visited him often. We talked and laughed about earlier days. Frank had called me, Considine, and himself the Three Musketeers. He thought that was very humorous.

For the next four and a half years, Frank's health grew progressively worse. Some days, when he felt strong, he would come to the office and see me. We had wonderful, warm chats. Then he would go home and I wouldn't hear from him. I would phone Liz and drive out to see him. He continued to lose weight and his spirit sagged. To lift his courage I teasingly suggested that he vote Republican. That always got Frank's Democratic dander up. He would challenge me with much of his old fire.

In the last stages of his life Conniff was paralyzed and could barely speak. He was in and out of the Rusk Institute, the Manhattan rehabilitation center. Mercifully, Frank finally died in May of 1971 at the age of fifty-seven. Just before he passed away, Frank and Liz tried to decide where to ship his thousands of books when the end came. They chose the Danbury State Prison. Frank believed they would offer some prisoners new hope.

I see Liz very rarely now. She's working and proud of her children, all successful. The last time we met I asked her how she was. Liz replied, "Bill, I miss the news business. Terribly."

"Yes," I told her, "and I have missed our having a Hearst paper in New York every day since Widget closed in 1967. Every single day. That's the truth. I have. For twenty-four years."

In February of 1973, at the age of seventy-nine, Berlin retired. He had been with the company for fifty-four years. Dick was succeeded by Frank Massi and later John R. Miller, both longtime Hearst executives. Actually, he was eased out of the corporation because he had been suffering from Alzheimer's disease for several years. Before leaving, Berlin summarized his attitude toward our newspapers, "I'd be willing to sell everything but the wife and kids if the price was right."

Berlin left our chain in poor shape. As he sold and merged, other news groups like Gannett, Knight-Ridder, and Newhouse were modernizing their plants as well as starting and buying new papers.

Berlin killed new magazine plans by the president of that division, Dick Deems. He also was ready to let eighty-year-old *Cosmopolitan* fold (it was then losing money), until Deems got author Helen Gurley Brown to take over the magazine. Helen made it one of the most successful publications in the country. She's still going strong after more than twenty-five years as editor.

Berlin's departure was deliberately low-key. The official word was that he would remain with the company as a consultant. He retained his executive office suite for several years, but as his Alzheimer's got worse he was moved to an out-of-the-way office. Berlin continued to issue memos and, at times, a flood of telephone commands. Our executives ignored them.

The action to break Berlin's strong influence on the board of trustees— eight of the thirteen were non-family members—didn't become known to our family for some time. Members acted secretly to assure better relations between company executives and our family. With Berlin gone, organizational matters began being discussed openly—with little or no behind-the-scenes maneuvering—and then being voted on. Eventually, our family had an effective voice on the trustees' governing board and the corporate boards of directors. With Berlin gone and new faces on the board, the company made decisions more objectively.

Berlin's health continued to decline. His wife and children were very concerned about him on several occasions. Once he slipped away from his male nurse and disappeared in Central Park with his dog. He was eventually found, but not the dog. Another time, he left the family dinner table and went to the office, believing it was the next morning and time to begin work.

I became even more concerned after an incident in my office. Berlin showed up and stood before Ralph Mahoney of our staff with a dozen or so of those yellow Post-it slips pasted to various parts of his suitcoat. They were reminders to do things and see various people. Mahoney said Dick looked like a yellow Christmas tree. Berlin introduced himself saying, "Hello, I'm Ralph Mahoney. We need to talk." Mahoney was completely taken aback, but recovered and said, "No, I'm Ralph Mahoney. You're Mr. Richard Berlin." Berlin said, "Oh," and wandered out the door.

We had had our differences in the past, but my heart went out to Dick and his family as he battled Alzheimer's. Eventually, Berlin stopped coming to the office. He died at the age of ninety-two at his home in Rye, New York.

In all these twenty-five years since the passing of the *Journal-American,* I have never understood why such a devoted family man as Berlin would scuttle a family operation. There were many financial reasons—and others too—why I've questioned that decision. We were the largest afternoon paper in the country, with a solid daily circulation of more than 500,000, and considerably higher on Sunday. Sure, we had been losing money for several years, but we had been hit by a strike and had plenty of other problems. But all were solvable. We needed some plant modernization, added investment, and guts. We could have made it. And the proof lies in the success of other large newspaper chains that moved ahead despite similar problems.

There was another fundamental reason why I was convinced we could have made it—a dramatic breakthrough in 1966 by Joseph Kingsbury-Smith, who had become publisher of the *Journal.* Kingsbury-Smith, who was a good friend of Arthur Ochs "Punch" Sulzberger, contacted the *New York Times* publisher. Joe thought it might be possible to have the *Times* print the *Journal-American.* That would have given the *Journal* the benefit of state-of-the-art production facilities. Most of the *Journal*'s composing room, printing plant, and other production facilities were obsolete. Some of the presses were forty years old. The idea was to pay the *Times* a reasonable price for the use of its facilities. It had spare presses that weren't needed every day of the week.

Joe and his executive staff did a study of what would be saved by getting the benefit of modern equipment. This would have enabled us to compete more effectively with the *World Telegram & Sun* and the *Post* in the evening field. We also would have the prestige of being associated with the *Times*.

Kingsbury-Smith and his staff had come up with a plan that showed the *Journal* could not only be pulled out of the red but operate at a moderate profit until we could build up our circulation and advertising. Joe submitted the plan to Berlin. He was skeptical. However, we and the *Times* agreed to have the respective experts on both papers study it. Because of the large Sunday circulations of both papers, the *Times* was unable to handle the Sunday *Journal-American*. We then sounded them out on the possibility of their printing the *Journal* on a five-day basis. The *Times* said it was prepared to consider that.

Joe rushed to Berlin with the good news. Dick's response was astonishing. He said that if we took such a route he would have nothing to sell if he wanted to get rid of the *Journal*. Our equipment was already outmoded, and much of our large plant on South Street would go unused and become almost useless. Other problems also would be created. Kingsbury-Smith pleaded with Berlin. Joe's repeated financial analysis showed that the *Journal* could not only survive but prosper as a five-day paper. He begged Berlin to give him and his staff a chance. Dick said no. He wanted a merger and that was it.

I, and just about all of us at the *Journal,* were convinced that we could have kept the paper alive because we did care about one another. We really were longtime brothers and sisters, and we had the will, especially under the pressure of survival, to save one another. I've learned one lesson above all others in my long life. All else is secondary to one's family, including the work of great individuals—even that of my father. Let it be said in the case of this Hearst that, at the end of all his ups and downs, he was a family man—at work and at home.

XII

THE GLOBAL VILLAGE

I 've been writing a Sunday editorial column called "Editor's Report" for nearly forty years. Frank Conniff originally assisted me in preparing the column, while Joseph Kingsbury-Smith has done so in later years. The datelines have ranged from New York to New Delhi, from Paris to Beijing, from the Middle East to Moscow. I've interviewed most of the world's leaders during that period—from Konrad Adenauer to Deng Xiaoping, from Gamal Abdel Nasser to David Ben-Gurion, and every U.S. president. The world has indeed become a global village in these years, with not only instantaneous television transmission but also supersonic commercial jet airliners that give you breakfast in Cairo, lunch in London, and dinner in New York.

In 1952 I began twice-a-year news trips to Europe and elsewhere, interviewing heads of state, important political figures, military leaders, U.S. ambassadors in various countries, and others from all walks of life. Three years later I formed the Hearst Task Force of Conniff, Kingsbury-Smith, and myself (Considine came on farther down the road), not only to interview international figures but to cover major stories like the explosive Middle East, the war in Vietnam, and the election of popes.

*

Churchill was the greatest international figure I ever met. He and my father had been lifelong friends, so he always welcomed me. Contrary to those who believe great leaders must be saints or sinners, Churchill was a man in the middle. Perhaps that is why he understood the world so well. The wartime prime minister was known as a man of extraordinary leadership and eloquence. But I believe he would not have attained this stature without his most basic quality: shrewdness. Churchill saw through to the core of issues and men. In my chats with him, he had an uncanny knack for getting quickly to the heart of a problem and into the minds of those involved. That's what made him great.

I'll never forget a 1961 lunch that I had with Churchill and his attractive eldest daughter, Diana, in the oval dining room of their penthouse suite at the famous Hôtel de Paris, overlooking the harbor at Monte Carlo. Churchill greeted me in his sitting room, nattily attired in a gray worsted suit and waistcoat. We chatted over an aperitif. He had read the morning newspapers over his café au lait, and just finished a prolonged argument with his valet over trimming his hair. So Sir Winston was well informed and feisty. We discussed his day. He planned to go for a long drive after lunch, then spend several hours on his voluminous mail, don his black tie and jacket for dinner, and play the roulette wheel in the nearby casino until God knows when. Churchill mentioned that he was still painting and writing—he recently had produced a short book that combined both, *Painting as a Pastime*. Sir Winston had just celebrated his eighty-seventh birthday and said he was now slowing down in his retirement. I burst out laughing. What slow down! What retirement!

The Churchills served filet mignon and a lovely French wine. Sir Winston then poured several shots of 100-year-old brandy. His hand was as steady as a surgeon's. I was about to collapse under the table from the effects of all his hospitality, when Churchill presented me with his *pièce de résistance*—a very expensive-looking cigar. I rarely smoke and didn't know what to say. "Go ahead," Sir Winston said, urging me into even more dangerous waters. "It's the perfect complement to a good lunch."

I took the cigar, lit up, and looked out on the beautiful harbor. Paradise itself seemed to be drifting before my eyes. The sun shone brightly in a clear, blue sky. Watching the pale smoke climb into the vast expanse, I instinctively knew that I'd remember the moment for years. I would be able to tell my grandchildren that I had smoked one of the famous Churchillian stogies in the company of the great man himself.

In the chill January of 1965 I flew over to attend Churchill's funeral in London. I simply had to say farewell.

Along with thousands of his countrymen, I walked past his coffin, set high and precisely in the center of 900-year-old Westminster Hall. Some 90 feet above us, the lacy Gothic arches made of oak gave an impression of warmth to the 250-foot-long stone-walled and stone-floored hall.

Four bemedaled naval officers, their heads bowed, stood at the corners of the lighted catafalque. I noted that not a single man or woman ahead of me in the long line was dry-eyed as they looked for the last time on their wartime leader. They knew that the man receiving the honors reserved only for kings and queens was really one of the common folk.

*

Some international leaders so totally repelled me that I never cared to meet or interview them. The Ayatollah Khomeini was one. The Iranian leader was a madman who cloaked his fanaticism in the robes of religion.

Charles de Gaulle was another. Although I met the French leader casually on a couple of occasions, he projected such arrogance that I found it impossible to suffer through his pomposity. De Gaulle cut an aristocratic and impressive figure nevertheless, and he rated very high with me as a genuine French patriot. However, without U.S., British, and other Allied troops, de Gaulle would never have returned to France. I was, therefore, deeply dismayed by his petulant withdrawal from NATO, and his simultaneous ousting of American troops and Allied headquarters from his country. The decision was an inexcusable insult to the thousands who gave their lives and limbs in two world wars so that France might be free.

The haughty Frenchman, despite his limited military and political leadership during World War II, had never forgiven the English-speaking Allies for not making him equal to the U.S. and British officers who fought the war. But this was inappropriate on his part because French forces had been of minor importance to the outcome. Since Allied commanders were wary of de Gaulle's playing the grand figure, especially in making announcements, they never disclosed their invasion plans to him. De Gaulle later envied and resented the vast power of the United States. He was a man whose personal arrogance compromised his destiny.

Jawaharlal Nehru also deeply disappointed me. I interviewed the Indian prime minister once and was completely turned off by his racist tenor. It was our first and last meeting. Nehru seemed obsessed with race. He camouflaged it in the term "Western imperialism," and it took me some time in our interview before I understood his real meaning. I was trying to get precise answers as to why he objected to so many U.S. policies. But Nehru kept telling me that the Americans and British thought they knew it all, yet they understood little and had even less in common with most people around the globe. His anger boiled over on how he and other Indian intellectuals had been treated socially by the British. Nehru was imperious, arrogant, and perhaps even more conceited than de Gaulle. He came across as a pompous, petulant little boy.

*

After Churchill, the three most memorable leaders I met were West German chancellor Konrad Adenauer, Israeli prime minister David Ben-Gurion, and Irish prime minister and, later, president Eamon de Valera. All played the same role as George Washington—fathers of their countries.

Adenauer was elected chancellor in the first Democratic elections in Germany after World War II. He led West Germany for fourteen years—from 1949 to 1963. Adenauer gave the appearance of being a simple man, a familiar old shoe. It was said he deliberately limited his vocabulary to about 800 words, so every German would have no doubt what he said and meant. Adenauer had an extraordinary human touch and reached the common man better than any German leader except, unfortunately, Hitler. As a member of the German resistance, he had fought the Nazi leader.

I shall never forget an interview that Joseph Kingsbury-Smith and I had with him in 1955. For one solid hour he looked us directly in the eyes—never deviating—while saying over and over to us: The Soviets hoped to wean West Germany out of the North Atlantic Treaty Organization and away from the West. He said Moscow was then engaged in a phony relaxation of tension, and was trying to lead the West into a false sense of security. He knew what Moscow was up to and said that as long as he was chancellor, West Germany would never cut a deal with the Communists and compromise the Western alliance. Adenauer spoke with simple clarity and emphasis.

Adenauer was a Catholic from the Rhineland who projected a saintliness that one usually associates with a prayerful monk, not a politician. Based on various interviews with him over the years, I think he was perhaps the most truthful foreign leader that I ever met. (Ireland's de Valera was on a par. I never doubted a single word either ever said.) More than any other leader in Western Europe, Adenauer was responsible for the strength and unity of NATO. The German chancellor was totally committed to NATO and carried the West German people with him in that bond.

Adenauer was a superb gardener who raised splendid roses. He would light up like a child when anyone recognized their beauty. He lived across the Rhine from Bonn in the wooded mountains, and commuted daily by ferry like any ordinary German workman. Yet the greatest beauty in Adenauer's life was not his roses but his own plain-spoken truthfulness. That is the way I remember him so well: direct, simple, precise, and unwavering.

*

I first interviewed Israeli premier David Ben-Gurion in 1955. It was obvious, merely looking at and listening to Israel's legendary first leader, that he was a man of exceptionally strong will. As he spoke from behind his desk in Tel Aviv, Israeli and Egyptian troops clashed in periodic firefights along the Gaza Strip. Ben-Gurion had one message: If war was to be avoided in the Middle East, the United States must match the arms shipments that the Soviet bloc was sending Egypt.

Ben-Gurion taught me a lesson: No man can truly be a leader without total commitment. That seems like an easy cliché in the abstract, but it becomes charged dynamism when carried out in human character. Ben-Gurion was neither a large nor physically impressive man like de Gaulle. But he had an inner strength and dedication that flowed from his mind and body to all those with whom he came in contact. That dynamism is often unexplainable until one feels it in a simple setting. That was what made Ben-Gurion a leader. He communicated greatness and strength of will in ordinary human contact. His personality transformed a simple moment into an unforgettable experience.

*

I interviewed Eamon de Valera on numerous occasions. De Valera had been born in Brooklyn of an Irish mother and a Spanish father. After his father died, de Valera's mother sent her child back to Ireland, where he was raised by a grandmother and then an uncle. Mrs. de Valera married again, but Eamon remained in Ireland.

De Valera took part in the 1916 Easter Monday Rebellion against England. The Proclamation of the Republic on that day is one of the most stirring declarations in Irish history: "Irish men and Irish women! In the name of God and of the dead generations from which she receives her old tradition of nationhood, Ireland through us summons her children to her flag and fights for freedom! And we pledge our lives and the lives of our comrades in arms to the cause of its freedom, of its welfare and of its exaltation among the nations."

English troops quickly put down the bid for freedom. De Valera was sentenced to life in prison, but was pardoned after an international uproar and the discovery that he was an American as well as an Irish citizen. The tall, thin ascetic became a rural elementary-school teacher. De Valera later became a professor of mathematics and the Gaelic language. He fought all his life to keep the Irish language alive. It still thrives today as the spoken tongue in Dingle, County Kerry, and other parts of Ireland.

I visited de Valera as much to know the man himself as to discuss Irish issues. He was a studious, old-world gentleman who was prime minister three times, for a total of twenty-one years, and president for another fourteen years. He thus led Ireland for thirty-five years, and would have continued longer if he had not gone virtually blind. Ireland became a Republic in 1949, with six northern counties still tied to Britain. We discussed mostly the troubles between Catholics and Protestants in northern Ireland, the European Common Market, Irish economic problems, and emigration to the United States and other countries.

De Valera was a deeply religious man, charitable and very forgiving. The Irish leader spoke softly, with great personal charm and not a little subtlety. He was proud of being an Irishman, but he greatly admired the

United States. I must say he loved everyone. I never heard him voice a single criticism of anyone. Not even the English! De Valera had a secret source of personal magnetism and power. It was an exceptional sense of loyalty—to his wife and seven children, his church, and his country.

De Valera repeated his respect for Pop each time we met. He said, "Your father helped us to be a nation." (Israel's David Ben-Gurion had said the same thing to me.) Speaking with him often, I came to learn that he never deviated in the slightest from his basic loyalties, no matter what new events or political developments might tempt him. He used to quote the Irish patriot Daniel O'Connell: "I take my religion from Rome, but my politics from Ireland."

He always distinguished sharply between Church and State. De Valera never forgot that during the 1922–23 civil war he and other Republicans were denied the sacraments by the Catholic Church because they were judged "not worthy to receive them." He found many priests who defied the ban, but the hierarchy was not yet ready to let political figures rise to their social level.

It mattered little to de Valera what I might say or write of him, but he cared greatly about what was said of Ireland in the context of church and family. To him, the Emerald Isle was the United States, Europe, Asia, Africa, and the Middle East rolled up into one. It was not that he ignored or played down the importance of the others; rather, he considered Ireland a sacred land and his a priestly calling.

De Valera addressed the U.S. Congress in 1964, the greatest international triumph of his life. He died in 1975, in his nineties. De Valera was buried in the shadow of Daniel O'Connell's towering tombstone in Dublin, amid the gray granite graves of ordinary folk—except for where, a few tombstones away, Charles Stewart Parnell, Michael Collins, Arthur Griffith, and other Irish heroes lay waiting to receive him.

*

I met many other world leaders—Israel's strong-willed Golda Meir, Egypt's ambitious Gamal Abdel Nasser, and a farsighted Anwar Sadat. Saintly popes like John XXIII and Paul VI. And such widely different individuals as Indonesia's Sukarno (a perennial playboy) and Kenya's stable Jomo Kenyatta; Italy's studious prime minister Amintore Fanfani,

France's Georges Pompidou, thoughtful François Mitterand, and Britain's "Iron Lady," Margaret Thatcher; South Vietnam's dedicated Ngo Din Diem, Taiwan's ill-served Chiang Kai-shek, and China's ill-advised Deng Xiaoping.

I still try to keep up with Mitterand and Mrs. Thatcher (even though she has resigned), because their grasp of world events, particularly in Europe, is first-rate. Mitterand has steered French socialism to the free-market economy, a very significant feat, and has proven to be an excellent intermediary between Washington and Moscow on certain issues.

I have had the good fortune of knowing Mrs. Thatcher since she became Conservative opposition leader in the House of Commons in 1975. A dozen years ago, when she became prime minister, I began meeting with her in her cozy study on the second floor at Number Ten Downing Street. I found her quite different in the prime minister's residence than when she had led the Tories in the House of Commons. There, she sometimes seemed brisk and perhaps aggressive. In parliamentary debate she could be strident, with an acid wit. At Downing Street, during my last interview with her in 1990, she was relaxed, soft-voiced, feminine, and charming, despite her long, tiring agenda.

I shall never forget Mrs. Thatcher taking time out of a hectic schedule on a cold, rainswept day in London, in May of 1986. The prime minister unveiled in Grosvenor Square, across from the U.S. embassy, a monument to the legendary American Eagle squadrons. These were American volunteers who fought with the Royal Air Force in the Battle of Britain before we entered World War II. It poured rain as Mrs. Thatcher spoke beneath the simple, graceful statue of an American eagle in flight, with uplifted wings pointing to the sky. Our company was proud to donate the memorial. Charles Sweeny, an American living in London and a good friend of mine since childhood, helped create the Eagle squadrons. I still see Sweeny every time we visit London. On the other side of Grosvenor Park there is another statue—that of FDR. I always visit the park when we stay in London.

After the ceremony all of us hurried out of the rain to nearby Claridge's for a reception. When Mrs. Thatcher came in a waiter offered her a cup of tea. She replied, "Hell, no, I'm chilled. Give me a strong whiskey!"

During my 1990 interview with Thatcher in London, she said that Iraq's Saddam Hussein must be forced to withdraw completely from Kuwait. She added that, if necessary, she would join Britain's military forces with those of the United States to drive Hussein from Kuwait. She, and her successor, John Major, kept her word and the U.S. and British forces performed magnificently.

As I was standing to leave, Thatcher put out her cheek for a kiss. I froze. My mind darted back to the ceremony in Grosvenor Square four years earlier, honoring the American Eagle squadrons. After Thatcher had unveiled the statue, I tried to give her a peck on the cheek, but she instinctively pulled away. Now she offered it. I gave her a good buss and we smiled. Perhaps she remembered my futile attempt that rainy day, perhaps not. But I was very moved. It's not often that an American gets to kiss a British prime minister!

*

All these leaders were, in one manner or another, formidable personalities. After some reflection, I have to say I concur with the obvious—individuals may not always demonstrate particularly distinguished qualities on the road to national and international leadership, but once they assume such a role, the full strengths of their personalities become clear. The demands of leadership serve like adrenaline once power is assumed. The good journalist studies not only policies but evaluates the personalities driving them.

Of all the world leaders I have met, I wish I had studied Deng Xiaoping longer and better. I recall visiting him with my wife and family and Joseph Kingsbury-Smith, in 1980, during a five-week trip of interviewing Asian leaders. Deng couldn't have been more gracious or more forthright about the liberalized direction of his policies. Quick-witted and good-humored, Deng said that China's feet had been unbound, and he was going to modernize his country with Western technology, investment, and internal free-market changes. I was captivated. Here was a soft-spoken, charming individual who would right the wrongs that had left China behind in the twentieth century.

I left Beijing convinced that the brutal rule of terror, instituted by Mao Tse-tung more than three decades earlier, had been buried with the late dictator. History shows how wrong I was. Deng—no different from Mao—ordered young protestors calling for limited freedoms, some of which already had been promised, shot down in cold blood in Tiananmen Square on June 3–4, 1989. I grieved for them.

Today the diplomatic word coming out of China is that Deng privately admits his assault was a mistake, and that it set back China's economic plans and future for years. I would like to hear that from his own lips. Perhaps it would ease some of the pain I have felt from being so completely taken in by Deng's statements about freedom. I'm not sure that I'd believe him, but at least I would like to see his face when he admits his tragic mistake.

*   *

During nearly a half-century of world travel on news assignments, I've visited about eighty different countries and wound up with enough diarrhea and other travel ailments to bed down a company of U.S. Marines.

The most traumatizing times of those years were my trips to Vietnam. I was recently looking back through my old columns and found the most prophetic one I ever wrote. It appeared in our papers on April 11, 1954, many years before the United States made any significant troop commitments in Vietnam. President Eisenhower had sent a small cadre of military advisers there after the Communist victory over the French at Dienbienphu. The column said:

> It is about time that President Eisenhower and Secretary [of State John Foster] Dulles tell the people of the United States more of what is on their minds and what they see in store for this country in relation to the war in Indochina.
>
> The American people will run any risk and make any sacrifice if they are convinced it is vital to their own or their children's preservation as a free people.
>
> But they will grow resentful and even balk if they are handed any "Papa knows best" treatment and kept in the dark as to the direction in which national policy is leading them. The time has come to put the cards on the table.

President Kennedy later sent several thousand advisers to Vietnam, and of course our troop level there soared to a massive 500,000 men under President Johnson. Not one of these presidents ever sufficiently explained or convinced Americans of the need for U.S. involvement in Vietnam. Millions of Americans ultimately rebelled at the conduct of the war.

Nevertheless, Vietnam provided one of the most heartwarming—and humorous—sidelights among our trips abroad. In 1970 my son Will, Joseph Kingsbury-Smith, and Bob Considine spent two weeks in Vietnam and Cambodia. Will, Kingsbury-Smith, and I were headed for Israel. Considine was going home to New York via Hong Kong, Tokyo, and San Francisco.

U.S. Air Force Captain Robert Peck had adopted an eighteen-month-old Vietnamese orphan and planned to bring her home to his wife in Austin, Texas. When it was time for Peck to rotate home, the U.S. military and Vietnamese government documents necessary to take the child out of the country were hung up in both bureaucracies. So he talked Considine into following through for him.

Considine ran into a stone wall with both the American military and Vietnamese, so he passed the buck to me. I called U.S. ambassador Ellsworth Bunker and Vietnamese vice-president Nguyen Cao Ky. Bunker had someone work the military side and Ky, a flamboyant fellow, told me not to worry. He had enough official government stamps in his desk to approve almost anything. I gave him the child's name, Ngo Tai Lam (we called her "Buttons"), and we hustled over to Ky's office to pick up her stamped passport. Bunker came through with the military papers, so Considine marched through Vietnamese customs and up the ramp to our Pan American plane, carrying his typewriter, newspapers, and the baby in his arms. It was quite a sight.

Bob had a problem and it was to last all the way to New York. Buttons was wetting her pants and his. And he didn't know how to change diapers. As a matter of fact, he had no diapers. So he ordered a double Scotch from the stewardess to mull it all over. Meantime, the waterworks had dripped down both his pants legs. The stewardesses were giving him the glass eye. The rest of us were laughing our heads off, while Considine stewed and gave us a few sharp looks.

Finally, he sheepishly asked the stewardesses if they had any diapers. They didn't. That called for another double. But word was getting around. The stewardesses asked three U.S. Army nurses seated in the rear of the plane if they could help. Of course. So Bob got up and carried Buttons back to the nurses, to the amusement of observant passengers. The giggling nurses used Pan Am napkins and handed the kid back to Bob.

Considine said he was jumping out an exit without a parachute unless Joe, Will, and I shared Buttons. We agreed, and carried her back to the nurses for a quick change each time she leaked badly. At Tokyo, however, we and the nurses deplaned.

Poor Bob! He was on his own again, flying in his wet pants all the way to San Francisco and New York. He never mentioned the flight again. The parents-to-be, I was told, were overjoyed. So much for the glamour of being a foreign correspondent.

*   *

Here at home, for more than seventy years, I've been a president watcher. There is not a more fascinating study in the United States. And no news assignment is more interesting than a private interview with the president.

The watching began in 1916 when I saw President and Mrs. Woodrow Wilson riding in a Pierce Arrow with the top down during a parade in New York City. I was only a boy but I remember that both wore black— he in a high, silk stovepipe hat and black overcoat with velvet collar, and she with a broad-brimmed black hat and black fur. If that's what a president wore, I told myself, the job wasn't for me.

I attended my first convention—without knowing what it was all about—in San Francisco during the summer of 1920. I was twelve years old, and all I can remember was that Warren G. Harding was president. My grandmother was able to get me into the convention hall, since she had entertained some of the dignitaries.

When President Harding died, his unprepossessing vice-president, Calvin Coolidge, inherited the White House. I later met President Coolidge at the ranch in San Simeon, when he stopped by to see my father. He was a very taciturn, slight gentleman who spoke sparingly in a sort of nasal voice with a funny twang. Somebody subsequently told me that was New England talk. Pop invited Coolidge to lunch. The president didn't indulge in alcohol. My father drank very sparingly. However, he did serve a Moselle wine and recommended that the president taste it. The repartee went something like this:

Coolidge: "Alcoholic?"

My father: "Oh, no."

Reassured, Coolidge tasted it, smacked his lips, and commented: "Tastes fine."

During the course of the meal, the president blithely enjoyed several more glasses, still smacking his lips and repeating: "Fine. Very good."

I leave it to the reader to decide who was kidding whom.

I remember the 1924 convention because it was the first time that radio played a role in the presidential process. Foghorn voices blared the names of the states, and the announcing of their votes for candidates seemed very dramatic.

The only thing I recall about the 1928 campaign was that I was upset because some voters held Al Smith's Catholicism against him. The campaign left a bad taste in my mouth.

I remember 1932 very well because my father played a prominent if not dominant role in the nomination of FDR. The anti-Roosevelt coalition held firm for the first three ballots and it looked like FDR was a dead duck if he didn't win on the fourth go-around. The wise money was betting that the Democrats would then nominate a compromise choice, who would lose to President Herbert Hoover.

Joseph P. Kennedy, later to become FDR's ambassador to England, phoned my father, who was a major influence in the Texas and California delegations. Pop had gotten involved with both groups. Roosevelt needed two-thirds of the votes to capture the nomination. Kennedy asked what Pop wanted to help move these two state delegations to Roosevelt on the next vote. Pop shot back, "He has to promise House speaker Jack [John Nance] Garner [of Texas] the vice-presidency."

Kennedy then got FDR on another phone and said, "Hearst says he'll release the Texas and California delegations to you if you'll promise Garner the vice-presidency."

Roosevelt fired back, "Promise him anything, including the White House."

The switch assured FDR's nomination and he went over the top on the next ballot. FDR then named Garner as his running mate. Pop later split with Roosevelt because he ran for a third term and attempted to pack the U.S. Supreme Court. The old man told me that FDR seemed to feel he owned the White House and the presidency.

One bright memory of the GOP convention in 1932 was a story written by Damon Runyon after Herbert Hoover was nominated. Hoover's victory was about as much of a surprise as the sun coming up in the morning.

Damon wrote the kind of delightful but surprising baseball ending that made his style so distinctive:

> You know the old story.
>
> Man with a cold in his neck. Can't lift his chin off the first button of his vest.
>
> Goes to a balloon ascension with a friend. Waits around for hours, able to see only the ground in front of him.
>
> He keeps asking, "Has she gone up yet?"
>
> Says the friend, "No, not yet."
>
> Finally: "Has she gone up yet?"
>
> "Yes."
>
> Says the man with the crooked neck, "Let's go home."
>
> The balloon went up here in the Republican convention at three-fifty-five this afternoon.
>
> "Let's go home."
>
> "It's Hoover and Curtis."
>
> "Herb and Charley."
>
> "Same old battery."

In 1936, for the first time in his life, Pop strongly supported a Republican, Alf Landon, for president. His campaign was a huge flop, and our friends—and enemies—had a big laugh on the Hearsts.

I remember the packed galleries in 1940 supporting Wendell Willkie for the GOP presidential nomination at the Philadelphia convention. When the 1944 conventions came, I was away covering the war. In 1948 I thought I was demonstrating sage analysis in writing that Harry Truman couldn't beat Tom Dewey, because FDR hadn't allowed any Democrat to develop and shine during his autocratic reign. Boy, did I eat those words!

*

My close analysis of each president didn't begin until Dwight Eisenhower's era. But I've been an even more ardent president watcher ever since.

Instead of supporting the New Deal, our newspapers called for a new deck. We backed the Eisenhower-Nixon ticket because we felt the Democrats had been in power too long and that power had bred a lot of reckless spending, corruption, and cynicism. Ike was a man's man. If he got mad, he could cuss. And if he felt like a drink, he'd pour one for everyone around without hesitation. He walked straight, talked straight, and tried mightily to hit a golf ball straight.

Eisenhower defeated Adlai Stevenson handily, twice. One reason was that the Illinois governor often projected a superior, aloof personality that didn't wash well with many Americans. Of course, that wasn't the only reason. Ike's war record and down-home touch accentuated the differences between him and Stevenson. And it cut sharply into the strength of Adlai's quick wit.

I've heard the stories about Eisenhower's being a Democrat at heart, that he wasn't too bright, and that his responses to the press at White House news conferences often rambled. But it was, as they say in Ike's hometown of Abilene, Kansas, a lot of hogwash. If Ike was really a Democrat, he sure fooled a lot of Republicans—and Democrats too. His fiscal policies were highly favorable to the business community, and his strong defense position sounded like it was written by the joint chiefs at the Pentagon. Before he left office Ike did warn the country of the dangers of the nation's military-industrial complex; however, he was talking about procurement and other abuses, not the intrinsic value of the military and industry to the nation's defense system. The nation is still fighting the close financial and job links between the two, but we've begun to make progress in curtailing abuses.

Suggestions by some newsmen (I'm sorry to say) and others that Eisenhower wasn't too smart were laughable. I talked with Ike numerous times and found him not only intelligent but extremely well informed on government and most other topics. As for Eisenhower's rambling at White House news conferences—he simply needed time to think in the clamor and frenzy of questions being fired at him. The prima donna antics of reporters to capture personal attention began under Ike and then became a disgusting mania under Kennedy and later presidents.

To his credit, Ike lived up to his promise to end the Korean War, and he kept the U.S. economy humming during his eight years in office. He wasn't the global theorist that so many liberal eggheads of those days felt was necessary if we were to win the Cold War, but he managed to strengthen our military and keep the peace. I believe that Eisenhower was underrated by his critics and that history will vindicate him as one of this century's finest chief executives.

*

Our family had known the Kennedys for more than twenty-five years before Jack became president. My father and Joe, the patriarch of the clan, had been close friends until Joe tried to scoop up all of our magazines for little more than a dime on the dollar during the Depression. Kennedy had been asked, as a friend, to give my father advice when the old man was in financial trouble. Kennedy's counsel was to sell the magazines; he planned to pick them up for little more than nothing. When Pop was informed about what Joe tried to pull, he was shocked. I don't think I ever saw him so taken aback. He had looked on Joe not only as a trusted friend but as a gentleman. Kennedy's attempted manipulation so dismayed the old man that the two were never close again.

I liked Jack Kennedy. He was a very personable, intelligent, and often humorous (in a charming, self-deprecating way) individual. There was much to admire in him because he brought a youthful spirit to the White House and the nation.

Today, as I reflect on Kennedy and the many columns that I wrote about him, one aspect of his presidency takes on a crystal clarity: Jack Kennedy was very much a political president. He based much of what he said and did on whether or not it was good politics. Compared to presidents Truman or Eisenhower, Kennedy easily won the questionable distinction of putting what was good politics over other considerations. Truman was, of course, an astute, lifelong politician, but Ike often acted in an apolitical manner.

Many may argue that this is a short-sighted view of Kennedy, since he projected so much idealism in the Peace Corps and in getting more young people involved in politics and government. However, the observation is not meant as a total appraisal of Kennedy's tenure. It is an attempt to focus on one critical aspect of his term. Most Kennedy decisions centered on the overriding factor of what would be the political fallout. From his cynical choice of Lyndon Johnson as a running mate to his self-righteous spin on his failure at the Bay of Pigs, Kennedy was the consummate politician. The president was a split personality—a pragmatist who cloaked his politics in idealism. I believe that will be the ultimate conclusion of historians a century from now.

Yet, as I look back, there was no president in whose company I would rather have been. Kennedy exuded so much charm and wit that one couldn't help but like him. Like Ronald Reagan, he projected the personality of a "nice guy" with whom you'd like to have a beer or cup of coffee. But that is not the stuff of achievement or history.

I believe that FDR, Truman, Eisenhower, and Ronald Reagan were better presidents than Kennedy. But, to be fair to Kennedy, he didn't have enough time to prove himself. Richard Nixon, Lyndon Johnson, and Jimmy Carter wounded their own presidencies.

*

LBJ was probably the most complex man to become president in this century. He was an outgoing leader who loved to press the flesh, but inwardly Johnson was one of the loneliest men I ever met. He was one of the most down-to-earth realists ever to grace the Washington political scene, yet also a frustrated showman. Johnson disliked being labeled, but he put a label on almost everyone else. He was cussedly hard-headed, and sometimes brutal to others, but he had a tremendous hankering to be loved. He was a superb local politician, though he never seemed to get a grip on foreign affairs. But when all was said and done, I liked him.

If Vietnam was LBJ's Waterloo, civil rights was his greatest triumph. The fact that a southerner was instrumental in passing the 1964 Civil Rights Act will always remain a monument in U.S. history. His big-spending Great Society created false expectations and was a socioeconomic failure, but several excellent programs, like Head Start, endure today.

I visited LBJ in the White House and at his Texas ranch. He and his wife, Lady Bird, were very gracious hosts. And I got a feel for the man who loved that hardscrabble land. Johnson may have been viewed as a Washington powerbroker—and he was—but to me he was more of a stereotype of the hard-working farmers on the rugged, rolling land along the muddy Pedernales River. Those people had to be tough and perhaps even mean to survive, but they never let go of their hopes. That was LBJ: tough, sometimes mean, but seeking better times for ordinary folks.

I never believed Johnson was happy as president. Contrary to those who say his monumental ego demanded the pinnacle of power, I am convinced that LBJ's happiest days were when he was the Senate majority leader. He loved wheeling and dealing with other political pros in their specialized fields, especially outfoxing "those Ivy League Harvard and Yale boys." Like fellow Texan Sam Rayburn, the longtime House speaker, Johnson was totally at home on Capitol Hill. But he was a fish out of water in the White House. Many people with whom he had to deal there didn't speak his language. LBJ was vulgar and common. They didn't understand how you counted noses to assess political power, and didn't appreciate his down-home ways. He didn't understand foreigners, and they couldn't fathom him.

I believe Johnson was often maligned unfairly and maliciously. Sure, he could be devious and play his cards close to his vest. And he certainly had a Texas-sized ego. But many eastern intellectuals were very demeaning toward him. This included many of the Kennedy crowd, who looked on Johnson as a big hick. But LBJ was not impressed with eggheads, since he had regularly spanked them in his Senate school of politics.

Johnson was the quintessential American. He came from ordinary folk, raised himself by his own bootstraps, had no guilt about American economic or military power, and was a patriot, totally committed to the United States and its people. Some of the more cynical Washington crowd joked that LBJ always believed God was an American. I found no fault in Johnson's Americanism. If LBJ is to be faulted, it is because he never leveled with the American people about the cost and escalation of the war in Vietnam. That was a disastrous course, and he paid for it in bitter personal agony during the last years of his life.

Let it be said of Johnson that no one ever took his place in the Senate. The country could use his leadership there today.

*

In 1948 Richard Nixon, a young congressman from California, and his pretty blond wife, Pat, walked into the small garden of our home in Washington on a summer evening. They were neighbors. I hadn't met the Nixons before, but had heard about him. He was heavily involved in the battle against Communist subversion in the United States. I believed that

America's fight against communism—at home and abroad—was a valuable public service.

My impression of the young congressman, after the evening of cocktails and an informal dinner, was that he was very intelligent but also overeager; that he lacked self-confidence and a sense of humor, and was somewhat impetuous and very ambitious. Nevertheless, Nixon was alert and serious. I concluded that he was a real political comer.

Because of my interest in California, I followed Nixon's career closely. During his years in Congress and as vice-president under Eisenhower, we became warm friends. I watched his growth, especially his travels around the world, including his famous Kitchen Debate with Soviet Premier Khrushchev. By then he was still ambitious but had become much more mature with the years.

Dick moved to New York after losing his presidential bid and then being handily defeated by Democratic incumbent Pat Brown in the 1962 California governor's race. The Nixons bought the apartment two floors above us on Fifth Avenue. He practiced law with a prestigious New York firm. Another neighbor in the same building was Governor Nelson Rockefeller, who later became vice-president. It was all very cozy—parties, dinners, and all that sort of stuff. While working for the law firm, Nixon traveled a great deal, read considerably, and spent a lot of time campaigning for Republican candidates. It was clear to me that Nixon planned to make a political comeback. He may have lost to Kennedy and Brown, but he was never defeated. Nixon had incredible resilience.

I saw Nixon off and on after he won the 1968 presidential campaign against Vice-President Hubert Humphrey and his 1972 race with Senator George McGovern. Others offer complex reasons about Nixon as a political survivor, but I believe he rose from the political dead because he knew what he wanted. He never deviated in his drive for political power.

Nixon was superb in foreign affairs. It took him time to end the war in Vietnam, but there was never a doubt in my mind that he would do so. His peace efforts in the Middle East could not have been more diligent. And his opening to China was brilliant.

I applauded his attempts to cut the cost of government and the power of Washington. Unlike the young congressman I had met more than two decades earlier, President Nixon was now a man of solid experience and self-confidence. He took on the boys in the ivory towers like LBJ had never done, and this drove them crazy. He contested not only their ideas but their longstanding luxury of going unchallenged. No wonder so many of the Democratic intelligentsia despised Nixon.

On May 6, 1973, about fifteen months before Nixon resigned in disgrace over the Watergate scandal, I began to waver on his innocence. It was very painful because a twenty-five-year friendship started to wash out to sea. I was deeply disturbed after Nixon went on television. He had just fired John Dean, the White House counsel, and accepted the resignations of Attorney General Richard Kleindienst and two of his chief assistants, H. R. Haldeman and John Ehrlichman.

Nixon sounded as if he were reading a road map, clipped and methodical. My God, the government and its moral integrity were collapsing before our eyes, and the president was treating it like so many miles to the next town. Instead of appointing an unimpeachable investigator from outside the government to explore and explain the ramifications of Watergate, he appointed Elliott Richardson, an able man but a presidentially appointed government official. On hearing that, I was amazed. I believed that Nixon owed the American people a much clearer and deeper explanation of what had really transpired.

I tried to be fair to Nixon by suspending final judgment on his guilt or innocence. But the charges of his lying about certain events and the condemning evidence on the tapes mounted. So did accusations of a deliberate presidential cover-up.

Nixon continued to slide downhill. Finally, because I no longer believed the president, I publicly broke with him in my column of May 5, 1974. That column was the most reluctant that I had written since beginning the "Editor's Report" twenty-two years earlier. I had read with genuine shock the latest transcripts of the White House tapes. I then wrote: "I have never heard anything as ruthless, deplorable and ethically indefensible as the talk on those White House tapes. Like a gang of racketeers talking over strategy as they realize that the cops are closing in on them. Scene after scene sounds like a corny old movie. How can we cover up this and that? How much dough do we need to pay off so and so? Who's going to take the rap for this and that?"

Nixon had taken advantage of the American people's faith in government and the presidency. I concluded my column: "Today, sitting here in stunned sorrow, it is hard for me to imagine why any informed person would not see the inevitability of impeachment."

Nixon's resignation and leaving the White House in disgrace was a traumatic experience for me. I was angry because he had been such a close and trusted friend and I had backed him editorially in our newspapers. I felt bitter betrayal.

A bigger man would have left office with an apology for lying to the American people. Not Nixon. He had the consummate gall to announce he was quitting merely because he had lost the political support in the Congress needed to conduct the affairs of government. He showed none of the humility that accompanies true greatness. There was little that was really human in Richard Nixon at that moment. It was as if a clockwork robot had read some wooden words of farewell and then walked out on the American people.

Nixon has since made another comeback, writing excellent books on national and international policy and being a good-will ambassador to China and other foreign governments. He is to be applauded for this. However, he still suffers from a fatal moral weakness: He has never had the magnanimity to apologize for his lying to the American people. Unless and until he does that, Nixon will remain a sad, lonely exile who can never return among equals in the history of presidential politics.

*

I supported President Gerald Ford's pardon of Nixon. I simply believed the hatred and distrust that the former president had brought to the White House and national scene had to be swept away if we were to concentrate on so many neglected problems before the country.

Ford was a good interim president. He restored a sense of decency and dignity to the office.

*

Jimmy Carter was a well-meaning man who understood little about how Washington worked when he arrived and little more when he left. He was a mystery man when he entered the White House and a Lone Ranger when he departed.

Carter was honest, God-fearing, hard-working, and sincere. That clearly came across when I interviewed him. However, although Carter knew just about every detail of an issue, he frequently failed to understand the problem itself, much less the Washington avenues to a solution. It has been said by some that bad luck—the U.S. hostage crisis with Iran—was the major cause of his loss to Ronald Reagan in 1980. That's nonsense. Carter lost because, despite his intelligence, Americans believed that he was generally inept.

Much can be said in Carter's behalf once he left the White House. He has undertaken many foreign missions, including overseeing free elections in Nicaragua, and has displayed courage and an extraordinary ability to mediate between enemies. He had already exhibited that by getting Israel's Menachem Begin and Egypt's Anwar Sadat to sign the Camp David peace accord. He has never sought to enrich himself from his presidency. Carter still radiates an inner peace and joy that make him a very attractive human being.

*

Ronald Reagan was an easy man to like. He was an up-front, easy-going, humorous person, and a first-class storyteller. He had the same Irish wit as Frank Conniff, with perhaps a bit better timing. I remembered him from the days when he was president of the Screen Actors Guild, which was then loaded with Communist sympathizers. He did a lot to make the guild more objective.

It may take a century to evaluate Reagan's presidency fully. However, it now seems safe to say he changed the American political landscape by sufficiently explaining the conservative philosophy to millions of voters so that they revolted against the Democrats.

Despite eight years of solid economic growth under Reagan, there is still sharp criticism of his economic programs, especially the deficits run up during his administration. However, Congress is to blame for the big spending—not Reagan. Now, with Washington hovering around a $2 trillion debt, everyone seems to have gotten the message that the days of federal wine and roses are over.

I also believe that Reagan's strong defense politics helped convince Soviet leaders that the Cold War with the West had to end. Obviously, there were other factors—a devastated Soviet economy falling farther behind the West technologically, and the growing restlessness in Eastern Europe. But Reagan played a significant role in forcing the Soviets to make the hard choices.

I think Reagan taught us two lessons, apart from the day-to-day politics of the office: One doesn't have to be obsessed with the job, as Carter and LBJ were, to be a good president; and all presidents should strive to get their message across by effective personal delivery on television. It took Reagan to demonstrate how to develop massive presidential power via the tube.

*

I believe President George Bush does well on TV because he's so relaxed. Bush doesn't strive for dramatic effects, as Reagan did, but he is direct, simple, and very clear. That is a big plus, giving him immense power among the American people.

It would be imprudent to draw any major conclusions about the Bush presidency at this stage, except to point out three obvious factors that seem sure to influence the outcome: the vast federal deficit, combined with the savings and loan scandal; winning the peace after winning the Persian Gulf War; and the President's ability to assist the emergence of genuine democracy in the Soviet Union, Eastern Europe, and China. The challenges facing Bush are as great as those confronting any president in the post-World War II era.

*

It would be a breach of faith for me not to mention some of the outstanding Democratic nominees I knew who never made it to the White House, particularly Adlai Stevenson and Senator Hubert Humphrey. I respected both of them and believe that each would have made a good president. The Illinois governor was a first-rate intellect and gentleman. Perhaps more than any candidate of this century, Stevenson lifted the tenor of presidential debate and campaigning. His grandfather, Adlai Stevenson, vice-president in the second Cleveland administration, was a good friend of my grandfather's while George Hearst was a senator in Washington.

Humphrey loved politics perhaps more than any man I ever met. The Minnesotan seemed born to it. Hubert was a liberal who fought hard for everything in which he believed. He was an eminently fair person with a quick sense of humor and much good will. It's a pity the two men aren't with us on the political scene today.

*   *

In the 2,000 or so Sunday columns that I've written these many years, four public issues consistently flow through the decades: the construction and safety of a modern U.S. transcontinental highway system, American military defense, New York as the cutting edge of big-city problems, and freedom of the press. Now, in the twilight of my life, I often look back nostalgically on these four issues as milestones in my career and in the history of twentieth-century journalism.

*

In 1952 our newspapers began a national drive called "The Hearst Better Roads Campaign." Our thesis was simple: With more than 50 million motor vehicles on our roads, the nation needed a more adequate interstate system. Our newspapers were the only large chain in the nation to undertake a prolonged editorial campaign to construct such a system. Our rationale could not have been more succinct: If we were to expand and prosper as a nation, we must have adequate roads. The sooner the better. Of course our national security also was involved. So was over-crowding on our highways as the use of cars and trucks soared.

It was generally conceded that the National Highway Act of 1956, which bolstered construction and safety, was due in large part to our campaign. In 1958 the Congress approved spending $1.5 billion in federal and other highway funds for apportionment among the states.

President Eisenhower had appointed me chairman of the President's Committee for Traffic Safety in 1959. Presidents Kennedy, Johnson, and Nixon followed suit. I went around the country off and on for about fifteen years giving all kinds of speeches—though I never particularly cared for public speaking—and making a nuisance of myself over highway safety. In many ways, this was the most important work of my life, because our safety efforts may have helped save countless lives.

In 1902 the United States had no national highway system. We had 23,000 motor vehicles and 17 million horses on our dusty roads. Today the United States has a 43,000-mile transcontinental highway system that handles 21 percent of all vehicle miles traveled in the nation. Some 176 million vehicles motor across those highways from coast to coast. It has cost federal taxpayers more than $100 billion to build the system. Billions more are still being spent. And the system is worth every dime.

*

Alexander P. de Seversky made a lifetime impression on me. Born in the Soviet city of Tiflis in 1894, de Seversky became a Soviet military pilot who fought in World War I and became a flying ace, shooting down thirteen German planes. He lost a leg in action. Five months after the Communists seized power, he fled to the United States.

De Seversky soon became a U.S. citizen and a major in the air corps. He flew as a military test pilot and set many aviation records. De Seversky later became a scientist, engineer, and inventor of aeronautical devices. He designed and built some of the world's finest planes. He was also an authority on the strategy and tactics of air and space warfare. Major de Seversky became famous largely because of his book *Victory Through Air Power,* published in 1942. He predicted that air power would be of paramount importance in future warfare.

I met de Seversky at a flying club on Long Island shortly after the end of World War II. We became friends because of a mutual interest in planes and air power. He came under fire for some of his predictions, including warnings about the menace of the Soviet military build-up.

I listened closely when, in 1947, de Seversky warned of the Soviet Union's increasing air power, and urged our political and military leaders to maintain this country's invincibility in the air. His concerns were largely ignored, but I was impressed when he analyzed the U.S. and Soviet military budgets and said that Moscow was spending as much if not more than we were in building up its military machine. De Seversky stressed that the United States had to change its entire military philosophy. We must place greater emphasis on the use of intercontinental ballistic missiles and man-made earth satellites. In 1957 the Soviets became the first to put such a satellite in orbit. Sputnik put our entire nation in a state of shock.

De Seversky changed my priorities in the complex mix of critical issues facing the nation. He convinced me that America's military defense of freedom was the most crucial subject that I would ever cover and write about. Through the years, I've learned as much as I could about U.S. defense, and have strongly supported its funding. I've backed a strong U.S. military for some forty-five years, and done as much as I could to enlighten our readers about it. Writing about communism and the Soviet military threat occupied a significant part of this commitment. That interest was deepened when Khrushchev said communism would bury us.

Times have, of course, changed. The Soviets are still a formidable military power, but they no longer pose such a direct and immediate threat to the free world. I believe our military strength helped bring that about.

I feel strongly that Soviet leaders have changed. They do desire a better life for their people, rather than continuing the nuclear arms race with the world living in a twilight of terror. Nevertheless, mankind has seen too much betrayal and too many unexpected developments in the past 2,000 years not to be prudent about the future. We must proceed to better our relations with Moscow—but with caution.

*

I cannot conclude these thoughts without referring to my love of New York.

Heaven knows, the city has gone far downhill in the past two or three decades. Violence, drugs, and crime have skyrocketed, setting new records almost every year. Yet there is still a good side to New York—the financial, communications, theatrical, cultural, fashion, and restaurant capital of the nation. Wall Street, the major radio and television networks, magazines, book publishers, wire services, advertising, theater, music and dance, the world-class museums, auction houses, and the best American fashion designers, and shops for collectors of all types still make New

York unique—and attractive to ambitious young people from across the country. And they still hold millions of New Yorkers of all ages enthralled.

My mind still beats to the rhythm of the city—its noise, earthy talk, international bill of top entertainment, and sweeping array of other attractions. I sometimes dislike what New York is becoming, but I can't leave it. That's the test of friendship—not to walk away even though you're hurt. At night, when I look at New York's unforgettable skyline, I still get goose bumps. And, like actor Telly Savalas, I ask, "Who loves ya, baby?" I always reply: "I do."

XIII
THE NEW GENERATION

On March 4, 1887, my father set his name on the masthead of the *San Francisco Examiner.* Today, more than a century later, his little four-page daily has grown into one of the largest communications companies in the world.

Every day millions of Americans read one of our many newspapers, magazines, other periodicals, or books. They watch our TV stations and cable programming and listen to our radio stations. Millions of others around the world read our overseas publications as well as view our broadcasting. Our comics and other features span the globe.

This indicates how far we have come and what the new generation of Hearsts is inheriting. We have a dozen daily and five non-daily newspapers located around the country. These include the *San Francisco Examiner, Seattle Post-Intelligencer, Houston Chronicle, Albany Times Union, San Antonio Light,* and other papers in Texas, Michigan, and Illinois. We're the largest publisher of monthly magazines in the nation, with a total circulation of more than 21 million among fourteen publications. These include *Good Housekeeping, Cosmopolitan, Harper's Bazaar, Connoisseur, Town & Country, Esquire, House Beautiful, Popular Mechanics, Sports Afield,* and many trade publications, such as *The American Druggist.* We own a large, thriving publishing company in England; this subsidiary publishes six magazines in ten languages, which are distributed in more than seventy countries. We also publish books under William Morrow and Company, Arbor House, Avon, and other imprints. King Features Syndicate and similar enterprises are still going strong around the world.

Our organization owns six TV stations. These include WCVB in Boston, WTAE in Pittsburgh, KMBC in Kansas City, WBAL in Baltimore, WISN in Milwaukee, and WDTN in Dayton. We also have seven radio stations in Milwaukee, Baltimore, and San Juan, Puerto Rico. We are expanding continuously in cable television. These holdings include joint ventures in cable television's Arts and Entertainment network (A&E); Lifetime, an advertising-supported network addressing women's interests; the ESPN sports network; the New England Cable Newschannel, covering regional news and events; Ellipse Programme, a French TV production company; and various other television production companies.

Some 12,000 people work in the 135 different businesses of the Hearst Corporation. This includes a data-bank information service—Electronic Publishing Services—and large real estate, timber, and livestock holdings. That's quite a mix!

My mother and father would be very pleased. However, I am sure they would recall our hard times and the struggle to survive. I do.

The changes in America since I was born in 1908 have been profound. Then the life expectancy of a child was fifty years for a boy and fifty-three for a girl. Today a boy can expect to live for nearly seventy-two years while the average girl will reach seventy-five and a half years. We have increased our life spans by more than two decades through providing more nutritious food, cleaner water, better shelter, and much more advanced health care.

When I was a youngster, millions of families canned their own food. Tens of thousands of food-poisoning cases occurred each year and hundreds of persons died. Now, one case of botulism from canned food creates headlines from coast to coast.

In the year I was born, New York City reported about 20,000 deaths from cholera and other diseases caused by flies and insects that thrived on horse manure. The horses were used, of course, to transport people, produce, and freight. Today there's wide concern about the pollution caused by motor-vehicle exhausts in big cities. But I'll take the smog any day. And that too will be conquered.

When I was nine years old, America and the world were hit by a massive flu epidemic. More than half a million Americans died of the disease, while the toll around the world was estimated at about 20 million people. We still have outbreaks of flu, of course, but modern medicine has been able to bring it under control. And no longer do the scourges of diphtheria, smallpox, typhoid, polio, measles, tuberculosis, or pneumonia devastate our society.

We had a national work force of 31 million when I was born. Three million were unemployed. Today we have a work force of more than 126 million (including military), with about 6 million unemployed. Not only is total employment now vastly greater but joblessness is proportionately much less.

I remember twelve-year-olds working in factories, mines, and sweatshops. They often worked twelve-hour days or longer. The average work week was then fifty-seven hours. The average hourly wage for all ages was twenty-five cents. The average annual earnings for all workers in every industry was then $543. Today, the average work week is about thirty-five hours—down twenty-two—with an average hourly wage of $9.66. Obviously, life costs more today, but the wage difference is still enormous. The average annual mean (income divided by families) income is now more than $38,600. Again, a vast leap.

A hundred great technical advances of one kind or another have been made in cars, airplanes, television, electronics, satellites, telephones, computers, medicine, and many other fields.

We have gone a long way toward bringing all minorities into the mainstream of society.

I submit that my generation didn't do a bad job in bringing about economic, social, and political opportunity, along with personal dignity and racial equality in the United States.

I've tooted the company's horn and that of my generation, but the notes are bittersweet. Three of my brothers are now dead. George passed away in 1972, following a long illness. He was buried with Pop in the family mausoleum outside San Francisco. His last wife, Rosalie, got him off booze and other excesses, and George was a superb human being at the close of his life. It is ironic that, when he died, George was probably as happy as he had ever been. The twins by his first wife—George, Jr., and Phoebe—are active in the corporation.

John died in 1958 at the age of forty-nine and was buried in New York with our mother. He had been ill, but his passing came as a shock. John had four children: John, Jr. (Bunky), by his second wife, as well as two daughters—Joanne and Deborah—and another son, William, by his last wife. Bunky has worked for the company for many years and is now a trustee.

David died in Los Angeles in 1986 and was buried at Forest Lawn. He's the only one of the five brothers who married just once—to lovely Hope, who is still with us. The two were wed in 1938 and had two children, David and Millicent.

Randy, David's twin, is now chairman of our corporate board. He had five daughters by his first wife, charming Catherine. They are Catherine, Virginia, Patricia, Anne, and Victoria. Patty was splashed in national headlines and TV coverage after being abducted by a terrorist group. She was the first American victim of the same type of terrorism that later swept the Middle East. Virginia has been voted on the company board of directors.

Mother died in 1974 at the age of ninety-three and was buried in New York. She left an estate of about $2.5 million, which was divided among us five sons. The persistent claim that the families of George and John received no inheritance isn't true. Mom gave George his inheritance before she died, and paid all his debts. She did the same for John earlier—buying him houses, paying mortgages, and clearing his debts.

Randy and I each have a 20 percent interest in the family trust, which owns the Hearst stock. The other 60 percent is held by the children of our deceased brothers. Randy's and my share will pass to our children when we die.

As for the new generation, my two sons are married. Our son Will has two children, including grandson William Randolph Hearst IV and grand-daughter Adelaide. Will is publisher of the *San Francisco Examiner.* Our other son, Austin, is a vice-president and director of special projects at Hearst Entertainment Distribution, Inc. Both sons serve on the corporation board of directors.

My sons, Will and Austin, are independent thinkers. Each has a strong work ethic. My wife and I drummed that into the two from an early age. We privately spared no one in the family if they didn't work properly.

From their childhood I told Will and Austin that their futures would depend on themselves—just as their success in the company will depend entirely on themselves. Austine and I told the boys that their name might be Hearst but they had better work as if it were Jones or Brown. Like Pop, I believe every member of the family must be professionally prepared to hold any job in the company.

On the surface, Austine seemed an easy disciplinarian, but she was after our boys all the time to study, behave, go to church, and dress properly.

I disciplined and lectured the boys, but only on occasion. I recall one episode clearly. We were having breakfast on a Sunday morning and Austin wouldn't finish his eggs. I told him it was wrong to waste food and he should eat everything that he had put on his plate. He rebelled. So I took an egg in my hand and mashed it over his face. Both of the boys were very surprised, but cleaned off their plates after that. Neither of us allowed the boys to feel that they were people of wealth. We told them: Life is tough.

Will was a sensitive youngster. I remember taking him to San Simeon on vacation about 1953. He commented on the deserted airstrip and the tumbleweed blowing down the runway. As we drove up the hill to the castle, he said to me, "Pop, this place is so beautiful and big, but nobody's here. I get a strange feeling." It was only after we had a swim in the outdoor pool and went horseback riding that he felt comfortable.

I reflected on Will's words. How differently his grandfather had seen the place. How would the old man have responded to his grandson?

The gulf between Will's and his grandfather's generations was epitomized in a simple but significant gesture during the company centennial in 1987. Our advertising agency asked Will—as publisher of the *San Francisco Examiner,* where Pop had launched the company—to take part in the centennial publicity.

Will had been changing the paper, modeling it on the *Miami Herald* and *Boston Globe.* He put a lot of emphasis on local and international news, and sought major improvement in its columns, feature writing, the arts, and other sections of the newspaper. It was clear that he was going to continue making as many changes as needed to bring the *Examiner* around to his own model of a newspaper.

Will had agreed to do a television spot that would reflect some of the changes he had made. He sat in his office with a large portrait of his grandfather on the wall above. The ghost on the wall addressed his grandson, asking, "Are you sure you know what you're doing, Will?"

Will replied, "Did you?"

The words just came out. One generation looking at another.

Will said later that he wanted the family and the *Examiner* to be less distant, friendlier—ordinary people trying to produce a living newspaper rather than two awesome giants standing amid a collection of old documents.

Will doesn't think at all like Pop. That's because papers, magazines, and television have changed in format and color, in featuring briefer stories yet longer news analysis, and in expanding live coverage by television. He sees news undergoing constant revolution with the media in a continuing state of flux. Of course he's right.

At the same time, Will has long defended his grandfather's reputation as a newsman. He conducted a study of Pop's direction of the *Examiner* on its hundredth anniversary in 1987. He concluded that the major reason for the old man's success with the *Examiner* was his sophisticated choice and placement of important news. Pop was the first editor in San Francisco to feature, regularly, top foreign and Washington developments as well as details of state and local government, including major investigative reporting.

Austin is interested in TV production and video, not in newspapering or publishing. He sees national and international TV and video as the wave of the future. He doesn't want to see company progress tied to newspapers. There is little or no chance of that with our magazine and television properties doing so well, but Austin is leading the charge toward greater involvement with TV and video. He sees the international exchange of such programming as extremely important. He explains:

> I believe the day my grandfather died that we had peaked in the newspaper business. There was no one strong enough to take his place. Whether you liked William Randolph Hearst or not, you got a feeling of action, style, direction. As a businessman with ideas, conviction, and drive, he would have made Donald Trump look like a wimp.
>
> The biggest professional mistake that my grandfather ever made was to become involved in politics. It was as great an error as his relationship with Marion Davies. For her part, she should have gone out and married someone. My parents never once mentioned her in our presence.

I understood that and appreciated their feeling. Yet, affairs are ordinary stories these days. I think politics cheapened my grandfather much more than the Davies affair because he had to make all those compromises to survive. By temperament, he was not a compromiser. Politics was a waste for him. It was silly. He would have been a greater man if he had remained only in the media. I think he would have been one of the real pioneers in television. That was always his way—to be first.

Reliable indicators show that Austin is right. The great growth in communication will be in television, not newspapers. Daily newspaper circulation increases have not kept up with population gains for most of this century. Only two-thirds of Americans read a newspaper most days, compared to three-quarters two decades ago. Television, direct (junk) mail, suburban dailies and weeklies, and "shopper" tabloids have slashed advertising—about two-thirds of most daily newspaper revenues—in virtually all big-city newspapers. Newspaper competition itself has caused less advertising in individual papers.

Nevertheless, about 113 million adults read a daily paper every week day, an increase over 93 million such readers in 1967. Even so, the latest totals represent a smaller percentage of available readers. Circulation gains have not kept pace with population increases.

TV obviously is the major reason for newspapers' loss of readership. But another major reason is that many more women now work, and they don't have the time they once had to read papers. Reading has become a lost art among many Americans. Many claim they don't have the time. Simultaneously, the country has had a steady loss of literacy.

In 1690, when *Publick Occurrences,* the first colonial newspaper, was published in Boston, the colonies were the most literate place in the world. Today, many nations are more literate than the United States.

I have been very concerned about this, because reading and thinking are very closely related. To retain our freedoms in every aspect of life and make progress in others, including international economic competition, we must read. Newspapers are much more informative than television. If we don't use them, the American people lose a vital source of information for informed decision making and will be less able to compete at home and in global markets.

I was reading recently about David Sarnoff, one of the founders and longtime leaders of NBC radio and television as well as the Radio Corporation of America. Sarnoff was born in the Soviet Union near Minsk and was of Russian-Jewish background. He was brought to this country as a child. His first job as a youngster was selling Yiddish newspapers on New York's East Side. Biographers say he studied English by reading city newspapers pulled out of garbage bins.

My father began his New York newspaper operation by producing a newspaper that would not only attract the masses of poor and foreign born but also teach them to read. It is indeed ironic that, nearly a century after Pop talked about teaching people to read, we are still supporting the same need.

Newspapers are now changing their design, content, marketing strategies, and are accommodating new requests from advertisers. Cleaner type and page layout, more color, shorter and simpler stories, new sections on music and other interests—these are only a part of current changes. Some papers work closely with advertisers by furnishing them with demographic information that will allow firms to target customers more accurately. Newspaper circulation, delivery, and promotion are being changed as well.

However, newspapers and the written word have diminished greatly since television began making the world a global village some four decades ago. That's the short-term view. In terms of history, the written word still retains a vastly more important place in society than TV. And it will continue to do so, because I believe television is generally far less effective in explaining the profound complexities of government, science, and other aspects of public endeavor.

Television's greatest impact has been to create an unprecedented era of greater knowledge and awareness among the globe's billions of poor, illiterate, and even many lower- and middle-class citizens. It has done much to inform and educate, and bring myriad cultures into the homes of the world. However, the written word—its depth of information, logic, and analysis—is today, and will continue to be, the most effective way of communicating our most needed knowledge: the profound understanding needed to run nations, economies, industries, and businesses and to achieve scientific, political, and social advancement in the areas of health, education, legal justice, welfare, and other systems.

The majority of Americans now get from television not only most of their news but also the preponderance of their cultural, entertainment, and sports information—all packaged in living color and beamed toward their couches, where they are are enjoying a soft drink and popcorn in their bathrobes and slippers.

While some TV broadcasting is compelling and substantive, much more of it offers superficial answers compared to the detailed information and analyses contained in many books, specialized journals, and certain newspapers and magazines. To know what's really happening in science or health, for example, we must turn off the TV and read.

These views are obvious to anyone with leadership, economic, and social responsibilities in modern society. Nevertheless, they need to be reemphasized because depending on television as a sole source of information is inadequate and can even be injurious. Thirty-second news bites do a woeful job of covering any story. They may not only distort reality but degenerate into little more than emotional bursts that encourage prejudice. And these quick takes can be misleading and unfair. I don't understand how many people can vote merely on the basis of the scanty knowledge of candidates and issues presented on TV. The detailed reporting and analysis provided in responsible journals, newspapers, and magazines offer a much clearer picture of political developments than what is delivered on television.

While TV may affect the public at large, the world can function without it. However, modern society cannot carry out its many complex responsibilities without the written word, the ultimate means whereby our most critically needed knowledge is communicated. Without it, not only would the modern world stall but our future would slow to a crawl.

Less reading is one of the most ominous developments in modern society. I hope that my children and grandchildren will help change this drift. They must hold the door open to the detailed understanding of thousands of years of documented human development—from scientific advances to great literature, art, music, and the rest of man's endeavors. Much history and culture will wither and never influence the lives of multimillions of people if this mindless trend away from reading continues. Reading is one of the reasons why I've been thinking so much about the Hearst family and the company that will further evolve after I've gone. Only the new generation can change our direction.

In terms of the crucial advertising dollar, newspapers are competing not only against TV but among themselves for a greater share of the bucks. TV is gathering more viewers not only because of a long and clear shift in public habit but because literacy has become a significant problem in the United States.

Despite all their problems, I have a sentimental attachment to newspapers. And for all the hand-wringing about their future, I am still very optimistic about papers. The main reason is, they are so much more substantive than radio or TV. The world is becoming ever more complex, and the need for all print media increases in proportion. Another reason is these newspaper totals in 1990: The nation's 1,626 dailies generated about $32 billion in advertising—$5 billion more than all TV services. Plus they had a circulation of some 62 million, and employed more than 475,000 people.

Newspapers will be around long after many more generations of Hearsts, although they may have a different format, such as being faxed into homes or shown page by page and perhaps subject by subject on TV screens. But that is for Will, Austin, and my nephews and nieces to work out. Life and the future are rarely clear and always unpredictable.

Will and Austin found that out as they began their careers. That new generation of Hearsts received the greatest shock of their lives. As a matter of fact, so did the old. Patty Hearst, only nineteen years old, was abducted in 1974 by a bunch of crazies. The kidnappers called themselves the "Symbionese Liberation Army." Actually, they were eight ragtag radicals—seven whites and a black—who fantasized a revolution of the poor and oppressed. Patty, a sophomore in art history at UC Berkeley, would bring them ransom money and put their cause on the front page.

The details have been reported extensively. She was confined for endless weeks in a closet, and released only to be brutally terrorized and raped. She was forced to tape tirades against her family, carry a gun in a bank heist, and otherwise follow the orders of her captors.

Patty was finally captured by the FBI and police in a hideout, along with some of her abductors. She was tried and sentenced to prison for the bank job. Patty was no more guilty of a crime than any of the foreign hostages held by Arab terrorists. She simply followed orders to survive. All of us found it incredible that a kidnap victim would be jailed for a crime. Yet Patty was ultimately sentenced to seven years in prison.

Randy and Catherine Hearst and their four daughters went through hell. They faced a $2 million ransom demand. The media drove them into hiding. Patty's face stared out at them from newspapers and TV news

major reason why, at the age of eighty-three, I keep writing
olumn. I'm carrying the flag for them. And I will not let it
die. I want my sons, grandchildren, and great-grandchildren
the tradition.

why Austine got me to write this book: tradition.

to see the work of people like John Mack Carter (editor-in-chief
Housekeeping and director of new magazine development) and
urley Brown (editor of Cosmopolitan) and our other top editors
iters continued—especially their spirit of innovation. They've al-
leaped into the twenty-first century.

ost of all, I pray we can keep the ranch at San Simeon. It's such a
nificent place—the rolling hills and rising mountains standing above
fresh, clean air rolling in from the ocean.

My Episcopal burial service will be exactly like Pop's—simple, with
o eulogy. . . . And someone will read his poem, "The Song of the
River."

My spirit will watch over San Simeon, because that's where I spent so
many happy times with my mother and father, my brothers, my wife and
children, and my grandchildren. I especially hope that Pop and I will meet
spiritually again there, climb the hills together, look out, and thank God
for our family, love, and divine forgiveness.

Publisher's note: Austine McDonnell Hearst died on June 23, 1991 in
New York at the age of 72.

shows from morning to night. The FBI and police questioned them endlessly. Patty had become "Tania," a guerilla fighter. There was speculation that she might have been put on mind-bending drugs.

The $3,700 robbery, with Patty holding a carbine on bank officials and customers, was unexplainable. Was she a willing participant in the heist? Patty's trial was almost unbearable to all of us. How could the government try the central victim of the crime? Wasn't it obvious that she had been brainwashed? None of us could go anywhere without people staring at us, asking questions, probing for explanations that none of us had.

Patty was finally released from prison in February of 1979, nearly five years from the day of her kidnapping. President Jimmy Carter granted her clemency after almost two years in jail. Repeated appeals were made to President Reagan to grant her a pardon, but they were ignored by Reagan for reasons that are still unclear. The pardon attorney for the U.S. Department of Justice recommended that Patty be pardoned. His recommendation was put on hold in the office of the attorney general, who refused to discuss the matter.

It was indeed ironic that Patty had been imprisoned in Pleasanton, near the beautiful hacienda of her great-grandmother. And ironic, too, that our family had been unable to take part in the campaign to release her lest we be accused of seeking special treatment.

I wrote little about Patty during her ordeal, simply because the situation was so delicate. Austine, our sons, and I visited her in prison. Every one of us suffered because we knew Patty as a vibrant, eager young woman. In prison, she seemed aged and worn with little of the spark that once shone in her face. One weekend we saw Patty four different times. We tried to give her courage.

Meantime, throughout Patty's torment the lives of all the Hearsts changed. It was, as Patty put it, like a "tidal wave had engulfed the family." There was widespread speculation in the media about a Hearst empire—from family mansions to lavish jewelry, priceless art, yachts, and other riches. Much of it was nonsense. However, amid reports of such a vast fortune, many of us felt we had become targets for kidnappers and robbers. Everyone was concerned about personal safety. We became nervous and suspicious of strangers. Some bought guns. Others hired bodyguards. Everyone without an unlisted phone number got one. We changed our living patterns, taking different routes to office and home, and not making restaurant reservations in our own names. As a family, we were determined not to draw attention to ourselves. To this day some of us continue to keep a low public profile.

Patty eventually married and now lives on the East Coast with her husband and two beautiful daughters. She was wed to Bernard Shaw, one of her bodyguards, after release from prison. Patty smiles today when someone asks her if she had been a rebel fighting in a class struggle. She simply asks: Have you ever been taken hostage?

It was inevitable that some of the grandchildren wanted a larger piece of the pie after all the publicity about family riches and company wealth. However, there was no way that their grandfather's will could be broken to obtain more money for them.

In one case, Randy and I got company jobs for a granddaughter and her husband, even though some of our executives felt they were not qualified to hold them. It was against my own rule and better judgment, but I wanted to help them. This same granddaughter and her husband later gave interviews that didn't reflect well on others in the family. I smiled ruefully at that because of the caring assistance that we had offered when they asked.

I've deplored some of the talk among a number of my brothers' children. Several of them—and their husbands—foolishly made false statements to persons working on books that turned out to be unfairly critical of our family. I've been deeply hurt by these criticisms and by their complaints about not getting big jobs in the company. Some were also motivated by anger over the amount of their inheritance, although all those entitled received it fully.

As one of Pop's two living sons, I am still receiving my full share of his trust, as does Randy, the other surviving son. However, through the years, I have given part of those funds to our children.

These developments pose questions that will be critical to the company's future. Will individual interests of family members eventually cause the corporation to go public, break up, or be sold in some leveraged buyout or other deal? I cringed when the Bingham family was forced to sell the *Louisville Courier-Journal* because of family differences. The Binghams had a long tradition of professional excellence and public service.

Over the past century, we have had similar traditions. Today, the growth, diversity, and magnitude of the company has never been greater.

Our magazines, broadcast u... cable television operations, ... nesses are among the best. Our ... triple what they were at the start ... running more than $2 billion a year ... *Forbes* magazine called us "one of th... the world."

The relationship between our 100-per... board of trustees, and our top managemer... A. Bennack, Jr., president and chief executive... extremely well since he was put in charge in 1... came up through our ranks over the past twen... of the more innovative and future-oriented m... country.

My father's trust will expire at the death of th... grandchildren who were alive when he passed away. ... be sometime in the next thirty to fifty years. Hearst C... will then be distributed to the remaining heirs of his five s...

I believe the company can remain intact and privately o... next thirty years or so. However, a sale or public stock offe... missible under terms of the trust. No one can predict what ... generations will do.

There is another trouble spot that must be guarded against. All the ... cannot run the company or share equally in its management. For ... present, the trustees manage the corporation for the benefit of the hei... I hope they will make sure that the cream rises to the top and that family members will be employed—if they join the corporation—on the basis of merit and ability. Some may well feel that their talents have not been properly recognized. Such squabbles could eventually break up the company.

I dread the prospect that such squabbles could splinter the company and that the name Hearst could disappear from the nation's media. But why, at my age, should I bother thinking about it? There's not a lot that I can do. The reason I care is because I loved Pop and the company with my heart and soul—and all the remarkable and sometimes wacky people who were such great reporters and editors: Considine, Conniff, Kingsbury-Smith, Runyon, St. Johns, the Kilgallens, and so many others. To me, if we sold out it would be like turning our back on my father's life.

That's the ...
my Sunday ...
fall until I ...
to carry on...
That is ...
I wan...
of Goo...
Helen ...
and w...
ready...
M...
mag...
the...

INDEX

२

Journal

NE

AN AMERICAN | PAPER | FOR

No. 24,875—DAILY

MONDA

Pulitzer Prize to W. R.

Conniff and Smith Share

A Pulitzer Prize for international reporting was awarded today to William Randolph Hearst Jr., Kingsbury Smith, general manager of International News Service, and Frank Conniff, Hearst's editorial assistant.

The top American journalism award went to the reporting team of Hearst, Smith and Conniff for their historic and unprecedented series of interviews with the top Soviet leaders early in 1955.

In January and February, 1955, Hearst, editor-in-chief of the Hearst Newspapers, Smith and Conniff interviewed Soviet Foreign Minister V. M. Molotov, Communist Party boss Nikita Khrushchev, Defense Minister Georgi Zhukov and newly-named Premier Nikolai Bulganin.

MALENKOV REPLACED.

Bulganin had replaced Georgi Malenkov, Stalin's hand-picked successor, only four days before.

The 1956 award for fiction went to MacKinlay Kantor for his Civil War novel, "Andersonville," the story of a Southern prisoner of war camp.

Frances Goodrich and Albert Hackett won the drama prize for "The Diary of Anne Frank."

W. R. HEARST JR.

The local reporting journalism award went to sports columnist Arthur Daley of the New York Times for his coverage and commentary on sports in his daily column, "Sports of the Times."

DETROIT REPORTER WINS.

Lee Hills, Detroit, Mich., Free-Press, received the prize for local reporting against edition time and for his reporting of the United Auto Workers' negotiations with Ford and General Motors for a guaranteed annual wage.

The other awards went to:

For history, Richard Hofstadter for his book "The Age of Reform."

For biography, Talbot Hamlin for "Benjamin Henry Latrobe."

For Poetry, Elizabeth Bishop

Winning Aces!